KENNETH D. ALFORD

M●NETARY MEN

The Allies' Struggle to Recover and Restore Nazi Gold, Silver & Diamonds

Schiffer Publishing Ltd®

4880 Lower Valley Road · Atglen, PA 19310

Cover design by Danielle Farmer
Type set in Benton Bold/ times Roman
ISBN: 978-0-7643-4836-5
Printed in China

Published by Schiffer Publishing, Ltd.
4880 Lower Valley Road
Atglen, PA 19310
Phone: (610) 593-1777; Fax: (610) 593-2002
E-mail: Info@schifferbooks.com

For our complete selection of fine books on this and related subjects, please visit our website at www.schifferbooks.com. You may also write for a free catalog.

This book may be purchased from the publisher. Please try your bookstore first.

We are always looking for people to write books on new and related subjects. If you have an idea for a book, please contact us at proposals@schifferbooks.com.

Schiffer Publishing's titles are available at special discounts for bulk purchases for sales promotions or premiums. Special editions, including personalized covers, corporate imprints, and excerpts can be created in large quantities for special needs. For more information, contact the publisher.

Dedicated to the Monetary Men
of the European Theater of Operation:

Colonel Bernard Bernstein

Colonel William G. Brey

Commander Joel Fisher

Lieutenant Herbert DuBois

Mr. Frank C. Gabell

Mr. Edwin P. Keller

Mr. Frank J. Roberts

And the sixty-one finance officers of the infantry,
armored, and airborne divisions.

CONTENTS

PREFACE

I began this book in the early-1980s after reading a two-page description in an Army History Series book, *The US Army in the Occupation of Germany,* by Earl F. Ziemke, regarding the recovery of tons of Nazi gold in a salt mine in Merkers, Germany. This was the beginning of more than thirty years of research on the subject of valuables looted during World War II that has resulted in the publication of seven books.

My first trip to the archives was in search of the disbursement of this cache of gold. Here I hit a stone wall regarding this subject. After several years, I recovered sufficient information on how the gold was acquired in Germany, but not what happened to the monetary gold afterwards. I could track the bulk of the gold that had been transferred to the Bank of England and Federal Reserve Bank in New York but here I hit a dead-end.

On June 15, 1983, I filed a Freedom of Information Request with the US Department of State for information regarding the Tripartite Gold Commission, the agency responsible for the distribution of the gold acquired in Germany during World War II. A few redacted pages were sent but nothing of any substance. A year later after considerable correspondence and several trips to the Department of State, I filed Civil Action number 84-0538-R with the United States District Court in Virginia. In response, the US Department of State made a ninety-nine-page declaration to the court stating that I had reviewed 1,689 documents and that documents requested from file 91C were denied in whole or in part and all documents in file 91D were denied. The document in file 91C and 91D were needed to determine what had happened to the gold.

The case continued for a year, until Friday, May 17, 1985, when the clerk of the court phoned and requested my presence in the chambers of Judge David Dortch Warriner. Upon arrival the judge introduced four well-dressed representatives as members of the US Department of State and the FBI. The judge stated these four individuals had requested that he issue a warrant for my arrest for treason! I was stunned as the sympathetic judge told me that he would give me until Monday to return with a lawyer to explain why he should not issue the warrant. The judge said: "They have unlimited legal resources and the FBI working for them. Now I cannot tell you but I advise you to return with a well qualified attorney."

The attorney had "connections" with the court and after a weekend of work the question of the arrest warrant was quickly dismissed. The following day the headlines of all major newspapers carried the headlines of the arrest of John Anthony Walker Jr. a United States Navy chief warrant officer and communications specialist for spying for the Soviet Union. Walker lived in Virginia, the same state as me. This frightened me! Coincidental, or was the author to have been arrested with Walker? Regardless of the outcome from the publicity, I would have been fired from my job with a large financial firm on the East Coast. Shaken, I dropped my civil action case with the United States District Court. I would not pursue the disposal of the Nazi gold acquired by the US Army.

In 2013, by chance, while searching an unrelated subject I found a document requested in my 1985 Civil Action. The document was in the format of a pdf file in the William J. Clinton Presidential Library and accessible through the internet. I spent two weeks analyzing the documents; downloading them and printing thousands of pages. This was the material needed to complete this book. Most unfortunately, what the US Department of State was hiding from me all these years, for the most part, were large quantities of boring documents. Thus the story of the distribution of the gold is a bit lackluster, but the chase for the gold is adventurous and thrilling. Most of the information in this book is published for the first time, but some recently found material is related to previous books. A quick look at Appendices A and B will help the reader with the timeline and sequence of valuables collected by the US Army.

I sincerely hope the reader takes as much pleasure in this book as I did in the research and writing.

ACKNOWLEDGMENTS

I am thankful to the many people and institutions who have helped with the research and writing of this book. A special thanks to Fred Pernell (Ret.), Rich Boyland (Ret.), M'Lisa Whitney and Greg Bradsher, National Archives and Records Administration. I also extend my appreciation to Da Capo Press for permission to use material from my earlier book *Nazi Plunder*. I pay tribute to my wife, Edda. Without her support the tasks that I undertake would be unattainable. Photos are courtesy of the US National Archives and the author.

INTRODUCTION

For centuries, the United States' Allies of Western Europe—specifically Belgium, England, France and Holland—obtained their wealth and power from the exploitation of colonies. They extracted raw materials such as rubber, oil, and cotton at low prices and paid low wages to their subjects in Africa, Asia, and the Pacific area. Much of the income from the sale of these products was invested in the development of Australia, Canada, and the United States in the form of railroad construction and financial institutions. Tremendous wealth was invested outside of Europe, which made the governments of Western Europe powerful. The land surface of the forenamed Western European countries is nine percent of the globe, but in 1935 they controlled eighty-five percent of the world's land surface and seventy percent of its population. The United States itself played a limited colonial role in Cuba, Puerto Rico and the Philippines, but England was the predominant leader in colonialism and in comparison with the Europeans, the United States was a junior partner.

World War II was extremely expensive and liquidated a very large part of this wealth. In view of the widespread devastation of war and the apparent demise of colonialism, the European Allies intended to regain their wealth by forcing the Axis powers into feudal roles. Germany and Japan would become agricultural societies with reduced standards of living.

To ensure the economy of the Western Allies at the conclusion of World War II, a conference was held on July 1, 1944, in Bretton Woods, New Hampshire. The Allies' plans included a unified Germany, not the division of East and West Germany. They intended to reduce Germany's economic and industrial power so it would not be a threat again to Europe. Since World War I, the Germans had rebuilt a remarkably strong industry that produced a powerful military force. The war was then five years old and the attitude of Allied leaders was reflected by Henry Morgenthau Jr., secretary of the Treasury, who stated he wanted Germany turned into a pasture. President Roosevelt told his cabinet that as far as he was concerned, the Germans, "could live happily ... on soup from soup kitchens." In this frame of mind, forty-four Allied nations assembled at Bretton Woods to establish a permanent bank for the reconstruction and redevelopment of the European Allied countries. The bank was to stabilize world currency, and assist Allied members with long-term loans through private financial agencies with the bank, guaranteeing and participating in the loans. This policy would prevent the complete collapse of British sterling and provide a smooth transition from wartime to a peacetime economy. The conference recommended that a universal currency be established for all Allied countries. This was rejected by England, who insisted the English pound be the universal currency.

As part of establishing a World Bank, the forty-four Allied countries planned to divide the spoils of war. Bretton Woods Resolution VI was adopted, which legalized the looting of Germany and neutral countries. Resolution VI required all neutral countries to compile a list of German assets in their countries; items of particular interest were bank balances, gold, gems, art objects, stock, real estate, investments, patents, and all commercial, industrial, and financial holdings. Regarding Germany, Resolution VI stated ample evidence existed to show all German prewar gold stocks had been exhausted and any gold in Germany's possession could be presumed looted. All gold recovered in Germany would be assumed unidentifiable unless there was convincing evidence to the contrary. All looted property and German assets would be consigned to the Allies following the defeat of the Axis.

For special emphasis, Resolution VI was telegraphed to the following neutral countries: Ireland, Morocco, Portugal, Spain, Sweden, Switzerland, and Turkey. Additional procedures validate Switzerland received the telegram. The Allies were aware that the Swiss had purchased eighty tons of gold looted from Belgium and suspected them of purchasing over 200 tons of gold from Germany.

The proposals at the Bretton Woods Conference were ambiguous and each country interpreted the rules to its own advantage, but the primary thrust of Resolution VI was clear. In July of 1944, more than 400 tons of gold lay in the Reichsbank vaults in Berlin. The Allies intended to obtain all of it and determined to offer Germany no other choice than accept Resolution VI or continue fighting. Resolution VI was in effect a decree to proliferate the Allied Gold Pot for reparations expected by the Allies.

This declaration was issued because Germany had acquired more than one million pounds of gold from the following countries:

Belgian gold reserves in custody of France	435,664
Luxembourg gold reserves in custody of France	9,524
Austrian gold reserve	201,919
Wiener Bank Austria	1,883
Netherlands gold reserves, contribution to help finance the war against Russia	142,549
Netherlands gold from pilot ship 19	20,591
Belgium, France, Holland paid for defense of foreign exchange	118,784
Italian gold reserves	134,612
Gold from the Sudetenland (Czechoslovakia)	31,680
Total pounds	1,397,000

The gold had been concealed by the Reichsbank in a series of five hidden accounts, kept as secret as possible even within the Reichsbank. Balances of these accounts were reported under "suspense" or "miscellaneous" in financial reports. These five accounts follow:

Konversionskasse—A journal stating the complete development of all gold transactions, with the exception of gold transactions which were considered "secret matter of the Reich."

Asservaten Senderkente—The gold account listing the entries of weekly bank statements regularly published in newspapers.

Goldankauf—Originally a listing of gold deposited with foreign-issuing banks, later an accounting of the bank's over-the-counter gold business with the public. During the war the assessment of Dutch gold was was hidden in this account. The total value of Dutch gold deposited to this account was $70,960,356. Holland contributed funds to finance the war against the Russians on the Western Front.

Treuhandgesellschaft von 1933 Konte "GR"—Listing of all gold purchased by the Reichsbank institutions within the Reich. This account was known as the new Juliusturm—a reference to the gold reserves built up for World War I and hidden in the Julius Tower in Spandau prison.

Assert "Der"—The most active and largest of the hidden accounts. Most gold amounts were entered and were exclusively destined for the purpose of the war effort. The gold came from Germany and territories occupied by German troops.[1]

In 1943, the Allies requested the Swiss Government to cease acquiring gold from Germany and disallow Germany any Swiss currency. The Swiss Bank would not honor this request because they were in fact the international bankers financing the war for Germany. The Swiss continued to purchase

Belgium-Luxembourg gold throughout 1943 and 1944. Some of this gold was sold to the Turkish Central Bank with the original smelt numbers 949 to 1021 inclusive, with the year 1939 stamped on each bar. The secrecy of the Swiss banking system served Germany well; no German banks ever were established in Switzerland.

The Reichsbank needed the Swiss National Bank to procure and establish foreign exchange credit with neutral countries. During World War II, the bank purchased 984,667 pounds of gold from Germany. The Swiss National Bank in Bern, acting as the Bank of International Settlement, transferred large quantities of German gold to Spain and Portugal. Between May 1943 and February 1944, 280 truckloads of German gold bars went from Switzerland to Spain or Portugal. The gold was shipped from the Bank of International Settlement in Bern and the Swiss national emblem appeared on every truck.

In June of 1944, for example, the Reichsbank packed 119 boxes of gold weighing 5,664 pounds, and shipped it by train from Berlin to Aschaffenburg, Germany. From there the gold was loaded onto German Army trucks and sent through French territory to Spain. Also during June, 616 pounds of gold went by air from Berlin to Portugal.[2]

In 1943, the United States and Britain launched the Safehaven program. This program was to thwart Germany's financial transactions worldwide. The Allies' idea was to prevent the Nazi regime from successfully transferring funds to neutral and non-belligerent countries In order to cut short all attempts at German rearmament. To do this it was necessary to track down and freeze German assets all over the world.

During January 1943, and on two occasions during 1944, the American and British governments issued "Gold Warnings." In these declarations and in diplomatic notes, they drew the attention of all countries, and especially the neutrals and non-belligerents, to the practice of plundering by Germany. They warned the neutral government against buying gold from Germany because, in their judgment, there was a high probability that this was looted gold. They declared that they could not recognize such transactions after the end of hostilities.

Finally, towards the end of the war and immediately after the German surrender; the Allies defined their reparation policy toward Germany at a series of conferences. At Yalta, in February 1944, they fixed the global amount of German reparations at $20 billion. At the same time they adopted the principle that all German assets outside Germany should be confiscated by way of reparations. At the Potsdam Conference in August 1945, a decision was reached on an apportionment between the Western Allies and the Soviet Union: the German assets in the three Western zones and the countries of Western Europe should be liquidated for the benefit of the Americans, British, French and fifteen other Allied countries, while the German assets in the Soviet zone and in Central and Eastern Europe would revert in their entirety to the USSR and the victorious countries of Central and Eastern Europe. Finally, in December 1945, eighteen Allied countries created the Inter-Allied Reparations Agency in Brussels. These countries instructed the United States, Great Britain, and France to open negotiations with the neutral countries concerning the handing over of German assets to this agency.

PART I

NAZI GERMANY'S ACQUISITION OF GOLD, SILVER, AND DIAMONDS

CHAPTER 1

THE ACQUISITION OF THE AUSTRIAN, POLISH, AND NORWEGIAN GOLD

Having masterminded the phenomenal growth of Germany's military power in the 1930s, Adolf Hitler could now use the threat of force to secure territorial gains and the respective booty earmarked for the Reich. Austria was the first victim. Germanic in blood and language, it had been part of the German Confederation, but a true union was forbidden, unwisely so, by the Versailles Treaty. Hitler began undermining the Vienna government by cajoling it with false promises and inciting internal Nazi-led revolts. At 8:00am, on March 13, 1938, *General* Heinz Guderian, Germany's architect of tank warfare, crossed the Austrian border with the Second Panzer Division and the *Leibstandarte* SS Adolf Hitler Division to annex that country without resistance to the Greater Third Reich. By incorporating Austria, Hitler secured two great strategic advantages: he forced Benito Mussolini to support him and his cause, and he encircled Czechoslovakia in Nazi territorial pincers.

After German occupation, the gold reserves of the Austrian National Bank were appropriated by the Reichsbank against payment of the Reichsmarks. The Austrian National Bank set up a liquidation account with the Reichsbank on March 17, 1938, and soon after six shipments of Prussian state mint gold bars were transferred from Vienna to Berlin. The major part of the Austrian gold had been deposited in the Bank of England and after Nazi occupation the gold was transferred by way of the Bank of International Settlement in Bern, Switzerland, to the Reichsbank in Berlin.

Prior to World War II, it was unlawful for German citizens to own monetary gold, such as coins and gold bars. (These same monetary laws applied in the United States until 1972.) After Austria's annexation, these laws applied there also. The Austrian Reichsbank purchased all of the gold owned by the Austrian people and shipped it to the German Reichsbank, where it was mixed with the other gold reserves.

A coin collection was established by the Nazi regime for the future Linz museum, with the main part of the collection taken from thirteen Catholic monasteries in Austria. Coin collectors complained of the havoc wreaked on the market by the high prices paid by government officials. In the Third Reich, an American five-dollar gold piece was selling for $800.

The year 1938 was a favorable one for the Reich. After the annexation of Austria, the French and British, awed by Germany's Luftwaffe and the West Wall, preferred an uneasy peace to the dangers of war. Hitler demanded that Czechoslovakia allow Germany to annex the German-speaking Sudetenland, which was achieved by the infamous Munich Accord of September 30, 1938. By acquiring her mountain passes and munitions works, Germany deprived Czechoslovakia of power and tactical positions for future resistance.

Neville Chamberlain, Prime Minister of England, was pleased with the Munich Accord and told the British people this agreement provided, "peace for our time." In less than six months, Czechoslovakia was dismembered and became a puppet state of Nazi Germany. After first Bohemia and then Moravia became protectorates of Germany, the Reichsbank replaced Czechoslovakian currency with German Reichsmarks. Three days after Prague was occupied by German troops, the National Bank for Bohemia and Moravia ordered the Swiss National Bank to transfer 1,845 bars of gold from their account to the Berlin Reichsbank.

A German supply column on the march through the Norwegian mountains.

The prelude to World War II ended on September 1, 1939, when Germany invaded Poland. Honoring an existing defense pact with Poland, England and France declared war on Germany.

As the Germans advanced eagerly toward Warsaw, the panicking Polish government loaded its gold reserves aboard a train and fleet of trucks and sent them to the southern city of Luck. The gold from other banks was also shipped to Luck, which became a central collection point and was then loaded onto a single train that sped through southern Poland and Romania to the port city of Constanta on the Black Sea. While in Romania, the Polish minister for foreign affairs made an urgent request to British and French diplomats to charter a ship for the gold transfer. The British located the creaky 4,000 ton tanker *Eocene* that was totally unsuitable for the task, but was the only available vessel. On September 15, 1939, the gold was loaded onto the deck of the tanker. Expecting attacks from the Luftwaffe, the small vessel hugged the coast of Romania, Bulgaria, and Turkey and proceeded to the Straits of Constantinople.

There, the French and British agreed the *Eocene* was too small and slow to make a dash for safety across the Mediterranean. The gold was then loaded aboard a train and shipped south across Turkey and Syria to the port city of Beirut. The French dispatched the fast cruiser *Emile Bertin* at full speed to take aboard the seventy-five tons of Polish gold. In the confusion, fifty-seven tons were loaded onto the *Emile Bertin* and the destroyers *Vauban* and *Epervier* took the remaining eighteen tons to Toulon, France, and put it aboard an armored train, which took it to Nevers, 125 miles south of Paris, where the gold was deposited in the vaults of the Bank of France.

The conquest of Poland in less than a month was a brilliant feat of military strategy. The northern *blitzkrieg* or "lightning war," which overran Denmark and most of Norway's leading ports and cities in half a day, was even more of a miracle. Troops secretly concealed in ore ships had been escorted by destroyers, safe and unobserved, a thousand miles up the Norwegian coast. Surprise attacks overwhelmed the port cities, and an expedition slipped past the forts protecting Oslo and captured the Norwegian capital that afternoon.

During this surprise attack, the finance minister of Norway gave orders to ship the Norwegian gold reserves north. That very morning, 120,000 pounds of gold in 1,538 boxes traveled by truck to Lillehammer, ninety miles north of Oslo. One week later, as the Germans advanced northward, the gold was loaded onto freight cars and sent 150 miles farther north. At the end of the railroad line the British cruiser *Galatea* was waiting for the shipment. Under cover of darkness, the gold was being loaded aboard when German planes began to bomb the ship and news came that the Germans were nearing the city. With only 200 boxes of gold loaded, the captain rapidly weighed anchor and sailed, leaving 1,338 boxes of gold sitting on the wharf.

Once more the gold was loaded onto twenty-five dilapidated trucks and sent north. The Germans knew of the gold mission and bombed the trucks incessantly; several trucks were hit, four broke down, but the gold continued northward to the coastal town of Molde. Within forty-eight hours Molde was aflame.

Again the gold-laden trucks headed north, and again made it to the coast. There, they were abandoned and their precious cargo loaded into five fishing boats. The convoy continued its northern trip, harried by torpedo boats and German bombers. During the trip the five boats off-loaded the gold to two larger fishing boats. A full three weeks later, the gold reached the city of Tromso, where it was gathered aboard the British cruiser *Enterprise* and sent directly to England. In all, the Norwegian gold was unloaded and reloaded thirty times before it reached its final destination, the Federal Reserve Bank of New York. Thus, Norway was the only country to escape Nazi gold looting.

CHAPTER 2
The German Invasion of Western Europe

The German war with France and England was stalemated for six months and became known as the "sitzkrieg." During this time the Bank of England shipped its entire gold reserves of more than 1,600 tons to Canada, where it was stored in the vault of the Sun Life Insurance Company in Montreal, Canada. The French also used this lull to transfer part of its phenomenal 2,430 tons of gold to fifty-one caches outside France.

On May 10, 1940, the stalemate ended and a furious attack on Western Europe began. Ninety-four German divisions assaulted the Allies through Holland, Belgium, Luxembourg, and France. The Dutch fought heroically for four days but surrendered on May 14.

During the Wehrmacht's attack on Holland, the Dutch, like the Norwegians, frantically began loading their gold reserves onto ships in a race to remove all valuables before the German troops arrived. On the eve of the invasion, May 9, 1940, approximately thirty-five percent of the roughly 192,360 kilograms of total gold stock was still in the Netherlands Bank. A part of this remaining gold was stored in the vaults of the head office at Amsterdam and the remainder was being kept at the Rotterdam branch. As soon as the German offensive had started the gold stored in Amsterdam was shipped to London via the port city of Ijmuiden in two freighters of the Royal Netherlands Steamship *Cy*.

An attempt to convey 937 gold bars from Rotterdam to England that same night failed; the Germans had dropped high-explosive mines from aircraft into the waterways to impede the shipments from Holland's port, and the Dutch pilot boat 19, carrying the gold struck one of the mines and sunk. The force of the explosion was enormous and tore the boat in two. Within seconds, sixteen Dutch crewmen perished, and the vessel's valuable golden cargo lay at the bottom of the Nieuwe Waterweg Channel. Remaining in the vaults of the Rotterdam Branch was a quantity of 102,732 kilograms of fine gold.

The occupying Germans, between then and July 1940, located the contents of the 200 steel-bound boxes embedded in mud and salvaged 816 bars of gold weighing 9,571 kilograms. Despite protests from the Netherlands Bank, the Germans declared this war booty and deposited the gold in the Reichsbank. The gold at the Rotterdam Bank, 975 bars and 1,886 bags of coins, was taken under "a payment imposed on occupation Netherlands territory for a so called external occupation cost."

In following with Germany's laws that prohibited citizens to own gold, all residences of the occupied Netherlands were required to sell or transfer all their fine gold to the Netherland Bank. Collected from the citizens were 35,476 kilograms of gold. The larger portion consisting of 886 bars and 560 bags of coins, was transported to Berlin in 1940 and 1943.

On February 24, 1945, after Allied forces had occupied the southern part of the Netherlands, the remainder of the Dutch gold, one bar, and two boxes and thirty-four bags of coins, was transported to the Reichsbank Wurzburg, Germany. The gold was earmarked for the account of De Nederlandsche Bank with a receipt dated February 26, 1945.

The following were the Dutch claims for gold:

> 816 bars, recovered from sunk ship
> 866 bars and 560 bags of coins taken from the public
> 3,015 bars of gold—occupation cost
> 975 bars and 1,886 bags of coins—occupation cost
> 32 bags of coins from Arnhem
> One bar, 34 bags, and two tin boxes of coins from Meppel
> **In total, 145,674 kilograms of fine gold**[1]

Belgium fared about the same as Holland. The Germans poured across the Belgian border in large numbers and prevented the Belgians from blowing up their bridges. The Germans took the "impregnable" concrete fortress of Eben Emael in thirty hours by a massive airborne attack.

During this rapid assault, the National Bank of Belgium transferred its gold to the Bank of France for safekeeping. The gold was packed in 4,944 wooden boxes marked "B.N.B." This included ninety boxes of gold from the Bank of Luxembourg.[2]

At the same time, three freighters carrying diamonds were on the way from the Belgian Congo and Portuguese Angola colony to Antwerp. The whole cargo consisted of 332,000 carats of crude diamonds from the Belgian Congo that was the property of Society International Forestry and Minerals of the Congo, or Socété de Cordination Industrielle, or Forminiere, a Belgian company. An additional 195,000 carats of the cargo, from the Portugal colony was the property of the Portuguese company "Companhia de Diamantes de Angolia." The diamonds were in the steamer ship *Elisabethville*, an ocean liner built in 1921 for Compagnie Belge Maritime du Congo. In 1930, the company became Compagnie Maritime Belge. She was used on the Antwerp-Matadi route. In 1940, *Elisabethville* was requisitioned by the Ministry of War Transport for use as a troopship. In its vault, the *Elisabethville*, was carrying 295,318 carats of Congo diamonds, and 66,141 carats of Angola diamonds

The Belgian transport ship SS *Leopoldville* was a passenger liner later converted for use as a troopship. In the ship's safe was 35,809 carats of Congo diamonds. The *Leopoldville* was struck by a torpedo fired in the English Channel on Christmas Eve, December 24, 1944. As a result, approximately 763 American soldiers died.

The SS *Thysville* passenger liner was built in Hoboken, Belgium and its maiden voyage was to the Belgian Congo on February 2, 1922. Converted to a troop transport ship in 1939; a year later the Steamer *Thysville*, was carry in its vaults 129,499 carats Angola diamonds. The three ships were carrying a total of 526,777 carats or 248.14 pounds of diamonds secured in their safes.

Soon after the German occupation, the Belgium military administration was informed these steamers were underway at the outbreak of the war to Antwerp without having reached their destination. Therefore inquiries were made to Forminiere about these diamond consignments resulting in the findings that the *Elisabethville* and *Leopoldville* had reached the French harbor of La Pallice. Here the French admiralty confiscated the diamonds and deposited them with the Bank of France, La Rochelle. On June 18, 1940, the diamonds were loaded into the military transport ship *Golo* and sent to an unknown destination. It was reported the ship "probably" had left for Casablanca. Apparently reaching the port later, the diamonds on board the steamer *Thysville* were also confiscated by order of the responsible French Navy department, but they were sealed and left in the safe of the ship. The *Thysville* left the harbor of La Pallice on its own accord on June 16, 1940, and was later directed to England by the British Navy.

In the meantime, the capture of Eben Emael, Belgium opened the way for the invasion of France. On June 14, Paris was declared an open city. Three days later France announced in a radio broadcast that it was seeking an armistice. The 1940 armistice allowed Germany to occupy all of northern and western France. In effect, the country was at the mercy of the Germans.

During the invasion the Bank of France loaded five warships at Lorient with 1,200 tons of its own gold. At the same time, the French warship *Victor Schoelcher* was loaded with the Belgian, Luxembourgian, and Polish gold, the Polish gold being sent from Nevers, 300 miles north. The convoy sailed from Lorient, France, on June 16 and 17, 1940, hastening to the open sea under German air attacks. The ships linked up with other auxiliary cruisers and the aforementioned transport *Golo* with its cargo of diamonds. For unknown reasons, the convoy did not steam to the safety of Halifax, Nova Scotia, which was the port designated to receive the valuables, but instead proceeded to Casablanca where it docked on June 21. The diamonds were off-loaded and stored in the vault of the d'Etat de Marco. The same day, orders were issued for the gold convoy to sail immediately for Dakar, the main port of Senegal, Africa (then French West Africa). French sailors toiled in the heat and manhandled the heavy gold crates aboard a train that carried them nineteen miles inland to the tiny military camp of Thies, which was no more than a cluster of huts surrounded by barbed wire and guarded by a small contingent of soldiers.

The gold at Thies was tempting, and the British and Free French under Charles de Gaulle began planning an attack on Dakar. The gold, they reasoned, could be used to equip the Free French forces. On September 22, 1940, the Royal Navy provided powerful backing for an invasion by the Free French forces under the command of General de Gaulle. Through the thick sea mist an all-out gun battle began with additional engagement of aircraft and submarines. Several attempts to land Free French forces were made but abandoned due to intense resistance on the part of the Vichy French defense force.

An old house had been converted by Vichy forces into a strongroom to contain the gold. The windows were bricked up, a deep moat was dug around the perimeter and thirty armed guards were posted for a twenty-four-hour watch.

The Germans soon began to put pressure on the French to remove the gold from Dakar and threatened to use the Luftwaffe to assist matters. The French delayed and stalled for almost two years, but eventually the gold was airlifted to Marseilles where the Germans transported it to Berlin in twenty-four separate rail shipments over a period of a year and a half, ending on May 29, 1942. Shortly thereafter, the Reichsbank transferred title for the gold from the National Bank of Belgium and Luxembourg to the account of the German Reichsbank. The Bank of Belgium would not accept payment for its gold from the Germans, but the Bank of Luxembourg did accept payment in Reichsmarks for its 357 bars of gold, the Germans considered this a legally acquired purchase. Following the seizure of the Belgium-Luxembourg gold, the Reichsbank melted it down and recast large quantities, shrewdly stamping the gold bars with prewar dates.

The Germans immediately turned their attention to the Polish gold, insisting that it be shipped to the Bank of Poland in Warsaw. The French again stalled by arguing that Poland was a divided nation with the German and Russian occupation, and that they only recognized the exiled Polish government in England. Thus the Polish gold continued to sit in the military camp at Thies.

In July 1941, the occupying German military government of Belgium found out about the steamers from the Congo and their diamond cargo. They decided to investigate with the help of Forminiere Company officials, promising the firm part of the diamonds as an incentive. Their investigations of the transport steamer revealed the *Golo* had really sailed to Casablanca a year earlier. The German Consulate General in Casablanca was told the diamonds in question had been given to the French commerce and industry.

Undaunted, the Germans assigned John C. Urbaneck to the case, and he found out the complete consignment of about 397,000 carats of diamonds was actually stored in the vaults of the Banque d'Etat de Marco in Casablanca in November 1941. Based on photostats of bank documents, the German Armistic Delegation for Economy filed a claim with the French government for restitution of the diamonds for Belgium. The French responded the diamonds had been requisitioned for French commerce and sold to the Socété de Cordination Industrielle, in Vichy, therefore it was impossible to restitute the diamonds formerly belonging to Belgium. Urbaneck found out the Socété had been formed in late 1941 with the purpose to take over the diamonds. He further found that French officials were partners of the Socété de Cordination Industrielle and trying evidentially to profit from the Congo diamonds. Owing to this reason alone negotiations with the French government would be very difficult.

The Germans requested Forminiere supply a written certification authorizing the Germans to act as their legal agents, but the Belgium company was reluctant, fearing reaction to their large estates in the Congo if England should know they had been cooperating with the German military administration. Finally, the Belgian Ministry of Economy, under control of the occupying Germans, issued the requested certification. The Forminiere company officials were promised the return of the diamonds, grade them and sell the diamonds at the price valid during the fall of 1940 on the Antwerp market.

Two years after the diamonds were seized by France, at a conference in Paris with representatives of Forminiere, the German Armistice Delegation, and French minister of production, it was agreed to settle the claim. During these negotiations, the French government stated they were willing to sell 160,000 carats of diamonds to the German armament industry and declared expressively these were not part of the confiscated diamonds, but those held in stock by the French economy. The price was 200 Reichsmarks per carat. Very high prices considering the Germans were purchasing diamonds from the Netherlands and Belgium for two to five Reichsmarks per carat. From the inventory it was quite clear these were not from the confiscated lot, therefore the Germans decided to purchase the diamonds. Thus, they were brought to Paris for examination and at first sight it was obvious to the diamond experts that the diamonds had come from the Belgian Congo and were indeed property of Forminiere. These 160,000 carats were immediately confiscated by the German Security Service.

After new lengthy discussions with the French minister of production, he was willing to restitute the 397,268 carats to the Belgium firm Forminiere but 81,000 carats of these diamonds had already been used by French industries and an additional 16,000 were demanded to meet a one-year supply for manufacturing need. Now the French threw another demand into the negotiations, belonging to the Portuguese Company were 66,141 carats that were included with the valuables. The French refused the restitution of these Angola diamonds. After several weeks, the Germans produced an authorization from the Portuguese Companhia de Diamantes de Angola to act as their legal agent in the disposition of the diamonds. The French, incidentally, made one final attempt to frustrate the claim of the Forminiere company by stating that the diamond experts were not entitled to act as representatives of Forminiere, because the company was not Belgian-based but headquartered in the Congo. After a lengthy discussion, the German Reich ordered the French minister of production to turn over the diamonds to the Belgian firm. Finally all difficulties were overcome on March 15, 1943, with a final regulation of the restitution of the diamonds, and they arrived in Brussels a week later.

John C. Urbaneck of Frankfurt, Germany received special congratulations for his work in the negotiations for these Belgian Congo diamonds. He also received some of the diamonds and shared the lot with his relatives J. Wilhelm Urbaneck and Franz Urbaneck of Neu-Bamberg, Germany.[3]

The Germans then simply purchased the diamonds from Forminiere. During World War II, Belgium supplied the German armament industry with about 925,000 carats of industrial diamonds, which was enough to meet Germany's demand throughout the war.[4] Generally, industrial diamonds are too badly flawed, irregularly shaped, poorly colored, or small to be of value as gems, but they are of vital importance in metalworking and mining industries.

Later, a surprising Allied victory in North Africa caught the Vichy government off guard and the Polish gold had not been removed from Thies, Senegal. The United States dispatched two destroyers, the *Breeman* (DE-104) and *Bronstein* (DE-189) on March 23, 1944. The following day, the two destroyer escorts put into Dakar, French West Africa, and began loading an unusual cargo— fifteen tons of gold belonging to the Bank of Poland. The two warships departed Dakar on March 26, and proceeded to New York by the most direct and safest route and arrived there on April 3. The ships were relieved of their precious cargo by an army of policemen and armored trucks. The gold was deposited in the Federal Reserve Bank of New York.

The Ustasha Croatian Gold

During the turbulent days of World War II, Yugoslavia consisted of six provinces, Serbia, Croatia, Slovenia, Bosnia and Herzegovina, Macedonia, and Montenegro. From the beginning of its history the eastern and western districts were conflicting, not only politically but in cultural and religion as well. The Croatians and Slovenes became Roman Catholic and adopted the Latin alphabet, while the Serbians became Byzantium Christians and adopted the Cyrillic alphabet.

Following World War I, the Kingdom of the Serbs, Croats, and Slovenes was established as a sovereign state. On June 28, 1921, the new state acquired its first constitution despite the fact that the Croatian Peasant Party, the major political force among the Croats between the two world wars, abstained from voting. The Croatian leaders wanted the new state to be organized on federal principles. In 1929, King Alexander I dissolved the parliament, abolished the constitution and all political parties, and proclaimed the new states the Kingdom of Yugoslavia.

A year later, the Croatian Revolutionary Organization known as Ustasha was formed. Its leader was Ante Pavelic, a native of Zagreb and a lawyer by profession. This was an organization that sought to create an independent Croatian State. Pavelic was closely connected with Italy, for in 1932, he and about 500 followers had been invited to Italy, where in a training camp they were instructed in shooting, hand grenades, assassination, sabotage, secret writing and other subversive activities. Armed with Italian weapons, Pavelic and his men returned to Croatia.

Pavelic was best known for his part in the assassination of King Alexander. On October 9, 1934, the king arrived in Marseilles to start a state visit to the Third French Republic. While Alexander was being driven in a car through the streets a gunman shot the king, who died instantly. After his assassination this regime of royal dictatorship continued, with a regent acting for the then-eleven-year-old King Peter II.

On April 6, 1941, Yugoslavia was attacked by German and Italian armed forces. After ten days of bitter fighting, the Yugoslav armies were crushed. The youthful King Peter II and the cabinet fled the country and spent most of the war years in London. Yugoslavia was divided by the Axis powers. Some provinces were annexed outright while the others were given small degrees of self-government.

Fortunately the National Defense Council of Yugoslavia decided in May 1939/40 to send the major portion of their gold reserves to the Bank of England and Federal Reserve Bank, New York. On November 26, 1940, in view of the unfavorable events, the National Bank of the Kingdom of Yugoslavia packed the remaining gold coins into 166 cases and the gold bars into thirty-eight boxes and loaded the 204 containers onto trucks and drove the valuables to one of the Bank Branches in the city of Uzice. This gold was stored in a special constructed vault in the Bank Branch.

In the wake of the German attack on April 6, 1941, the gold was moved by trucks to the Bank Branch in the town of Mostar. Upon receipt of a wireless transmission it was to be moved again, as German forces were advancing, to the town of Niksic. The gold was loaded into trucks and offloaded into a railway car and arrived in Niksic on the morning of April 15, 1941, then reloaded onto trucks and hidden in a cave in nearby Trebjesa Mountain (Trebjesa Grotto).

It had been the intent of the Yugoslavian government to remove the gold by air, but the quick advance of the Germans and destruction of the Yugoslavian Air Force prevented this plan from being executed. Although when King Peter II, the third and last King of Yugoslavia, fled his country into exile, six of these cases accompanied him and his supporters.

During the king's departure on April 16, 1941, 100 cases of gold were removed from the cave loaded again onto four trucks under the command of Lieutenant Jonkovic, and sent to the town of Centije. At the same time ten cases were removed and driven to the Ostrog Monastery, a complex of cavelike churches built on the face of a mountain. Hiding out in this monastery was Patriarch Gavrilo V of Serbia, who was later arrested and sent to the political area of the Dachau Concentration Camp. Gavrilo had accepted the ten cases of gold and placed them under his safekeeping.

The Gestapo, in collaboration with the Wehrmacht, had discovered an important part of the Siberian State treasure concealed in the inaccessible mountains of Montenegro. The coterie that surrounded the young King Peter had previously, like so many others governments in alliance to England, endeavored to convey the state treasure to the British Isles. This attempt failed in Serbia as 375 million dinar, as well as ten chests of mint gold, were seized. In addition, the Patriarch of Yugoslavia, Gavrilo V, one of the principal instigators of the war against Germany, was arrested in the Greek Orthodox Convent of Ostrog, the last refuge of the former king and his followers.

The raid began on April 25, 1941, at 5:00am with German troops in Niksic, a small Montenegro provincial town, whose importance was due to the fact that it was located in a wide valley surrounded by high mountains. Located here was the aerodrome from which the plane left that carried the ex-king Peter and his close associates out of the country; the scene of the last act of his short career as Serbian King. It was at this airport that everything that could not be carried off in rapid flight from German troops was left behind; millions in banknotes, gold, state documents, and personal property.

The town of Niksic was still asleep when German troops led by a general and a few Gestapo agents left by motorcars and trucks via a narrow winding, one lane road that went up the mountain. The mountain scenery was wildly romantic, filled with ravines and steep rocks, and with a swift running stream many meters below. Here the soldiers caught sight of the Orthodox Monastery of Ostrog locasted in an almost perpendicular mountainside. The convent seemed still asleep when the Germans arrived, except for the "monotonous chanting" of the monks in the chapel; but the place was soon awakened by the German soldiers. The gatekeeper, "whose appearance betrayed a bad conscience," appeared and seemed at once to understand what the soldiers were after. He stated that the abbot was still in bed but was informed that the abbot's presence was required. The residences of the monastery were awakened and assembled in the reception room of the monastery administration building before the beginning of the search. When the German general asked whether everyone was present, he was told that all were there, except two monks who were in the church situated within a cave on the upper level of the monastery and dedicated to the Holy Cross.

Taking his word, the Germans began their search. A locked door had their interest. From the outside it appeared to be the entrance to a storeroom. The servant of the abbot assured them that it contained nothing important, but they were anxious to investigate. Finally, after the servant noticed the Germans had hammers and crowbars, the abbot produced a key. Having opened the door, they found themselves in a comfortable furnished room with chairs, a round table and more. There was a door opening to another room, and who should they find here, but the Patriarch of Yugoslavia, Gavrilo V.

Gavrilo V had just finished putting on his richly ornate official vestments when the Germans showed him two pistols he had hidden away in his cupboard. "Apparently the Patriarch was prepared to fight against Germany with other than merely spiritual weapons," concluded the Germans. Later they found other arms, rifles, numerous pistols and a large store of ammunition. "There was no doubt that it was only their sudden appearance which prevented these weapons being used against German soldiers."

Although the Gestapo had quite reliable clues that led to this monastery, the Patriarch maintained that he knew nothing of the treasures. It was only after forcefully making him understand that he might be shot for having concealed the weapons that he requested them to follow him. The Germans were led down to into the mountain cellar, closed by an iron door. By the light of their torches, they saw piles of boxes, officer's equipment and state documents. They then proceeded through a narrow damp passage where there was a small amount of food. A bit further along was the storeroom of the monastery, filled with countless numbers of sausage, hams, sacks of flower, sugar, coffee and other food; also more sacks with strong canvas, fastened with chains and locks. These were dragged up to daylight and they contained 375 million dinars that were loaded on a truck. More important were the ten chests containing gold coins and bars, each so heavy that two men had difficulty in carrying them.

The German forces then investigated the upper level church to search for the two monks missing from the previous assembly. They hurried to the romantic convent on the side of the cliff, climbing up countless steps. The two monks, looking pale and frightened, were there waiting. One was elderly and the other considerable younger. They led them through the church that was built into the rock, full of winding passages with beautiful views of the countryside. In contrast to the narrow cells in the tiny chapel below, the storeroom here was also wide and filled with many things. Here the Germans found a little chest filled with coins that had apparently come from the cache of gold below. After a thorough search, Gavrilo V and his private secretary were taken in cars by the Gestapo and interned as special political prisoners in Dachau Concentration Camp. The ten chests of gold were shipped to the Berlin Reichsbank.[1]

The remaining 204 cases of gold were scattered throughout western Yugoslavia; ten boxes recovered by the Germans, six chests taken by the king in exile and the remainder tracked down by the Italian Army. On April 24, Italian forces reached Niksic and removed the eighty-eight boxes of gold that had been left behind in a cave in nearby Trebjesa Mountain. The fifty cases sent from Niksic to Cetibje were recovered, and forty-two additional chests from Cetibje to Heroegnovi were removed by the Italians. An additional ten cases, hidden enroute to Heregnovi, were discovered and removed by the Italians, who shipped the gold to Rome in five shipments between May and December 1941. Thus, the 204 cases of gold were all accounted for by Bank of Italy officials. Five years later, eighty-one bags of these gold coins would be found buried in a shed on a dairy barn in Austria.

After the German blitzkrieg through Yugoslavia and Greece in March and April 1941, they dismembered Yugoslavia. The so-called independent state of Croatia was established on April 10, 1941. The Germans then established a puppet government under the leadership of the Croatian Ustasha, an organization based on religious racism and an ally of Nazism. Of all the pro-fascist, Axis supported, paramilitary organizations formed in central Europe during the 1930s, the Croatian Ustasha was the group that started out with the smallest popular support yet succeeded in compiling a record of murder and terrorism not even equaled by the murderous German SS.

When German troops entered Zagreb, the capital of Croatia, there was gold remaining in the National Bank of the Kingdom of Yugoslavia in Croatia. This gold (35,037.947 Troy ounces) was transferred to the newly established Croatian State Bank by Ustasha officials.[2] The National Bank of Serbia was seized immediately by German officials. During the war years, under occupation by the Germans and Italians, both banks continued to collect gold coins and bars from the citizens of that country, looted from Serbs, Jews and hundreds of thousands more.

Ante Pavelic, the leader of the Ustasha Party, remained in partial obscurity until the 1941 German-Italian invasion of Yugoslavia. The Italians sent Pavelic by motorcar to Zagreb where, with the help of the Second Italian Army and a body of about 1,000 Ustasha men, he was appointed head of the independent State of Croatia. On May 18, 1941, Pavelic traveled to Rome where he was received by the Pope. Here, he formally placed Croatia at the disposal of King Victor Emmanuel. The crown of the new kingdom was offered to King Victor's cousin, Aimone of Savoy, Duke of Spoleto. In spite of his acceptance, he never visited his kingdom, although he did maintain a firm foothold in the administration and economy of Croatia. At the same time a twenty-five-year agreement was signed guaranteeing collaboration and a frontier agreement that favored Italy. Thus, Italian troops flooded into Croatia, outnumbering the occupying German forces.

The Ustasha tried to closely follow the pattern of the Nazi Party with an Ustasha Political Party, Ustasha Youth, Ustasha Women's Organization, and Ustasha Military. But, in spite of a declared independent Croatia, the Ustasha Party was a failure from the beginning with the people.

The Ustasha established the Jasenovac Concentration Camp in the Independent State of Croatia during World War II. It was the only extermination camp that was not operated by the Germans, and was among the largest camps in Europe. It is estimated that about 90,000 people were murdered

After the establishment of the independent Croatian State, Croatian guard units are given a grateful reception by the population of Sarajevo.

here. Those exterminated were Jews, Greek Orthodox, Freemasons, and Serbs. Whole villages were destroyed and looted. This continued throughout the war.[3]

During this war, there were two large Yugoslavian military forces in opposition to the Axis. General Draza Mihailovich led the nationalist Chetniks who stood for the reestablishment of pre-war Yugoslavia, administrative centralism, and the dynasty. Josip Broz, also known as "Tito," led the communist inspired partisans who advocated a new Yugoslavia organized on a republican and federal basis. In actuality, a civil war existed between Mihailovich's chetniks and Tito's partisans. As the mighty Red Army rolled into Yugoslavia, the position of those chetniks who advocate cooperation with the Germans, was strengthened by the fact that the Nazis would be forced to evacuate Serbia. This would be the signal for a showdown between Tito's communists and the nationalists. Mihailovich therefore cooperated with the German army while it was still in Serbia, in order to lessen the effectiveness of Tito's partisans. By emphasizing the common fight against communism, Mihailovich would obtain as many weapons as possible from the Germans. He felt that he would be able to take over the German positions easily once the German army left. Informal negotiations between them were said to have been initiated. Regardless, in September 1944, the Soviet armies came to Yugoslavia in pursuit of the retreating German forces and ensured the partisans a victory in the internal struggle for political control. At this time a temporary "unity government" was formed including the representatives of King Peter II and Tito.[4]

In these closing days of the war, specifically one day before the end of World War II, on May 8, 1945, the extraordinary commissioner and Ustasha officials Dr. Mirko Puk and his associates Lt.Col. Cirilo Kralj and Major Mirko Vutuc fled into Austria with 3,779.384 Troy ounces of gold from the Croatian State Bank. In 1945, this amounted to a sum of $132,278.44. The gold was taken from the vault of the Croatian State Bank and loaded into a truck driven by Major Mirko Vutuc and guarded by a few gendarmes. The truck, along with a column of cars, carrying suitcases, pillows and other household goods, started from the bank at about 10:00 in the morning. The traffic was dense as the German Army, along with their Axis powers and collaborators, were in full flight. Trying to force their way through the traffic was demanding, resulting in Major Vutuc using force as described by Mato Crnek. "Vutuc often provoked incidents on the way being awfully rude, he was menacing with a revolver in his hand everywhere. At a crossroad not far from the frontier, Vutuc provoked an incident again. I [Mato Crnek] went forward and at that moment I saw four German officers aiming at Vutuc with their revolvers and forcing him to turn aside from the road into a meadow."[5]

Also entering Austria in these closing days of World War II, was Ustasha leader Ante Pavelic with a party of up to 1,500 Ustasha and $5-6 million in gold. Many of these Ustashas were quite wealthy. Most surprising, they were not treated as the enemy, even though they had fought with the Nazis, but accommodated as war refugees. They were quite surprised at being treated as refugees instead of enemy prisoners; after all their regime had declared war against the Allies, murdered, robbed and persecuted their victims by the tens of thousands, and delivered multitudes of Jews and other innocent victims to the Jasenovac Concentration Camp. Most of the Ustasha party members were interned in war refugee camps supplied by the United Red Cross, and many of the wealthy rented rooms in the better hotels in Salzburg including the fashionable Stern Hotel.

This gold was hidden in Austria until it was recovered and used in part to finance anti-communist activities aimed at Yugoslavia and also to maintain Pavelic in exile in Argentina. Other portions were used to maintain the Ustasha in Italy. A large number of the Ustasha members had fled Austria and moved into a large transit refugee camp in Bologna.

Yugoslavian Prime Minister, Ivan Subasic, shared confidential information with the OSS. From Subasic and Tito's point of view, they knew only too well that the Vatican was trying to organize a federation of Catholic states into which Croatia was to be included, and that he favored Tito's feeling that Croatian separatists would avail themselves of the opportunity when Allied troops landed in Yugoslavia to march against the partisans.[6]

The College of San Girolamo Degli Illirici in Rome, which provided living quarters for Croatian priests studying at the Vatican during and after World War II, was a center of Ustasha covert activity and a Croatian "underground" that helped refugees and war criminals to escape Europe after the war. The prime mover behind this activity in Rome was the secretary of the College, Father Dr. Krunoslav Stefano Dragonovic, who was also an Ustasha colonel and former official of the Croat "Ministry for Internal Colonization," the agency responsible for the confiscation of Serb property in Bosnia and Herzegovina.

Regarded as Ante Pavelic's "alter ego," the Croatian-born Father Dragonovic had been a professor of theology at Zagreb University. In 1943, he went to Rome, allegedly as the representative of the Croatian Red Cross, but probably to coordinate Ustasha affairs in Italy. Taking advantage of contacts inside the International Red Cross, and other refugee and relief organizations, Dragonovic helped Ustasha fugitives illegally emigrate to South America by providing temporary shelter and false identity documents, and by arranging onward transport, primarily to Argentina.

In July 1945, US Intelligence Officer, Captain Marion H. Scott, took the lead in the search for Ante Pavelic with the help of Heda Stern. Although she was a gentile, her Jewish husband had been a well-known, wealthy industrialist in Yugoslavia. Mr. Stern committed suicide ten days after the German occupation of Zagreb. After two years in Zagreb, Heda Stern made her way into Italy where she acquired a job with the US Military Government Forces, G-5, due to her many language skills.

Heda disguised as an American Red Cross worker, along with Captain Scott, visited the Ustasha refugee camps in Austria and Italy seeking information regarding their government officials. Most of the information gleamed from this investigation came from letters given to Mrs. Stern from inmates in the camps addressed to relatives or acquaintances in other camps. She then read all this correspondence looking for intelligence information. Captain Scott and Stern did not discover the location of Pavelic, but learned that Minister of the Interior Andrija Artukovic was in a camp in Spital an der Drau in the British Occupation Zone of Austria. Artukovic had been declared a war criminal by Allied forces, but the British released him with a diplomatic passport. With full knowledge of his true identity, the Swiss government issued Artukovic travel papers in the name of Alois Anich. He fled from Switzerland to Ireland, and then to California in 1948. He remained in the United States for forty years until his extradition to Yugoslavia for war crimes. There, during legal proceedings, he died of natural causes.[7]

Little is known of Pavelic's whereabouts for about eighteen months after war's end. The British occupation authorities in Austria definitely housed and took care of him and a thousand or so of his henchmen. The bottom line had to have been payoffs to the British, for all requests from the US Army and Yugoslavian authorities for the extradition of these war criminals were ignored by the British. Pavelic was then tracked to Rome where under the guise of the Vatican he was hidden. London informed Washington D.C. that the war criminal they were seeking for Yugoslavia was now a refugee behind Vatican walls. American intelligence did not pick up Pavelic's trail until his arrival in Argentina in November 1948. Here he shared his wealth with a few select Ustasha friends as he and his family created a miniature homeland and lived a life of luxury. At the age of seventy, Pavelic died in Spain in 1957 from wounds he had received two years earlier in an assassination attempt in Buenos Aires.

In 1951, Dragonovic worked with the US Army Counter Intelligence Corps (CIC) to organize the escape of anti-communist informant and Nazi war criminal Klaus Barbie to South America. In mid-October 1958, a few days after the death of Pope Pius XII on October 9, Dragonovic was ordered to leave the College of San Girolamo by the Vatican secretary of state. The indications are that Dragonovic lived quietly in Yugoslavia where he died in July 1983.

CHAPTER 4
The Italian Gold

In November 1942, the United States invaded North Africa in the first offensive by the US against German and Italian forces. By May 13, 1943, the American forces, under General Dwight D. Eisenhower, had forced the German troops to abandoned Africa completely.

From North Africa, the Americans and British invaded Sicily, after which Italy was the next logical target. The Italians, sensing this, forced Benito Mussolini to resign and the government was taken over by Marshal Pietro Badogilo. Mussolini was arrested and imprisoned. On September 3, 1943, the day of the Allied invasion, Badogilo signed an armistice with the Allies. Within two weeks on September 12, 1943, a daring glider raid led, by Otto Skorzeny, rescued Mussolini from a remote ski lodge at Gran Sasso, in the Abruzzi mountains, in central Italy. A few days later, Mussolini was back in Rome as the Prime Minister of the Italian Social Republic. The real power in Italy was, of course, in German hands. Not so much in military hands, who were largely engaged in holding off the Allies farther south, but in the hands of that same ruthless and highly trained instrument of suppression that the Germans used for policing all territories they conquered—the SS. However, the Germans remained in Italy and mounted a fierce opposition to the Allied invasion.

On September 20, 1943, with Rome under occupation by German forces, the commissioner of the ministry of finance, of the newly organized Republican Fascist Government, pursuant to order issued by the German Commander in Italy, instructed the governor of the Bank of Italy to immediately make arrangements for the transfer to northern Italy of all gold that remained in the vaults of the Bank at Rome. As evidenced, by the following letter the Governor of the Bank, V. Azzolini, thereupon ordered the Central Cash Department of the Bank to make the transfer:

Rome, 22 September 1943
No.87034:
To : Banca d'Italia, Central Cash Department, Rome
You are authorized to send by rail to our Milan Branch, through Messrs. Giacomo Strinasacchi and Alessandro Cembran, escorted by German military, the following:

162 Kegs, containing gold belonging to the Bank of the gross weight of Kg. 26,072.8 (including packing), corresponding to Kg.21,763.861837 of fine gold for 1.465,338,070.57 weight

20 bags, as above, containing gold coins of the gross weight of Kg. 1,320, (including packing), counter value of L.24,829,815.49;

13 kegs, containing gold coins, bars and platinum belonging to the Royal Treasury of the gross weight of Kg. 2,177.4 (including packing).

The kegs and bags containing the above gold will be kept in custody by the Milan Branch, intact and as sealed by the Cassa Centrale, and will be deposited in the vaults for safe custody; the gold belonging to the Bank will be at the disposal of this Head Office and the gold belonging to the Royal Mint will be at the disposal of the General Direction of the treasury. This letter will be kept in the vaults in place of the gold shipped to Milan

THE GOVERNOR
/s/ V. Azzolini[1]

Therefore, between September 20 and September 28, all of the gold was packed, transferred to the railroad station on German military trucks, and loaded onto railcars for the journey to Milan. The shipment was, at all times, accompanied and guarded by officials of the head office of the Bank of Italy and German troops. Upon arrival at Milan, the gold was entered onto the books of the Milan branch and deposited in its vault. Of the three keys to the vaults, one was retained by the German commander, and the other two were held by officials of the Milan branch.

In November 1943, looking for a safe place to store the Italian gold Berlin Reichsbank Official, Albert Thoms, traveled to northern Italy and inspected the old fortress at Fortezza, built in 1833 by Ferdinand I of Austria. Thoms found that the long abandoned fortress was two separate units built of two-meter square, stones. The upper fortress was about fifty meters above and overlooked the Alpine Brenner Road. The lower fortress was an ammunition storeroom. Thoms noticed that both fortification were very susceptible to air attacks. In the course of further examination, Thoms noticed a large semicircle tunnel in the center of the forts. The larger had sufficient granite rock to protect it from the heaviest bombardments. It needed a thorough cleaning and electric lighting installed. Most importantly, the front and back of the tunnel needed armored doors with a threefold lock as required by the treasury of the Reichsbank. Thoms also requested the ammunition be removed to some lower buildings. Of primary importance, the fort had a spur track that connected to the main Brenner railroad.[2]

Thoms then traveled the short distant south to Bolzano and informed the German Wehrmacht to make the necessary repairs and provide sufficient guards. He was told that the SS did not have a force that could help, and also, no suitable men were available to make the necessary repairs to the tunnel.

Albert Thoms definitely had influence, for within hours of being denied help with the tunnel, a meeting was arranged with General Karl Wolff, supreme commander of the Waffen-SS, and police chief of Nazi-held Italy, along with Rudolf Rahn, Italian ambassador. General Wolff an explosive, hard, blond Aryan had been a personal adjutant to Heinrich Himmler. Coming to Italy from a high post at Führer headquarters, he was rightly regarded as a favorite of the Nazi upper crust, and derived great prestige from that assumption. Adolf Hitler had assigned a trusted German diplomat, Rahn, as his ambassador to Mussolini's government, and he was given the additional title of Plenipotentiary of the Reich.

After this meeting, work was started to convert the tunnel in Fortezza to a vault. The debris was removed, wood was placed on the stone floor, and electricity was installed. The entrances were closed with steel reinforced concrete and an iron trellis, while waiting for the armored door with the three locks to be completed. Meanwhile, Thoms had secretly inventoried the Italian gold in the Bank of Italy vault in Milan. By making notes from index cards kept by the bank, Thoms surmised the vault contained 626 barrels of gold and 543 bags. This was more than had been reported by the bank to the German embassy. Moving the gold was proving more difficult than the construction of the vault in Fortezza, as it required the approval of Mussolini and the Italian minister of finance. These negotiations took several days.

On December 16, 1943, at 8:00 in the morning, the gold was loaded onto six trucks, that had to make multiple trips, and then driven to the train station where they were loaded into twelve boxcars. This process took nineteen hours and proved to be hard work, considering that each barrel weighed 180 kilos and each of the burlap bags of coins, seventy kilos. The bars were placed two each into a burlap bag and then placed in the barrels. After loading, the train doors were wired shut with steel wire, and the lead-seal of the Bank of Italy was stamped on each boxcar. The train was heavily guarded by eighteen policemen with machine guns, hand grenades and automatic pistols. The train then began its trip to Fortezza, but due to Allied bombing, the dual set of tracks had been mostly destroyed, and traveling and passing other trains on a single set of tracks proved difficult and slow. The following night, the transport arrived at its destination.

A local workforce of sixty men began to unload the gold and store it in the newly constructed vault. Due to the weight of the gold and age of the men, this proved to be an almost impossible task. After a delay, fifty Russian prisoners of war were brought to Fortezza to unload the valuable cargo. Finally, with such a concerted effort, the gold was finally stored in the afternoon of December 19. The now secure vault was guarded by twenty-six police guards and two bank officials. These officials, from Bolzano, moved into the vault and remained there day and night.[3]

The minister of finance of the Republican Fascist Government, in agreement with the German authorities, had ordered that the gold in Milan be removed and stored in the tunnels at La Fortezza near Bolzano per authorization of the following letter:

Rome, 28 December 1943
Banca d'Italia
Administration Zone Centrale

TO: Dr. M. Bernhuber,
Manager of the Reichsbank,
German Embassy, Rome

No.101817
Yesterday I perused the statements signed by the representatives of the Banca d'Italia, and by the delegates of the German Embassy, officials of the Reichsbank. in connection with the transfer of gold from Milan to Fortezza, which transfer is being effected following agreements between the Italian and German Governments and in accordance with precise instructions given by the Italian Minister of Finance.

As you are aware, the site at Fortezza was chosen by the German Military Authorities as offering greater security against eventual enemy air raids in view of the fact that the gold is stored between the remarkably: thick walls of underground rock tunnels. Although the gold is not stored in the vaults of one of our branches, the Banca d Italia which, as shown; also by your repeated assurances, is the sole owner thereof, will provide an appropriate guard through one of our Branch Manager's and other Bank employees. Until further notice, the security measures for the integrity of the tunnel will be entrusted to German Military authorities.

In view of the fact that the said gold is deposited at Fortezza for account of this Head Office, I would request your assistance in order to obtain that our Manage be put in the position of communicating with both our Como and Bolzano branch, the latter having undertaken the accounting records of the gold in question.

Awaiting your acknowledgment, and thanking you in advance.

The Governor
Sgd: V. AZZOLINI[4]

In March 1944, the Swiss government notified Germany that the Swiss National Bank and Bank of International Settlement had loaned the Italians a large sum of money in 1939 to help finance the war. Furthermore, the loan had come due in 1943 and the Italian government had failed to repay it. The Swiss claimed that the value of the loan, including delinquent charges equaled fourteen-and-a-half tons of gold. The Swiss pressured the Germans for a repayment.

On April 19, 1944, under the supervision of Thoms, eighty-nine locked and sealed barrels containing 1,068 gold bars weighing 405,251.418 Troy ounces were packed for shipment to the Bank of International Settlement in Basel, Switzerland. An additional seventy-four barrels containing 891 bars, weighing 346,715.329 Troy ounces, was packed for the National Bank of Switzerland.

After considerable concessions by the Germans, to influence the Swiss Government in continuing to provide banking services, the requested gold was then transported to Chasso on the Swiss border in German military vehicles, where it was then transferred to Swiss National Bank trucks. Under the protective custody of Swiss guards, the gold continued its journey into Switzerland to its final destination, the Swiss National Bank.[5] Thoms noted that 288 barrels and 108 bags of gold remained in Fortezza.

A few months after regaining power, Mussolini signed a decree; "The power to dispose the Central Bank gold reserve is exclusively committed to the state."[6] Thus, Mussolini gained complete control over the gold in the Bank of Italy. On February 5, 1944, he assigned a large amount of the gold to the German ministry of foreign affairs, as a trustee. The gold transfer was to include the sequestered Yugoslavian gold.

On March 3, 1944, the first shipment of the remaining Italian gold arrived in Berlin, by train; consisting of 175 barrels of 1,863 gold bars and 238 bags containing 20,680 coins. The gold was delivered directly to the Reichsbank and stored in the main vault, except for 135 bags of coins, which went to the foreign office of Joachim von Ribbentrop. On May 4, an additional sixty-two bags were transferred to the foreign office account, for a total of 197 bags of gold coins.[7]

The second shipment of Italian gold, consisting of 135 barrels and fifty-three bags of coins, arrived in Berlin on October 25, 1944; the entire contents was delivered to the Reichsbank. The 1,620 gold bars were individually identified by a serial number assigned by the Reichsbank, that was printed on a slip of paper and pasted to each bar. The bags of 8,560 coins were identified in a similar manner. The gold was to be purchased by the Reichsbank. A partial payment of eighty million Reichsmarks was made toward the first shipment, and fifty-five million more for the second shipment.[8]

The Italian gold also included 14,740 pounds of the precious metals that had been confiscated from the National Bank of Yugoslavia as noted in the previous chapter, all of which had been shipped to Berlin with the two shipments. The gold had been transported from Fortezza to Berlin under the supervision of Albert Thoms and vice directors of the National Bank of Italy, Mr. Gigle and Dalla Torre who were ordered to accompany the valuables.

A large amount of this gold was placed under the supervision of Bernd Gottfriedsen, a thirty-three-year-old member of the ministry of foreign affairs in Berlin, who reported to Joachim von Ribbentrop, a handsome, arrogant man and foreign minister of Germany. During the war years, Gottfriedsen held this position and was responsible for exchanging gold for foreign currency that was used to pay agents operating in countries outside greater Germany. Under orders from Berlin, forty-one sacks of gold had previously been shipped to a house in the forest near Ballenstedt, located in the Hartz Mountains. Staying at the chalet was Margaret Seifert, Gottfriedsen's young, attractive secretary. But with the gold from Italy, Gottfriedsen was instructed to sent forty-one sacks of this gold to the Julianna farm in the village of Heiligenstedten, about forty miles north of Hamburg. This farm was a popular safe haven for the wives and children of ranking Nazis in Berlin. On or about April 6, 1945, Gottfriedsen, his wife and Mrs. Mary May, a close friend of the von Ribbentrops, arrived with a large furniture van, filled with carpets, tapestry, two large wireless radios, and eight heavy boxes of gold which were all placed in the cellar of the large farm house. Mrs. May was a personal advisor to the interior decoration of the numerous houses of von Ribbentrop as well as the embassies in the neutral countries of Spain, Switzerland and Sweden.

A few days later, the bags of gold were removed from Heiligenstedten by the security service and sent 228 miles south on a truck to Ballenstedt, where it was stored with the previous forty-one bags of gold. About two tons of gold remained in the cellar of the Julianna farm.[9] On April 1, 1945, Gottfriedsen telephoned Miss Seifert in the Hartz Mountain forest house and told her to have the gold ready for immediate transfer to the Fuschl Castle, fifteen miles south of Salzburg, Austria. She was informed that the shipment of the eighty-two bags of gold by truck was under her supervision. Two days later, the gold arrived and was placed in the cellar of the castle where it remained under the care of the Wittman Security Group.

The Fuschl Castle had belonged to the Baron and Baroness von Remitz. Von Remitz had been an early, outspoken Reich opponent. As a result of his opposition, the Baron was arrested as an enemy of the state. His castle was seized by the Gestapo and requisitioned by von Ribbentrop, who used it as a home and headquarters. The Baron would die in a concentration camp, before the eighty-two burlap bags of gold were stored in his former cellar along with another 135 bags that had been sent there in the meantime.

With the US Army fast approaching the Austrian border, Gottfriedsen was instructed to go at once from Berlin to the Fuschl Castle and take charge of the gold. He left Berlin with several bars of gold, and two days later arrived at the castle. Von Ribbentrop was supposed to meet there but he did not arrive. Gottfriedsen took it upon himself to move the gold deposit. He examined the eighty-two bags and noticed that one bag was torn and coins had fallen out. He then sought advice from the local Nazi leaders regarding the safeguarding of the gold.

Art and gold guarded by a German soldier and U.S. Sergeant Wallace E. Holen at Fortezza, Italy. Destined for Germany, these valuables were abandoned by the Germans when their trucks ran out of fuel.

The head of the Farmers Association informed Alois Ziller, a forty-three-year-old local dairy farmer near Hintersee, that he was to attend an urgent meeting with a high official of the ministry of foreign affairs. During the meeting, Ziller was told that it had been decided to conceal a large quantity of valuables on his farm. He was instructed to dig a deep hole in a wooden shed to the right side of his barn. The hole was to be large enough to contain two large packing cases. Ziller was told to "observe the strictest silence on the matter." He was informed that the valuables would arrived on the night of April 27, 1945, and at nightfall he should wait at the crossroad of Baderluck bei Hof to act as a guide for the truck driver. Ziller arrived punctually at the agreed spot, spent two hours waiting, then returned home. Later that night, a truck accompanied by Gottfriedsen arrived with two packing cases and forty-one bags of gold coins. The packing cases were removed and placed in the hole, and then one case was filled with the forty-one burlap bags of coins. Ziller recognized that the bags were filled with coins and in his mind estimated that the bags weighed about 130 pounds each. When the door to the shed was shut, Gottfriedsen told Ziller that he would return before daybreak with another load of gold coins.

Ziller waited in vain until daylight but the truck did not return. In the early hours of April 29, 1945, Gottfriedsen arrived, requesting help. Ziller accompanied him back about one mile to the truck that was stuck in the mud and snow. They could not free it. Leaving a guard, Gottfriedsen and his helpers returned to the Fuschl Castle. The following day they freed the truck with another vehicle and proceeded to the dairy farm. The contents of the truck, forty bags of gold, were placed in the remaining packing case. The cases were closed and Ziller filled the hole with dirt. When all traces of digging had been smoothed out, Gottfriedsen, again, reminded Ziller that he must remain silent, promised him a reward for his work, and wished him goodbye. (Years later Ziller complained that he never received the reward.)

On May 1, Gottfriedsen loaded the torn bag and three other bags of coins, including the bars he had brought from Berlin, into a large truck and drove sixty-nine miles south to Bad Gastein. The town mayor (Bürgermeister), along with Gottfriedsen, buried the gold contained in a small packing case in the backyard of a house at number 89, Böcksteiner Street, Bad Gastein.[10] Gottfriedsen will return in a later chapter.

The Italian gold was shipped from Berlin to the Kaiseroda salt mine in Merkers, Germany on February 11, 1945, a location that was, as we shall see later, a significant one in the history of Nazi plunder.

After the collapse of Mussolini, and during the retreat from Italy, the Germans did a great deal of plundering under the guise of aiding their ally in carrying her art treasures to safety. The systematic burning of Italian libraries, and the looting of villas and palaces occurred when discipline was lax and feelings ran high against Germany's former ally. During the shipment of these valuables, the Italian fascist government clamored for the return of the art to Italian control. Their ambassador in Berlin protested to von Ribbentrop, who promised to speak to the Führer. But it was to no avail. The Germans intended to keep what valuables they had obtained. These *objets d'art* were destined for Alt Aussee, but, because of a lack of fuel, only a few of the most valuable items left the rocky Italian outpost at Fortezza. A considerable amount of gold remained in Fortezza.

By May 1945, units of the US Fifth Army, operating under combined Anglo-American Command, occupied the Bolzano region. On May 6, 1945, the Fortezza tunnels were opened for inspection by British and American military authorities. Officials of the Bolzano branch of the Bank of Italy were still there when Allied forces took over. After inspection, the gold remaining in the tunnels was placed under guard of Fifth Army units until May 17 when it was returned to Rome. It was then placed in the vaults of the Bank of Italy under custody of the Allied Financial Agency to hold the gold under instructions from the Combined Chiefs of Staff.

After the return of the gold to Rome, the Bank of Italy, upon request of the Allied commissioner, checked the gold returned against the lists compiled in 1943 when the shipment to Milan was made. The gold remaining at Fortezza consisted of 23,088.176 kilos, indicated as belonging to the Bank of Italy; 1,678 kilos indicated as belonging to the Royal Mint and 146.95 kilos, indicated as belonging to the Ministry of the Treasury. Apparently, none but bona fide Italian gold was recovered by the Allied forces.

CHAPTER 5
The Netherlands' Diamonds

"Market Garden," the airborne operation, conceived by British General Bernard Montgomery, began on September 17, 1944. It was designed to lay a carpet of airborne troops along a narrow corridor, extending approximately sixty miles into Holland from Eindhoven northward to Arnhem. The airborne troops were to secure bridges across a number of canals, as well as, across three major water barriers—the Maas, the Waal (the main downstream branch of the Rhine), and the Neder Rijn (Lower Rhine) Rivers. Through the corridor opened by the airborne troops were to pass British ground troops in a prompt push to Arnhem. The principal objective of the operation was to get Allied troops across the Rhine. Three main advantages were cutting the land exit of those Germans remaining in western Holland; outflanking the enemy's frontier defenses, the Siegfried Line; and positioning British ground forces for a subsequent drive into Berlin.

The supreme commander, Eisenhower, endorsed Montgomery's strategy and provided him General Lewis H. Brereton's 1st Allied Airborne Army. Later, Eisenhower agreed to divert supplies from other fronts to Montgomery's 21st Army Group, therefore setting the scene for one of the Allies most disastrous errors in northwest Europe.

During the initial assault of Arnhem, the Germans had reason to be concerned: the diamonds from the Amsterdam diamond industry had been ordered to be removed from that city and stored in the bank vaults of Arnhem. Mr. Erich Hagen and Herr Plumer were dispatched from Hamburg to Arnhem with instructions to seize the diamonds still there. Hagen and his associate were to travel to Holland in a diesel-powered Mercedes supplied by the German army, but for some reason the army was unable to supply the men with a car and Hagen and Plumer had to drive Plumer's big American made Oldsmobile to Arnhem. The Oldsmobile used a lot of gasoline and as there was not enough available for the trip, the two agents were forced to buy limited gasoline on the black market in each small town, in order to reach their destination.

Once they reached Arnhem, Plumer visited the Bank of Amsterdam and explained to the Dutch officials that he was to remove the diamonds from the besieged city to the safety of the Reichsbank in Berlin. Both Plumer and Hagen tried to convince the Dutch bankers that the diamonds would be inventoried properly and stored in the safety of the German Reich. They stressed that the Germans would be totally scrupulous in handling the diamonds, and that the German vaults would never fall to the enemy, but still, Hagen noted, the bankers looked puzzled.

Hagen, realizing he could not get the bankers voluntarily to open the vault and safe deposit boxes, demanded a list of the contents. He received a typewritten list of diamonds on deposit. The *Sprengkommando* (blast commandos) were then dispatched to the bank. They blasted the vault and then dynamited open the individual safe deposit boxes. Valuable items were destroyed during the powerful explosions.

The Germans removed 23,995 carats of diamonds from the vaults. These were packed in brown envelopes, and in the upper left corner was written, "Service State Office for Trade, Industry, and Shipping." In the middle of the envelope the name of the owner was printed. The brown envelopes were placed in larger yellow ones pre-stamped "German Treasure Agents." During the blasting and removal of the diamonds, Hagen remarked, "It should be noted, that on the Dutch and German side, much was stolen during the move at Arnhem."[1]

The diamonds were taken to Berlin by car and deposited in the Reichsbank. Toward the end of the war, they were removed from Berlin, and in May 1945, were uncovered by the US Army at the Friedrichshall Salt Mine and stored in the US Foreign Exchange Depository in Frankfurt, Germany as Shipment 22.

PART II

THE FOREIGN EXCHANGE DEPOSITORY

A Quick Look at the Foreign Exchange Depository

The Foreign Exchange Depository was a successor organization of the Currency Branch, Supreme Headquarters, Allied Forces Europe. This branch was created on September 7, 1944, and its primary function was receiving, holding and supplying occupation currency for Allied Armed Forces and Military Government, and was under the supervision of the Finance Divisions.

Actual operations began on April 10, 1945, when the Currency Branch under the command of Lt.Col. Henry D. Cragon arrived at Frankfurt/Main, Germany with the mission of establishing and operating the depository. The large Reichsbank (State Bank) building, on Adolf Hitler Anlage, then occupied and in use by Reichsbank officials was requisitioned. This was done principally, due to the efforts of Colonel Bernard Bernstein, who was chief of the finance division and responsible for the collection and control of the great variety of assets that later came into the depository. Possession of the building was established on April 17, when the three keys to the main vault were turned over to the US military government by the director of the Reichsbank. Certain structural alterations were necessary in order to provide greater secure storage capacity than was afforded by the existing vaults of the Reichsbank. For this purpose the air raid shelters in the sub-basement were strengthened and sealed.

The first shipment from the Merkers Mine arrived at the depository on April 15, 1945. Some of the Currency Branch personnel had traveled to the mine, located between Fulda and Eisenach, to supervise the loading and distribution of this enormous hoard, consisting of gold bullion, gold and silver coins, platinum, jewelry, a large quantity of SS loot and various currencies including 2,700,000,000 Reichsmarks (a 1945 value of $270,000,000) bags, boxes, parcels; there were approximately 11,750 containers in this shipment alone. The long caravan of trucks that brought the valuables, identified as Shipment 1, from the mine over a period of days was provided with a strong military escort of army trucks, motorcycles, guards, and fighter planes in order to eliminate the danger of loss. Seventy-five additional shipments were received at the depository during the remainder of 1945. These mainly came from the US Zone of Occupation in Germany, but some shipments were from Austria, Czechoslovakia and other areas taken by the US army. By the end of 1945, the depository contained the largest single collection of wealth in the world, with the possible exception of the valuables at Fort Knox, Kentucky. The gold holding alone was only second to those at Fort Knox.

During June 1945, three US treasury agents arrived to inventory the contents of the depository. The bars of gold were identified by bar number and arranged in piles of thirty each. Shipments were not separated and a location chart was drawn of each compartment with the first bar number of each stack of thirty clearly identified. The bags of gold coins were stored in a similar fashion and also identified by a location chart.

The treasury team inventoried the valuables on worksheets that included the date they were received by the Reichsbank, the name of the original smelter of the bar, the name being copied from the bar, the name of the assayer or multiple assayers, the bar number or numbers stamped on the bar, gross kilograms, and the fineness of the gold based on assay certifications and weight. This treasury inventory report, known as the "Howard Report," remained at the Foreign Exchange Depository and contained 234 worksheets covering gold, platinum metal and odd bars, 108 worksheets on gold coins, silver and rare coins, and five large folders of worksheets on silver bars.

Meanwhile, the personnel of the Currency Branch, consisting of some sixteen officers and 130 enlisted men, proceeded with the laborious task of inventorying, sorting, orderly storage and cataloguing the contents of the depository. Within two months, it became apparent that the space in the Reichsbank building would not be sufficient to store all the assets that had been taken into control by various army agencies primarily under Military Law 53; therefore these properties were held in various Reichsbanks in the US Zone as a temporary measure.

An elaborate security system modeled on that used by the US Mint was instituted. Triple control was established for the main vault where the most precious items were kept, and dual control for all other strong rooms. No person could be admitted to the main vault without the concurrent cooperation of three officers; each carried keys to dual locks under his exclusive control. In addition, the vault door had a combination lock, known only to the three officers. No person could enter any vault or strong room unless two of the three officers were present. Additionally, an infantry company of the 29th Infantry Division was assigned the duty of guarding the building, premises and all vault approaches. Barbed wire barriers and flood lights were maintained around the building of which only had one entrance.

The large Reichsbank building in Frankfurt was home to the Foreign Exchange Depository.

This cache was discovered by the U.S. Army in the Merkers salt mine where it had been deposited by the Berlin Reichsbank for safety from Allied air raids.

Locked cages with bags of gold coins.

Sealed cages with gold bars on the floor.

Large metal containers containing currency from nearly every country in the world.

In the main vault, through wire netting, could be seen rooms filled with gold bars stacked three deep from wall to wall. The bars had an average weight of twenty-five pounds and a 1945 value of $12,500 each. In one cage was a gold nugget, approximately the size of a grapefruit, that was said to be the largest nugget in the world. In another was the gold of the German Foreign Office, called the Ribbentrop gold. In another was virtually the entire Hungarian gold reserve. Still another compartment housed boxes of diamonds of all sizes, and specially processed metals. One compartment was devoted to super precious metals such as platinum, iridium, and palladium. Several sections were filled with sacks of gold from different countries. Also in the massive vault system were the famous crown jewels of the Hungarian, Hesse, and Hohenzollern dynasties.

One large room contained about 200 suitcases or small trunks of SS loot. Included in this loot was an untold quantity of money and personal jewelry stolen from victims of the Nazi regime. There was also 600 pounds of gold fillings extracted from the teeth of concentration camp victims. The two air raid shelter vaults were stacked to the ceiling with boxes of alarm clocks, most of them inexpensive; all part of the SS loot. No attempt had been made to evaluate the SS loot but from a cursory glance it was apparent the value was a very large figure.

Of interest to the Monetary Branch was the hoard of English pounds sterling buried by the retreating Nazis. The money was declared counterfeit by experts dispatched from Scotland Yard, but were pronounced to be so well done as to be virtually indistinguishable from genuine notes. The face amounts of these notes were approximately $8,000,000 in denominations from 5 to 100 pound notes. They were all neatly stacked and bill-strapped as if they had just come from the printing press and were quickly shipped to the Bank of England.

As these gold shipments arrived on a daily basis at the Foreign Exchange Depository, Colonel Bernard Bernstein and his staff kept each shipment separate and confined to a specific area in each compartment of the large vault. This one vault contained eighteen separate secure compartments

The valuables were divided into the following four classifications of definitions:

Monetary gold: Gold held as part of a country's reserves in a government's central bank or other monetary authority at the time of wrongful removal by German forces.

Non-monetary gold: Gold that was seized or obtained under duress by the Nazi government and later confiscated by the US Army. Such gold is unidentifiable as to national or individual origin, or it originated in various concentration camps regardless of geographic location. This classification also included valuables such as silver, diamonds, platinum, and other small items of high value.

Returnable gold: Gold surrendered to the Germans by individual residents of occupied countries still in its original form and identifiable as to individual ownership.

German gold: Gold held under Military Law 53: neither: monetary, non-monetary, nor returnable. This classification also included silver and other valuables seized under Military Law 53.

Military Law 53 was effective in May-June 1945 and the acquisitions from this law were covered under Article III as follows:

Within 15 days of this law all of the following classes of property shall be delivered, against receipt of therefore, by the owner, holder or other person in possession, custody or control thereof, to the nearest branch of the Reichsbank, or as otherwise directed: Currency other than German currency. Gold or silver coins; gold, silver, or platinum bullion or alloys thereof in bullion form.

Because of Military Law 53, thousands of Germans in the US Zone turned in silver, US currency, gold coins, and gold bars to their local bank. The central banks were scattered in the American Zone, such as Mannheim, Ulm, Karlsruhe, but the largest bulk of the coins were confiscated in Munich.

The gold was sent to Finance Division, External Claims Branch, Frankfurt/Main. Gold coins in this category were taken from some 3,000 individual Germans in the US Zone. Bars, mostly small, were also seized; one of the larger amounts was taken from August Wolf Reinhardt of Heidelberg, consisting two bars (38.03 ounces). German citizens were given a receipt for their valuables preprinted in German and English and signed by a local German banker.

German valuable and property not seized by Military Law 53 could be subject to Military Law 52, which had been passed in September 1944 soon after US troops crossed the German border. Military Law 52 made all property in Germany subject to seizure by the US military government.

The first page of Military Law 53.

Surrendered property to Reichsbank Dessau
according law Nr.53

I. German silver coins (currency money)

Nr.1	Städtische Kreissparkasse, Dessau	RM	1850.—
2	Stange , Dessau	"	200.—
3	Füg "	"	1000.—
4	Müller "	"	1000.—
5	Kratz "	"	1000.—
6	Cords "	"	1000.—
7	Boitin "	"	1000.—
8	Faust "	"	935.—
9	Volksbank e.G.m.b.H., Dessau	"	4997.—
10	Wolf, Karl, Dessau	"	1000.—
12	Spieß, "	"	984.—
13	Welckenbach "	"	180.—
14	Angelmeier	"	1000.—
15	Anhalt-Dessauische Landesbank, Abteilung der Adca, Dessau	"	109.—
18	Wyrzykala, Dessau	"	17.—
19	Schmidt "	"	400.—
20	Schüler "	"	1000.—
21	Dr.Gerd Huppertz,Dessau,Hindenburg-Allee10	"	28.—
22	Dr.Adolf Mittelstraas,Dessau, Schlageterallee 4 I	"	300.—
23	Hertha Lachenwitz, Dessau	"	2000.—
24	Friedel Diepolder, "	"	1000.—
25	Johannes Fügner, " Körnerstr.12	"	218.—
26	Gertrud Koop	"	1000.—
27	Willy Junker, Dessau, Bugenstr.4	"	50.—
28	Wilhelm Lindemann, Dessau, Johannisstr.12	"	595.—
31 ✓	Elsa Usener, Dessau, Fischereiweg 21	"	2.—
32	G.Polysius A.G., Dessau	"	226.—
33	Käthe Graf, Dessau, Sclageterallee 58	"	102.—
35 ✓	Frau Olga Bode, Dessau,Hindenburg-Allee 10	"	2.—
37	Ewald Paragenings, Dessau, Flössergasse3	"	257.—
46	Franz Ziegler,Dessau,Ludwig-Würdigstr.12	"	336.—
47	Karl Stoye, Dessau, Friederikenpl.32	"	79.—
48	Auguste Elze,Dessau,Damaschkestr.99	"	150.—
51	Reichsbank	"	18.861.—
		RM	42.878.—
(57)	Dr.Curt Wittig,Dessau, Goethestr.24. registered under Nr.III)	RM	29.—

II. German and other silver coins (not currency)

Nr. 30	Margarete Brauns, Dessau, Albrechtstr.16	Mark	17.—
(35)	Olga Bode, Dessau, Hindenburgallee 10	"	1.—
40	Otto Rummel, Dessau, Böhmischestr.41	"	253.30
(31)	see also under Nr.I Elsa Usener, Dessau, Fischereiweg 21,S.S.2.—		
(57)	registered under Nr.III Dr.Curt Wittig,Dessau	XM	50.—

38

Military Law 53: one sheet from thousands of pages of listed receipts from German civilians.
This account is Shipment 34 from the village of Dessau.

The officers and enlisted men at the depository had hardly started on the inventory when the drastic redeployment program caused a halt in this operation, so that all but the most essential currency functions came to a halt in October 1945. Col. Bernard Bernstein returned to the United States for discharge and believing the fate of all the assets in the Foreign Exchange Depository had been left to the then German Government, or as he told the author: "Those valuables were left to the Adenauer régime." The colonel was misinformed, as Konrad Adenauer, a German statesman and later chancellor did not assume control of the valuables in the Foreign Exchange Depository.

The Supreme Headquarters Allied Expeditionary Forces, SHAEF, had also disbanded and it commander, General Dwight D. Eisenhower and the military leaders, returned to the United States. Assigned to the Foreign Exchange Depository at this time was civilian, Lewis S. Harris, who had been sent to the European Theater as a fingerprint expert. Now he, along with three more "displaced" well-paid civilians working for the Army, had been assigned to the depository as security officers. They were the complete staff in a run down, dark, building with the ceiling collapsing; "it just looked like desolation." When later asked about his duties, Harris responded: "As I say, we probably did nothing as Security Officers; except to visit vaults about twice a week."[1] The depository remained mostly dormant; collecting dust, for six months until a reorganization of forces in Europe took place under the authority of the Occupation Forces Government of the United States, OMGUS. During this dormant period, Allied nations had been filing claims for valuables that had been collected by the US Army and shipped to the Foreign Exchange Depository, only to be ignored.

This was an embarrassment to the US Department of State. Something had to be done. In March 1946, Col. William G. Brey of San Francisco was appointed Chief of the Foreign Exchange Depository, assisted by civilians, Frank J. Roberts, Frank C. Gabell and Edwin P. Keller. Operating under the endorsement of OMGUS, the depository was completely reorganized. The staff was beefed up to twenty-two military and US civilians, six technical experts in gold and diamonds, and sixty-five German employees. The security officer was Col. Brey's son-in-law, Capt. Francis D. Ruth who was responsible for the security of the depository. The depository staff was well qualified including one German civilian, Albert Thoms, the former officer in charge of precious metals for the main Reichsbank in Berlin. He had been captured at Merkers.

When Brey took over the FED, the main vault had not been entered since the Howard inventory in the summer of 1945. The cement floor had uncrated bars of gold stacked in square piles, large heaps of fifty canvas bags, each weighing about 100 pounds, filled with gold coins, tied and tagged, all in one large room with burned out light bulbs and dust. The coins had been weighed to gross amount, which presented Brey and his staff with a large problem. The actual amount of gold could only be obtained by separating the coins by country as each one had a different appropriation of gold for their coins. They were reweighed and separated by country and placed into smaller twenty-pound bags. About ten bags were then placed into wooden boxes and banded with a steel strap. For the smaller English sovereigns, eleven bags would fit into a box. The empty 100 bags would be turned inside out and the lining checked for small gold coins. (While doing research in the National Archives the author opened a small cotton bag and found several dime size gold coins. He then contacted the proper authorities, and they secured the gold coins.)

One of the more knowledgeable German workers, Albert Thoms left the depository for several months on May 8, 1946, Thoms wrote and signed a statement concerning SS deposits of gold, silver and foreign currency taken from concentration camp victims and deposited in the Reichsbank. Then on May 15, 1946, he went to Nuremberg and was a valuable witness at the trials of Nazi war criminals. Thoms, like most Germans, would deny in one breath that he ever knew about the concentrations camps and in the next, excuse himself by saying had he done or said such a thing he would have been thrown into one.

It is not clear if Thoms was charged at this time with a minor role in war crimes, but this much is known: on October 13, 1946, Claims Chief Frank J. Roberts drove a jeep to the railway station in Frankfurt and met Thoms. After considerable discussion concerning Thoms' light sentence, and subject to the enrollment in the denazification program, Roberts determined that Thoms was eligible for reemployment at the Foreign Exchange Depository. He was to prove helpful in managing the paperwork involved in tracking the movement of valuables during the war and in processing the claims submitted by the various countries and individuals. Fortunately, uncovered at Merkers, were the books and records of the Precious Metals Department of the Berlin Reichsbank. A multitude of these claims were filed by Albania, Austria, Belgium, Czechoslovakia, Greece, Italy, Luxembourg, Netherlands, Poland and Yugoslavia.

Under Colonel Brey's control, an inventory began for a great variety of valuables, concentrated in the vaults estimates to be worth in excess of $500,000,000. The inventorying of jewelry and precious stones began in April 1946, with the arrival of the first jewelry experts. Up until then, the priority had been given to the inventory of SS loot recovered at Merkers Mine, Buchenwald and Dachau concentration camps. Most of these valuables were unidentifiable as to ownership. The jewelry, precious and semi-precious stones, beads, and costume jewelry was sorted into many containers, resulting in the separation of thousands of carats of precious stones of all types. Accounted for were thousands of watches, rings, brooches, jeweled ornaments and tons of scraped silver from damaged tableware. Inventoried were the jewel collection of Hermann Göring's wife, Emmy, and Hitler's mistress, Eva Braun. As late as August 13, 1947, there were hundred of boxes and bags that had not been inventoried, mostly shipments from Military Law 53, including six boxes of jewelry and personal effects from Dachau concentration camp from Shipment 52E. These items in individual envelopes were identifiable and would be returned to country of origin. During this time of upheaval, it is interesting to note that jewelry serves no military purpose. Its use is universal among all races and ages. Every civilization has lavished their most talented artists and craftsmen in making jewelry and its only function is to bring attention to oneself as a personal adornment.

In August 1946, on authority of the US Army Commanding general, and under Colonel Brey's command, 1,013.345 tons of gold bars and coins were returned by train to the Hungarian National Bank of Budapest along with 813 bag of rubles turned over to the Russians. The German government was "loaned" forty tons of silver for the purpose of reactivating the German silver economy in the American Zone of occupation. Strangely enough, the Currency Section of the Foreign Exchange Depository was responsible for processing payments to over two million former German prisoners of war.

During November and December 1947, released by the Foreign Exchange Depository to France for deposit to Belgium and Luxembourg were 2,436.17 tons of monetary gold for France, and 1,041.35 tons for the Netherlands.

The year of 1948 would be busy, starting with the shipment of all remaining monetary gold to the Bank of England. These shipments of 4,576.70 tons of gold were made in several deliveries by commercial aircraft. Many assets taken under Military Law 53 were returned to the originating bank for evaluation and disposal prior to July 31.

All non-monetary gold and currencies originating from SS sources, along with thousands of unidentifiable diamonds, jewelry and other assets, were delivered to the Intergovernmental Committee for Refuges (IGCR), later renamed the Preparatory Commission of the International Refugee Organization (PCIRO). For example, on February 9, 1948, twenty large boxes of gold and silver bullion were shipped to London. These valuables were to be at the disposal of victims of Nazi persecution for resettlement and rehabilitation.

Col. Brey retired from the military in July 1948 and returned home. He was replaced by Frank C. Gabell who took over a dissolving department consisting of himself, one US civilian and six secretaries/labors. The US Army was removing itself from Military Government functions and relieving the army from the responsibilities of the Foreign Exchange Depository. In the process the remaining assets of the depository were transferred to the Bank Deutscher Länder and the Landeszentralbank von Hesse, subject to further instructions from the Occupation Military Government of the United States (OMGUS).

After December 1950, the Foreign Exchange Depository ceased to exist. Its few remaining assets consisted of unclaimed personal items, some platinum bullion, German securities, and an odd assortment of foreign currency and industrial diamonds. This material was transferred to the Bank Deutscher Länder, which had already taken over most of the FED building (the former Frankfurt Reichsbank) a year earlier. Ironically, at least one of the platinum bars and some of the securities had come from the Merkers cache in April 1945. Albert Thoms, the man responsible for shipping the Berlin Reichsbank assets to Merkers, was one of the two representatives for the Bank Deutscher Länder who accepted custody of the Foreign Exchange Depository's remaining assets. Several items were processed up and until the end of 1951.

The story of the Foreign Exchange Depository still continues. During the summer of 1948, most of the records of the Reichsbank's Precious Metals Department were partially microfilmed by the US Army and, interestingly enough, turned over to Albert Thoms, who continued working for Bank Deutscher Länder. These records have subsequently disappeared in Germany, and there has been a search for them in 1998 in the belief they would shed light on how much non-monetary gold (e.g., dental gold) was melted down and mixed with the monetary gold (i.e., central bank gold) and thus indicate how much restitution still should be made to victims of Nazi persecution and their heirs. Thoms died in 1977, and some of the missing documents were found in his estate records during an extensive search in 1998.[2]

During his service with the Foreign Exchange Depository, Col. Brey was asked: "Would this be a true statement? A final accounting of the contents of this building and what is gotten out of it depends to a great extent on the honesty of you and the people working for you." Col. Brey answered: "Yes, the integrity of my staff and myself. I have a staff whose integrity is beyond question."[3] His "yes" was absolutely the truth and the US Army was most fortunate to have such men as Col. Bernard Bernstein and Col. William G. Brey serving our country during and immediately after World War II.

The Merkers Gold Cache

In the morning of April 4, 1945, the village of Merkers was cleared by I Company, 3rd Battalion, 358th Infantry Regiment, 90th Infantry Division. The advancing soldiers were told by slave laborers that the mine contained some German equipment and money. One regiment remained behind to guard the treasure as the rest of the division pushed ahead. All roads were lined with liberated slave laborers, some walking aimlessly, becoming slowly accustomed to their freedom, some walking determinedly, burdened by huge packs, with their eyes firmly fixed on the road that led to home. Days later, the 90th Division Military Police discovered the mine contained the largest treasure hoard ever found.

Located within the Kaiseroda Mine at the village of Merkers in Thuringia Province, was the most valuable prize of World War II—the main cache of Germany's gold reserves. The mine was owned by Wintershal Inc., the leading German producer of potash, chemicals, synthetic gasoline, and rock salt that was refined into table salt. Extensive mining over the years had created more than thirty-five miles of underground tunnels. At the entrance to the mine were several large, five-story brick buildings in which were housed electrical generators powered by coal. These generators produced electricity for lights, air ventilation fans, and power for the large elevators used in the mineshafts.

In July 1943, as a safety precaution from the incessant Allied bombing of Berlin, the German Reichsbank decided to move twenty tons of gold stock from to various provincial banks in the smaller cities of Germany. In February 1944, the Berlin Reichsbank ordered that a part of the gold (seven tons) be sent back to Berlin as a preliminary move in an operation to evacuate most of the Reichsbank gold to a salt mine in Merkers, Thuringia for greater safety.

Deposits began arriving at Merkers with twenty-two railroad cars of gold bars and coins, eighteen of which were delivered on February 11, and four more on March 18, 1944. The gold was of course very heavy and only one layer was loaded into each railroad car. (Normally a bag of gold weighed eighty-one pounds and a single bar weighed twenty-seven pounds.)

Albert Thoms, officer in charge of precious metals at the Main Reichsbank, Berlin, accompanied the shipments. Thoms and the Reichsbank officials could not remain with the gold because they did not have enough of the required ration stamps to buy food. Despite their easy access to this fortune in gold and currency they had to return to Berlin to avoid starving in Merkers.

Millions of Reichsmarks, US dollars and other paper money arrived regularly at Merkers during the early months of 1945, and was first unloaded at the small train station, then carried by truck across the cobblestone main road and up the service road to the mine entrance, located about 500 yards from the station. On one side of the train track lay Merkers, on the other, the industrialized mining area.

Trains with government, commercial and personal belongings for storage arrived almost daily from cities in Germany and Austria. The Henschel family, for example, owners of a giant engineering and locomotive works, used the mine to store business and personal belongings for themselves and their many wealthy friends. Family shipments began arriving in May 1944, and the Henschels employed several people at Merkers just to care for their personal property. Dr. Joseph Goebbels, minister of propaganda, had the Luftwaffe store 40,000 bottles of the finest liquor available in Europe. (Several instances of drunkenness among the mineworkers forced the Kaiseroda mine managers to complain about the storage of the volatile spirits.)

The SS Office for Economy and Administration, that operated the concentration camps, also requested their loot held by the Reichsbank to be sent to Merkers for safekeeping. From August 26,

1942, until January 27, 1945, the SS made seventy-six deliveries to the Reichsbank of property seized from concentration camp victims. This stolen property was received for a holding account in the name of "Melmer," named for SS Captain Bruno Melmer, who made most of the deliveries. Gold jewelry was sold abroad; gold of some fineness was sold either to the Prussian Mint or to Degussa, a large German industrial firm that engaged in the refinement of precious metals. Securities, foreign currency, and similar items were purchased by the Reichsbank. Much of the miscellaneous jewelry was sold through the Berlin Municipal Pawn Shop. Once the transactions took place, the proceeds were credited to the account of "Max Heiliger," codeword for Heinrich Himmler and his SS. By early 1945, much of the loot had been processed, but a significant amount still remained with the Reichsbank.

The confiscated property on hand in March 1945 consisted of all kinds of gold and silver items ranging from dental work to cigarette cases, diamonds, gold and silver coins, foreign currencies, and gold and silver bars. These were placed in eighteen bags, and the remainder of the loot was placed in 189 suitcases, trunks, and boxes and, along with other items, were sent by rail to Merkers on March 18. The shipment was under the control of Albert Thoms, head of the Reichsbank's Precious Metals Department.

On February 3, 1945, 937 B-17s of the 8th US Army Air Force dropped 2,300 tons of bombs on Berlin, causing considerable damage to the Berlin Reichsbank and destroyed the printing press used for Reichsmarks. No longer able to print money, the Germans realized that an acute shortage could be averted only by shipping money from Merkers to Berlin. Therefore, on April 2, Albert Thoms, Dr. Werner Veick, and Thomas Frommknecht were sent to Merkers to transport currency back to Berlin. Upon arrival at the mine they met the Reichsbank Director Pohl and another Reichsbank official, Kaese, who went immediately into the mine and promptly began senting money up the large elevator and loading into a 2½-ton truck. A considerable amount of US and Swiss currency was also put on the truck. Veick overheard Pohl and Kaese discussing that they were, "taking something which was important to Berlin."[1] Veick did not know what the important item was loaded onto the small truck that left in great secrecy at 3:00pm that afternoon with Kaese. The truck went through Erfurt, Halle and Magdeburg distributing money to Reichsbank branches in these towns as it headed towards Berlin.

After this activity, a railroad car was loaded from 3:00pm until 7:00pm by twenty displaced Polish workers under the supervision of the Reichsbank officials. The next day the train began its return trip to Berlin with 1,000 bags of Reichsmarks valued at one billion marks—a 1945 value of 100 million US dollars.

Fate intervened, however, as one of the bridges the train had to cross was found to have been destroyed by Allied bombing. The train was forced to reverse its route, and the 1,000 bags of currency were returned to the Kaiseroda Mine. The following morning, fifteen Polish workers supplied by the mining company, Wintershal, began unloading the railroad cars. Dr. Veick was working in the mine and Mr. Frommknecht and Thoms were supervising the operation when, after approximately thirty minutes, Thomas Frommknecht, the official in charge of money distribution, informed the workers that American troops were within two miles of Merkers. Frommknecht then went down into the mine to close the main vault door in tunnel number eight.

About 200 bags of currency had been returned to the vault. Frommknecht tried in vain to lock the door with a key, then used a hammer to force the vault closed. As the US 358th Infantry advanced, Dr. Veick and the workers continued to unload the Reichsmarks, stacking 400 bags of currency near the vault door and 450 bags at the bottom of the elevator shaft in the mine. When the Americans finally arrived that morning they searched Veick, Thoms, and Frommknecht, inspected the Polish workers, and checked the identification papers of the Reichsbank officials. The soldiers noticed the unloading of the railroad car and asked, "what is this." They glanced at the money, but had no great interest in the work party and considered this a routine Reichsbank operation. From here the 3rd Battalion pushed rapidly forward to capture the resort town of Bad Salzungen as their mission was to secure a bridgehead over the Werra River before dark. They were a well-organized, frontline combat outfit with a war to win. Safekeeping was for the follow-up echelons.

Meanwhile, after burning some papers, Frommknecht said to Thoms, "Let's go to the entrance and see if we can slip away."[2] As they started walking down the road towards Erfurt, an American jeep pulled up and they ran for the woods. Frommknecht got away but Thoms was captured and brought back to Merkers for questioning. That was the last anyone would see of Frommknecht.

Dr. Veick did not attempt to flee, as the fifty-five-year-old bank official's health was deteriorating after a 1944 bombing that had broken his collarbone and severely damaged his back, causing his left foot and leg to be somewhat immobile. He also felt he had "an ace in the hole" as his wife and nineteen and twenty-one-year-old sons were living in the United States. Veick's explained that his family was in the US since his wife was Jewish and that he had remained in Germany. As a result of this marriage, his family life had been destroyed and he did not receive any promotions at the Reichsbank. But in actuality, he divorced his wife and she remarried before leaving Germany and relocating in Cooperstown, NY. Veick married a pure Aryan in 1939 and lived in Berlin with this wife.

After the capture of Merkers, there were many rumors of recent gold movements from the German Reichsbank in Berlin to the Kaiseroda. The rumors persisted but no witnesses were located until the morning of April 6, 1945. Two military police, PFCs Clyde Harmon and Anthony Kline, stopped two displaced French women from Thionville, who were violating an order prohibiting all civilians from movement around the 90th Division command post at Keiselbach. One of the women was pregnant and was being accompanied by the other in a search for medical assistance. After questioning by the military police at the XII Corps Provost Marshall Office, the women were driven the two miles to Merkers by an army private.

Upon entering Merkers the private saw the large buildings and tops of the elevator lifts at the Kaiseroda Mine and inquired as to what sort of mine it was. The women said flatly that it was the mine in which the German gold reserves and valuable property of the National Art Museum of Berlin had been deposited. They stated that the gold had been left in the mine and local civilians and displaced persons had unloaded and stored the gold and currency. However, they did not know the quantity or value of the cache, but said that it took seventy-two hours to unload and store it.

The stunned private reported this conversation to one Sgt. Matthews of Headquarters Company of the 90th Division and retold the story to Lt.Col. William A. Russell, Military Government Officer for the 90th Division. Lt.Col. Russell proceeded immediately to the Kaiseroda mine where he interviewed displaced persons in the area about the gold stored in the mine. The women's story was confirmed.

Russell then confronted the mine officials who admitted that gold was in the mine and that other mines in the immediate area contained many valuable objects. During these interrogations, Sgt. Walter Farager, captured in 1940 at Dunkirk as one of the more than 200 British prisoners working in the mine, came forward to state that he had worked as a machinist's assistant for the past year at Kaiseroda and had helped in storing the gold. Russell also found Professor Paul O. Rave, assistant director of the National Galleries in Berlin, who admitted he was in Merkers to protect the paintings stored in the mine. The gold, he said further, was reportedly the entire reserve of the Reichsbank in Berlin!

With this further corroboration of a large cache of gold in the Kaiseroda mine, Lt.Col. Russell requested the 712th Tank Battalion to proceed to Merkers to guard the mine entrance. One of he GI asked wonderingly: "But who in the hell is going to guard the tankers."[3] At this time it became known that the mine had thirty-five miles of tunnels and five entrances, and the entire US 357th Infantry Regiment was diverted to guard it. The Kaiseroda Mine was thus secured by reinforced rifle companies, antiaircraft guns, tanks, tank destroyers, and jeeps mounted with .50 caliber machine guns. Additionally, Russell told the mine officials that they were technically under arrest and were to be confined to their homes.

First Lieutenant Ray Griffin, of the 712th Tank Battalion, from Aurora, Nebraska, considered his guard duty at Merkers the most pleasant combat duty ever performed by the 712th or any other combat outfit.

Griffin reported:

> We were in comfortable quarters … we had regular and hot meals … we got clean clothes … there was no training … guard duty was at minimum … All in all, it amounted to a nice rest period. During the guarding of the salt mine, I saw a movie of my family. I had told my men to be strictly on the alert for an 8mm projector, while doing their routine looting, which was customary whenever we moved into a new area. During our stay in Merkers, I got wind that there was an 8mm projector in town. After a check with some of the 357th Headquarters personnel, I got on the trail. Sure enough there was an 8mm projector, but there wasn't a take up reel. Not to be stopped by such a small item, I decided to run the film out on the floor.[4]

During the time that the 712th guarded the mines, the front lines advanced and a field hospital moved into a nearby area; the combat troops at Merkers thus had the rare experience of talking to American female nurses. This, to most of the combat troops, was a more memorable experience than guarding the vast treasure.

Securing the mine and verifying the presence of a large treasure trove had taken the 90th Division three days. On Saturday, April 7, the Americans decided to examine the contents of the tunnels. The steam generators were fired with coal to provide electric power for the elevators and ventilators. Lt.Col. William A. Russell; Col. Joseph Tulley, Assistant Division Commander; Maj. Joseph Brick, Judge Advocate General; Capt. James McNamara of Los Angles, Public Relations Officer for the 90th Infantry Division; and the POW Sgt. Farager entered the mine. The group was accompanied by Dr. Werner Veick, Reichsbank official, US Signal Corps photographers, and several US enlisted personnel.

They found 550 bags of Reichsmarks at the base of the elevator shaft and Captain McNamarra asked Dr. Veick if this was the entire stock of Reichsmarks. Dr. Veick shrugged his shoulders; where upon Sergeant Farager stated there were 140 additional bags of currency in a different passage and showed them the location. These bags were part of the 1,000 bags returned to the steel vault on April 4th and abandoned because of presence of the 358th Infantry. Each bag contained one million Reichsmarks with a 1945 value of $100,000 per sack and was bound securely with strong cords with lead clipped to both sides of the cords. These lead fasteners made it somewhat difficult to open the bags.

Dr. Veick accompanied the military personnel into the mine and Lt.Col. Russell ordered him to open one bag of currency. The bag was cut open by Dr. Veick, and a second bag was opened by one of the American soldiers. Some of the currency was removed, photographed and returned to the damaged containers and tied with additional string. The two opened bags were located next to the vault's steel door. Then Lt.Col. Russell made several unsuccessful attempts to open the vault door with the keys, after which force was applied to the door handles and they were sheared off completely; the door was impossible to open. In frustration, Russell suggested entering through the wall, but Tulley suggested that blasting an entrance in the vault wall the following morning would be easier. The party then moved on to examine the art works found in different mine passages. That afternoon Veick told Russell that the gold was in one room behind the vault door.

The following morning, Lt.Col. Russell asked Dr. Beil, chairman of the Wintershal board, and Mr. Kurzel, Wintershal's lawyer, to meet with him at their home office in nearby Dorndorf. The purpose of the meeting was to review the only copy of records of the items stored in the Kaiseroda mine. The records were stored in a tall cabinet in the Wintershal Building. The two men waited for Russell for a long while and finally had a US medical sergeant telephone him. During the wait however, an American lieutenant came to the home office and removed the secure cabinet with the

The gold bars recovered from Merkers were stacked in long rows between the visible bags, containing gold coins. Hundreds of boxes of currency are stacked on the left side. A narrow gauge railroad track runs through the center.

complete file. The story went that the American troops had shown the lieutenant the contents of the cabinet on that Sunday morning. All of the records were clearly marked "Secret." The files contained the only copy of what was stored in the various mines of the Wintershal Corporation. The lieutenant then had his name and the engineer battalion names written on the door of the cabinet as it disappeared. US Military Intelligence could not locate this lieutenant and accused the Wintershal staff of destroying the cabinet. Because of this mysterious removal, the treasures removed from the mines could not be validated against inventory records. For years this missing file led to many speculative and unverified stories of valuables stolen by Germans and US Army personnel.[5]

But Lt.Col. Russell had not kept his appointment with the Wintershal staff because on that Sunday morning he and Gen. Herbert L. Earnest, Commander of the 90th Division, had reentered the Kaiseroda Mine. This time Russell would not be denied entrance to the vault. He brought members of the First Battalion, 357th Combat Engineers for reinforcements. As they reached the vault door, they had the two bags of currency reopened and the contents shown to Gen. Earnest. Photographers made pictures of this event, and additional pictures were made of two engineers sitting on top of the bags of currency with 100 Reichsmarks bills spread out in a fan. After the photography session, approximately half of the bags were moved from directly in front of the vault to one side. After the move, Lt.Col. Russell attempted unsuccessfully to locate the opened bags and suggested that they were evidently at the bottom of the new pile. He searched through the pile but did not locate them. It was evidenced by now that some of the money was missing from the previous day.

The combat engineers then attempted to dig a hole through the three-foot brick vault wall, but found it impregnable. Explosive charges were set into the wall, and as the men sat on the stacks of money, the detonation blasting out an entrance approximately four by eight feet. The vault itself was approximately 75x150 feet with a twelve-foot ceiling, and well lit but not ventilated. A narrow-gauge railroad track ran through the center.

What the men saw astonished them. The treasure was in twenty, long, single rows with a 2'6" separation between the knee-high rows of 7,000 bagged gold coins and gold bars. Bales of currency were stacked along the side. Eighteen bags, and 189 valises and trunks were heaped in the back of the vault. Each bag contained a packing slip describing the contents and containing a tag bearing the name "Melmer." These 207 packages contained thousands of gold and silver dental crowns, bridges, plates, silver tableware, watch cases, eyeglasses, gold wedding rings, pearls, precious stones and assorted currency. They cast a dark shadow over the vault. It was a mute reminder of Nazi atrocities.

Bags of gold coins were opened, examined and more pictures made of Gen. Earnest and other military personnel in the vault. In order to examine the contents of the bags, the Americans had to break open the seals. At one point, a bag of gold coins was opened and part of the contents were poured into a steel helmet, photographed, and returned to the bag. Each bag of these gold coins weighed eighty-one pounds.

A partial inventory was made that indicated that there were 8,198 bars of gold bullion; fifty-five boxes of crated gold bullion; hundreds of bags of gold items; over 1,300 bags of gold Reichsmarks, British gold pounds, and French gold francs; 711 bags of American twenty dollar gold pieces; hundreds of bags of gold and silver coins; hundreds of bags of foreign currency; nine bags of valuable coins; 2,380 bags and 1,300 boxes of Reichsmarks (2.76 billion Reichsmarks); twenty silver bars; forty bags containing silver bars; sixty-three boxes and fifty-five bags of silver plate; one bag containing six platinum bars; and 110 bags from various countries. Immediately, a sentry post and two machine gun posts were established in the mineshaft near the vault's entrance. Additional security patrols were put on roads in the area, and foot patrols were placed along the railroad tracks near the mine.[6]

The men of the 90th Division were participating in an event most could only dream about: stumbling upon 285 tons of gold bars and gold coins and $519,805,802 in cash. The cash, incidentally, was listed on the records as being assets of the German Reichsbank. Capt. James McNamara said: "Gee I never saw so much money in my life as when I walked into the room and saw those bags stocked against the wall."[7]

Many more valuables were found in the thirty-five miles of tunnels. These include the following:

Sculptures: These were large, important works of the Italian Renaissance from the Kaiser Friedrich Museum and ancient Egyptian sculptures looted from Northern Europe.

Paintings: More than 1,214 crates of priceless artworks by Raphael, Van Dyke, Rembrandt, Dürer, Renoir and the works of Italian artists from the fourteenth to the sixteenth centuries were discovered.

Textiles: 140 rolls of oriental carpets

Museum Collections: Also included were Greek vases, pottery, porcelain, and works of Egyptian antiquity gathered in groups from various museums.

Miscellaneous: In addition, the search found two million valuable books from the German State Library in Berlin, music, books and costumes of the Prussian State Opera, city archives and genealogical records and patent records including hundreds of tons of blueprints and specifications for Luftwaffe materiel and ammunition. These later items were plans for rockets, jet fighters, and heat-seeking missiles, which made the patent records as potentially valuable as the gold.

CHAPTER 8
The Seizure of Germany's Gold Reserves

Col. Bernard Bernstein, Director of US Military Government Finance Division transferred with General Eisenhower's Headquarters from London, England, to Versailles, France. The Finance Division staff consisted of British and American officers with offices in the building called the Grand Ecurie, the big stable at Versailles Palace. In Versailles, Bernstein continued planning and training personnel to serve as military governors for the occupation of Germany.

On Sunday, April 8, 1945, Col. Bernstein had a late breakfast at the officer's mess and then walked over to his office with a copy of the military newspaper *Stars and Stripes* under his arm. Before starting to work, he read the frontpage story that told of American troops finding a great quantity of gold and other treasures in a salt mine at Merkers, Germany.

Shortly thereafter, Col. Bernstein's telephone rang. It was Gen. Frank J. McSherry from the advanced headquarters at Rheims, France. He said Gen. George Patton had asked Gen. Eisenhower to take over the responsibility of handling and safeguarding the Merkers treasure. That afternoon Col. Bernstein used the small plane taxi service between Paris and Rheims and proceeded to Rheims for the takeover of the treasure in the name of the commanding general, European Theater of Operations, United States Army.

The following morning Bernstein spoke to Gen. Lucius Clay who had recently reported to the forward headquarters and was to be Eisenhower's deputy in the military government of occupied Germany. A secure area had to be found to store the treasure and Clay suggested the use of Fort Ehrenbreitstein at the junction of the Moselle and Rhine rivers at Coblenz, Germany. Clay reminisced about the depot at Fort Ehrenbreitstein when he was there as a young man during World War I causing Col. Bernstein to think to himself, "I was just a young boy in 1919. I was eleven." At the conclusion of the conversation, Clay stated that no information of any kind was to be passed on to the press concerning the treasure, and that there was to be no publicity except the taking of official pictures. He asked Bernstein if he had any questions and the colonel said, "Only one, general. May I act as it seems to me wisest to do?"[1] Clay assented.

Bernstein then drove to Coblenz. On inspecting Fort Ehrenbreitstein, he discovered that structure was already filled with archives and art. The records of the former rulers of the Grand Duchy of Luxembourg and the royal records of the Netherlands had been stored there early in the war by the Germans.

Bernstein and his party then drove to Frankfurt, approximately sixty miles away, and decided that the Reichsbank there would be an excellent building for storing the gold, currency and art treasures from the mine. On the basis of the colonel's inspection, the German employees in the bank were removed and arrangements made with the mayor of Frankfurt to requisition the building, located on the corner of Taunus-Anlage and Mainzerlandstrasse in downtown Frankfurt. The three-story building was constructed of large square brownstone blocks and was located directly across from the large Grueneburg Park. On the far edge of the park was a spacious highrise office building belonging to the I.G. Farben cartel. Untouched by bombs and with hardly a window broken, it seemed to be the only building large enough left standing in western Germany to house the Allied supreme headquarters. Because of the condition and location of these two buildings, Gen. Walter Bedell Smith cabled Washington to insure that Frankfurt would not be assigned to the French occupation zone. As a result, the headquarters building would be less than a mile from the Reichsbank, which would be most convenient for Col. Bernstein's staff. A complete inspection of the now empty Reichsbank building was performed by a bomb disposal squad. No explosives were found and a twenty-four-hour guard was posted at the empty building to prevent booby traps being placed in the building.

The 1306th Engineer General Service Regiment rehabilitated the building to the extent necessary to provide adequate security and protection from the weather. It had not been damaged by the war, but had been neglected during the past few years due to shortage of building materials. That same day, April 10, Bernstein drove the eighty-five miles to Merkers and reported to the 357th Infantry Regiment. After making a preliminary inspection of the Kaiseroda Mine and its contents, he left instructions with the officers to call up selected personnel and assign them to handle valuables in the mine. Bernstein interrogated Dr. Veick and Dr. Otto Reimer, the chief cashier of the Berlin Reichsbank, and learned there had been movements of large amounts of gold and currency into southern Germany and Austria. Veick told Bernstein that he did not know that much about the gold, but Thoms knew all about the gold. Bernstein was further informed that valuables were stored in other mines in the immediate area.

The indefatigable colonel then drove over to Patton's Third Army command post located near Merkers to explain to Gen. Patton that the valuables must be moved from Merkers to Frankfurt as quickly as possible. Patton, however, was opposed and said, "There is no chance the Germans can push me out of this area. It is safe to leave the gold and other treasurers down in that mine." Bernstein, determined, responded, "I don't for a minute question the correctness of your statement, but under the Big Three arrangement, this part of Germany will be taken over by the Russians for military government control after the fighting ends and we certainly want to get all of this out of here before the Russians get here." Patton was astonished at Bernstein's statement. "I didn't know that at all," he said "but I will do everything possible to facilitate your mission."

On April 11, Bernstein set up a command post for Headquarters, European Theater Operations United States Forces, at the mine building in Merkers. The necessary office equipment, mess, billeting and other facilities were brought forward to the area. During the day, Bernstein went into the mine and began an inventory. Years later, the colonel explained, "Because of my background with the Treasury Department and working for a large law firm that provided attorneys for the old Farmers Loan and Trust Company in New York, the first thing you do is, you want to know what you have got. Make sure that you are accounting for it properly."[2] An inspection was made of the art treasures with Dr. Paul W. Rave present to furnish information. A number of cases of art were found in a developing pool of water and Bernstein arranged for these cases to be moved to higher ground within the chamber.

In the afternoon, Lt. George Stout, US Navy, and a British officer reported to the colonel with expectations that they would take over the responsibility for protection and removal of the art. In civilian life, Stout had been the chief of conservation at Harvard University and was considered an expert on the techniques of packing and transporting objects of art. Stout and the British officer started for the mine to review the vast collection of art, but to their surprise Col. Bernstein denied them entrance. The colonel assured them that he was in command and they needed his permission to enter. Upon Stouts insistence, the colonel produced a letter from higher command authorizing him to decide who went into the mine. Much to the chagrin of the British officer, he was denied entrance, but Bernstein agreed to let Stout view the treasure and begin preliminary work for its evacuation.

That same afternoon, Bernstein toured the nearby mine in Mezengraben. Unfortunately, for the colonel, the power failed and he and his party had to remain in the mine for five hours until it was restored that night. When the colonel returned to his quarters, there was a message that Gen. Patton had called instructing him to be at the entrance of the mine the following day at 9:00am. Col. Bernstein and his staff arrived at the mine early on the following morning and continued the inventory. At 9:00am, Bernstein took the elevator to the entrance, but as no one had arrived yet, he paced nervously back and forth. At about 10:30 he saw the front end of a jeep bearing a plaque with five stars in a circle. Bernstein automatically straightened up—he knew there was only one person entitled to that designation in this theater and as he saluted, he found himself looking into the faces of Gen. Dwight D. Eisenhower, Gen. George Patton, and Gen. Omar N. Bradley, all three in one jeep.

Gen. Manton S. Eddy joined the group as they approached the elevator to descend into the mine. The elevator was suspended in a 1,600-foot pitcher-black shaft and due to the late arrival of the generals; the operator of the elevator was a German. Standing on the wooden elevator platform Bernstein ponders, "We were fourteen stars and just a colonel in the hands of a German who could have really upset the whole plan at that point. If that German running the elevator had been a fanatic, you never know what might have happened." Nevertheless, the group did descend safely into the mine. As they stepped out into the semi-darkness at the foot of the shaft, after a split-second hesitation, the US Army guard saluted and was heard by all to mutter "Jesus Christ."

Gen. Eisenhower was interested in learning about the contents of the mine. He sat on a large stack of currency smoking a cigarette as Bernstein told the generals about the gold, currency and valises filled with loot from the concentration camp victims. Eisenhower looked through a number of valises; one ladies' small traveling bag still had the fresh aroma of perfume inside.

The generals looked at the artwork that was later ascertained to constitute about twenty-five percent of the contents of the vast Berlin Art Museum. They examined also the plates of the Reichsbank used for printing currency. As they walked through other tunnels, Bernstein explained the plan for the inventory and removal of the treasure from the Kaiseroda Mine. The tour lasted over an hour and at one point, Eisenhower saw some writing on the wall. It was in German and Eisenhower asked Bernstein to please translate. Bernstein didn't know German but knew enough Yiddish to read the writing which said, "The state is everything and the individual is nothing," causing Eisenhower to assert, "What an appalling doctrine."[3]

Upon viewing this priceless artwork, Patton wrote in his diary "The ones I saw were worth, in my opinion, about $2.50, and were of the type normally seen in bars in America."[4] He was looking at paintings that included 202 of the world's greatest paintings, valued at $80,000,000.

During the afternoon, Bernstein telephoned Capt. Henry Morgenthau III, the son of the Secretary of the Treasury, who was with the forward combat units and on Patton's staff. Bernstein wanted to discuss the treasure found at Merkers with him, but Morgenthau was not available. Giving up, Bernstein went to bed around midnight, but about fifteen minutes later a soldier came in and shook him. He said, "Capt. Morgenthau is on the phone." The colonel answered the phone and Morgenthau said, "I suppose you are calling me about what you heard over the radio." Bernstein replied: "No I don't have time to listen to the radio," Morgenthau announced, "President Roosevelt died." Bernstein returned to bed once more, but did not sleep, thinking what a terrible thing this was as he tossed and turned.[5]

At breakfast the following morning, Bernstein's staff was sitting around looking sad. Lt.Col. Barrett arrived late and asked, "What is all this mourning about?" After he was told about Roosevelt's death Barrett joined in the general gloom. A little later the men returned to the mineshafts and their work.

Later that morning Gen. Frank J. McSherry, Deputy Assistant Chief of Staff, G-5, phoned to say that Gen. Eisenhower had not heard from Col. Bernstein in twenty-four hours and wanted to know what was going on. Bernstein told McSherry to tell Eisenhower that work was going on around the clock to carry out the program the supreme commander had approved. Bernstein had the feeling General Patton had discussed with Eisenhower the fact that the area was to be taken over by the Russians and that the US certainly wanted to get the treasure out before the Soviets got there. The way the war was going, he knew it might end in a very short time.

During this time, Stout went to the Ransbach Mine about ten miles away and spoke with Rave, who explained that that were forty-five cases of art in that mine but could not be inspected as the elevator was not working. Stout returned to Merkers and made a spotcheck of some of the boxes and crates of artwork in that mine. He found that, in addition to the crated items, some four hundred paintings were lying loose. He had seen enough to know that he needed proper packing materials and that the art constituted great wealth. The next afternoon he returned to Ransbach to prepare the items there for the move. Upon his return to Merkers, Bernstein told him that the art convoy would leave on the 16th.

The inventory of the Kaiseroda Mine continued with the major work performed by Lt.Col. Omar V. Claiborne, Lt.Col. Tupper Barrett, Lt.Cmdr. Joel A. Fisher and a civilian, Maurice St. Germain. These men had arrived on April 12, at 1:30 in the afternoon. St. Germain, an employee of the Guaranty Trust Company of New York City, had been working in Paris prior to this assignment. Cmdr. Fisher, United States Coast Guard Reserves, was assigned the responsibility of inventorying the other mines in the immediate area. Fisher also was to analyze all the testimonies of Reichsbank officials captured at the Kaiseroda mine and gather financial and property control intelligence.

That afternoon St. Germain, with the assistance of Barrett, inspected the mine and made an estimate of the situation and after consulting with Mason, outlined a plan for operations. During the day, under the direction of Moore, four teams were organized to make an inventory of the contents of the mine based on the information shown on the tags. Two teams worked on the gold bullion and coins, and two worked on the other loot. Also that day, thirty-two ten ton trucks from the 3628th and 4263rd Quartermaster Truck Companies were made available for the move and their commanders were told to report to Merkers early the following morning.

During this frenzied activity, Bernstein met with Stout, Dunn, and Bartlett to discuss the arrangements for the movement of approximately four hundred tons of art stored in different parts of the Merkers mine. It was agreed that loading would begin at noon on April 16, but the mission actually begun earlier, for at midnight on the fourteenth, Bernstein ordered Stout to prepare three truckloads of art, which were to be mixed in with the gold to make the loads lighter.

On April 14, ten days after the capture of the mine, the treasure was ready to be removed. Trucks arrived at 7:30am, and guards watched over each truck upon arrival. Prior to loading, large tarpaulins were laid out flat in the trucks; after loading, the tarps were folded over the gold to conceal the treasure. Security was doubled in the salt mine area as the transfer of gold began at 9:00am. A broken elevator in shaft two, large enough to carry a jeep trailer, was repaired by a nearby engineer regiment. This shaft was used to remove the gold and the elevator in shaft one was used for carrying currency and miscellaneous items.

Lt. Ray A. Griffin worked the second shift and went into the mineshaft at 7:00pm. The movement of the treasure had been proceeding for ten hours when his shift began. He took one of the big freight elevators to the main vault level, entered the main room and observed the remaining gold. Even with approximately one half of the valuables removed, the cache was still impressive to see. Griffin lifted one of the bars and said later, "A person really gets a surprise the first time he tries to lift one of these bars. One of the first ones I tried, I thought it was nailed down."

He observed the procedure for removing the gold. Two enlisted men carried the bullion from the storeroom to the blown open passage way placed it into a jeep trailer. Each bar or bag of gold was counted by an officer of Bernstein's staff and a pre-printed number attached to each bag or bar. After the trailer had all it could carry—and it did not take very much gold to make a load—it was hitched to a jeep. Lt. Griffin would sign for the gold and take the pre-numbered ticket with the inventory. It was then pulled to the elevator shaft by the jeep, unhitched, put on the elevator and taken to ground level. The gold then went onto the trucks. The inventory was checked again during unloading by another officer of Bernstein's staff. Once it was re-verified, Griffin was relieved of responsibility for that trailer load and returned to the mine to get another. During these trips, he wondered, "What would happen if I was short one or two bars? It would take a long time to pay for one of these with a first lieutenant's pay."

During the loading of truck number 43, a canvas bag of gold coins broke open. Griffin asked the British officer who was verifying the gold if he could have a coin for a souvenir. The officer declined; Griffin later said, "All I got out of being around all that money was losing a night's sleep."[6]

During the loading, the two bags that had been cut open by Lt.Col. Russell were spotted and placed inside the main vault. The last items into the jeep trailers were the SS loot. The two bags that had been opened were loaded into the last jeep along with some other damaged packages. This load with the damaged containers was given special security treatment with Lt.Col. Barrett and Col. Bernstein accompanying it up the elevator. Bernstein then gave Capt. Kurt L. Walitschek a special order to ride in the ten ton truck loaded with the damaged packages.

Colonel Bernard Bernstein in Frankfurt, Germany 1944, and in his Manhattan apartment in 1994.

Loading the treasure continued throughout the night. As each truck was filled, its driver and his assistant would go to sleep in the vehicle. At 7:45 on the morning of April 15, 1945, loading was completed. Three truckloads of fine art and twenty-seven truckloads of gold and currency were ready to move. The shipment was made to fit into thirty trucks by overloading each of the ten ton trucks by approximately ten percent. At one point after the trucks were loaded, Bernstein insisted a military guard ride up front with the two drivers. He then asked Lt.Col. John H. Mason, Commander of the 357th Infantry Regiment, if he was willing to allow one of his soldiers to stand on the back of each truck to prevent the possibility of some German trying to hop on and taking some gold or money. Mason looked at Bernstein and said, "I think we are better off taking our chances with the Germans. These are very tough soldiers."[7]

Bernstein understandably was worried, but the convoy was under tight security by the First Battalion, 474th Infantry Regiment. On the morning of the gold shipment, companies A and B had been moved from their bivouac area to Merkers, while companies C and D proceeded to Frankfurt to clear and isolate the Reichsbank and establish a perimeter defense and interior guard for the immediate area. At Merkers, companies A and B of the 474th were supplemented by reinforcements of the 785th Military Police Battalion. All roads and intersections were blocked and no traffic was allowed on the eight-five-mile route to Frankfurt. At 8:15am, a quarter ton truck with military police left Merkers to ensure that the route was secure and no traffic was on the road. Fifteen minutes later, additional military police, accompanied by two M8 armored tanks, preceded the convoy. The M8s had 37mm guns mounted in their cast turrets, augmented by .30 caliber machine guns. The drivers were briefed: no smoking, no passing, a speed limit of twenty-five miles per hour, and one five-minute stop near Alsfeld, the halfway point. At 8:45, the convoy left Merkers, in two separate, but identical serial of vehicles. Each serial consisted of:

- 2 military police on motorcycles
- 1 quarter ton military police truck with police captain and crew
- 1 M-20 tank with a four-man crew equipped with four .50 caliber machine guns
- 1 quarter ton truck with infantry guards
- 2 mobile antiaircraft multiple-mount guns equipped with a 37mm gun combined with two .50 caliber machine guns
- 5 ten ton cargo trucks loaded with gold (numbers 1-5)
- 1 M8 tank with a four man crew equipped with a 37mm gun and a .30 caliber machine gun
- 5 ten ton cargo trucks loaded with gold (numbers 6-10)
- 1 M8 tank
- 1 two and a half ton truck with two 12-man rifle squads
- 1 mobile antiaircraft gun
- 5 ten ton cargo trucks loaded with gold (numbers 11-15)
- 1 M8 tank
- 2 two-and -a -half ton trucks with four 12-man rifle squads
- 1 quarter ton truck with military police
- 1 three quarter ton truck with infantry squad
- 1 mobile antiaircraft gun
- 2 military police on motorcycles to patrol column of vehicles

The second serial was a duplicate of the first, followed by a rear unit of:

- 3 wreckers
- 2 ten ton trucks (spares)
- 2 M8 tanks
- 1 ambulance with a battalion surgeon and four medical assistants
- 1 two-and-a-half ton wrecker

While pulling out of the mine's factory area one of the trucks broke down and was placed under tight security until repaired. The convoy left Merkers under cover of P-51 Mustang fighter escorts and constant radio contact with a Piper Cub spotter aircraft. Military police, riding motorcycles and jeeps, crisscrossed back and forth through the convoy during the trip.

During the time that the treasure was being loaded at Merkers, companies C and D of the 474th Infantry Regiment had arrived at the Reichsbank in Frankfurt and placed the area under tight security. Five heavy machine gun squads surrounded the bank building and three additional heavy machine gun squads were in place at strategic roadblocks. All surrounding streets were closed and ten six-man rifle squads stood in fixed positions while twenty-four infantrymen patrolled all streets and alleys within a three-block area of the Reichsbank. Additionally, twelve infantrymen patrolled clockwise and counter-clockwise in the immediate area of the building.

The convoy arrived in Frankfurt at 3:45pm without incident. The defenders were then supplemented by reinforcements from the convoy; eight M8 tanks and ten antiaircraft guns were added to the existing security already in place. There were now over 700 combat infantry troops guarding the gold from Merkers.

Unloading began immediately with 150 US Army engineers. It continued throughout the night and into the next day until 1:30pm on April 16, 1945. During the unloading of truck assigned number 43, driven by Cpl. Roy A. Stiebritz, a hole was noticed in bag number 3362 containing gold coins. Five smaller bags were contained within the large canvas bag that was torn and one of the smaller bags also was torn. The content was counted by Capt. Paul A. Mitchell and Lt. Duel F. Bunch. They discovered thirty-four Dutch ten-guilder gold coins missing. A thorough search of the truck and tarpaulins by Lt. Bunch and Capt. Mitchell did not turn up the coins. One week later, when questioned about the missing gold coins, Cpl. Stiebritz replied, "When they got through unloading, Lieutenant Bunch said they were short something. I stood around there and waited a while. I gave him my name and truck number and he told me to go on out."[8]

After the unloading and during inspection of the valuables in the lower vault level at the Foreign Exchange Depository a discrepancy was found in the amount of paper currency that had been removed from the mine. The two bags opened on April 7 did not contain the full amount of currency. One bag was short 460,000 Reichsmarks ($46,000), and the another was short 8,800 Reichsmarks ($880). These happen to be the two damaged bags on the last jeep at the Kaiseroda mine. Despite an investigation by the commanding officer, European Civil Affairs Currency Section, the currency and gold coins were never recovered.

That afternoon, as the unloading was taking place, McSherry visited the Reichsbank and directed that a tentative inventory be prepared of the gold, silver, and currency. This inventory was completed at 10:00pm and handed to McSherry. The next day, April 18, Eisenhower cabled the War Department with a rough estimate of the Merkers find. Two days later, Eisenhower's chief of staff sent the Combined Chiefs of Staff a preliminary inventory of the Merkers treasure. It indicated that the value of the gold, silver, and currency was over $520 million. In his cover letter he pointed out that a large quantity of the loot appeared to have been taken by the SS from victims and suggested that proper agencies be contacted to send representatives to review the loot in terms of being evidence in war crimes proceedings.

A partial inventory made on April 8, 1945, by Lt.Col. William S. Moore identified as missing some English currency and one bag containing $12,470 in US currency. The American money disappeared between April 8, and April 11, at which time Col. Bernstein established his command post at Merkers. There was no investigation to recover the missing American currency.

At Frankfurt an analysis was made of the German records for currency deposited at Merkers. The German records indicated that $175,873 in US currency had been placed in Merkers by the Germans, but not recovered by Bernstein's task force.

The Americans, Germans, and a British POW had an excellent reason to destroy the records in the file cabinet removed from the Wintershal office on Sunday, April 8, 1945. Without these records it was impossible to accurately verify what had actually been placed in the Kaiseroda mine at Merkers.[9]

What happened to the missing money? Did Thomas Frommknecht take some of the currency with him? How about Albert Thoms?

Sometime during the afternoon of April 17 or 18, Bernstein, now back at Frankfurt, learned that his colleagues had uncovered in Merkers a series of account books belonging to Thoms's Precious Metals Department, which Thoms had earlier informed Bernstein had been sent back to Berlin. In interrogating Thoms on April 18, Bernstein asked him to explain the books. Thoms indicated that the books were a running inventory of the gold bars and gold and silver coins held by the Reichsbank for its own account and the account of others. The books also provided specific information about each bar held at either Merkers or Berlin. Bernstein believed the books should be useful as a checklist against which the discovery of the Reichsbank gold could be controlled and might assist in the location of all of the Reichsbank gold. It appears that this was a partial list and the complete inventory had indeed been sent back to Berlin. The foreign currency balance sheet was three pages of currency dated February 9, 1945. Back in Berlin was another foreign currency balance sheet of seven pages dated April 13, 1945, with the inventory of foreign currency sent to Munich, Mittenwald and other areas of Bavaria. Col. Bernstein was unaware of this balance sheet and all the currency recovered by US forces was believed to be accounted for in the three page February 9 balance sheet totaling $4,000,000. As we shall see in later chapters Thoms background becomes even more questionable.

This concluded the largest single treasure capture in military history. The US Army had seized 830 tons of Germany's treasures from the designated Russian occupation zone. This constituted the first deposit—569,726 pounds of gold—the beginning of the Allied Gold Pot This gold 6,836,709.834 Troy ounces was air freighted to the Bank of England in 1948 and deposited into the account of the Tripartite Gold Commission.

The Reichsbank building was surrounded with a barbed wire fence and was under constant surveillance by guards in watchtowers. At night the building was illuminated by floodlight.

Gen. Bedell Smith requested Bernstein to furnish him with five gold coins to make medals for President Roosevelt, Prime Minister Churchill, General Marshall, Field Marshall Montgomery and General Eisenhower. Col. Bernstein replied that this was an unusual request and that the army and American government had a fiduciary responsibility for the gold. Gen.Eisenhower might be subject to criticism for taking gold coins, he said. This was the colonel's diplomatic way of saying "no." Not to be denied, Gen. Smith asked Gen. McSherry to ride with him from the Supreme Headquarters building to the Reichsbank to get five gold coins. As they were driving, McSherry asked Smith if he had any idea what tight security Bernstein had set up. Smith told the driver to turn around and go back to headquarters. Thus Shipment 1 became the first deposit at the Foreign Exchange Depository.

CHAPTER 9
Task Force Fisher

Joel H. Fisher was commissioned as an ensign in the United States Coast Guard Reserve in May, 1942, and promoted to lieutenant commander in April, 1944, while on assignment in Alaska as captain of port activities. In 1944, the US Army organized a team to search the world for Nazi loot and the industrial assets of German companies. Lt.Cmdr. Fisher's background as an attorney with the US Treasury Department qualified him for this assignment. In early 1945, the twenty-five-year-old was assigned to the European Theater of Operations and accompanied assault troops into towns where his specific objective was to uncover hidden gold, securities, and other loot of the Reichsbank and large industrial companies.

Fisher's interrogation and investigation of the high-ranking Reichsbank officials at Merkers revealed that large amounts of foreign currency, gold and other valuables had been transferred into southern Germany, Austria and Switzerland. Immediately, Fisher made a plan to locate and capture the remainder of Germany's assets before they could finance the activity of the National Redoubt.

From the Reichsbank officials Fisher learned the locations of towns occupied by the Germans that contained additional deposits of Reichsbank gold. He formed a reconnaissance team, consisting of three jeeps with four men each. Additionally, two Piper Cubs were assigned to the group to assist in communication and quick reconnaissance in an emergency. The team was to proceed into targeted towns as soon as they were secured and locate the gold and valuables.

Organized by Col. Bernstein, the reconnaissance team consisted of himself, Fisher, and Lt. Herbert G. DuBois. This team became known as Task Force Fisher. It traveled in the Thüringen Forest region located in the southeastern part of Germany. Mostly undeveloped wooded mountain slopes, the region contained many small villages. They traveled north into the Harz Mountains to the town of Halle, arriving there at 6:30pm, Friday, April 20, 1945. Here, members of the US Army Counter Intelligence officers joined the team and the group went to the bank. As they walked towards the Reichsbank, Lt. DuBois could not help but notice the lingering pungent smell of human flesh that permeated the town.

The German Reichsbank officials were well dressed and had meticulous records of the contents of that Reichsbank. They seemed oblivious to the fact that Halle had been nearly ninety percent destroyed by Allied bombing. After five years of bombing and constant war hostilities, the German civilian population conducted business as usual during the American advance. A preliminary investigation of the Reichsbank financial papers revealed that there was gold and currency in the banks vault. Five rangers from the 5th Ranger Battalion were traveling with the team, so they immediately placed a guard on the vault.

When the Halle Reichsbank officials opened the vault doors, Col. Bernstein noticed sixteen wooden boxes, and also two larger chests. The seals on the containers were unbroken. There were sixty-five canvas bags of foreign currency and seven bags of gold coins. (Additionally, this vault, like all Reichsbank vaults contained several small blue steel handguns that very quickly became souvenirs for the American guards.) Shortly after the vault was opened, the captain in charge of the local military government arrived and provided four military police to help the rangers guard the vault and the Reichsbank officials who were now in custody.

Col. Bernstein requested that this large quantity of currency and 2,140 pounds of gold be transported immediately to the Foreign Exchange Depository in Frankfurt. But due to military protocol, the commanding general of VII Corps demanded written confirmation that Bernstein had authority to take the valuables. Confirmation was not received that night nor Saturday or Sunday, therefore Bernstein arranged for the local US military government to take over the job of safeguarding the contents of the Reichsbank vault. Thus, Bernstein turned over to Capt. Frank W. Murphy the six keys to the vault. As DuBois took Murphy to the vault, they checked each item against the inventory and then relieved Bernstein and his team of the responsibility. Capt. Elwood Taylor delivered Shipment 2 to the Foreign Exchange Depository in Frankfurt three days later on April 25, 1945.[1]

Members of the Foreign Exchange Depository began to inventory the items. Five bags, Shipments 2A and 2B, contained the following mix of US currency:

11,500	$100	$1,150,000
4,000	$50	$200,000
11,000	$20	$220,000
31,000	$10	$310,000
23,000	$5	$115,000
5,000	$1	$5,000
		$2,000,000

Shipment 2A: foreign currencies to include $1,000,000 U.S tagged sending Halle.

Shipment 2B: foreign currencies to include $1,000,000 US tagged sending Nordhausen but actually taken at Halle.

Shipment 2C: sixteen wooden boxes were gold bars of the firm of Dollfuss Mieg, of Muelhausen, Alsace that bore the seals of Societe Banque Suisse, Le Locle. Each box contained four gold bars and the total weight was 2,601 pounds.

Shipment 2D and E: The two wooden chests and seven bags were gold and foreign exchange assets of Banque de France customers located in Tours, Blois, Orleans, Chartres, Dreux and Chateaudun. Within each bag, or box, the property of each customer was wrapped separately and each package marked with the owner's name, "M. Emile Rivand—gold coins—820 US dollars, 2,430 French francs, two English pounds, twenty Danish crowns and five Russian rubles." Seven $500 and two $1000 bills along with a mixed amount of several thousand dollars of US currency were found in this shipment. These large bills bore definite evidence of ownership by individuals with French names and addresses. A one US cent coin was recorded as belonging to M. Albert Marie, a $500 and $1,000 US bill was taken from Dr. Maurice Grenier. It astonishes one that during the war, the Germans kept such meticulous records of their thievery.

According to a letter attached to the boxes, Shipments C, D and E were taken from France during the German Treasury Agents (*Devisenschutzkommandos*) retreated from Paris in September 1944. The total US currency included in these shipments amounted to $37,530.[2]

Shipment F consisted of four more bags of foreign paper currency and silver coins, reported to be an accumulation of the amounts received for the past three week during daily business transactions. Also, this shipment contained letters and diaries from the safe deposit box of Mrs. Lange, former wife of high-ranking Nazi Reichsbank Vice President Kurt Lange. These were taken for possible intelligence information as they might contain regarding Nazi activity. The personal letters had been sent to a German soldier, Klaus Pastuszyk in 1940-1942 by his family and friends. Also included was his diary and identification papers, the later an indication that he was deceased. An examination of the papers revealed no allusions to either military or political matters.

This shipment contained, "1 coin collection listed under name of Paul Volk & containing several hundred small envelopes."[3]

On February 17, 1949, "Miscellaneous currencies, jewelry, checks, gold bullion, scraps, et cetera, previously taken from safe deposit boxes of various French banks"[4] were removed from shipment 2 and returned to the French Mission for Restitution along with the US $500 and $1,000 bills. Despite the fact that the owners were identifiable, this gold consisting of 25,862.530 Troy ounces of gold was air freighted to the Bank of England in 1948 and deposited into the account of the Tripartite Gold Commission.

On January 21, 1949, the Klaus Pastuszyk letters were burned under orders of Mr. Jo Fischer Freeman, deputy to the finance advisor to the military governor, Berlin.[5]

The US currency from Shipment 2A and B would later be sent to the US Federal Reserve Bank, in New York.

Continuing their meticulous searches and inventories on April 23, Col. Bernstein's team traveled back on the *autobahn* approximately fifty miles towards Frankfurt to investigate gold shipments from the small town of Erfurt, and Eisenach, the birthplace of German composer, Johann Sebastian Bach. Maj. A.A. Hedstrom, the military government detachment commander, provided several guards to accompany the party to the Erfurt Reichsbank where they investigated the bank officials. After a period of questioning, the officers stated they had received about eighty bags of gold "about a year ago" but had sent all their gold and accompanying records to Berlin on the night of April 4, 1945. Bernstein requested a copy of the receipt that revealed the destination of the gold was Magdeburg. A search of the vault "revealed a bag of foreign notes including US dollars." [*author*: Their underline, although there are no records indicating US currency was in Erfurt.] The Reichsbank director typed a list, noting the foreign currency but it did not include any US dollars. Maj. Hedstrom suggested Bernstein take the bags, including the dollars, with him to Frankfurt.

After obtaining guards from the military government commander at Eisenach, the party proceeded to the Reichsbank and conducted a through investigation. At first the bank officials stated there had been seven bags of gold at the bank, then changed the story to ten bags of gold, and finally admitted, there had been eighteen boxes and seven bags of gold at the bank. They claimed that the gold had been brought to the bank in September 1944 by German treasury agents of France as part of the industrialized German Four-Year-Plan. The Reichsbank officials had the understanding that the gold had been taken from France by Göring's men. (The Reichsbank officials are describing the above Shipments 2C, D and E)

At Eisenach, Bernstein reviewed the balance sheet of December 31, 1944, and found an entry showing that the Coburg branch had received forty-one bags of gold for the Berlin Reichsbank. The vault contained a small amount of foreign currency and some silver coins. Valuables from Erfurt and Eisenach were sent to the depository as Shipment 9.[6]

Belgian, Polish, and Hungarian currency was delivered to the Foreign Exchange Depository, but US currency was not included. Why was there an underline in describing the US dollars? On November 28, 1945, Col. H.D. Cragon wrote a letter noting there was no receipt for receiving Shipment 9 and requested an explanation. There was no response.

After this tedious five-day reconnaissance, Col. Bernstein returned to Frankfurt to continue establishing procedures for the Foreign Exchange Depository in Frankfurt. This depository was a branch of the Finance Division, Office of Military Government (OMGUS) and its function was to take custody, inventory, and account for monetary valuables uncovered in Germany by the Allied forces.

Bernstein arranged for Lt.Cmdr. Fisher, and Lt. DuBois, and Reichsbank official Albert Thoms to continue developing leads on other hiding places for gold and foreign currency. Thoms's assistance would prove most useful as he was officer in charge of all precious metals at the main Reichsbank in Berlin.

On the morning of April 25, 1945, Lt.Cmdr. Fisher interviewed the Reichsbank officials at Hof, a small town next to the Czech border. After a prolonged session, the bank officials produced a large case containing a considerable amount of Yugoslavian and Hungarian currency.

After more detailed interrogation about SS loot, the Reichsbank official admitted that some valuables from Lublin concentration camp on the outskirts of Lublin, Poland, had been deposited at the local Stadt V. Kreissparkassee (city and local savings bank) at the direction of Dr. Richard Wendler, former mayor of Hof and later governor of the District Lublin, Poland. He had been living in Hof but disappeared before the occupation by US forces. The boxes contained the address; General Government Office of the Lublin District Governor, First Governmental Councilor [Mr.] Lodde.

Following instructions from Wendler, they had been deposited on April 7, 1945 by Mr. Christian Kroegel, inspector of governmental administrative services and a resident of Hof.

Following this lead, the reconnaissance party went to the savings bank, where it located the two boxes containing:

> One gilded metal chalice with motifs in relief.
>
> 24 gold plated silver plates with the initials S.L. surmounted by a crown
>
> One set gilded sliver tableware comprising 41 forks, 41 knives, 41 spoons. The spoons and forks had cast motifs in relief and were carved. The handles of the forks and knives were in porcelain adorned with color designs.
>
> The items all bore Polish markings and had been brought to the bank during the month of January 1944, by an SS captain and a civilian.

After discovery of the valuables in the Stadt V. Kreissparkassee, Fischer was advised that a number of large boxes had been deposited by Dr. Richard Wendler for safekeeping in the basement of a local spinning mill. The local US military governor informed Fischer that he had inspected some of the boxes in the cellar and they contained very valuable gold and silver tableware, china, etc with Polish markings.

Next, they proceeded to the cellar of the mill to examine the boxes and interrogate the officials of the spinning mill. Arriving, the military governor was surprised to discover that since his examination the prior day, three of the boxes had been completely emptied of their contents. Fischer proceeded with an intense interrogation of the mill's directors Schmidt and Wunderlich. Both, longtime standing members of the Nazi party, admitted that twenty-three cases had been deposited with the factory in July 1944 at the request of Wendler who said the property had been taken from the governor's house in Lublin, and would eventually be sent to Munich as property of the German state. Fischer suggested that steps be taken to examine all the boxes and safeguard the contents. The twenty-three boxes appeared to contain valuables taken from Catholic churches.

Fischer delivered the two boxes from the Stadt V. Kreissparkassee to XII Corps and they were sent to the Foreign Exchange Depository on April 27, 1945 as Shipment 3.

On October 11, 1948, twenty-four gold plated silver plates with the initials S.L. surmounted by a crown; a set of silver tableware comprising forty-one forks, knives, and spoons with handles adorned with colored porcelain designs and a large gilded metal chalice was signed for by a representative of the Polish Mission for restitution.[7]

Dr. Richard Wendler avoided arrest as a war criminal by using a false name and remaining in a US prisoner of war camp for several years.

Lt.Cmdr. Fisher, Lt. DuBois and Mr. Thoms then left Hof and traveled north approximately twenty miles to the town of Plauen. They arrived at 9:00pm on April 25, 1945, and phoned the local military government detachment commander to explain their mission. The commander said he would arrange for an interview that evening with the Reichsbank officials, but was unable to provide a place for the team to stay. Another phone call to the 87th Division Military Police insured the locating of the Reichsbank officials and the military police provided accommodations for the team. The interrogation began five hours later, at 2:00am, and lasted approximately one hour and forty-five minutes. The bank officials admitted fifty to sixty bags of gold were in the vault of the Reichsbank, but the bank had been destroyed by Allied bombing and the third key needed to open the vault was in the pocket of a dead cashier buried under the debris of his apartment.

Fisher and his team slept for three hours. At 8:00am, DuBois went to the Reichsbank with the bank officials and found the vault intact although the rest of the bank was completely destroyed. DuBois visited the deceased cashier's apartment building and learned from local workmen that it would take several days to locate the body under the rubble. Lt.Cmdr. Fisher then went to the command post of the 87th Division and explained the nature of his mission and the problems to Gen. Frank J.

Culin, commander of the 87th Division. The general made arrangements for members of an engineer company to blast open the vault and guard the bank.

Bulldozers removed the debris from the vault, and at 11:30am exploded the first charge of dynamite; withstanding several blasts, its doors finally blew open. It took an hour and half before the dust and debris from the explosions had settled and Fisher could enter the vault. It contained thirty-five bags of gold coins deposited in April 1944, in the name of *Reichsführer-SS* Heinrich Himmler. It weighed 1,955 pounds and contained 12,500 US $20 gold coins, plus additional gold coins from Switzerland, Holland and Norway. The vault also contained 18,000 silver five-Reichsmarks coins and 4,000 silver two-Reichsmarks coins.

Thoms and Fisher had a balance sheet, as of December 31, 1944, which showed sixty bags of gold had been deposited on April 12, 1944, by the German army for Himmler. Despite an extensive interrogation of bank officials by the US Army, the twenty-five missing bags of coins remained lost. Fisher and DuBois made a detailed inventory of the bags of gold and silver using the German serial numbers and markings on each bag.

Discovered in the vault were several private valises belonging to individuals in the Plauen area. An appropriate screening and examination was made by Lt. DuBois to determine whether foreign currency and other loot was in the valises, which were impounded while arrangements were made for the counter intelligence corps to inspect their contents in detail.

The next morning, at 8:00am, the 87th Infantry Division loaded a convoy with the treasure and left Plauen for Frankfurt to deposit the gold and silver in the Foreign Exchange Depository as Shipment 4A.[8] The gold in this shipment consisted of 25,296.075 Troy ounces was air freighted to the Bank of England in 1948 and deposited into the account of the Tripartite Gold Commission.

Twenty-five bags of German silver coins that were still legal tender were taken from the Plauen Reichsbank as part of this seizure and were placed in the Foreign Exchange Depository as Shipment 4B.

Lt.Cmdr. Fisher and his team worked around the clock as the towns targeted for their mission were all located in the future Russian Occupation Zone. In early July, after the evacuation of the Americans from Plauen, the Russians requested information pertaining to the removal of the gold. On July 9, 1945, the US Finance Division responded to the Russians: Our investigation revealed no information on the funds referred to in your basic communication.

On April 27, 1945, Fisher and his team drove thirty miles north to interrogate the Reichsbank officials in the small town of Gera. The officials admitted to receiving forty-one bags of gold from Saalfeld on April 3, which originally had been sent from Berlin to Saalfeld. The Gera bank records contained no entries for gold received. Under interrogation, the officials revealed that the gold records were in a secret book that was destroyed before the occupation of US troops on April 15, 1945, in accordance with instructions from Berlin. Reichsbank officials said the gold was sent in two shipments to the town of Zwickau, approximately ten miles from Gera.

The Zwickau bank officials told Fisher that the forty-one bags of gold had been sent to Aue, then the frontline for Patton's Third Army, and presently heavily defended by the German army. Fisher met with the chief of staff of the 89th Division and suggested that he make a prompt examination of the bank when it was captured, but before the US troops could capture Aue, the gold was transferred south to Munich.

Continuing on, Fisher and DuBois followed Patton's Third Army through central Germany and into Czechoslovakia. The retreating German army continued to send large quantities of gold and currency into the National Redoubt of southern Germany and Austria. Fisher advised the US government detachments to make a prompt examination of the Reichsbanks in the areas captured and to inventory, inspect and ship any valuables to the Foreign Exchange Depository.

Following additional leads, Fisher and his task force drove north and arrived in Magdeburg on April 28, 1945. Located on the Elbe River, Magdeburg is less than ninety miles from Berlin. The Elbe was the farthermost point in the Allies' advance to capture Berlin and to the complete surprise of Churchill and a number of American field commanders; Eisenhower made the decision to attack the German forces in a southeast direction, away from Berlin. This near reversal in the direction of attack put the Reichsbank gold, currency, diamonds, and valuable art, directly in the path of the US Third and Seventh Armies!

Arriving in Magdeburg on April 28, at 11:00 in the morning, Lt.Cmdr. Fisher contacted Capt. James R. Williams, commander of the military government detachment. The US 30th Division, which had captured Magdeburg, suspected the presence of valuables in the Reichsbank vault and posted guards around the bank. Reichsbank officials Walter Luebcke (who had been at the bank for only two weeks, replacing the previous official who had left for Oslo) and Bernhart Nicolai were questioned immediately and forced to open the vault and assist in examining the contents which included, 769 large silver bars, 5,273 small silver bars, thirty-four miscellaneous small silver bars, and 536 boxes of silver bars, coins, and miscellaneous records.

The vault contained ninety-four bags of records from the Bond Office in Berlin, twelve of which were identified by Mr. Thoms as the records of the Precious Metals Department of the Reichsbank. Also in the vault, were printing plates for currency. According to Mr. Thoms, the bags and plates had been removed from Merkers several days before US forces arrived.

The Magdeburg Reichsbank officials produced a letter showing that the deposit of silver in the bank originally was part of Hungary's silver reserve. On January 17, 1945, the silver had been released by the Hungarian National Bank to the German minister of finance and loaded into seven freight cars. The train proceeded to Vienna, but because of Allied bombing of the railway system, the silver was transferred to nine large trucks. These arrived in Magdeburg on January 29, 1945, but due to severe air raids, the bank did not have the personnel or equipment to make a complete inventory. The officials merely signed a receipt for delivery of the silver.

Further interrogations revealed that on April 5, 1945, eighty bags of gold and two sealed envelopes arrived from Erfurt, and on April 7, forty-one bags of gold and one sealed envelope arrived from the Reichsbank in Goslar. All of the gold went to Berlin on April 11, 1945, and apparently, the foreign currency that included $2,170,000 that had previously been sent from Merkers Mine. The bank officials stated they had no knowledge of the Hungarian gold reserves. Gold had not been discussed during the silver transaction, they claimed. US intelligence knew that the Russians had advanced through Hungary and surmised that the Hungarians and Germans had not allowed the Hungarian gold reserves to be seized by the advancing Russian Army.

Lt.Cmdr. Fisher arranged with the 30th Division for additional security precautions and on May 9, the 198,000 pounds of silver left for the Foreign Exchange Depository in Frankfurt as Shipment 17.[9] To make room for the silver, the art treasures from Merkers were moved from the air raid shelter to the ground floor of the depository, and the shiny metal was stored in the more secure area of the air raid shelter.[10]

The ninety-four parcels of records were accepted on that day as Shipment 17D. The upcoming phenomenon of the bags of records is revealed later in Shipment 104.

REICHSBANK
Nr. 58

Hinterlegungsschein

Wir bescheinigen hiermit, daß uns heute von *Herrn Capt. John D. Cofer, Military-Govt.-Officer, Fürth/Bay., Det. I 3 - B 3. für Herrn Walter J. Funke-Kaiser in Mehlem(Kreis Bonn) unter Beigabe* ~~eines verschlossenen~~ *eines Briefes* ~~mit der Aufschrift~~ *Holländische Gulden 23.900,- (in Worten: Dreiundzwanzigtausendneunhundert) und Französische Franken 37.000,- (in Worten: Siebenunddreißigtausend)* ~~zum angegebenen Werte von Reichsmark in Worten Reichsmark unter den auf der Rückseite dieses Scheines abgedruckten Bedingungen~~ zur Aufbewahrung übergeben worden ~~ist~~ *sind.*

Fürth/Bay. den *23. April* 19 *45*

Reichsbanknebenstelle

Zum Mitverschluß übernommen:

am	bis zum	Lagergeld R.M	Pf.	Versicherungsgebühr R.M	Pf.	Unterschrift der quittierenden Beamten
						Es sind entrichtet
19	19					
19	19					
19	19					
19	19					

Das Depot zurückerhalten am	Unterschrift des Hinterlegers als Quittung	Wieder eingeliefert am	Gebühren R.M	Pf.	Unterschrift der quittierenden Beamten
19		19			
19		19			
19		19			
19		19			
19		19			
19		19			
19		19			
19		19			
19		19			
19		19			
19		19			
19		19			
19		19			

In true German bureaucratic prose, the gold in the Furth bank was signed over to Captain John D. Cofer on a German form, as shown here.

Following the trail of gold, Fisher and his group backtracked to Eschwege, about twenty miles north of Merkers, and the first location outside of the Russian occupation zone to be searched. He was accompanied by a local military commander who interrogated the Eschwege Reichsbank official. The interrogation on April 29, 1945 revealed forty-one bags of gold, each containing two smaller bags, had been deposited in the bank during August 1943. Due to the approaching US troops, the bank officials considered burying the gold, but the rapid advance thwarted the plan and it remained in the vault. The eighty-two bars of gold weighing 2,873 pounds were Horchwertige bars—a partial deposit of the Belgian gold taken from France.

Five bank officials from the Ministry of Finance in Berlin were found hiding in a house near Eschwege. Fisher arranged with the military government to have the men taken to Frankfurt for questioning.

The following day, Fisher continued south to Coburg and questioned the Reichsbank officials there. Initially, they denied that the bank had any gold, but finally admitted they had buried it before the American occupation under a chicken coop, beneath a manure pile in the garden of a friend's house, one and a half miles from the bank. Fisher remained at the bank while Lt. Fredrick L. Howard, from the military government detachment, gingerly retrieved the bags of gold and delivered them to the bank; it also was learned six bags of silver coins were buried in the cellar of the bank. The 2,723 pounds of gold were positively identified as Horchwertige gold from Belgium.

The bags of gold from Eschwege and Coburg were shipped to the Foreign Exchange Depository on April 30 and May 2, 1945 as Shipments 7 and 10.[11] The gold in Shipment 7 consisting of 32,882.035 Troy ounces of gold and Shipment 10 that contained 32,667.532 Troy ounces were air freighted to the Bank of England in 1948 and deposited into the account of the Tripartite Gold Commission.

The dogged task force advanced south and arrived in Wurzburg on May 1, 1945, and met with Lt.Col. E.D. Stocker, Fiscal Officer, Military Government Detachment F1 A1. Stocker had been told by German bank officials that gold was in the Wurzburg Bank vault, but had not interrogated the bank officials. Fisher proceeded to question Mr. Kipple, the Reichsbank official, who said thirty-four bags and two boxes containing gold bars had arrived from Amsterdam on February 26, 1945. In addition to the gold from Amsterdam, the bank also received three boxes containing works of art in the name of Dr. Kuelmann, state secretary for justice of Holland. The gold and 750 million French francs had been sent to Nuremberg on May 26. The Wurzburg vault also contained 128 bags of Belgian currency, four bags of additional foreign currency and eight bags of German silver coins. Fisher discussed the importance of the vault contents with Stocker and made arrangements for Stocker to have the valuables delivered to Frankfurt as soon as possible. These items went to the Foreign Exchange Depository on May 3, 1945, Shipment 14. The Dutch gold was later returned to the Netherlands Bank.[12]

Immediately, Fisher went to Nuremberg arriving on May 1, late that night, and had the satisfaction of sleeping in a hotel suite that had belonged to Hermann Göring. The Nuremberg Reichsbank had been badly damaged by Allied bombing although the vault was intact. Here he met with Capt. Stewart Campbell, from the military government. The interrogations had to be conducted across the street in the former German military justice building. Under questioning, Reichsbank Director Weidmann admitted that he had burned all of the 750,000,000 French francs (1945 value $17,250,000, but mostly worthless in a month's time) because he thought the notes were no longer in circulation as the lawful currency of France. Albert Thoms felt this was not the real reason; he postulated that Weidmann instead simply wanted to destroy something that might be of value to the Allies.

The remaining bank officials holding the necessary keys to the vault were rounded up. They found thirty-four bags of gold, and one bag of gold foreign currency from Holland. Fisher made the necessary arrangements with Third Army headquarters for Capt. Campbell to deliver this gold to the Foreign Exchange Depository.

On May 3, 1945, Campbell traveled to nearby Nuremburg by truck and an escort furnished by the military police. Here, he had the bags of gold and currency loaded onto the truck. He had made previous arrangements to meet with Capt. John D. Coffer at Furth, a few miles away and in the direction of Frankfurt, to receive two locked metal boxes of gold Dutch guilders from the Reichsbank in Furth. Specific orders were given regarding the Furth gold; "No receipt is to be surrendered to the Reichsbank. The inventory for both banks was to be checked and witnessed in the presence of a United States Army Officer other than Captain Campbell."[13] On May 3, 1945, the Nuremberg and Furth gold was delivered to the Foreign Exchange Depository by Capt. Stewart Campbell as shipment number 15. He received a signed receipt certified by Capt. Paul S. McCarroll.[14] The gold in Shipment 15 consisting of 43,588.203 Troy ounces of gold was air freighted to the Bank of England in 1948 and deposited into the account of the Tripartite Gold Commission.

Nuremberg was the last reconnaissance of the hardy Task Force Fisher, which had traveled 1,900 miles and deposited 13,310 pounds of gold and more than 198,000 pounds of silver to the Allied Gold Pot at the Foreign Exchange Depository.[15]

From information gleaned at various interrogations, Lt.Cmdr. Joel Fischer had informed the commander of the Ninth Army of a large deposit of gold bars in the Zwickau Reichsbank. In the bank were forty-two bags containing eighty-two bars of gold with an estimated weight of one ton. The gold was delivered to the Foreign Exchange Depository on June 15, 1945 as Shipment 29. This shipment consisted of 32,637.948 Troy ounces of gold was air freighted to the Bank of England in 1948 and deposited into the account of the Tripartite Gold Commission.[16]

CHAPTER 10
Assorted Deposits

At 3:50pm, on April 28, 1945, a convoy under the charge of Lt. Victor D. Downer, Battery C, 172nd Field Artillery left Nordhausen for the Foreign Exchange Depository, Frankfurt. The convoy was escorted by two armored cars for added security.

Deposited in the Foreign Exchange Depository as Shipment 5 was the following:

> 240 numbered large sack containing 2,589,027,550 French francs
> One sack containing 500,000 Dutch guilder
> One sack containing 40,000 Guilder notes
> Sealed envelope with certified checks drawn on the bank of France for 3,500,000,000 French francs
> > Three bags of 10 wooden cases of bullion
> > > 12 bars platinum
> > > 6 packages platinum scrap
> > > 5 plated platinum
> > > 1 block palladium
> > > 2 plates palladium
> > > 1 bottle palladium
> > > 2 bottles rhodium
> > > 3 bottles iridium
> > > 2 blocks gold
> > > 4 packages gold scrap

Of interest, on June 4, 1945, France recalled all outstanding currency. The French franc was to be exchanged within twelve days. Only notes larger than 5,000 ($115 in 1945) francs could be exchanges during these twelve days. After that, all bank notes between 50 and 5,000 francs would cease to be legal currency. A family was restricted to 6,000 francs per head of family plus 3,000 for each dependant. Therefore, only notes of less than 50 francs ($1.15) would be legal tender. The large bulk of cash collected by the US Army would be worthless.[1]

The policy of the Allies was to return all currency recovered in Germany to the former occupied country. France had been assured of receiving the money recovered from Nordhausen, plus others areas of Germany. The exception; currency recovered from Hungary, Rumania, Bulgaria and Finland would be given to the Soviet Union.

On August 29, 1948, the certified checks were signed for by a representative of the French Ministry of Finance and under the authority of them, the currency, without count verification, was sent to a pulp mill in Frankfurt to be converted into cardboard boxes. On January 3, 1949, the platinum, iridium and rhodium were sent to the Bank Deutscher Laender.[2] The gold in this shipment consisted of 21.494 Troy ounces of gold was air freighted to the Bank of England in 1948 and deposited into the account of the Tripartite Gold Commission.

On April 28, 1945, Lt.Col. Berthel W. Peterson was contacted by Col. Bernard Bernstein and given the assignment of investigating a reported cache of silver near the village of Wertingen, Germany. From interrogations it was reported that the silver ingots had been owned by the German gold and silver smelting firm of Roessler, Frankfurt, Germany.

Peterson spent the following day studying maps and reviewing the combat situation of that immediate area. He further contacted by phone Capt. La Point of the US Seventh Army, who stated the suspected area had not been cleared of enemy forces. La Point also informed Peterson that he may well need some pneumatic tools or dynamite to break through a cement wall as a captured German prisoner had told interrogators this was the case.

Two days later, Peterson arrived at Seventh Army headquarters. Here, contact was made with Army Engineers to meet the colonel and Capt, Oliver D. O'Bryan, B Battery, 108th Anti-Aircraft Artillery, at Wertingen where they were joined by military police. The location supplied earlier to the colonel was incorrect, but O'Bryan stated he knew the location. At 6:30pm, on April 30, they arrived at the well-concealed and camouflaged location in a dense forest. Guarding the structure containing the reported silver were twenty-four soldiers of the US 4th Infantry Division. Concerned about themselves the soldiers immediately stated they were hungry and without any rations.

Concerning himself with his mission, Col. Peterson noticed the building was made of plastered bricks and decided it could be broken into with pick axes that were ready available. Thus once the wall was bashed in, the loading of the trucks began immediately. It had to have taken the soldiers several hours to load the trucks considering the cargo consisted of 297 large and 645 small bars of silver totaling twenty-two tons. Leaving with a contingent of security police, Peterson met the detachment of engineers that had been sent out to blast the building. The 2940th Engineers were given a brief explanation of the situation and informed that their assistance was no longer required.

The following morning, May 1, 1945, the colonel returned with the cache of silver by way of Heidelberg before continuing on to Frankfurt. He reported that he arrived in that city at 6:30pm after encountering nine flat tires, two malfunctioning truck carburetors, and towing one jeep. The following day, after a lighting power failure, the silver was turned over to the Foreign Exchange Depository as Shipment 11 at 2:15 in the afternoon.

Shipment 11. American civilian, Edwin P. Keller, holds a bar of silver that the inventory describes as "large and small bars."

In these times of electronic spread sheets, it is refreshing to read this actual inventory of the silver bars marked with lines in groups of five assigned to five trucks. The truck number is noted along with the driver's name and his military serial number.

On October 15, 1946, the silver with a gross weight of 20,077.149 kilograms was released to Col. Frank W. Fruitman, US Economics Division, Office of Military Government for Greater Hesse.[3]

Shipment 12 was of historical significance, for on April 27, 1945, after the capture of Nordhausen, seven American soldiers from the 350th Ordnance Depot, while inspecting the nearby Berntrode Mine for ammunition, found some 400,000 tons of ammunition in the fifteen miles of underground corridors. During their exploration, the men observed a masonry wall built into the side of the main corridor a quarter of a mile from the shaft, and not far from a large storage of dynamite. Noticing the mortar was still fresh, they made an opening; after tunneling through masonry and rubble to a depth of six feet, they uncovered a framed latticed door padlocked on the inside. Breaking through this, they entered a room divided by partitions into a series of bays, filled with paintings, boxes and tapestries, and hung with brilliant banners. The contents were grouped around four caskets; one was decorated with a wreath and red silk ribbons bearing the swastika and the name Adolf Hitler.

Capt. Walker Hancock, Monuments Fine Art and Archive Officer, was contacted and given the assignment of investigating the find. He traveled to the Bernterode Mine on April 29. After crawling through the opening into the hidden room, Hancock was forcibly struck with the realization that this was no ordinary depository of works of art. The place had the aspect of a shrine because of the symmetry of the plan, a central passageway with three compartments on either side connecting two large end bays. There was a dramatic display of the splendid banners hung in deep rows over the caskets and stacked with a decorative effect in the corners. In each of the three compartments on the right of the central passageway was a wooden coffin, placed parallel to the partition. To the top of each a label had been attached with scotch tape. Hastily scrawled in reddish crayon was written, "Field Marshall von Hindenburg," "Mrs. von Hindenburg" and "Frederick Wilhelm I, the Soldier

King." In the last compartment, on the left, was a great metal casket with no decoration of any kind. On the label was simply written, "Frederick the Great." Near this was a small metal box containing portraits in color of military leaders from Frederick Wilhelm I to Hitler. Here were the remains of some of Germany's greatest historical figures!

The banners were 225 Imperial regimental army standards dating from the early Prussian wars, and including many from World War I. Several of the older ones were tattered and mounted upon netting. All were unfurled, contributing to the dramatic display of Prussian militarism.

That evening at army headquarters in Weimar, Capt. Hancock made his report and received orders to remove all the contents of the macabre depository. The actual work of packing and hoisting consumed four days and ended on May 8, V-E Day. The caskets were the last to be removed. Frederick the Great was left until the very end, as the great weight and size of his casket might have caused problems. The Americans wanted to ensure that having the paintings and objects of more contemporary interest safely out of the mine should the elevator malfunction. Capt. Hancock had the unique experience of riding up in the elevator with Field Marshal von Hindenburg. When Hancock reached the surface, he waited while Frederick the Great was loaded into the elevator down below. His casket weighed at least twelve hundred pounds, and if it had been one-half inch longer not even the engineers could have gotten it aboard. For more than an hour, Hancock waited while the men struggled to squeeze the great weight into the elevator.

Meanwhile, a radio installed in the office alongside the shaft entrance poured forth-patriotic speeches and music in celebration of the victory in Europe. Finally the ready signal came and the men jubilantly started hoisting as slowly as the engines would turn. By one of the most whimsical of all coincidences ever arranged by the ironic fates, the radio at this instant began playing the "Star Spangled Banner." As the casket of the Prussian king rose to the earth's surface, the tune changed to "God Save the King."[4]

American soldiers load the heavy coffin containing Frederick the Great,
one of the Germany's great military leaders, idolized by Adolf Hitler.

Chapter 10

Early the next morning, a convoy of eight trucks, and two jeeps without escort, started on its journey to the Marburg collection point, a place of safekeeping for the gruesome cargo. For now, the caskets and corpses would remain at the Marburg collection point, but on May 2, 1945 were turned over to the Foreign Exchange Depository as shipment number 12. The Prussian crown jewels, originally from the Hohenzollern Museum, Berlin, included as follows:

1. Leather case of the crowns, the scepter and Imperial Orb used in the carination in 1701 in Konigsberg.
2. The crown of the King and Queen. Made for the coronation on January 18, 1701 of Frederick I and his wife Sophie Charlette in Konigsberg. Only the frames were kept. Both crowns were equipped with jewels for the occasion.
3. Imperial Orb, made for the coronation of Frederick I on January 18, 1702
4. The Imperial Sword, made for Duke Albrecht of Prussia in 1504-41 by Jobst Frender in Konigsberg.
5. Silver and Gilded Box for the safekeeping of the Reich seal, fashioned by the Berlin goldsmith Humbert and son, in the middle of the 19th century.
6. The Imperial Seal with the likeness of King Frederick I sitting on the throne. Made by Samuel Stall for the coronation.
7. Death Helmet of hammered and gilded copper that was carried various funeral procession with the crown insignia and fastened onto the coffins at funerals of male members of the royal household. It was first used for the funeral of the Great Elector, Frederick William of Brandenburg who died in 1688.
8. The Imperial Scepter that was made for the 1701 coronation.
9. The Elector's Sword, blessed by Pope Pius II and solemnly presented to him as a ceremonial sword to the Elector Albrecht Achilles in Mantua, Italy on January 6, 1460.[5]

The Prussian crown jewels remained in the Depository for four months and on September 17, 1945 they were signed for by Capt. Walter I. Farmer, Wiesbaden collection point. All of these valuables, and thousands more, were released on August 1, 1948 to the Minister President of Hesse.

The corpses would take another avenue, for in April 1946, Headquarters, Monuments, Fine Art and Archives, received a brief message from Gen. Lucius Clay, military governor of Germany and commander of US forces in Europe. The four distinguished corpses recovered from the Bernterode mine were to receive a suitable and dignified burial that would reflect no dishonor on the action of the US government. The assignment was given to the MFA&A personnel as it was felt the corpses were historical. The macabre project was dubbed "Operation Bodysnatch" and considered top secret. The Hindenburgs had an estate in the British zone of occupation, and a request was made for the burial of the field marshal and his wife at the estate. The British were quite distressed at the prospect and hastily referred the matter to the Foreign Office in London.

Temporally stalemated, the MFA&A officers began looking for a site where Frederick Wilhelm I and Frederick Wilhelm II could be buried. The kings were of the Hohenzollern family and two plots of their land were found, suitable for burial, in the French Occupation Zone and when permission was requested from the French, the answer was unequivocal: No.

Bad luck continued as the MFA&A officers investigated other Hohenzollern property and various Protestant churches. With delight, they finally discovered a church that seemed ideal. It was located just across the street from the Marburg collection point where the bodies were concealed. The St. Elizabeth Church had been used for centuries as a burial place for royal families of the region and had suffered no serious war damage.

Two separate sites in the church were selected for the final resting-place and approval was obtained from the surviving family members. But now, in the secret burial negotiations, the German authorities voiced violent objections to the entire plan. They stated that Germany's misfortunes were as attributable to Field Marshal von Hindenburg as to Hitler. They did not offer the same objection to the two kings, but made it plain that the burial in a church was too good for any of the four. The Germans strongly resented having the Hohenzollern and Hindenburg corpses handled by the MFA&A officers and their hostility was understandable, but after days of bitter disagreement the Germans were told the burials would take place as planned.

Shown here are a few of the thousands of wedding rings the Germans removed from their victims in order to salvage gold. The U.S. First Army found these rings, watches, precious stones, eyeglasses and gold teeth fillings hidden near Buchenwald Concentration Camp, near Weimar, Germany.

The coffins were secretly transferred at night and lowered into the open graves, sealed with a layer of steel and cement. A large sandstone slab was laboriously pushed over the tombs. It would be difficult for the disgruntled Germans to remove the coffins. That night a stonecutter etched simple inscriptions on the slabs, giving names, birth and death dates, and no titles. The MFA&A officers congratulated each other on how well the secret had been kept, but by the following morning more than 500 Germans had gathered at the church. It was sixteen months since the bodies had been removed from the Bernterode mine.[6]

Why had the US Army gone to such length to remove the bodies from the mine? Why not leave the corpses there and let the Russians take care of the problem? The Army knew this area was to be turned over to the Russians. The breach between the Western Allies and Russia had already begun and was playing itself out in many situations, such as this.

Shipment 16 was a deposit from Buchenwald concentration camp. On April 28, 1945, Maj. Howard M. McBee, the investigating officer of war crimes from the Judge Advocate Section, traveled to Buchenwald to investigate the atrocities and brutal treatment of the prisoners. Two German political prisoners who had worked in the disinfecting plant at the camp told McBee that a large deposit of valuable property was hidden in a cave at the stone quarry in the western part of the camp. McBee, the two Germans, and two prisoners who had worked in the quarry, found the spot where two air raid shelters had been dug to form a tunnel. The Germans had completely covered the entrances to the tunnels by blasting rocks over the entrance. Marks of the previous blast used to form the tunnels were visible near the upper rim of the quarry.

Twenty men went to the quarry and began excavating both entrances. After three hours of difficult digging, they made a small hole into the entrance of one of the tunnels. McBee crawled through and discovered several suitcases containing a wide variety of items, including US currency, US gold coins, rings, diamonds, precious stones, clocks, coins, razors, tools, tableware, dishes, and gold tooth fillings. The excavation of the second tunnel continued and the quarry was immediately placed under US military security. When all was completed, the retrieved valuables filled nine two-and-one-half ton army trucks. After clearing out the tunnels, the US Army engineers blasted the entrances closed. A bulldozer finished covering the opening with rocks so that no one would be injured should the tunnels ever cave in.

The loot was removed from the caves on May 1 and taken to a building in Weimar acquired by the Chief of War Crimes. The contents were then placed under the authority of Col. A.L. Hunter, Office of the Inspector General. Here, some of the items were sorted and the more valuable gems were separated. After making a partial inventory, and estimating that it would take a group on enlisted men fifteen months to complete a full inventory of the items, it was decided to turn the property over to the Currency Section in Frankfurt. The complete contents of the valuables taken from Buchenwald were packed into 319 boxes with an estimated weight of twenty tons.

On May 6, 1945, a convoy of six 2.5 ton trucks, and two armored cars, under guard with police motorcycles making frequent checks to insure no truck was diverted. That night they arrive at the Foreign Exchange Depository in Frankfurt and the following morning the boxes were unloaded as shipment number 16.

Valuable gems, previously inventoried, had been separated and were placed under the command of Maj. Windom, Finance Officer. There were three $100 checks drawn on Chase Manhattan Bank along with several $10 American Express traveler's checks in this shipment. The contents was insurmountable with an estimated 7,811 pounds of alarm clocks, 17,102 pounds of tableware, 4,030 pound of coins and sadly 134 pounds of children's toys. Many items were identifiable as to owner, such as a marriage certificate, passports, bank statements, bankbooks, graduation certificates and many Hungarian life insurance policies.

On April 26, 1948, six lots of Jewish religious objects, weighing 169 pounds, were delivered to J.A. Horne, director Offenback Archival Depot. On May 11, 1948, one savings book was delivered to the Deutsche Bank Finliale, Furth, Germany. On August 25, 1948, the Hungarian life insurance policies were handed over to Hungarian representatives.[7] It appears that the Foreign Exchange Depository made an earnest attempt to return the identifiable object from Buchenwald to the country of origin.

The American Army turned over to the Inter-Governmental Committee for Refugees (IGCR) millions of dollars' worth of accumulated SS loot taken by the Allies from Buchenwald, Merkers, and various individuals. Many of these valuables were sent to New York and put up for sale at public auctions.

CHAPTER 11
The Eagle and the Jackdaw

Each day throughout Germany, more gold and currency arrived in Berlin from Reichsbanks in towns that were to be overtaken by Allied forces. After days of devastating Russian bombing and artillery barrages, Hitler authorized the Berlin Reichsbank to prepare most of its remaining gold and currency for transfer to southern Germany.

Two German military trains with the code names "Eagle" and "Jackdaw" (a common European small black bird) were loaded with the valuable cargo on April 13, 1945, at the freight station Berlin-Lichterfelde West. The Eagle transported officials of the Reichsbank and other agencies. A baggage car attached to the Eagle contained a large amount of currency to supply southern Germany some 520,000,000 Reichsmarks (1945 value $52,000,000) that were urgently needed in the Munich area. The Eagle was to transport the Reichsmarks to Munich and the Jackdaw was to continue south into the National Redoubt area and deliver the foreign currency and gold to the village of Mittenwald.

Accompanying the trains were Dr. Walter Funk and Dr. Fritz Schwedler. Funk, president of the Reichsbank, was a shrewd moneyman, artist, musician, a notorious homosexual, and a habitual drunkard. Born on August 8, 1890, he was married, had no children, and made his home at the Bergerhof estate, near Bad Tölz. The property was a gift from a German business and was within the National Redoubt.

The trains were not able to take the direct route to Munich, due to Allied air observation and the rapidly advancing US army. The Eagle left the freight station first and took an indirect route through Czechoslovakia. Because of the advancing Allies and bombing of the railroads, it took the Eagle two days to reach Pilsen, Czechoslovakia. Because of the slow progress, the commander suggested that the eleven bags of foreign currency seized from Belgium by the Devisenschutzkommando (German Treasury Agents) go by truck to Regensburg. At first, the Reichsbank officials requested the German army transport the currency in their army trucks, but the transport commander flatly refused, therefore, the eleven bags of currency were loaded on a rental truck and driven by Reichsbank officials Fritz Mielke and Lothar Knape but due to the advancing US Army they did not travel to Regensburg but continued onward to Munich. Enroute, the truck came so near the front that for security reasons, Mielke removed the identifying Reichsbank tags and seals from the bags. On April 21, these bags arrived at the Reichsbank in Munich and on April 25, official Goller, from the Lindau Bank, removed 85,000 Swiss francs from one of the bags.

After six days of travel, the slow-moving Eagle reentered Germany in Bavaria at Eisenstein. Again, due to the delay, an additional sixty bags of foreign currency and 111,800,000 Reichsmarks were loaded onto trucks. Berlin Reichsbank director, Hans von Rosenberg-Lipinski, left the train with this cargo and headed to Munich, about 100 miles away.

The Eagle and Jackdaw continued on their southern route until they reached the Danube River at Daggendorf. The railroad bridge over the Danube had been destroyed by Allied bombing, so the cargo was ferried across and loaded on trucks for the remaining eighty miles. On the night of April 25, the valuable contents were turned over to Reichsbank officials in Munich.

Dr. Funk called Goller on the phone and instructed him to that the gold and currency that had arrived in the Munich Reichsbank should be taken to a military building in Mittenwald. Mielke hired a truck from private firm in Munich, along with the driver, and the valuables headed in a southern direction. During this trip, Funk left the shipment at Bergerhof and stayed at home with his wife. Dr. Schwedler preceded on to a lead mine in Peissenberg, in accordance with Funk's instructions. However, the mine was too wet so the trucks continued to Mittenwald, a small town fifty miles south of Munich on the Austrian border.

The shipment was under the supervision of Reichsbank official Mielke. He delivered the treasure to a military building in Mittenwald used as a casino/hotel for German officers. A telephone call was made to Funk, who agreed that the valuables could be accepted by an unnamed German army captain. Turned over to the captain at Mittenwald were twenty-five cases of gold, 364 bags of gold, nine envelopes containing records of gold shipments, thirty-four printing plates for German currency and ninety-four bags of foreign currency containing US $2,170,000 that had previously been in the Merkers mine, transferred to Magdeburg, and forwarded on to Berlin. This delivery included an equal amount in English pounds, Swiss francs and Norwegian crowns.

The gold and currency was accepted in the name of Col.Franz Wilhelm Pfeiffer, who was presumably quite familiar in the area. He was the regimental commanding officer of the Mountain Ranger School in Mittenwald and was expected to know a secure place to hide the treasure. Pfeiffer was forty-years-old, had served the German army on many battlefields and had been awarded Germany's highest award, the Knight's Cross for bravery. Because of his many combat wounds, Col. Pfeiffer, like many wounded veterans, had been assigned a noncombatant role.

That afternoon, April 26, the gold and currency was taken to a forester's home on Lake Walchen, approximately twelve miles north of Mittenwald. Mielke accompanied the shipment that was made in two separate trips in a German army truck under the direction of the German army captain. Fritz Mielke took an inventory of the items taken to the home of the forester, Hans Neuhauser, and prepared a receipt that was signed by the German army captain for Co. Pfeiffer. The treasure was stored in a shed at the rear of Neuhauser's home for two days.

The following day, it was removed by three civilians and several German soldiers who made two trips between 7:00 and 10:00pm using a German army cargo truck. Col. Pfeiffer and a select crew of German army soldiers then loaded the cargo onto pack mules and took it to a remote location. They dug six holes and buried the gold in three locations and the currency in the other three holes.[1]

Lt. Herbert DuBois had remained in Frankfurt for several days after the reconnaissance with Lt.Cmdr Joel Fisher. Then what the world had waited for, happened. The German high command surrendered on May 8, 1945, and the war in Europe ended. On May 9, DuBois left Frankfurt for Heidelberg with Albert Thoms and a military driver to discuss their mission with the US Sixth Army Group. A Maj. Cattier was stationed at the headquarters and had previously interrogated the Reichsbank officials in the Munich area about two trainloads of valuables codenamed Eagle and Jackdaw. Cattier made necessary clearance arrangements by phone and the reconnaissance team left for Munich and other areas in the Sixth Army Group vicinity.

DuBois' target area was in the Bavarian Alps which separated Germany from Austria. These mountains are almost 10,000 feet high and difficult to traverse, located in the foothills is Garmisch-Partenkirchen, a premier winter sports center and location of the 1936 winter Olympic Games. Ten miles southeast, in the valley of the Isar River, is the beautiful Alpine town of Mittenwald with the rugged Karwendel Mountain rising almost vertically above it. There, in the vicinity of Mittenwald, are several small, blue-green lakes, among them Lake Walchen and Lake Ferchensee.

The team arrived in Munich the evening of May 9, and contacted Capt. Theron D. Wilson, the local military government finance officer. Lt. DuBois and Capt. Wilson proceeded to the Reichsbank and interrogated Reichsbank director Goller who discussed the gold and currency that had been moved from Berlin through Munich and then to Mittenwald.

Here, at the Reichsbank in Munich, they found the following six categories of foreign currency:

A. 11 bags of currency deposited by the SS in Berlin and shipped to Munich on the Jackdaw. The bags contained mixed currency from Holland, France, England, Switzerland, and the US The US currency consisted of (18) $1 bills, (16) $5, (10) $20, half dollar, nickel and two envelope containing $825 burn. The total amount of US currency was valued at less than $300.

B. 5 bags of currency brought back from Mittenwald by Mielke containing English, Swedish, and Swiss currency and (305) $100 (620) $50, (1,110) $20, (1,920) $10 (2,517) $5, (605) $2, and (5,452) \$1, for a total of \$90,100 in US dollars.[2] It was recorded at the time that the five bags contained US \$121,067.

    C. 104 bags of mixed currency transferred to Munich from the Reichsbank in Graz, Germany.

    D. 5 bags currency accumulated by the Munich bank in the course of normal business.

    E. 4 large boxes from Stalag Luft VIII-C (Allied air force POW Camp). The boxes contained personal valuables and currency including US dollars. The US currency consisted of (22) \$1, (3) \$2, (2) \$10, (1) \$50, and (5) \$100. The boxes also contained 1,226 silver coins, 28 cameras, 2 pairs of opera glasses, 1 box with compass and ruling pen, 2 fountain pens, 2 razors, 1 pocket knife; 1 tripod, 9 metal watches, metal chains, rings and barrettes, 6 silver plated metal coffee spoons, (1) 14 carat gold wrist watch, and 9.1 grams of 20 carat dental gold.[3]

    F. 28 bags and three valises deposited by the SS and containing currency from Bulgaria, Rumania and Russia.

Schedule "A"

Claim & Item No.	Description	Unit	Quantity	Appraisal 1938 RM
	Property of Belgian Prisoners of War			
FED Form No.	**Owner** **Description**			
14858	* One lot of paybooks etc.			
15378	Charles Tytgat 7 groschen, Austrian metal coins			
	Noel Kumps 7 bearer shares for 7.50 Francs each Residence Palace Co. Bruxelles with dividend coupons and talons attached.			
	Jules Georges 1 watch, 1 chain and 1 key in envelope marked lot No. 5			
	August Bykans 1 watch with chain, 2 pieces of gold crown			
	1 wedding ring, gold, 1 wedding ring, metal in envelope marked lot No. 6			
	Richard Delval, 1 fountain pen. in envelope marked			
	Quai des Peniches 1 1 ring, metal Lot No. 7			
	1 identity card			
	unknown 1 bearer share for 500 Francs, Compagnie Belge des Mines Minerais & Métaux, with dividend coupons and talon attached.			
	unknown 5 bearer shares for 80 Francs each Société National de Chemins de Fer en Colombie, with dividend coupons and talon attached.			
	Larbi Khenaldia 1 savings bank book			
	Grosper Jean 1 savings bank book			
	Dupeux			
	Louis André Nacot 1 savings bank book.			

An inventory of the property of Belgian prisoners-of-war recovered in Munich that was deposited in the Foreign Exchange Depository as Shipment 18E.

Item B above had been reported to be US $120,000 contained in bag number 35 and removed from the cache of currency that was to be taken to Mittenwald. This money had been taken to the Munich Reichsbank by Fritz Mielke and returned to that bank by him.

DuBois removed these valuables from the Munich Reichsbank and sent them to the Foreign Exchange Depository as Shipment 18.

On May 10, 1945, arrangements were made for DuBois, Thoms and two enlisted men to continue south to Mittenwald. Upon their arrival, DuBois inspected the cellar of the casino that had been a hospital for German officers. There was no evidence of the treasure in the casino, so DuBois and his team went to the aforementioned forester, Hans Neuhauser's house on Lake Walchen. After questioning the forester, he said that the treasure had been removed from Walchen and sent towards Jachenau, which was in the general direction of Bad Tölz. DuBois did not go toward Jachenau since a large number of armed German soldiers were spotted in the woods near the lake. He wanted additional US soldiers before leaving for Jachenau. DuBois and his three men returned to Munich to re-interrogate Fritz Mielke and Mr. Goller since they suspected the bank officials withheld information.

DuBois made arrangements for additional U.S guards and trucks to accompany him on his return reconnaissance mission to the Lake Walchen area. At approximately 1:00pm, the party left Munich. They stopped at Bad Tölz to interrogate Mrs. Walter Funk, who was living with the Bürgermeister in Bad Tölz. She said Dr. Funk, had left Bad Tölz on May 6, a day before US troops entered the city. She also said she had not heard anything of the treasure at Mittenwald, but did remember one phone conversation in which her husband gave advice that gold should not be taken to Constanz. Mrs. Funk surprised DuBois by revealing that she had heard on the radio earlier that day that her husband had been taken prisoner by the US Seventh Army near Berchtesgaden. (Mrs. Funk was later arrested and imprisoned for several months along with Hermann Göring's wife, Emmy, and young daughter, Edda.)

DuBois thought Funk could supply some answers about the gold, so he traveled to Salzburg, headquarters of the XV Corps. The XV Corps finance officer, Captain Sattgast, informed DuBois that Funk was at the US Seventh Army Interrogation Center at Augsburg, Germany. Later that evening, DuBois and his reconnaissance team left Salzburg and drove to Augsburg, a three-hour trip. Capt. Zoller interrogated Funk. The doctor told the basic story of movement of the gold and currency, but maintained that he did not know the final destination. He did, however, believe the valuables had been put in a lead mine in the Mittenwald area. The Interrogation Center made it clear to DuBois that the procedure followed in the interrogation of Funk was within their control and no pressure whatsoever was exerted on Dr. Funk. Yet it was quite possible Funk knew more than he disclosed. DuBois sent a wire to Maj. Cattier of the Sixth Army Group advising him of the Funk interrogation and stating his intentions to return to Mittenwald.

That evening, DuBois and his party arrived at Lake Walchen and again questioned the popular forester, Hans Neuhauser, about the locations of mines in the immediate area. The only mine the forester knew about was midway between Wallgau and Vord-Riss. It was getting late and the team was hungry, so one of the rangers told DuBois to stand on a small bridge where the water flowed slowly beneath. The ranger then dropped two hand grenades in the water. After the concussion several large trout floated up under the bridge. DuBois gathered them up and Vera de Costra, a thirty-year-old Serbian woman staying at the forester's home, cooked the fish. DuBois and his reconnaissance team dined heartily on this unorthodox catch and stayed at the forester's home that night.

The following morning, May 14, the party covered the few miles to Wallgau to inspect the mine. Four bridges had been blown up along the road and it was necessary to walk four miles to reach their destination. They checked the contents of the buildings and talked to various employees but none had seen the arrival of any packages during the last days of the war. The mine could only be reached by a narrow 500-yard catwalk across the Isar River, and DuBois considered it quite unlikely such a heavy load could have been carried that distance over the catwalk and thought it inadvisable to inspect the mine.

DuBois returned to Mittenwald to investigate the locations of Col. Franz Pfeiffer and Dr. Fritz Schwedler. This exploration and the inspections of mines in the local area produced nothing. DuBois returned to the Foreign Exchange Depository in Frankfurt on May 17 to determine if any more inquiries were necessary.[4]

The POW valuables, Shipment 18E, were mostly identifiable and turned over to the country of origin. Items for US soldiers included a 10 Shilling note belonging to Kenneth Stearn, POW number, 80983; Check number 2/35704 for 8 Pounds payable to and from Robert Munro, POW number 82006 and Cashier check No.484331 for $11 payable to Jean Germak signed by Roger Duillard, POW number 427. These three negotiable items were signed for by the US Army. The remainder of this shipment, along with the other 18A through 18F, was signed for by the Landswzentralbank von Hessen on May 25, 1948.

CHAPTER 12

Shipments 27A-F

Shipment 27A: Maj. Harry G. Costello, Counter Intelligence Corps, VI Corps, on May 21, 1945, deposited, in the Innsbruck Reichsbank, gold bars weighing 1,535.418 kilograms or 49,364.835 Troy ounces with a 1945 value of $1,727,769.23. The gold was weighed in the Reichsbank and in the process some coins fell out of some of the wet and torn bags. These bags were replaced with new bank bags. The identification found with the gold was labeled "Coding Section of Foreign Office, Berlin." This gold was delivered by Capt. Charles L. Jenne, Seventh Army to the Foreign Exchange Depository on June 10, as shipment number 27A.[1]

The gold in this shipment consisted of 43,539.656 Troy ounces of gold was air freighted to the Bank of England in 1948 and deposited into the account of the Tripartite Gold Commission.

Shipment 27B: Found near Dorenwald and reported to be property of the German Foreign Office were forty bags containing seventy-nine gold bars delivered by also by Capt. Charles L. Jenne, Seventh Army to the Foreign Exchange Depository on June 10, as shipment number 27B.

Of the seventy-nine bars, fifty-five could be identified from German records as being resmelted from Russian gold during January 1940, which was before Russia was attacked by Germany.[2]

The gold in this shipment consisted of 31,707.201 Troy ounces of gold was air freighted to the Bank of England in 1948 and deposited into the account of the Tripartite Gold Commission.

Shipment 27C: Found in Lindau by Mr. V.S. Guinzbourg, 307th Detachment CIC, were twenty-eight parcels consisting of twenty-two wooden boxes numbered, four small boxes unnumbered, and two canvas bags unnumbered alleged to contain gold bullion. The valuables were reported to be property of Foreign Office, German Reich. Delivered by Capt. Charles L. Jenne, Seventh Army to the Foreign Exchange Depository on June 10, twenty-eight bags of gold coins and sixty gold bars as shipment number 27C.[3]

The gold in this shipment consisted of 49,342.112 Troy ounces of gold was air freighted to the Bank of England in 1948 and deposited into the account of the Tripartite Gold Commission.

Shipment 27D: Recovered valuables in St Johann, Austria that involved the capture of General Gottlob Christian Berger. In May 1945, General Berger had been in charge of Germany's prisoner of war administration and under great risk to himself had transferred the senior Allied POWs by train to Switzerland after Hitler had ordered their execution. Later, at the Nuremberg trials, Berger was convicted as a war criminal for atrocities committed in Russia and received a twenty-five-year prison sentence.

On May 22, Maj. Paul Kubala, Military Intelligence conducted an interrogation of Berger. During this routine questioning, Berger stated that he worked directly under Heinrich Himmler who had given him money to hide and said the money was the property of the Reichsbank, not his or Himmler's. He offered to show the Americans where the valuables were buried.

The following morning Berger and Lt. William S. Scheuer, Military Intelligence, met Capt. Harry V. Anderson, 101st Airborne Division, at St. Johann, Austria. Berger took them to a chief forester's home that was connected to a barn. They removed some floorboards in the barn, dug down four feet and removed eight large cloth sacks and one large metal box. They contained a million dollars worth of currency from twenty-five different countries. There was no US currency in this cache. This currency was sent to the Foreign Exchange Depository as shipment number 27D.[4]

Shipment 27G: Valuables recovered at Wallgau also involved General Berger. During more routine interrogation by Lt.Scheuer, it was learned that twenty-five boxes of gold had been hidden in the vicinity of Mittenwald.[5]

Investigation of General Berger's report was assigned to Lt. Elroy F. Perez, T Force, US Seventh Army. The T Force had been organized in the early stages of the war to recover gold, silver, diamonds, patents, advanced technology, and scientists who worked with jet planes, rocket ships and other modern weapons. Perez, Scheuer, Tec 5 Kuehn and a driver left Augsburg and proceeded to Ferchensee about four miles beyond Mittenwald. They familiarized themselves with the terrain, and cautiously interrogated local inhabitants concerning German mule teams or any unusual events occurring on April 26, 1945.

No leads were obtained at Ferchensee, so the team returned to Mittenwald. There, the mayor stated that a Capt. Berger of the Gebirgs-Pionier Camp was in charge of all the local engineering equipment and mule teams during the war. During the conversation, the mayor revealed that Berger and other officers from the camp were in a prisoner of war cage at the icehouse in nearby Garmish-Partenkirchen. Immediately, arrangements were made to transfer the prisoners to Mittenwald. Berger was questioned, but being quite elderly and short of memory, could not materially add to the information. His staff of twelve officers was interrogated and nothing was learned, except that a Colonel Pfeiffer, previously in charge of an officer's training school, was said to be the person who could help find the gold. The colonel had disappeared but his orderly had been seen in the town of Mittenwald.

While the Americans were searching for the orderly, a German by chance overheard the request for Pfeiffer or his orderly and asked why they were wanted. The reply was the party had business to transact with them. The German then took the group to the Alpine hotel where they were introduced to members of a German civilian organization working for the American counter intelligence corps. Now things began to develop. This group had reports on the gold and people involved with it. They introduced two men who were familiar with the area in which the gold was supposed to be hidden. Arrangements were made for these two to meet with T Force at seven the following morning to reconnoiter the area.

Lt. Perez contacted the CIC Detachment at Garmisch-Partenkirchen that had reports of the German civilian organization. The CIC responded they had already obtained the information from the Germans and they had nine men in custody who were connected to the gold case. They were to be sent to Supreme Headquarters Allied Forces Europe (SHAFE) in Frankfurt the following morning for questioning by the Finance Division at Frankfurt, so Perez decided to interrogate the men that night.

The CIC gave the T Force all the facts they had and located the nine men to be interrogated. Scheuer and Kuehn handled the questioning. The first eight men provided no information, but the last man, Captain Heintz Rueger, said, "I think I can help to locate the gold. My men and I unloaded the gold on the night of April 25 and 26 and if you take me with you, I think I may locate the spot where it is buried."[6] The cross-examination ended at midnight.

The following morning, June 8, Perez, Scheuer, Kuehn, one driver, the prisoner, Rueger, two German civilians and six engineers with mine sweepers set off for Obernach approximately 500 yards from Lake Walchen. They drove to the foot of Altloch Berg, then hiked up a trail for approximately twenty minutes. Reaching a point where the trail forked, Rueger requested that one of the minesweepers be put in operation up the left fork. About ten yards from the fork and five yards to the left of the trail, the minesweeper indicated the presence of a metallic substance over an area six feet square. It was well-camouflaged with a tree stump surrounded by moss.

After digging down about four feet they uncovered the gold. Excited by the discovery, Perez took one bar to 10th Armored Headquarters, where he called Seventh Army Headquarters to report they had found the gold. The civilians were returned to Mittenwald and the prisoner to the POW camp.

Immediately, additional US military personnel arrived at the cache, where the gold was removed and counted. This cache had 728 bars of gold and was put into the custody of the 10th Armored Division which delivered the gold in two French and one American truck to the Foreign Exchange Depository on June 10, as shipment number 27G.[7]

The gold in this shipment consisted of 290,584.409 Troy ounces of gold was air freighted to the Bank of England in 1948 and deposited into the account of the Tripartite Gold Commission.

Shipment 27E: This find at Oberbichl involved the 101st Airborne Division, for on May 26, 1945, officials of the 502nd Parachute Infantry Regiment were informed of the fact that a large sum of currency had been found in the neighborhood of Oberbichl, Germany. The money had been found earlier when villagers had noticed their dogs digging in a ravine just over the Austrian frontier. They investigated and found some canned food that had been unearthed by the dogs. The food sent a good part of the village to the area attracting the attention of a Reicharbietsdienst or Government Labor Service Battalion (Todt Organization) that had been assigned to the German 2nd Mountain Division. In need of food, they too went down to investigate and dig for some canned food. On May 21, this unit found a large cache of money that was assigned to a German major who was in charge and he in turn ordered the money buried by two responsible men for safekeeping. He informed the XIII SS Corps of the find. Unbelievably, the chief of staff of the SS corps informed Lt.Col. Patrick F. Cassidy, 502nd, 101st Airborne Infantry of the find.

The colonel notified intelligence of the information, but due to an ongoing investigation, the officer could not leave for about five hours. Therefore Cassidy called Capt. Joseph Pangerl Jr., US interrogator of prisoners of war, to accompany him to pick up the money. When they arrived at the headquarters of the German 2nd Mountain Division, they were told the money was up in the hills and they would send for it. Cassidy requested a German officer to guide himself and Pangler and they would pick up the currency. The German took them to the headquarters of the labor battalion where the major in charge said he had already sent for the cash. After considerable waiting, the money in a damp and dirty bag was turned over to Cassidy and Pangerl. The major told them the money had not been counted.

In addition to paper currency, including 10,055 Swiss francs, the bags contained forty-two gold French Napoleons coins and about four pieces of jewelry.

Delivered by Capt. Charles L. Jenne, Seventh Army, to the Foreign Exchange Depository on June 10, one box said to contain foreign currency and securities from the Hispano-Americana de Electricidad Company as shipment number 27E.[8]

The securities of the Hispano-Americana de Electricidad Company were transferred to the Landeszentralbank von Hessen on November 16, 1948. The remainder of Shipment 27E was allocated to the Intergovernmental Committee for Refugees.

Shipment 27F: On May 4, 1945 near Ober Siegsdorf, the 3rd Battalion, 115th Infantry found a sum of money in a Hungarian general's staff car in an open box and the majority of the currency was tied in small bundles. The remaining uncounted was delivered by Capt. Charles L. Jenne, Seventh Army to the Foreign Exchange Depository on June 10, as shipment number 27F.[9]

The final destination of this shipment is unknown.

CHAPTER 13
Alpine Gold Caches

Shipment 31

Shipment 31 taken from Rauris began in April 1945, with the establishment of an Alpine redoubt still being considered by the Nazis. SS General Ernst Kaltenbrunner ordered foreign exchange assets to be removed from the Reichsbank in Berlin and hidden in the mountains of southern Germany. More than 6,000,000 US dollars worth of jewels, gold, silver and securities were shipped south by trains, planes and trucks. On orders from Kaltenbrunner, SS Colonel Josef Spacil traveled by plane, on April 22, to make arrangements to conceal the assets.

Spacil planned to set up a main caches and a paying station approximately five kilometers apart with communications between the two locations by motorcycle. He then ordered Pfeiler to hide the valuables in the vicinity of Zell am See, Austria. A truckload from this hoard was in Salzburg, so Pfeiler took the truck to Breitwies, where, due to unforeseen delays, they remained for several days. As a result, Pfeiler was relieved of the assignment and the truck containing the valuables was turned over SS Lieutenant Schuster and SS Captain Albert Apfelbach along with the driver of the truck SS Sergeant Menzel. They drove to Zell am See, and with the help of Forest Meister Reisinger, they buried the trove near a sawmill during the nights of May 2-4.

A few days later at war's end, Spacil joined up with SS Captain Gerhardt Schlemmer's unit, taking the identity of a SS Corporal to conceal his identity. He was captured along with Schlemmer and placed in the Oklahoma Prisoner of War compound. Spacil discusses with Schlemmer the possibility of buying a discharge from the Americans with funds from a hidden treasure. Keeping a low profile, Spacil asked Schlemmer to approach an American officer to try and buy a discharge for himself and their second-in-command Lieutenant Walter Hirschfeld. Schlemmer disclosed to Tec 3 John E. Alter, military intelligence, the scheme Spacil was proposing for a discharge. They hatched a plan duping Spacil into believing a discharge could be bought. He furnished Schlemmer a letter and password enabling an American, namely Lt. Nacke to contact persons who knew where the treasure was hidden.

On June 4, 1945, Lt. Claus K Nacke, Tec 3 John E. Alter and SS Lieutenant Hirschfeld drove to Taxenbach to make contact with one of Spacil's liaison men who knew who had the stash. The only one to be located was Forester Reisinger who was convinced by the password and letter furnished by Spacil that he could show them where the treasure was hidden.

First in Rauris, gold coins were found hidden in a barn under the wooden floor and foreign currency was hidden behind a bricked-up enclosure in the attic of the home of Herr Urschunger. Other valuables in wet sacks were later found buried along the Rauris-Taxenbach highway on a steep slope under some trees about 100 yards from the road.

These valuables received as Shipment 31 from Capt. David W. Wallace, Military Government Detachment F1H3 on June 18, 1945 the following:

> 19 bags of gold coins
> 1 mail sack said to contain paper money
> 3 boxes of currency
> 3 bags of jewelry and silverware
> 1 mail sack containing wrappings removed from coins, bills etc
> 2 boxes and 10 bags of silver coins and bullion
> 1 envelope of gold coins, currency and jewelry

The foreign currency included US $160,679. This included a three cent coin from 1853, three nickels, six dimes, four quarters, one silver dollar, a $500 bill and the remainder in various US bills.

Unfortunately, a supplementary shipment would be added to this shipment a month later. It seems that on returning to the Oklahoma Prisoner of War cage, Tec 3 Alter was involved in a jeep accident and hospitalized. Removed from his personal belongings were: 220 gold French franc, 280 gold Italian lira, 850 British pound notes, nine assorted rings, four wristwatches and one jeweled cross with diamonds.

Strangely, on September 12, 1945, Lt. Robert B. Kelse contacted Ralph K. Oates, an agent of the US Secret Service and requested that he carefully examine the contents of one specific mail sack received with this shipment that was considered empty of valuables. Oates wrote:

> The bag was found to contain currency and coin wrappers and cloth bags of various kinds apparently used for coin, gold, silver, and jewelry as well as dismantled cardboard and small wooden boxes which had apparently contained jewelry or other valuables. On some of the containers the contents had been noted in ink or pencil. All of this material is in a state of decomposition and on the majority the writing is undecipherable. The following items of material value were found in this bag and subsequently delivered to you:
>
> 4 - Italian 20 gold Lire coins discovered in folds of a rotted gunny sack
> 1 - Small wooden plaque or etching of questionable value found loose in a large bag.
>
> In so far as could be determined this bag contained nothing of value or interest to this Service and the contents intact have been returned to you for disposition.

It is unknown what role US Secret Service agent Ralph K. Oates, was involved with or the reason for Kelse's letter but by September 8, 1945, two boxes of British currency from this shipment were released to the Bank of England with the belief it was counterfeit. And, indeed it was, as the Germans had successfully counterfeited tons of English notes during the war.[1]

The gold coins in this shipment, consisting of 332.667 Troy ounces of gold, was air freighted to the Bank of England in 1948 and deposited into the account of the Tripartite Gold Commission.

Shipment 21

While the 221st Counter Intelligence Corps Detachment was located at Degerndorf, John G. Hammond and Dale Shughart received a call from William Mark the commanding officer of the 36th CIC Detachment asking them to visit him some fifty kilometers farther west. A man of few words, Mark lost no time in displaying four footlockers which they soon discovered were filled with obviously stolen loot. The contents of the lockers were not organized, but each held an assortment of jewelry, diamonds, watches, American currency, gold coins, and other items.

Mark advised them that he desired to be relieved of his cache, and forthwith handed it over to Hammond and Shughart for removal to corps headquarters. He told them that he permitted each of his agents to remove one $20 gold piece as souvenirs, but other than the contents were exactly as he received them. The valuables, containing thousands of gold coins including 475 US gold $20 pieces, were dumped in haste. The chests were found by members of the 36th Infantry Division in the sewer of a cement factory in Eiberg. Shughart recalled; he was told the possessor of the valuables was Nazi Ernst Kaltenbrunner.

Indeed the treasure was the foreign exchange funds that had been kept in Ernst Kaltenbrunner's office for purchasing gifts and personal items for the chief of the Reich Main Security Office. It consisted of a half-million dollars of foreign currency, of which 100,000 was US dollars and also contained several small bags of gold coins weighing about twenty pounds.

The money was kept in boxes about three feet long, eighteen-inches wide, and two feet high. In April 1945, these were loaded onto a train in Berlin. Later, in Bavaria, US planes strafed the slow moving train and it was destroyed. Off-loaded from the smashed boxcars into two trucks were boxes of treasure, whiskey, and office files that were transported by trucks to Gmunden, Austria. The gold treasure was then to be transported approximately fifteen miles south to Alt Aussee. The files and whiskey were to be sent to Castle Glanegg, near Salzburg. In Gmunden, the cargo was to be divided for their separate destinations, but a mistake, either deliberate or unintentional, was made. The files and whiskey were sent to Kaltenbrunner and the gold was sent to the Glanegg Castle and from there it was further transported to Imst. These valuables destined for Kaltenbrunner contained six sacks of gold weighing sixty-six pounds each and 600,000 units of US dollars, Swiss francs and English pounds.[2]

How this treasure ended up fifty miles from Imst in a sewer of the Alpine village of Eiberg is unknown, but now, Shughart and Hammond had these heavy boxes loaded into their jeep and headed back for XXI Corps headquarters. With that much loot, they should have been escorted by an armed guard, but were not.

At corps headquarters, the lockers were unloaded and a receipt taken. Neither Shughart nor Hammond took any of the loot for souvenirs. The four boxes were turned over to the Seventh Army Interrogation Center in Augsburg and on May 19, 1945, it was delivered to the US Foreign Exchange Depository in Frankfurt, Germany as shipment 21A.[3] Most of Shipment 21A was turned over to the Intergovernmental Committee for Refugees. (See Appendix C: Inventory of Kaltenbrunner's cache.)

Shipment 21B consisted of two bags of various coins, jewelry and stamps that were from Col. L.B. Moye, Finance Officer, 36th Infantry Division. The colonel had obtained the bags from MSgt. Kraus during combat near Bad Tölz. Kraus stated the coins were taken from a prisoner of war camp near Weilhelm, Bavaria. Part of this stash consisted of $604.63 US currency that included two silver dollars and 1,618 pennies.

Some parts of Shipment 21B were given to the Intergovernmental Committee for Refugees. On May 18, 1948, the remainder of shipment 21B was forwarded to the Landeszentralbank von Hesse, Frankfurt. The US currency was eventually sent to the US Treasury.

Then in the summer of 1949, four checks drawn on an Albanian bank, these were presented to a representative of the Albanian Government and 4,231 cancelled and uncancelled stamps declared worthless were destroyed.

Shipment 21C consisted of three boxes of several types of coins that were received from Capt. W.F. Hartly, VI Corps. The captain had taken the currency from a group of 115 German prisoners who were captured by the 20th Armored Division in the vicinity of Hintsberg, near Laufen. The coins appeared to have been looted by the German soldiers.

Hartly also turned over eight bags of various coins as Shipment 21D taken by members of the 20th Armored Division from the Nazi Party office in Salzburg, Austria. The coins deposited in the Foreign Exchange Depository were shipment 21D. Included in the six-page inventory of these coins were U.S 150 pennies, eight nickels and fourteen dimes.

May 19, 1945, from the US Seventh Army Interrogation Center in Augsburg, Germany the Foreign Exchange Depository received the following shipments; 21E three boxes of Italian and Polish currency and including one watch, ring and silver cup, 21F one bag Russian Rubles, 21G three bags of Romanian Lei, 21H one wooden case of Lei, 21I three bags and four boxes containing Lei, and 21J three bags also containing Romanian Lei.

Shipment 21E was returned on September 3, 1948 to the Russian Mission for Restitution.

Shipment 21K was eleven boxes of gold and silver taken from the Reichsbank in Munich and turned over by Maj. Dennis W. Macken. The origin of the items was unknown. The gold weighed ten pounds and the silver 1,763 pounds. Shipment K consisted of:

1 bag gold medallions
1 bag small gold bars
7 boxes silver bars and silver scrap
2 boxes silver shot
1 box silver medallions.

On November 22, 1948, the silver from shipment K was taken into custody of the Bank Deutscher Laender and receipt signed for by Albert Thoms.

Of interest regarding Shipment 21B, is a letter written on August 31, 1949, signed by Frank J. Roberts, Acting Chief, Foreign Exchange Depository. It is to:

Chief 7752 Finance Center.

1. Enclosed is check dated 30 August 1949 to the order of Treasure of the United States for $79.10.
2. This check was issued as the redemption value of a quantity of US postage stamps found at the end of the war by US Forces in an Allied Prisoner of War Camp in the vicinity of Weilheim, Bavaria and turned in to this Depository without data as to ownership.

The previous day the unused postage stamps consisting of: 1,312 six cent air mail, eight three cents and eight two cent, and one envelope of torn pieces of airmail stamps were to be redeemed at the 24th Base Post Office in Frankfurt, Germany. The contents of the envelope were declared to be beyond redemption and rejected by the post office. The envelope was later destroyed by "cremation."[4] Also in 21B were seven Money Orders and American Travelers Check from $5 to $25, payable to Mrs. Johanna C. Paulsen, Mrs. C.W. Randall, Francis A. Rusch, George M. Brown and C.S. Eggleston. The negotiable items were turned over to the US Army.

The gold in shipment 21K consisted of 174.906 Troy ounces of gold was air freighted to the Bank of England in 1948 and deposited into the account of the Tripartite Gold Commission.

Shipment 52

On June 27, 1945, Fritz Rauch, former lieutenant colonel and minister of Hitler's chancellery, telephoned a civilian friend who contacted Helmuth Groger, a German interpreter working for the 512 Military Police Battalion, and informed him that Rauch knew of a large cache of gold and currency buried in the Mittenwald vicinity. Rauch had said in return for certain favors, he would disclose the location.

Groger relayed this information to Capt. Russell C. Rockwell, who discussed the conversation with his commander Maj. Robert M. Allgeier. Most skeptical, Allgeier requested proof of the cache. Groger obtained transportation and an escort to bring back proof of the cache's existence and an inventory of the valuables. Fritz Rauch, Helmuth Groger, and two military police drove from Munich to Garmisch-Partenkirchen to investigate.

For some unexplained reason, supposedly to minimize suspicion, the plan was for Rauch to proceed alone to Mittenwald from Garmish-Partenkirchen. In the woods, at the cache, Rauch discovered that two of the hiding places had been uncovered and the gold removed. He was not aware that some of the hoard had been removed previously by the 10th Armored Division. Rauch noticed the location of a small amount of gold remained untouched and there were signs of interference with the cache of foreign currency. He dug up one store of currency, loaded it into his car and returned to Garmisch-Partenkirchen, where he met his associates and the two military police and then continued on to Munich.

In the early morning of June 28, the investigators phoned Maj. Allgeier to come inspect the twenty-three bags of currency that they had opened. Some of the bags evidently had been sealed while others merely had been tied loosely with a string. Allgeier immediately placed the currency under armed guard.

Groger and Rauch informed Allgeier they had brought back as much currency as possible. They assumed "partisans" living in the hills moved the cache to another location and urged immediate action before the balance disappeared. Rauch stated that to the best of his knowledge there were twenty boxes with fifty kilograms (110 pounds) each of gold, additional gold coins and an unknown quantity of currency still at the cache.

Allgeier circumvented normal channels and immediately dispatched Capt. Rockwell with men and vehicles sufficient for securing and guarding against possible "partisan" activity during the mission. Upon arrival in the cache area on the morning of June 28, it was apparent to Rauch that at least sixteen boxes of gold and some currency had been removed shortly after his departure the previous afternoon. The military police dug most of the day and from four large holes removed four boxes of currency and two bags of gold coins. The recovered gold weighed 475 pounds. The boxes contained six bags of Norwegian currency and the following US currency:

70	$1,000	$70,000
40	$500	$20,000
6,150	$100	$615,000
199	$50	$9,950
2,150	$20	$43,000
10,597	$10	$105,970
28,100	$5	$140,500
19,000	$2	$38,000
219,294	$1	$219,294
		$1,261,214[5]

(The official total is $1,261,717. The author added and re-checked this from the inventory forms and could have made a mistake.)

Further questioning of Rauch showed he had not reported the treasure sooner because he was waiting for the political situation to clear up. He wished to turn the valuables over to the proper authorities without endangering his own position. Rauch estimated 350 bags and twenty boxes of gold had been removed from this cache. Unbeknownst to him, however, the US 10th Armored Division had removed 364 bags with two bars each, but twenty boxes were missing from the collection. The gold had been found and placed in the vaults of the Foreign Exchange Depository as shipment 27A.

The valuables recovered by the 512th Military Police Battalion were shipped to the Foreign Exchange Depository on July 7, 1945 as shipment number 52A.[6] The currency was tallied in this same day as seventy-two bags of foreign currency. It would be two years before the US currency was actually counted. The money would be returned to the US Treasury in Washington D.C. The gold in this shipment consisted of 5,697.387 Troy ounces of gold was air freighted to the Bank of England in 1948 and deposited into the account of the Tripartite Gold Commission.

In early June 1945, the previously mentioned German Captain Hans Neuhauser received word from a German prisoner of war that the Americans were looking for him. The captain, a University of Munich graduate, was living with his parents and convalescing from a war wound. The single thirty-year-old captain had an impressive war record.

On June 23, 1945, in the small village of Falls, eight miles from Mittenwald, a Lt. Chatel of the 574th Antiaircraft Battalion, was contacted by Capt. Neuhauser who arranged a meeting with him at the Bürgermeister's home. Through a German interpreter he stated he had certain information about a large cache of gold and said he wanted to surrender and give this information to a particular American colonel at the POW camp in Garmisch-Partenkirchen.

Chatel, Neuhauser, and the interpreter drove the few miles to the POW cage in Garmisch-Partenkirchen. They learned that the particular American colonel whom German captain Neuhauser had in mind either had left the camp or possibly did not exist.

Chatel insisted that the German captain disclose his story pertaining to the cache. Neuhauser replied he did not have American army discharge papers. All he had was his *soldbuch* (a small book carried in a soldier's pocket listing equipment issued; leave time and personal information, also used as identification). Neuhauser requested that Chatel help him obtain an early clearance from a POW camp, and that the Americans assist in the release of his father, who had been arrested by the Americans fourteen days after the war ended. The father, also a forester, had not served in the German military. Neuhauser was told everything would be done for him and his father that could be done through proper channels. The POW screening authorities would be told of Neuhauser's cooperation and that he had surrendered to the Americans, through Chatel.

The German captain then said while at home convalescing, he decided to go to Mittenwald, where he saw the gold and currency at the German officers' casino. On April 25, the treasure was taken from the casino at Mittenwald to his father's home where it remained for two days. Then Neuhauser and ten SS men took the valuables up the mountain by pack mules and buried them.

On April 28, a Reichsbank official and an SS officer, had come to the forester's home and showed his son, captain Neuhauser, a slip of paper stating they were authorized to remove the cache. Neuhauser took the two men up the mountain and showed them where the valuables were buried and then returned to his home. The two men returned to the Neuhauser's home after only three or four hours. It seemed strange to the captain that the treasure could have been removed in such a short time and after the two men left he went to the area of the cache and noticed that the two men had dug up and removed only twenty cases of gold. Neuhauser followed the men's tracks in the new fallen snow and located the new hiding place.

With this information the American soldiers and Neuhauser left the POW camp at Garmisch-Partenkirchen. Just before reaching Walchensee, near Neuhauser father's home, he gave directions to turn off the main road. The two jeeps and their occupants climbed the hills south of the main road and reached a spot pointed out by the German captain. Several large holes had been dug in the area. Some envelopes and papers with the German Reichsbank imprint on them were near the holes. It appeared American troops had been in the area, because chewing gum wrappers, K ration boxes and C ration cans littered the area.

Neuhauser informed the Americans that it was difficult to locate the treasure, because it was buried when there was snow on the ground. After approximately forty-five minutes of searching, he located the spot.

After considerable digging the first wooden box appeared. There were twenty boxes in the hole, all the same size, approximately thirteen by eleven by seven inches. Each box had a flat metal band sealing the box on two sides. They were loaded into the jeeps. Driving slowly with the heavy loads, the jeeps delivered the contents to headquarters at the 574th AAA Battalion in Falls. The boxes were intact and the seals were not broken.

The twenty boxes contained 1,918 pounds of gold coins and were shipped to the Foreign Exchange Depository on July 7, 1945, as shipment number 52B.[7]

The gold in this shipment consisted of 23,020.722 Troy ounces of gold was air freighted to the Bank of England in 1948 and deposited into the account of the Tripartite Gold Commission.

Lt. Herbert DuBois and other intelligence-gathering and reconnaissance teams had recovered 53,217 pounds of gold that had been shipped from Berlin on the Eagle and Jackdaw to finance the National Redoubt.

A large amount of currency also was in this shipment. The currency had been deposited in he Reichsbank and a balance sheet showed two categories of currency. From these records it was possible to reconstruct that $1,168,990 of US currency had disappeared from the time the currency left Berlin and was recovered by the Americans. Had these dollars vanished into the pockets of the conquering American soldiers or seeped into the wallets of the enemy, or both?

Thus, over several weeks, thousands of miles of travel, and exhausting searches, Task Force Fisher and others had ensured that a great portion of Germany's plunder and legitimate treasurers would not fall into the hands of the advancing Soviets or Nazis fleeing Germany.

Shipment 52C: On June 21, 1945, Col. E.A. Ball, 80th Infantry Division, delivered gold and silver coins, four packages containing wedding rings and one box taken from Dachau by the 36th Infantry Division and left with the 80th to Third Army Headquarters. This box contained (145) US $100 and were later delivered to the US Treasury.[8]

Shipment 52D: One tin box said to contain charred currency and coins. Later described as charred beyond recognition, or identification and declared worthless. This shipment was deposited to the Landeszentralbank von Hessen on May 25, 1948.

Shipment 52E Dachau: In the closing days of the war, Dr. Frei, Swiss Consul for Bavaria, met with an SS officer in charge of prisoners from the Dachau concentration camp. Under guard of the SS they had been marching towards Tyrol. When the concentration camp victims marched into Tegersee near Rottach, Germany, Frei pleaded with the SS officer on behalf of the prisoners who were in no condition to march and finally persuaded him to stop for the night. Later that night, the SS officer delivered to Frei three wooden cases, two packages, and one valise containing personal property such as jewelry, watches and other articles which belonged to the prisoners from Dachau. With American forces fast approaching, that night, May 1, 1945, the SS guard fled, the prisoners learning that there was no guard, also took off. Frei held on to the property and released it to Military Government Detachment E1 P3.

In statements during his trial for war crimes, Josef Jarolin told of this march. He stated that about 10,000 prisoners were sleeping in the woods without food. Jarolin reported that he visited SS Captain Degelow to report these conditions and was told by the SS officer he had orders to march them to Ötztal, (a valley in the Austrian state of Tyrol) and could do nothing else. Of interest, Jarolin told that on May 4, 1945, he was a witness to a conversation in which the valuables of the Dachau prisoners, watches, gold valuables with a value of over five million gold marks were to be buried in the mountains. One part of the treasure was to be buried between Tegernsee and Schliersee, the other at Zell am See, Tyrol, Austria. The burying of the valuables at Tegersee was under the supervision of SS Sergeant Schimpf, from the commander's office at Dachau, and in charge at Zell am See was SS Sergeant Otto from the administrative office of the SS Captain.

When Jarolin was eighteen-years-old he had joined the Munich Police force during the time Adolf Hitler made his bid for power in the unsuccessful Nazi Putsch. Jarolin was part of the force that quelled the riot resulting in the imprisonment of Hitler. Unemployed in 1931 due to Great Depression, he joined the SS on March 6, 1935. From then to the end of the war, Jarolin was part of the killing machines of the concentration camp system.

Jarolin further informed the investigators of war crimes that the bulk of the valuables hidden were on trucks driven by SS Sergeant Spenger Alois who lived along the railway road between Paffenhofen and Ingolstadt. Jarolin's story is vague, and he may have been trying to impress the Army interrogators, but there may be some truth in his Alpine lake hiding ill-gotten gains story as it took on a life of it own. A book has been written about the burial of these Dachau valuables, and the lake is now Lünersee near the small Austrian town of Brand close to the Swiss border.

Jarolin most pathetic statement: "I proved to the prisoners that they belong to a race or religion the same as me." But with statements signed by more than 100 people attesting to his brutality, Jarolin was justifiable executed for war crimes by the US army hangman on May 28, 1946.[9]

Thus Shipment 52E was delivered to the Foreign Exchange Depository on July 5, 1945 by Lt. Edward Sacks from Third Army Headquarters. Two of the containers from Dachau were opened at the Foreign Exchange Depository and were found to contain 2,826 separate sealed envelopes each identified by name, nationality, number of prisoner and bearing indications as to contents. The contents were primarily watches, rings, pens and pocket money. "The task of inventorying all the material held in the Foreign Exchange Depository is now under way, but many months may elapse before its completion." It was noted, "the property could be identified against individual claims for same if the claimant can give full information corresponding to that listed on the envelopes. … It would not appear advisable to attempt a general restitution to the individuals named on the envelopes or their heirs."[10]

Envelope No.	Nationality	Assigned Number	Name	Birth Date	Description
23	Poland	19914	Grzegorczyk, Wadaw	28. 8.19	1 ring
24	Poland	20145	Ziemiak, Jeczepan	2.12.11	1 small watch
25	France	17262	Lafdal, Ali	28. 1.17	1 watch with chain
26	France	19894	Drillet, Josef	10.12.20	1 wrist watch 1 fountain pen 2 rings
27	Poland	19876	Bolesta, Edzard	14.10.93	1 wrist watch
28	France	22711	Boxure, Pierre	5. 6.22	1 ring
29	France	19901	Eugene, Gaston	21. 6.24	14,50 Peseta
30 lutwen B.V.		21076	Schmitz, Daniel	16.10.03	1 wedding ring
31 German (R.D.		21152	Bischoff, Mathias	12.11.98	1 wedding ring, 1 ring
32 (R.D.		21135	Ferrari, Josef	9.10.08	1 wrist watch 1 wedding ring, 1 ring
33	Russia	21098	Jwlew, Nikolaj	.17	1 watch with chain
34	ø France	19864	Colin, Henri	28. 6.09	1 tie-pin with ston
35	France	19893	Domont, Louis	16.11.98	1 ring
36	France	20017	Rognier, Fortuna	24. 1.92	1 watch
37 her R.D.		22297	Neuefeind, Paul	15. 2.02	1 ring
38	Russia	19995	Obolonsky, Wladimir	18. 4.24	1 wrist watch
39 ? B.V.		19242	Funck, Georg	15. 1.12	1 ring
40 ? Aso		19814	Reinhardt, Albert	23. 6.08	1 ring with stone
41	Belgium	17289	Verstraete, Octave	17. 7.05	1 watch, 1 wedding ring
42	Holl.	17307	Feitsma, Yme	1. 4.07	1 wrist watch
43	Holl.	17314	Hemmer, Bernadus	24.10.07	1 wedding ring
44	Holl.	17322	Kolmer, Klemens	18. 8.13	1 watch with fob
45	Holl.	17350	Tourne, Hyronimus	25. 3.01	1 wrist watch
46	Russia	17226	Weres, Nikolai	27.11.20	1 ring
47	Tsch.	22303	Jakubka, Saawa	14.12.17	2 rings
48	Russia	21056	Pryjmotschuk, Wassil	11. 8.22	1 ring
49	Poland	22273	Lukasik, Czeslaw	20. 5.23	1 watch with chain
50 ? B.V.		22268	Wuertk, Josef	22. 1.16	1 wrist watch 1 ring

- 2 -

Shipment 52E inventory, a complete typewritten inventory consisting of 127 pages was made from this Dachau shipment.

On June 16, 1947, the Foreign Exchange Depository received a claim from Paul Bloch who wrote he had been imprisoned in Dachau for political persecution, and had two Swiss watches taken, which he describes in detail, also a wedding ring inscribed, "Mein Seelchen 2.5.1930" or My Little Soul" and wedding date of May 2, 1930. Bloch sent a photocopy of his Dachau release papers which included his inmate number 141 394. There are no indications that he received a response. Shipment 52E was turned over to the Intergovernmental Committee for Refugees.

Shipment 60:

This shipment is yet another strange yarn regarding the US currency seized above as part of Shipment 52A. The story is taken from Capt. Benjamin S. Schilling Jr.'s handwritten note:

> Memo re Shipment no.60
> On August 11, 1945 the following officers stated they had $4,000 in US currency to turn in:
> Lieutenant Colonel L.W. Varner, 0198797, Inspector General, U.S, 12th Army Group
> Lieutenant Roger Ernst, AUS, 02025785, US Army 12th Army Group
> When I asked about the circumstances surrounding the acquisition Colonel Varner referred me to Lieutenant Ernst who stated he had found it on a mountain near Mittenwald while searching for buried documents. Lieutenant Ernst stated he had placed the money in a box from which he had become separated and the box had turned up in the Berlin Documentation Center. (Where the buried documents had been sent.) Colonel Varner began an investigation which Lieutenant Ernst stated had been very thorough as far as he was concerned. I asked Colonel Varner for a copy of his Inspector General report, but he flatly and emphatically refused.
>
> s/Benjamin S. Schilling Jr.

The well intended Col. Varner took the 4,000 dollar bills and Lt. Ernst to the Foreign Exchange Depository on August 11, 1945 and Shipment 60 was signed for by Benjamin S. Schilling Jr.

It is obvious the box of currency was sent to Berlin by mistake and when discovered, the Inspector General's office was called in to investigate. Varner was given this task and apparently covered for Ernst.

Who was Lt. Roger Ernst? In Interrogation Brief 73, the famed Dr. Karl Haushofer, who was recognized as the originator of geopolitical theories, and whose knowledge was considered superior to that of any other scholar, reported this: "After the Allied Victory, I was visited by a commission from the US Political Department … Other Americans visited my farm, … Roger Ernst of the Central Military Government, Berlin arrived on 27 May … All of them treated me in a most scientific and courteous manner."

A year later Ernst was the assistant to the US Secretary. Ernst definitely had clout, and maybe Varner was not aware that $1,164,990 was missing from the original amount that had been buried on the mountain.[11]

Shipment 57

The information for Shipment 57 involving Kurt Hellmann is taken from the Weekly Report F1 H2, 20-26 July, 1945, as follows:

> The banking situation in Oberbayern continues to be satisfactory and deposits are increasing in most places.
> The detachment at Garmisch-Partenkirchen turned over to this officer a box of British pound notes estimated at roughly 25,000 pounds, (1945 value $100,750) and British coins weighing

about 500 pounds. Also records of British deceased aviators from whom this money was taken. The money will be turned over to E1 F3 and Lieutenant Colonel Baker of the English Army who is instrumental in finding this money request the records for the British War Office. This money and records have been stored in the Stadtsparkasse (City Savings Bank) Garmisch.

In checking bank vaults in Munich, 10 packages of foreign securities were found in the Dresdner Bank. These were placed there on March 29 by Kurt Hellmann. His wife wrote a letter to the bank on July 7 stating the securities were property of the Nazi Party. ... Mrs. Hellmann was brought in for questioning and stated that the securities came from Luxembourg and prior to deposit had been left at her home by Managing Director Emil Schreyer, her husband's boss.

On July 30, 1945 received from Lt. Charles W. Snedeker, Government Detachment E1 F3 the following:

1. A wooden box containing British Sterling pound notes
2. 15 bags of British sliver coins
3. 10 packages foreign securities including $3,380 US dollars. Surprisingly enough one of the bills was $1,000. The US currency was returned to the US Treasury.[12]

Items one and two had had been stored in the City Savings Bank, Garmisch-Partenkirchen and received from deceased British aviators.

Item 3 had been taken from the Dresdner Bank, Munich, by Emil Schreyer. He was described as about five foot, six inches tall, proportionally small, childish face without a beard, and spoke with a Sudetenland accent. He was about thirty-five-years-old, wore civilian suites, dark blue and grey with boots, trousers over the boots. Last seen in Bad Nauheim he was wearing a dark blue suit with a grey vest and a white shirt with necktie.

Schreyer was the financial representative of the Nazi Party Stiko Fund with an office in the town of Bad Nauheim. Working with Schreyer was Kurt Hellmann and Miss Trude Puls. It appears that one of their functions was to confiscate securities from political organizations and hospitals that had investments that were Jewish "tainted." These notes and bonds were sold immediately and the money deposited into the Nazi accounts controlled by Schreyer. Both Schreyer and Hellmann held the status of indispensable, which meant that they could not be drafted into the German army. But unfortunately for Hellmann, the military situation was so desperate that he was drafted.

In December 1944, driving his grey PKW car along with one employee, Miss Trude Puls, Schreyer traveled to Offenburg, collected several packages and deposited them in rented bank safes in various town in the Taunus Mountains. Schreyer and Miss Puls spent their Christmas 1944 vacation in Bad Nauheim. In February 1945, they traveled to Berlin and returned with more bonds and securities which were placed in safe deposit boxes in the Peoples Bank, Bad Nauheim. These containers included some securities from old Czarist estate and town bonds as well as railway obligations.

On March 27, 1945, with American Army the advancing rapidly, the ten boxes were transferred in such a rush that they were handed to Miss Puls and others, and a receipt prepared which stated the boxes were to be deposited in the near future with a representative of the appropriate Nazi party. Schreyer, Miss Puls, and joined by Mrs. Kindermann with their personal luggage, left Bad Nauhein in the overloaded PKW along with 20,000 Reichsmarks. Prior to leaving and disappearing, Schreyer burned most of the important papers in the office. Miss Trude Puls was located at her home in the Sudetenland, an area in Czechoslovakia inhabited mostly by German speaking people, and annexed by Germany shortly before the outbreak of war.

After this detailed investigation of Emil Schreyer, the ten packages of foreign securities were handed over to the Landeszentralbank von Hessen on March 15, 1949.[13]

There are no records regarding the disposition of the British currency, but most surely it was released to the proper British authorities.

CHAPTER 14
The Hungarian Treasures

The Hungarian Gold Reserves were seized by the 80th Infantry Division as Shipment 20. As the 80th Infantry Division of Patton's Third Army had advanced towards Spital am Pyhrn, at the beginning of May, 1945, two Hungarian bank officials, Edgar Tornay and Count Geza Bethlen, presented a letter from the National Bank to Col. E.A. Ball, the 80th Division military governor. The letter stated that the bank was located in Spital am Pyhrn, where the valuables were being guarded by the Hungarian Royal Police, and requested protection by US military authorities for the bank's valuables and its 680 employees and family members.

On May 10, 1945, Sgt. William DeHuszar, US 80th Division, CIC, reached the Austrian town and took into custody the Hungarian Bank's valuables, located in a monastery adjoining a church. The material consisted of tons of paper pengoes, documents, receipts coupons, bills and other paper securities, plus about 100 automobiles and various trucks. His first action was the arrest of Laszlo Temesvary, who had full power of attorney concerning the management of the bank. As DeHuszar reported; "Temesvary is considered a strong anti-Semite and believes in Szalasi."

On May 12, the following order was issued in the name of Gen. Bradley:

> It is desired that gold found in Lucky area, [General George Patton' Headquarters Third Army] whether or not in Austria be properly transported to Reichsbank at Frankfurt under proper security arrangements and delivered to Currency Section for Germany together with any documentary or other evidence relating to ownership interest in such treasure. Tally should be made prior to removal and delivered to Currency Section with treasure. Information requested relating to discovery, ownership interest, and contents of such treasures.

> By Command of General Bradley

It further stated that the Commanding Officer of the 317 Infantry Regiment would turn over to Maj. Lionel Perera the gold, currency, jewels and other valuables at Spital.

Perera took control of the more valuable assets of the Hungarian National Bank and on May 14, acknowledged he had the following valuables:

> a. 633 cases said to contain gold bullion and gold coins, net weight, 29,855.0465 kg.
> b. 2 cases said to contain foreign bank notes and coins
> c. 19 cases said to contain safe keeping deposits
> d. 3 containers marked I-3048, II-3048, III-3049
> e. 1 package said to belong to Hungarian Military Police and to weigh 3.315 kg
> f. 28 cases to have been deposited by the Trust Company for Orphans of Budapest
> g. 1 sack said to contain: one case of sealed envelopes regarding Jewish properties, one package said to have been deposited by Commercial Bank of Budapest

On May 15, Company K, 319 Infantry Regiment, loaded fifteen two-and-a-half ton trucks. Traveling two days, on a 400-mile trip, the US 3805th Quartermaster Truck Company delivered the entire gold reserves of Hungary, to the Foreign Exchange Depository in Frankfurt, Germany as Shipment 20. The receipt for this shipment as described above was signed for by Col. H.D. Cragon. Remaining in Spital am Pyhrn were the staff and family members of the Hungarian National Bank and tons of books, postal stamps, and documents including Hungarian paper money weighing 105 tons and consisting of about four billion Hungarian pengoes.

Dr. Julius Biber, Manager of Hungarian National Bank, concerned that the bank's valuables were removed, and also with the welfare of his staff wrote letters to the International Bank Settlement, Switzerland, the Federal Reserve Board, the Bank of England, and International Red Cross expressing concern that the US Army had taken over the assets of the bank. Biber was justifiable worried about his staff and wrote:

> "There remains, however one more problem to be solved, touching the most vital interest of the Bank's employees; that is the question of their eventual delivery to the Russians. The Bank and all persons belonging to it immigrated to Austria first of all to be safe from the Russians. The reason for that is to be found in the first rank—beside the generally known conduct of the Russian occupiers—in the bank's hundred per cent capitalistic policy / incompatible with bolshevism / … It is therefore evident that the delivery to Russians would mean the most intensive danger to life for each and every person belonging to the Bank."

His letters went on to request permission for the Bank's staff to be allowed to immigrate to Switzerland and noted their expenses for transportation, food and housing could be taken from the bank's foreign credit balances, which at the time included Swiss Francs valued at $72,000.

Dr. Julius Biber's letters involving the Hungarian gold must have had an impact on the Allies for on November 9, 1945, an international conference opened in Paris involving all the countries that had been at war with Germany. The purpose of the conference was to determine the amount of reparations payable by Germany following World War II. Surprisingly, at this meeting the Hungarian gold was specifically exempted from the Allied "Gold Pot" of 420 tons of Nazi tainted gold recovered in Europe.

The bank staff was allowed to remain in Spital am Pyhrn for a year later as the remaining items were being readied for shipment back to Hungary. The US Army Displaced Persons officer had no plans to force the separation of the Hungarians bankers at Spital am Pyhrn. The DP officer told Captain William R. Loeffer, who was in charge of sending these remaining items to Budapest; that the employees of the bank were out of favor with the present regime in Hungary, and therefore feared to return. Loeffer requested a list of the employees and also a separate list of the bank employees that wanted to return with the remaining records of the bank. Seventy to eighty people requested to go back with the restitution train.

Meanwhile, it was decided the four freight carloads of pengoes currency would remain in Austria as paper pulp, but it was then concluded that the worthless currency in Hungary was a more valuable commodity as waste paper in Hungary, than it was in Austria. Also, the sealed deposits were opened and examined for gold, foreign currency and securities. Unfortunately, there is no record as to what was found.

On the morning of August 30, 1946, twenty-four freight cars and four passenger cars chugged out of Spital am Pyhrn for Budapest, Hungary. The remaining Hungarians were allowed to resettle in Germany.

As inflation in Hungary spiraled and the economy was in chaos, Imre Nagy, the Hungarian prime minister, traveled to Washington, DC and negotiated with the State Department for the release of the gold and silver reserves seized by the Americans during the last days of the war. On June 14, 1946, the United States informed Nagy that the gold would be returned and on July 10, a preliminary conference was held between representatives of the Foreign Exchange Depository and the Hungarian Restitution Delegation to discuss procedural matters for the gold restitution. A Hungarian mission, headed by Dr. Nicholas Myaradi, minister of finance, arrived in Frankfurt, on July 3, to make arrangements for the return of the gold.

On July 31, Col. William G. Brey gave the order to break the ribbon seal on the door of compartments number five and six in the lower main vault of the Foreign Exchange Depository in Frankfurt, Germany. These vaults contained gold and cloth bags for packing the gold bars. After

1,300 cloth bags were taken, the compartments were immediately re-sealed. Brey then gave the order to open vault number seven in the lower vault, the one that contained the Hungarian gold. It had not been opened since the gold was first stored there on May 16, 1945.

A team of seven Americans and six Hungarians then assiduously checked and compared the bars of gold as they were removed from the ninety piles and packed into bags. A fifty-five-pound weight limit was set for each bag. They were numbered, sealed and removed to compartment number nine, which had been previously emptied. The bags containing gold coins were not repacked, but were opened and checked. A total of 1,222 bags were used: 1,184 contained gold bars and thirty-eight contained gold coins. The repacking took four days and was completed on Saturday afternoon, August 3.

On Monday, August 5, the removal of the gold from the vault began under guard of the 381st Military Police Battalion. The MPs loaded a small hand truck with five bags of gold and wheeled it to a ventilator opening and from there loaded the bags onto a fleet of sixteen trucks. The last bag was packed at 1:30pm. The trip from the Foreign Exchange Depository to the train station was made under tight security, and the utmost precautions were taken as the trucks moved through the streets of Frankfurt. Two tanks escorted each truck, and no incidents occurred during the transfer to the train station. The gold was then transferred into three large baggage cars that were locked from the outside with special 3/8-inch twisted iron bars. Three US military police with machine guns were posted in each baggage car. Every car had a sign in five languages stating that anyone who approached and tried to open the door would be shot without warning. The train consisted of three armed baggage cars, two sleepers, a lounge car and dining car; the lounge car had been Adolf Hitler's and one magnificent sleeper had belonged to Eva Braun. Now the train was the property of the US Army.

It left Frankfurt on August 6, 1946, at 6:00pm with fifty-six American soldiers as guards, including Col. Brey. Several officials of the Hungarian government also were on board. The 600-mile trip took two days. During the hot August days, the heat in the baggage cars became unbearable for the guards, who removed their jackets and shirts. During the journey, the train entered the Soviet Occupation Zone at Bad Enns, Austria, and two Russian majors boarded the train to escort it through Russian territory. The US Army proved a gracious host and served Coke, wine, beer, roast beef, asparagus, and coffee to the Russians and the Hungarian delegation.

At the Austrian-Hungarian border, several Hungarian official welcomed the train. From the border to Budapest, a distance of about 116 miles, crowds who had gathered to watch it pass greeted the train enthusiastically. This train contained the hopes of the Hungarians for an end of the depression caused by the war. The closer the train came to Budapest, the bigger the crowds at the stations and crossroads.

Thousands of people jammed the railway station at Budapest to greet the train when it arrived at 8:00pm on August 7, 1946. The station was decorated with Hungarian and American flags and guarded by a great number of Hungarian policemen. Officially welcoming the train was a large reception committee from the Hungarian government. Ambassador Arthur Schoenfold and Gen. George H. Weems represented the American government; also present were representatives from Russia. After a speech from the minister of finance, Ambassador Schoenfold presented a symbolic bag of gold to Prime Minister Nagy. The sack was opened. The sparkling yellow gold glittered in the station lights and both statesmen smiled broadly.

Under heavy police security, the sacks of gold were quickly and noiselessly loaded onto trucks by employees of the Hungarian National Bank and taken through the blocked-off street to the vault of the Hungarian National Bank. By 10:00pm, the last gold bag was loaded onto the truck and ten minutes later was in the vault. After one year and eight months, the gold had safely ended its trip and come home.

During January 1947, the Foreign Exchange Depository received a report from the Hungarian National Bank that it had received a surplus of gold coins in the shipment of gold reserves. Originally, the gold bars and coins had been placed in compartment number seven by Col. Bernstein and his staff and they had sealed the vault door. It was always assumed that the entire content of that compartment was the property of the Hungarian National Bank. The bags of coins were weighed and both the Hungarians and Americans agreed that the coins matched the available records.

But when the Hungarians revalidated the actual weights and number of coins, gold coins of Turkey, Japan, and Colombia were discovered. It would take a while to correct this mistake.

Because US forces in Germany recovered the Hungarian silver reserves, Shipment 17, there was a controversy among the Allies regarding their return to the Hungarian government. Despite the controversy, the US made a commitment to the Hungarian government to return the silver reserves. In the middle of March 1947, the Departments of Defense and State issued a joint directive to return the silver immediately to Hungary.

On March 21, 1947, work began in the Foreign Exchange Depository with an inspection of the vaults by Col. Brey and his staff to prepare for removal of the silver. It was necessary to type a full list by number of the location of each silver bar. Since some of the bars did not have the weight stamped on them, they had to be weighed in order to have a complete and accurate record. The vault operation involved the checking of the 6,783 silver bars against the prepared listings and the final check of the shipment was completed on April 9. The following day, a conference on transit problems and other arrangements was held at the depository, attended by Foreign Exchange Depository personnel and Hungarian representatives. Procedures for the loading of the silver, a train schedule, security preparations and publicity were reviewed and final adjustments were made.

On April 21, the 198,000 pounds of silver and other valuables were removed from the vaults at the depository to five freight cars at the main railway station in Frankfurt. Other items also were transferred from the vaults; these were items seized with the Hungarian gold reserves but not returned with them. They included foreign currency, gold coins, gold bars, platinum, the personal property of former President Ferenc Szalazi, and deposits of the Trust Company for Orphans of Budapest.

Photographs and motion picture cameras recorded various phases of the transfer of the valuables for posterity and documented proof.

Two additional baggage cars containing jewelry and crated art objects were attached to the train at Regensburg. The art was valued at $20,000,000 and consisted of fifty-one paintings and 340 drawings. It included works by Da Vinci, Raphael, Rembrandt, Van Gogh and Dürer. The trip was similar to the gold delivery except one silver-laden car developed a hot box in the wheel assembly. An additional baggage car had been provided for such an emergency. Col. Brey, the off-duty MPs, and Hungarian officials transferred the silver to the extra car.

Karl Kristof, of the Hungarian paper *Vilag,* was invited to Frankfurt to cover the story of the return of the Hungarian Silver. It follows:

An American military policeman guards the loading of the Hungarian silver at the Foreign Exchange Depository in Frankfurt.

At the border town of Hegyeshalon, Hungary the "Silver Train" bound for Budapest stopped for minor formalities and to pick up Hungarian officer escorts. Many peasants lined the tracks to see the "Silver Train" return the silver reserves to Hungary.

Frankfurt on the Main, in a small undamaged section of the city and situated on a large square a huge building, the Foreign Exchange Depository. There is no admission to it. The Americans have taken charge of the building and within it they guard the treasury stolen by the Nazis. In the company of the capable chief of the Hungarian Commission, Alexander Ham, I enter the building. At the door leading to the hall of the vault room our papers are checked one more. Now we turn to the immense basement located in the Depository. A heavy steel door is opening and we are within a treasury chamber. In long rows the silver bars are piled up, 50 bars piled on top of each other form one pile. The ordinary bar weighs 30 pounds, the larger ones 66 pounds. We are showed to a place surrounded by iron bars. Here thousands of diamonds, cut and raw ones lie on tables, Pitiful contents are seen in boxes guarded by members of the M.P.s; gold teeth torn from the mouths of victims of Auswitz.

On Monday morning at eight o'clock the loading of the Hungarian valuables is started. German labor service men place the silver into trucks. On the way to the station one jeep proceeding and another one following every truck. The trucks tore through the town with sirens on full blast. Soon the 97 tons of silver was loaded in the railroad carriages. As the train approached Wiestal, an axel of one of the carriages broke down. The train stops. All of us crowd around the breakdown. We all take part in the reloading of the silver. During the night the train stops at Regensberg. Here two further carriages are attached to the train. In one is loaded the art collection of the Museum of Fine Art. At the frontier of the Russian Zone four Russian army officers board our train. They speak excellent English and they are most amiable. They accompany the train to Budapest. A great number of American reporters came to Budapest.[1]

Thus ended a second successful mission that should have provided Hungary with another step forward in its struggle for financial and economic rehabilitation from the destruction of World War II.

Shipment 82: As noted previously in 1945, the Hungarian gold reserves had been deposited in the Foreign Exchange Depository as Shipment 20. The gold bars and coins were always kept in a separate sealed compartment numbers 5, 6, and 7. On August 5, 1946, the entire contents of this particular compartment were received by Hungarian bank officials. The bags containing coins were not opened, but only weighed as they were checked against the available inventory records. As reported previously, in error according to the Hungarian National Bank, Turkish, Japanese and Columbian gold coins had been sent to Hungary with Shipment 20. The Depository declared: "They may or may not belong to the Hungarian National Bank." Regardless the FED requested the return of the coins in question.

The bags were:

749	Yen, bag number 6545	250.46 Troy ounces
2,269	Turkish, bag number 6546	520.03
1,185	Columbian Pesos, Bag number 6547	309.49
		1099.98

Thus, in question, were 91.66 pounds of gold with a 1945 value of $38,499.30. Officials of the Foreign Exchange Depository concluded the gold coins were sent with the original deposit, but did not belong to Hungary. They concluded that the coins should not have been delivered to Hungary and as such they were still the proper custodians of the gold coins now in the Hungarian National Bank and the safekeeping was under its jurisdiction. The Foreign Exchange Depository could push the issue; for at that time they held the trump card as the entire Hungarian silver reserves were still in the FED.

After much debate between the Army and Department of State, the coins were signed for Col. Stephen W. Beda, Allied Control Mission for Hungary, in Budapest on December 18, 1946 with a caveat: "On instructions calling for taking possession of the gold coins for the purpose of returning same to the Foreign Exchange Depository at Frankfurt, whereas instruction from the American Legation called for requesting the Hungarian National Bank to return the gold coins to this Mission for the purpose of keeping them in custody here until final disposition is made. Since it was the American Legation who communicated with the Hungarian National Bank and the Hungarian Government in connection with the Hungarian Gold, the coins were taken over for the purpose of keeping them here for later decision."

Col. William G. Brey would have none of this and wrote on February 5, 1947: "Please advise date when you will return coins to Frankfurt or whether you desire Foreign Exchange Depository Representative to take delivery in Budapest." At the end of the month the two following officers were cleared to perform a secret mission to Budapest with an effective date of March 19, 1947:

William G. Brey, O-6499, Colonel, GSC
Born 27 August 1888
Place of Birth: Milwaukee, Wisconsin

Beacher H. Brewer O-1312272, Captain, Infantry
Born 28 December 1910
Place of Birth: Perry, Ohio

They were cleared to travel by military aircraft or rail. Their trip is not recorded, but on March 24, 1947, in Budapest, Hungary, the gold coins were presented to Brey by Beda. The coins were deposited in Compartment 8 Lower Main Vault on March 25 as Shipment 82. There is no information regarding the disposal of this shipment in this game of one-upmanship.[2]

Personalities

Eva Braun

Shipment 76 contains some of the personal items of Mrs. Adolf Hitler, the name his young mistress, Eva Braun held until her suicide less than forty-eight hours after their marrage. It began with Walter W. Hirschfeld, (Involved in Shipment 31) one of the more intriguing minor players and unscrupulous individuals in the drama of World War II. He was born on July 21, 1917, in Grossröhrsdorf, Germany, joined the Hitler Youth in 1933, and was subjected to a great deal of propaganda describing the material advantages of joining the SS. Therefore, after finishing high school in 1936, he enlisted in the SS. Hirschfeld served on many fronts during the war, primarily in the East. During this time, he attended SS officers school and was commissioned a lieutenant.

On June 5, 1945, Hirschfeld managed to land a job working for the 970th Counter Intelligence Corps, US Seventh Army. He was given the undercover assignment of tracking down former SS members. He had a natural talent for covert work and knowledge of the complete setup of both the Nazi regime and structure of the SS. Most helpful was Hirschfeld's SS tattoo, the blood type tattooed under his left arm. This mark alone gave him entry into SS circles.

Hirschfeld's first assignment was informing the CIC with respect to Col. Josef Spacil's last assignment with the SS Security Main Office.

Eva Braun (right) and her sister, Margarete Berta "Gretl" Braun, enjoy themselves at the Berghof in their glory days as members of the inner social circle of Adolf Hitler.

On September 19, 1945, Hirschfeld received instructions from the commander of the CIC to contact and win the confidence of General Hermann Fegelein's parents. The CIC was aware Fegelein's parents had been living at Fischhorn Castle. Hirschfeld knew from the start it would be very difficult to win the confidence of the elder Fegeleins as previous interrogations by others had revealed them to be greedy.

Hirschfeld decided to pose as an SS officer with a major part in the so-called "Bernhardt Project" of the SS Security Main Office: that project was the passing in neutral countries and German occupied countries of counterfeit British currency made in concentration camps. These counterfeit notes were used to pay off agents, and to purchase jewelry and other precious metals. Hirschfeld had become acquainted with this project while working in the CIC with Josef Spacil at Taxenbach.

On Hirschfeld's first visit in Munich with the elder Fegeleins, he told them in a realistic manner he had buried valuable supplies of precious metals, gold and diamonds in Austria as the war drew to an end. He represented himself as a fanatic SS officer in possession of great secrets. He said he was trying to establish communication with their son in order to turn over to him, one of the last high-ranking representatives of National Socialism still at large, the maps and sketches showing the hiding places. The Nazis then could use the valuables in the future. Hirschfeld told the Fegeleins he was in Munich to sell some rings he had taken from one of the hiding places. To gain the full confidence of Mr. Fegelein, and to convince him of the truth of his statements, Hirschfeld gave him 15,000 Reichsmarks—supposedly surplus cash received from the sale of the rings. The Fegeleins, however did not need the money; they had even given large sums of cash to acquaintances visiting their home.

The elder Fegelein then told about a chest of gold that had been sent by his son to him while he was staying at the Fischhorn. He had taken the gold and loaded it onto his horse and wagon and gone to a farm belonging to Walter Andreas Hofer, director of Göring's art. At the farm near Bruck, Austria, Mr. Hofer buried the chest of gold under an abandoned automobile along with his son's riding trophies and various articles of jewelry in a hay shed; "so deep" Fegelein said "that they are sure not to be found."

During their conversations, the Fegeleins said Eva Braun had sent all of her things to them, and that they had stored them with a Doctor Winkler in Zell Am See. Mrs. Fegelein added that, "The doctor has a large, fine house and surely no one will look for them there." Regarding their trip from Zell Am See, Austria to their current residence in Munich, Germany, Mrs. Fegelein stated, "We did not bring much with us because we were afraid everything would be taken from us at the border. With the help of a few bottles of schnapps we were able to get everything through."

Hirschfeld told the Fegeleins he had to go to Austria to see what his group was doing and Mr. Fegelein said, "Naturally I would appreciate if you would stop and see my daughter-in-law (Gretl Braun Fegelein) in Garmisch. I will give you a message to take along. Please keep us in mind. Perhaps you could bring us something tomorrow. Cash is all right though we'd rather have jewelry." Mr. Fegelein cautioned Hirschfeld, "If you visit Gretl, be very cautious. I think things are not right from here. I am not being watched, but my daughter-in-law is certain to be watched. The Americans are correct there, however. They took my daughter-in-law to a hospital for delivery of her child after the Germans had refused to accept her."

Before departing, Hirschfeld asked about their son Hermann. Rising up due to a sore leg, the elderly Fegelein said, "Do not be taken in by rumors that my son was shot on orders from Hitler because he was found running around in civilian clothing. That is nonsense. Herr Hirschfeld, you can believe me. I have told you no funny stories. I know for certain that the Führer and my son are still living; otherwise my life would be finished." In a continuing conversation with Hirschfeld the old man continued to fantasize his fanatical SS beliefs.

On September 23, 1945, Hirschfeld called upon Gretl Fegelein and Mrs. Herta Schneider at their dwelling at 49 Hoellentalstrasse, Garmisch-Partenkirchen. He was received with some skepticism, which was not overcome by the introduction from Mrs. Fegelein's father-in-law. The two women, especially Mrs. Schneider, would not answer any of Hirschfeld's questions, but instead subjected him to a close cross examination on the personalities of the SS Security Main Office, the Waffen-SS and the general staff of the Wehrmacht. Mrs. Fegelein mentioned repeatedly the CIC investigation at the Fischhorn. She had visited Fischhorn personally with an American officer and had gotten exact information about Germans working as undercover agents for the US Army.

Eventually, in the conversation that lasted until midnight, Hirschfeld overcame the doubts about his identity. He offered Mrs. Fegelein 15,000 Reichsmarks. She declined the offer, saying she did not need the money, but invited Hirschfeld to stay overnight in the apartment.

By the next morning Hirschfeld had gained Mrs. Fegelein's confidence. She took him to a hiding place and showed him Eva Braun's jewelry, saying her sister had sent this jewelry at the end of the war and also a will naming her, Gretl Braun Fegelein, as principal beneficiary. The hiding place was in Mrs. Fegelein's bedroom in the drawer of a little stand. The jewelry itself was in a small, red leather chest. Upon opening it revealed a complete set of turquoise and diamond jewels, various diamond rings and a gold bracelet with nine 14-karat diamonds.

The will, which was also the last letter written by Eva Braun was one of the articles in the drawer with the jewelry. The letter reads partially as follows:

Berlin
April 23, 1945

My Darling little Sister,

I would like to wear the gold bracelet with the green stone until the end. Then I'll have it taken from me, and you are to wear it just as I have always worn it. Unfortunately I gave my diamond watch for repair here, so I'll write down the address below. Perhaps you will be lucky and get it yet. It is to belong to you. You always did want one. The bracelet and topaz clip, gift of the Führer on my last birthday, are also to be yours. I hope that these, my wishes, will be respected by others.

In addition, I must request the following. Destroy all of my private correspondence, especially the business papers. Under no circumstances are bills from Heise to be found. Destroy also an envelope which is addressed to the Führer and is in the safe in the bunker [Berchtesgaden]. Please do not read it. The Führer's letters and my answer book, blue leather book, I would like packed watertight and if possible buried. Please do not destroy them. I owe the enclosed bill to the Heise firm. There might also be further outstanding items. They should scarcely exceed RM 1,500 however. I don't know what you should do with the film and albums. In any case I beg of you, destroy everything only at the last moment, except for the business and private letters and the envelope addressed to the Führer. These you may burn right away.

Now I wish you, my darling little sister, much, much luck. Don't forget you will surely see Hermann again.

With heartiest greetings and a kiss
I am yours Sister
Eva

As she was closing the chest, Mrs. Fegelein said her mother, Mrs. Fritz Braun, whom she had recently visited, had taken part of Eva's jewelry. According to Mrs. Fegelein, she intended to give these jewels to their third sister, Miezi, in accordance with Eva's will.

Under general questioning about Adolf Hitler's personal belongings, Mrs. Fegelein stated she was unable to concern herself with the personal effects of the Führer. She stated Julius Schaub arrived at the Berghof in Berchtesgaden drunk and in the company of his mistress. Schaub, born 1898, had been a constant companion of Adolf Hitler for more than twenty years and had been sent by Hitler to destroy his personal papers. He had brought the keys to the cabinets with him from Berlin and did not use the assistance of Hitler's two secretaries, who had been with Hitler for twenty years, but instead with his mistress went through the files and burned them. Mrs. Fegelein believed Schaub selected the most interesting items with the help of his lover and hid them away.

As Hirschfeld prepared to leave, Mrs. Fegelein remarked that she had 18,000 Reichsmarks but could use his offer for the 10,000 Reichsmarks. To retain her confidence Hirschfeld gave her the money and said she would inform Hirschfeld if she should hear from her husband. Mrs. Fegelein would never hear from Hermann Fegelein again as he was the last man to die from orders of the Führer.

Based on the undercover work of Walter Hirschfeld, Special Agent Robert A. Gutierrez, MSgt. William J. Conner Criminal Intelligence Corps, Seventh Army, recovered were the personal items of Eva Braun, diamonds owned by Hermann Fegelein, photographs, motion pictures depicting the life of Eva and Hitler, stamp collections, and the suit worn by Hitler during the attack on his life on July 20, 1944. Many of the valuables were turned over to 307th CIC Detachment Eva Braun's valuables were taken into the Foreign Exchange Depository, Frankfurt, Germany, on November 8, 1945, and designated shipment number 76.[1]

From the Foreign Exchange Depository "History of Shipment No.76" (Eva Braun Jewels):

On 8 November 1945, items said to be property of Eva Braun were received in the Foreign Exchange Depository from Major Marc M. Spiegle G-2, [Army Intelligence] Documents Control Section, United States Forces, European Theater.

According to information furnished later from the files of G-2, this property with the exception of the brooch, belonged to Eva Braun, mistress to Hitler. Shortly before the German capitulation it was given for safekeeping to SS Oberführer Josef Spacil head of Amt II of the Reichssicherheisthauptamt [Main Security Office] in Berlin. Spacil transported the property to Austria where he turned it over to S.S. Hauptsturmführer [Captain] Franz Konrad at the S.S. Horse Farm, Fischhorn Castle, near Zell am See, Austria. It was found in the possession of Konrad on 21 August 1945 when he was arrested by Counter Intelligence Corps agents at Kirchberg, Austria.

The diamond broach belonged to SS Gruppenführer [General] Hermann Fegelein who entrusted it to S.S. Hauptsturmführer Erwin Haufler. The later gave it to Konrad on whom it was found at the time of his apprehension.

Deposited as Shipment 76 on November 8, 1945:

> Personal items of Eva Braun
> Set of silverware, in the form of violins, decorated with a Polish coat of arms
> 24 large services (knives and forks)
> 12 large forks
> 12 dessert services
> 24 coffee spoons
> 1 spoon for powdering
> 1 sugar tong
> 4 pieces of hors d'oeuvre service with ivory handles
> 2 gravy spoons
> 1 salad service with ivory handle
> 1 soup ladle
> 1 cake spoon with ivory handle
> 1 asparagus tong
> 24 large knives, steel blades, ivory handles
> 24 dessert knives
> <u>24</u> fruit knives, silver blades, ivory handles
> 156 pieces

In a box the following:

> A woman's gold bracelet-watch, having on each side of the watch, a motif of a half-roll decorated with diamonds (trade name Rix)
> A man's gold watch, leather bracelet, (Universal watch)
> A man's 14 carat gold watch with winding knob (international watch Company)
> A man's gold watch with leather bracelet (Omega)
> A man's 14 carat: gold watch with double case in front and back and winding knob (American Waltham)
> A pair of 14 carat gold cufflinks oval shape,
> 2 metal pieces shaped like bobbins

In a small black suitcase:

6 large knives, 6 large forks, 6 dessert spoons, steel blades, silver plated handles monogrammed E B with plate leaf decorations

A rectangular shaped brooch, having in the center, 3 principal motifs formed of one diamond in a square strewn with diamonds—the rest of the brooch is strewn with diamonds. [General Fegelein]

A silver necklace forming a curb-chain containing a medal of the Virgin.

5 US $100 bills
3 US $20
17 US $20
<u>1 US $10</u>
Total $1,000

1 English 10-pound note
105,725 Reichsmarkss
Miscellaneous
21 dress shields
5 zippers
1 black leather wallet
12 blue skeins of yarn
18 brown skeins of yarn

The Eva Braun jewelry, along with Shipment 70, the jewels of Emmy Göring, was inspected by representatives of the Rothschild family and it was definitely stated that none of the jewels corresponded with the missing Rothschild gems. The 156 pieces of silverware, with the Polish coat of arms, was inspected by the Polish Military Mission and they rendered their opinion that the silver was not of Polish origin.

On December 6, 1946, the *Stars and Stripes* published a frontpage article that the Eva Braun valuables had been sent to the White House for usage by the president. The president, Harry S. Truman hotly denied this report as he would not eat from Nazi tainted silver. The story quickly investigated by the Army proved untrue as the valuables remained in the Depository.

On July 13, 1948, all of these valuables including the currency and yarn were given to the Amtsgericht-Hinterlegungstelle (District Court Depository) for disposition pursuant to applicable German Law.[2]

Reichsmarschall Hermann Göring

On September 15, 1945, the wife of the Reichsmarschall, Emmy Göring was visited by US Treasury Agent Emanuel E. "Duke" Minskoff along with an interpreter and reporter. He asked her many personal questions as to her past and present friends. Frau Göring was most candid with her answers describing her days as an actress and her marriage to Göring. When Minskoff questioned Emmy Göring about Kurt Hegeler, her former chauffer, she told him about some missing jewels and stated that Hegeler denied stealing the jewels and now wanted to meet with her and rectify himself.

Telling about the jewels was a mistake, for at that point Minskoff asked about the remaining jewels and proceeded to confiscate four different lots of jewels from the surprised Frau Göring. He took one lot consisting of ninety-seven valuable pieces. The more expensive items, described as inventory numbers 15 and 37 follow:

Sergeant Virginia M. Wood of Lorton, Virginia examines Eva Braun's 18th century silver set valued at $300,000. This silver service was uncovered with her personal effects by the U.S. Seventh Army.

Flexible platinum bracelet made up of five motifs, each having in its center an emerald surrounded by diamonds, the body of the bracelet covered with round diamonds and baguette diamonds.

Platinum tiara adorned with laurel leaves strewn with diamonds and eight emerald cabochons. Platinum setting decorated with baguette diamonds.

The second lot was described as jewels of Frau Emmy Göring and consisted of forty-nine items. The third lot was fourteen pieces of jewelry belonging to Edda Göring. Two of the pieces were described as "one bracelet with lucky charms" and the other "one bracelet with diamonds." The fourth lot was twenty-four pieces that belonged to the Reichsmarschall himself. Minskoff simply gathered up the valuables, put them in a sack, and gave Frau Göring a receipt. He took the sack to Nuremberg and gave them to Eldon J. Cassidy.

On October 15, Emmy Göring and her sister, Elsa Sonnermann were all ordered to pack a small bag, arrested and imprisoned in the Straubing jail. Edda was placed in an orphanage. After seven weeks she was moved into the small jail with her mother. They remained there until February 28, 1946. After leaving jail, they lived in a small cottage without water or electricity in the woods near Veldenstein. Emmy Göring died a natural death in Munich in 1973.

On October 7, 1945, Eldon J. Cassidy arrived at the Foreign Exchange Depository with a sack of Göring's jewels that he wished to deposit. Col. William Brey, Chief, Foreign Exchange Depository was skeptical of the deposit and refused to receive the bag. Four days later, Cassidy convinced Brey to accept the bag of jewels. The jewels were checked against an inventory list and then sealed in a bag with Mr. Cassidy's signature on the seal. Brey observed that the jewels appeared to be personal jewelry of Emmy Göring and Edda, her seven-year-old daughter, as a gold bracelet forming a medallion contained a picture of her daughter. The bag did indeed contain fourteen items from the child and twenty-four pieces of the Reichsmarschall's collection. It was placed in the Foreign Exchange Depository as Shipment Number 70.

Hermann Göring's uniforms always signified his position as the second most powerful figure in Nazi Germany. He stole a fortune in valuables and acquired the largest private art collection in the world during the war.

Brey insisted on a written statement regarding the jewels, that Cassidy promised to send, but reneged as the statement was never received. Further investigation by Col. Brey revealed that Mr. E.E. Minskoff accompanied by an interpreter and reporter, sometimes during the period between September 14, and October 6, 1945, was at the Veldenstein Castle, for the purpose of questioning Emmy Göring. During the interrogation, he demanded and obtained possessions of her jewels and gave her a receipt. She forwarded it to her lawyer, Friedrich Strobel in Nuremberg.

Brey and the officials at the Foreign Exchange Depository were at a loss as to the disposition of the bag of valuables. In December 1945, they considered releasing the jewelry to the Inter Government Committee for Refuges as looted property. An undated letter from G.H. Garde depicts the disposition of jewels: "Certain property alleged owned by Emmy, Edda and Hermann Göring is now deposited in the Foreign Exchange Depository. Since the Military Government no longer has any reason to retain this property, it has been decided to release it to the Amtsgericht-Hinterlegungstelle [District Court Depository] for disposition pursuant to applicable German Law. *** arrange to accept this property and take possession thereof on 6 July 1948."

Thus the bag of jewels was transferred to the Federal Republic of Germany.

On April 14, 1949, the French Restitution Mission provided the Foreign Exchange Depository with a claim (No.25373) for the Göring jewels. The claim had been completely copied from the Foreign Exchange Inventory, word for word including jewelry descriptions and appraised francs valuation. After some questions of the French regarding the assertion it was determined that there was strong evidence of fraud or collusion and the claim was ignored.

During December, this shipment of Göring and Shipment 76, Eva Braun jewels were checked against the inventory for the missing Rothschild's gems. The jewel experts at the foreign exchange determined these did not match.

The Grand Ducal House of Saxony-Weimar

Shipment 79: The German province of Thuringia, which was created by Federal German Law of April 20, 1920, was first included as a municipal association Sachsen-Weimar-Eisenach, the territory over which the Grand Dukes formerly presided. The municipal association was dissolved effective April 1, 1923, and the assets of the Weimar District became the property of the Land of Thuringia The Grand Duke, beginning on January 21, 1921, would each year receive from the Territory of Weimar an annuity of 300,000 marks out of which all claims of the Grand Ducal family to civil lists, maintenance and other gratuities would be paid; that the allowance would continue to be paid to existing male descendants of the Grand Duke after his decease; that upon extinction of the male line, a reduced amount of 100,000 marks would be paid to his female descendants; and that as further settlement for the concessions made by the Grand Duke, particularly in ceding highly valuable collections and objects d'art the Grand Duke shall be paid a special compensation of three million marks.

The annuities under the 1921 Agreement continued to the Grand Duke's heirs until 1945, when the income ceased as the war had been lost by Germany and the Allies would not make these payments.

In October 1946, the Grand Duke smuggled out of the Russian Occupation Zone gold, silver, and jewels worth $5 million dollars. The valuables were from the Grand Ducal House of Saxon-Weimar-Eisenach. On the morning of October 7, 1946, a representative of the Counter Intelligence Corps Detachment stationed at Eschwege, Germany contacted Mr. Irwin A. Urbantke, US Civilian, Property Control, and informed him by phone that the CIC Detachment had in its possession an extremely valuable assortment of gold, silver and jewels believed to have belonged to the former Grand Ducal House of Saxon-Weimar. The proceeds had been seized by the German Border Police after having been smuggled out of the Russian Occupation Zone at the nearby town of Wanfried.

Officers of the CIC were requesting advice as to the proper disposition of the treasure. Urbantke consulted with Mr. Everett P. Lesley, US Civilian of the Monuments, Fine Art and Archival Section. An hour later, with a guard detail from the US First Constabulary Brigade, Lesley and twelve guards left for Eschwege. His convoy to Eschwege consisted of four ¼-ton trucks, each carrying three armed guards with automatic rifles, one sedan, and one 2½-ton truck. They arrived that night at about 7:00 and reported to the military authorities. The CIC had kept the discovery a secret and the valuables were housed in their headquarters building located on 2 Bahnhofstrasse. Lesley and his cohorts presented their credentials and were shown the entire collection. The property had been completely inventoried with each piece tagged and provisionally estimated between $2,500,000 and $5,000,000. This property contained several items of high value including a diamond necklace, a beautiful silver necklace with pendant of diamonds and emeralds, a set of gold table service with hand painted porcelain handles which were deemed irreplaceable and several jeweled crowns.

At that hour there was no possibility of packing and loading the property and returning to Frankfurt. Therefore, the next morning the decision was made to transport the valuables to the Foreign Exchange Depository. The items were rechecked, inventoried again resulting in twelve typewritten pages containing 380 numbered items. Loaded on the trucks that afternoon at 6:00, the convoy left and arrived at the Foreign Exchange Depository later that night. The trucks containing the property were left under guard at the Depository. The following morning, October 9, 1946, the treasure was unloaded and receipts were signed and these valuable were given the designation of Shipment 79. The entire seizure and movement of the valuables was kept completely secret.

On December 10, 1947, at 10:30 in the morning, the property of the Grand Ducal House of Saxon-Weimar-Eisenach was released in its entirety to Theodore A. Heinrich, Chief US Monuments, Fine Art & Archival Section, Occupation Military Government Hesse.[3] In the late-1960s the property was turned over to the officials of the West German Government.

The Royal Hohenzollern Treasures

Shipment 87A & B: The thirty-four-year-old Princess Hermine Reuss married sixty-three-year-old Wilhelm II in 1922, four years after he abdicated as German Emperor, following the disaster of World War I. He spent the remainder of his life exiled from Germany with Hermine as his constant companion. Upon his death in 1941, Hermine returned to Germany and lived on her husband's estate in Silesia, Prussia. As the massive Soviet Army advanced, she and the former German emperor's family—as the Kaiser and she had no children—shuttled east to Frankfurt an der Oder.

As the Soviets overran the city the family remained. Two years later in May 1947, Wilhelm II oldest son, Prince Ferdinand, along with his forty-one-year-old mistress, Vera Herbst, arrived in the American Zone of Berlin with ninety-five valuable pieces of jewelry belonging to the heirs of the late Empress Hermine von Hohenzollern. After arriving in Berlin, the twenty-five pieces of these gems were stolen. The US Criminal Investigation Division (CID) looked into the robbery. Subsequently, the seventy-six remaining items were taken to the Foreign Exchange Depository on July 22, 1947 as Shipment 87A.

Apparently, the enterprising agents of the CID found the twenty-five missing pieces for on September 10, 1947, two sealed suitcases reportedly containing twenty-five pieces of jewelry were deposited a Shipment 87B. The appraisers at the Foreign Exchange Depository inventoried this last batch and found twenty-seven items in the suitcases. Not on the accompanying inventory was, "1 platinum chain and adorned with 2 pearls. 1 gold and silver earring with 1 imitation pearl." Strangely, during the check-in of these packages, there was a restrictive clause that these assets were only to be released by the Foreign Exchange Depository in accordance with instructions issued to the FED by Chief Agent, CID, Headquarters Berlin Command.

Six months later the CID requested the return of the items to themselves. But upon accepting them, signed by Col. William Brey, were specifications that the valuables would be released to the chief agent of the Criminal Investigation Division. There was some confusion regarding the definition of chief agent and the colonel would not release this shipment. Apparently, Brey suspected, something was working through the US Army Legal Division on March 4, 1948; this large shipment of valuables was released to Dr. Walter Schmidt of Berlin, curator of the estate of Hermine von Hohenzollern.[4]

Shipment 111: The largest war trophy brought home by returning American soldiers from World War II was taken by the 175th Infantry Regiment, 29th Infantry Division. The prize was forty-four teakwood boxes full of silver service, enough for 500 people. The silver service included elaborate table ornaments and expensive glassware. The treasure was kept at the Baltimore Armory in Maryland. It was then valued at $800,000. The silver had been the property of the Royal Hohenzollern family.

These items had been taken from Germany by the 175th when on May 1, 1945; they had met with representatives of the German Rocket Division who offered to surrender the entire division.

Tag Nos.

1   One white gold linked diamond necklace with two large pendentive blue stones, each surrounded by diamonds in settings. Attached to larger blue stones are three diamond-incrusted fleur-de-lis, two connecting to necklace, one to the smaller blue stone immediately beneath. The fleur-de-lis embrace a total of *medium sized cut   *12 diamonds. (Enclosed in brown suede jewel case 14" x 7" imprinted with jeweler name Sy & Wagner).

2   One white gold hair ornament, front-piece with 35 tapered spears, incrusted with diamonds graduating from medium to small. (Enclosed in red collapsible leather case 6" x 2" with imprinted name Kuester-Perry, Munich, Berlin).

3   One large pearl necklace with pendentive six-sided amethysts in diamond incrusted settings, eight diamond-incrusted gold pieces spaced thoughout small pearls in band design (enclosed in dark blue leather jewel case 10" x 5" bearing name Sy & Wagner).
Note: Indentation in jewel case indicates another item of jewelry which was not present.

4   One yellow-white gold tiara, line of fifteen graduated emeralds, each emerald surrounded by a ring of diamonds, remainder of tiara strewn with diamonds set in petals, center section consisting of seven of above 15 emeralds detachable.

5   One white gold forehead piece in floral design, entire center design consisting of six large diamonds pear or petal shaped removable, immediately below is found the largest diamond of all, to left and right of center design another petal shaped ensemble each consisting of nine large diamonds, remainder of piece incrusted with diamonds, some rather large.

6   One 14 piece arm band, seven pieces enameled in clock faces, 6 in eagles, center piece in 8 point star design (enclosed in 8" x 2" plush jewel box, bearing jewelers name W. Lameyer & Sohn, Hannover).

7   One gold crown with 12 cameos.

Page 1 of 15 listing the Hohenzollern inventory of jewels deposited as Shipment 87.

The offer was considered as the German unit sought to escape capture by the Soviet Army. On May 2, the unit was allowed to cross the Elbe River as prisoners of war. During this time the silver service came into possession of the 175th Infantry.

Reported missing, following the war, the Army investigated and after checking all War Department records failed to find any documentation relating to the silver. Something this large and valuable could not be kept hidden. As the Department of State began to apply pressure, Col. William Purnell, wartime commander of the 175th, officially disclosed the silver's whereabouts to the War Department and expressed hopes it would be regarded as a legitimate spoil of war. The colonel said the silver bears the crest of the former German royal family. He stated the 175th was asked by a German division to take the silverware before the Russians arrived. But at the time Col. Purnell was in the hospital recovering from a wound inflicted by a mortar shell. He further stated that the treasure was declared to New York Port Immigrations authorities upon the regiment's return to the United States on August 21, 1945.

In December 1946, the *Baltimore Sun* wrote an article regarding the silver and the War Department ordered the Inspector General to begin an investigation. The Army inquiry did determine that the silverware was taken to Bremen and shipped from that port with the full knowledge of the US port authorities. On February 17, 1947, the War Department officially took custody of the seven tons of Hohenzollern silverware captured at the Elbe River from the V-2 Rocket Division by the 175th.

This elaborate dinner service, a wedding present, was given to the former crown prince, who became Kaiser Wilhelm. It had been on display in a Berlin Museum since the end of World War I. The silverware was placed in the National Gallery for safekeeping pending a formal legal decision deciding if the 175th Regiment would be permitted to keep the trophy.[5]

The Hohenzollern silverware would not be returned to the 175th for on January 7, 1949, the Commanding General; Office of Military Government received a radio message apprising him of a valuable shipment arriving in Germany. The shipment was forty-four boxes containing Hohenzollern silver and china. The outside of each box was stenciled with a large black diamond insignia and addressed to the commanding general. The shipment was to be stored in the Foreign Exchange Depository as Shipment 111.

The USAT *General Patch* arrived in the US Zone of Occupation Port City of Bremerhaven, Germany on January 20. The boxes were loaded aboard baggage car Frankfurt 105845, accompanied by one Security Officer, one Department of Army civilian and nine enlisted men with a time of arrival at 10:26 in the morning of January 21 at the Frankfurt Main Station. The train actual arrival was 1:10pm with the unloading beginning twenty minutes later. Ten minutes later Dr. Ferdinand Friedensburg, Deputy Bürgermeister of Berlin arrived along with his associates. The boxes being extremely heavy (200 to 400 pounds) and carefully packed were unloaded with some difficulty were placed in separate vault compartments under a lock affixed by the Bürgermeister.

Four days later, a shipping ticket was filed out and signed as being received by Dr. F. Friedensburg. The property remained in the vaults as it was deposited by Berlin officials to the safekeeping of the Bank Deutscher Laender.[6]

Ursula Heinze-Freisler

Shipment 88: Ursula Heinze-Freisler, attractive, intelligent and twenty-five-years-old, is the main source for the valuables in Shipment 88. She was under the command of SS General Ludolf von Alvensleben in the Crimea during 1941-1944. Previously, Ursula had attended SS Police School in Erfurt.

In January 1944, she married Wolfram Heinze, thirty-four-years-old and a captain in the Wehrmacht. Prior to the war, the captain had been a lawyer, then joined the SS and was assigned to the finance division of the organization—Amt II. He was originally appointed to duty in Norway, then at his request, to Berlin. During this time, he entered service in the German army. As the war continued, he, like most men in Germany, was sent to the Russian Front. Here, he served as a liaison officer between various subdivisions of the Jagdverband, a unit of top ace pilots in the Luftwaffe during the last months of the war, fighting against forces of the Soviet Union.

As the powerful Soviet Army forced its way through Czechoslovakia, Ursula with her husband, sister-in-law and other members of the Jagverband fled across the Czech Border to the German town of Zwiesel and found a haven in a mountain chalet. Plans were made for the capitulation of Germany and the women in the group were given liquid vials of poison. Wolfram Heinze had made connections with the commander of the nearby Deggendorf concentration camp and obtained forged identification papers for all the members of his party, plus a large quantity of valuable jewelry. The gems were split amongst them as everyone changed into civilian clothes and awaited the now advancing American army.

They did not have long to wait. During April 1945, the US Army arrived. Using her feminine charms with an American officer, Ursula obtained travel permits for her husband and other members of her group as they moved from Zwiesel to Deggendorf. Here she, her husband and sister-in-law lived in harmony until Wolfram became a liability for Ursula, she reported his previously association as an SS captain and this resulted in an automatic arrest for Wolfram Heinze.

With her husband in a POW internment camp, Ursula "gained the confidence of several American officers" that secured her employment as an interpreter, and better than average living quarters. Using the jewelry from the Deggendorf concentration camp she was able to obtain furniture, food and other luxuries.

For almost a year Ursula was living the good life until complications arose from her fifth abortion and she was sent to the local hospital where she stayed for a month.

It's not clear, but while in the hospital Ursula became involved in passing written messages enclosed in food. Somehow, a Mr. Kline working for the US Military Government was involved. Regardless, this puzzling event led to her release from on February 14, 1946, to be placed in the Deggendord jail. Her cellmate was a Canadian woman who spoke fluent German. The Canadian, Madeleine Geeger from Kitchener, Ontario, told Ursula that her husband had been forced to join the SS when the Germans invaded Yugoslavia in 1942. The women agreed that forcing foreigners to join the SS and others sent to Germany as forced laborers was a bad thing.

As this the conversation continued, Ursula told Madeleine about her early childhood; her first husband and quick divorcé. Afterwards, Ursula moved to Berlin where life really began for her. She met a general with the intention of marrying his son. Traveling with the general, she went to the Crimean Peninsula on the northern coast of the Black See. Ursula was the only woman in this remote outpost of Ukraine, which was a training base for high-ranking SS officers. Here she met Wolfram Heinze, who was a most important SS officer. They married and Ursula took the required SS oath of obedience and also joined the Nazi Party. They then moved to Berlin and lived in the best hotels, had wild parties, and met the higher class of the SS, including their wives and girlfriends. Ursula emphasized to Madeleine these were the best times of her life. She stated she would never forget those six years and the many good times she had. Now she intended to divorcé Wolfram as she was the sweetheart of an American officer.

It is not known why the Canadian, Madeleine Geeger was in jail, but disgusted with Ursula stories and feeling some patriotism, she went to the US Counter Intelligent Corps with her story. Ursula was arrested by American authorities and her home was searched on February 18, 1946. The poison vials were found with enough poison estimated to kill ten people. It is not explained but during this investigation/search 147 pieces of valuable jewelry were recovered from Ursula Heinze. She claimed her husband made the purchases of jewelry in Prague, Czechoslovakia. Ursula was placed in an internment camp and later tried in the German People Court (Spruchkammer). She was released as a result of their findings.

On September 29, 1947, this jewelry along with several other unrelated items from the Rothenburg Museum were deposited in the Foreign Exchange Depository as Shipment 88.

Following are the first five items from this 147-itemed inventory:

a. ring white gold, stamped 585, 1 little diamond square setting, left and right 3 ribs graved
b. ring white gold with square white plate, 1 diamond, left and right Onyx
c. 1 small golden ring, 3 diamonds side by side, 3 small splinters
d. formed golden ring 3 diamonds and 10 little roses, one of which is diamond set in Chaton
e. gold ring with rosette, 4 blue sapphires, 1 small diamond, 8 little roses

Apparently, with help from her American officer boyfriend, on October 19, 1947, Mr. Allan Mather, US War Department civilian requested a reinvestigation of her case. He was instructed to submit the request in writing through channels. Nothing happened and the gems were later released to the intergovernmental Committee for Refuges. Clearly, Mr. Mather had an axe to grind, for on January 10, 1950, three years after his initial contact and after the jewels had been released to the IGCR, he visited the FED and requested to read the CIC report on Ursula Heinze. His request was denied.[7]

Pierre Laval

Shipment 61: Born into a peasant family and trained as a lawyer, Pierre Laval (1883-1945) was elected (1914) to the chamber of deputies as a Socialist. He fought in World War I, and from 1925 on he held various cabinet posts under different premiers. Laval was Prime Minister in 1931-1932. After the fall of France in 1940, Laval reached new prominence as an appeaser with the occupying Germans and obtained the title of Premier. Predicting a German victory he was willing to deport 20,000 Jews from the unoccupied section of Vichy, France. Of the thousands of children deported Laval declared that the children did not interest him. After the Allied invasion of France in 1944, he fled to Germany with the retreating German Army and became part of the phantom French Government Committee. Contemplating his future, Laval took the necessary steps to invest $500,000 in the La Pampa Province, Argentina.[8]

Laval then went from Germany to Bolzano, Italy. Here, on the morning of May 2, 1945, he proceeded to Barcelona, Spain on a Junkers Ju 188 equipped with new engines. The plane stripped of all armaments and secret radar equipment had been painted with the official insignia of the commercial Lufthansa Airlines. It was piloted by twenty-three-year-old MSgt. Gerhard Boehm, and twenty-five-year-old copilot Sgt. Helmut Funk. Accompanying Laval were his wife, the French Minister of Justice, Maurice Gabolde, French Minister of Education, Abel Bonnard, and two other French Government Officials. When the plane landed that afternoon at Barcelona, it was met by Antonius F. Corria, the civil governor of Barcelona. On June 2, as the war was over, the two pilots were released as guests of the Spanish government.

The French government immediately demanded that Gen. Dwight D. Eisenhower use his military might to have Laval removed from Spain. After considerable maneuvering between Eisenhower's Headquarters, and the US embassy in Madrid, the decision was made by the Spanish to invite Laval to leave Spain.

On July 29, German pilots Boehm and Funk were summoned to Corria's office and told that Laval had to leave Spain in accordance with arrangements made with the American embassy in Madrid. Corria further explained that Spain did not want the world to think Laval was being turned over as a prisoner to any power, but was merely being escorted out of the country by the two pilots. They were further informed by Corria that it had been arranged with the embassy that upon delivery of Laval they would be free to return to Spain with the plane. The pilots were instructed immediately upon landing to notify Eisenhower's Headquarters so the news could be flashed back to Spain that everything was in order.

Originally, it was planned that Laval would leave the country alone but his wife was given the choice to join, and she did. No oxygen masks were available in the plane and the pilot, Boehm, asked Madam Laval to sign a statement absolving him from any claim in case of her accidental death during the flight. This she refused. Laval was under the impression that he was to be flown to Lisbon, Portugal. The pilots insisted the Spanish authorities inform Laval of his ultimate destination. Boehm further requested that he be armed incase Laval should threaten him while he was in the air to change course. He was then issued a Spanish pistol. At 6:30 on the morning of July 31, on the tarmac, Laval was told of his ultimate destination of Salzburg in the US Occupation Zone of Austria. At that time the Spanish told him that he could depend upon American generosity and could expect help from his son who was a resident of the United States. As the plane taxied out Madam Laval spoke sharply to her husband about: "entrusting his fate to two German pigs."[9] This did nothing to endear the two former Luftwaffe pilots for their passengers.

The German Cross in Gold worn by German pilot, Master Sergeant Gerhard Boehm, impressed the American airmen at the Horsching Airport, Austria. Today, these medals and documentation are fetched by military collectors for $5,000 or more.

They flew towards Salzburg with dead-reckoning and a compass with no radio contact. They avoided all French airspace, flying over the Mediterranean Sea and Northern Italy, upon spotting Linz, Austria they came down for a look at the ground and saw planes with US markings so they landed just before noon at Horsching Airport in Linz, Austria. As the pilots had overshot their planned airport by eighty-five miles, they were not expected. Upon touchdown the airmen of the USAAF 70th Fighter Group were surprised as two German pilots exited the plane wearing their former Luftwaffe uniforms and were most impressed with Boehm wearing his Nazi medals that included First and Second Iron Crosses, and most notably the German Cross in Gold.

The pilots and two passengers were immediately taken into custody and placed under guard by the Col. Martin, commanding officer, 70th Fighter Group and Laval and his wife quickly searched for any concealed suicide implements. In Laval possession were twenty US $500 bills, ten one thousand Swiss franc notes with a 1945 value of $2,300 plus some Spanish pesetas notes. His wife was also searched by an American nurse without anything being taken. The Lavals were separated from the Luftwaffe pilots and placed in a small room with the only furniture being two small beds, a table and a chair. The couple disapproved of the GI meal served them for lunch and ate sparingly, although the pilots had indicated Laval had lost considerable weight in the past two months. Laval appeared composed and made an attempt to discuss politics, assuring his captors that he had worked against the Germans and could prove it with the material he was carrying. Quickly informed that the airmen would not discuss politics, the conversation ended.

The money was seized by Col. H.C. Anderson, Finance Officer, 65th Infantry Division. The serial number of each $500 was recorded. Laval was given a receipt for the currency. At 4:00pm that same day Laval, carrying the receipt, and his wife left in custody of Gen. John Copeland for the French Zone of Occupation. The destination of Copeland, Assistant Commander, 65th Infantry Division, was Innsbruck, Austria, Headquarters, French Occupation Forces. They arrived that night and Laval was swiftly transferred to Paris. Several days later the Luftwaffe pilots, Boehm and Funk, were interned in a German prisoner of war camp.

In Paris, Laval was tried for treason, sentenced to death, and after an unsuccessful attempt at suicide, he was executed on October 15, 1945.

The Laval valuables were received at the Foreign Exchange Depository on August 20, 1945, as Shipment 61, and at the time, kept a secret from the French. Two years later, the French Director of Finances was notified that the Depository was in possessions of property seized from the late Pierre Laval. On March 8, 1948, the Foreign Exchange Depository was instructed to grant the monies taken from Laval to the French authorities upon presentation of the receipt given to Laval three years earlier. Five months after the Department of Army, Washington DC notified Frank C. Gabell, Chief of the Foreign Exchange Depository that the widow of Pierre Laval was in possession of the receipt and refused to release it to the French authorities. The Department of Army stated the receipt could only be procured through a lengthy court battle. The Army in DC requested instructions as to whether the money could be released to the French authorities by using a photostat of the receipt and assurances against indemnity agreement from the French government.

On September 2, 1948, Mr. Gabell received a letter from the Office, French Military Government, Berlin that they were indeed in possession of the receipt delivered by Lieutenant Col. H.C. Anderson, 65th Infantry Division, to Pierre Laval at the time of his capture. They also requested the monies.

Dubious, the Chief of the Foreign Exchange Depository had the Army legal staff review the release and agreed to hand over the currency with the surrender of the original acknowledgment, and, "a signed receipt and indemnity agreement in quadruplicate by a duly authorized French government official authorized to accept the funds and execute the receipt and indemnity agreement. The signing of the note and indemnity agreement must be witnessed by at least one United States Citizen representing the United States in the transaction and preferable three persons, at least two of whom are United States citizens."

After all this, the money was released to the French authorities on September 29, 1948.[10]

Although frequently referred to as neutral, Spain was not impartial in World War II, but a non-belligerent power allied with Germany, Italy and Japan. Hundreds of Laval's cohorts left Madrid on Iberia flights with the destination of Buenos Aires, Argentina, including Georges Guilbaud, with a death sentence on his head imposed by the French courts. He had hidden negotiable assets abroad for Pierre Laval. In the late-1960s, Guilbaud moved to Switzerland with the benefits of these assets and worked in banking.

In his glory days, Premier Laval and his daughter, Josee, arrive at Union Station, Washington DC, where they are met by General John J. Pershing, hero of World War I.

Erich Viehmann

Shipment 64 is an intriguing story about an injust seizure of Erich Viehmann's gems. It begins when Mr. Eduard Imgrund founded the jewelry firm bearing his name in 1868 at 24 Sandeldamm, Hanau, Germany. The Eduard Imgrund Company was purchased in 1888 by Jean Viehmann, but retained its original name. Jean and his wife prospered, and on December 29, 1909, she gave birth to a son, Erich. Upon the death of Jean Viehmann in 1926, his wife took possession of the firm as sole owner. Thus, the firm had been in possession of the Viehmann family without interruption since 1888 and was cutting diamonds, and dealing with jewels, and creating fine pieces of jewelry.

Erich joined the Nazi party on May 1, 1933, and a few years later the war interrupted his life and business as Viehmann was conscripted into the German army. The five foot-nine inch, 160-pound Viehmann served in Germany for two years, obtaining the rank of sergeant but was released due to a war injury. Returning to his jewelry business in 1940, Viehmann made numerous trips to Paris and other cities in the Greater Reich conducting his business. In 1941, he was arrested and brought before a court of the Nazi party as he was engaged to a Jewish lady. He was not known as a fanatic Nazi, and within a month after the end of the war, Viehmann married his long time fiancé, Gertrud Deines.

But fate was not with Viehmann as he was reported to the US Counter Intelligence Corps as a member of the Nazi SS—that was an automatic capture by the US Army. Thus, on August 18, 1945, Viehmann was arrested by members of the Counter Intelligence Corps, and all his raw diamonds, cut diamonds and pieces of jewelry were confiscated by US forces. The firm of Eduard Imgrund was by now one of the most successful jewelry business in all of Germany. Because of this, Viehmann was denounced to the Military Government as a member of the SS. This smear was made by two jealous competitors, K. Weber and his friend Laughans, the later now working for the Counter Intelligence Corps. Two days after his inventory was taken, Viehmann was requested to make a written inventory of the confiscated items. He pointed out that a few of the valuable items were missing and without further questioning, Viehmann was placed in jail by the US military government.

The Counter Intelligence Corps concluded with an examination of Viehmann's Travel Pass, "revealed uncounted trips abroad which confirmed the suspicions of this office as to the real activities of Viehmann. … Large quantities of diamonds, inconsistent with the declared former activities of the subject, were impounded by Military Government since their proveniences was suspected from illegal sources in former German occupied territories. Subject is a dangerous and cunning individual." Thus, Viehmann was locked behind bars in the US Internment Camp at Kornwestheim and was still there on January 28, 1946. Then he was transferred to Camp 75 in Ludwigsburg. His release date is not known.

On August 24, 1945, Viehmann completed the inventory that was deposited by Lt. Francis R. Paternoster, Military Government Detachment E5, in the Foreign Exchange Depository as Shipment 64. Almost immediately, the Netherlands Restitution Mission requested an investigation of the diamonds and an interrogation of Viehmann. The American authorities denied the Dutch request.

The US Occupation Forces required former Nazi party members to be "denazified" before they were allowed a competent job or credibility. This was accomplished by a mandatory appearance before a German judge in a denazification trial. Viehmann was summoned in December 1946. After an investigation of several months the court (*Sprunchkammer*) found that Viehmann had never been a member of the SS, and was also arrested by the Gestapo for dating a Jew. He was cleared by the denazification board but his diamonds remained in the Foreign Exchange Depository.

In October 1947, after denazification, Viehmann reactivated his business and was quickly successful, exporting to his prewar American customers about $75,000 worth of jewelry. He then filed claim with the Americans for the return of his valuables, noting the results of the court. The director of the Foreign Exchange Depository noted the findings of the court were completely inconsistent with the Counter Intelligence Corps and played "hard ball" with Viehmann's request. They asked him to supply an inventory of some of items in the Foreign Exchange Depository. On January 20, 1948, Erich Viehmann wrote a two-page description of twelve of the more resounding items. Here is the first:

> Item 1: One ring with a diamond which has been estimated at 6.60 carats by the taxation of the [U.S.] Military Government, weights 7.08 carats according to my list of articles and my balance. I bought this stone in 1941 as a raw stone of 20.50 carats and I cut it. The color of the stone is yellowish-green to brownish and has slight faults. The cut is modern and well executed. The original tag of the stone is marked with a capital U.

These descriptions were subsequently found to accurately describe twelve pieces of the inventory. But identification as to all the diamonds could not be accomplished due to the fact that the stones were no longer in the original Viehmann wrappers, and, additionally, they had been regrouped and resorted through several handlings. The same with the Dutch diamonds, or in other words they had been mixed with other shipments of loose diamonds.

The Foreign Exchange Depository had a visitor on January 13, 1948, as Mr. A.J. Fould, partner of Calumet Importers, New York, spoke in behalf of Viehmann, recommending him, as a business associate, and inquired as to the steps necessary to regain the property claimed by Viehmann. Fould knew the "ins and outs" as he had previously been employed by the military government in Germany

On October 21, 1948, Viehmann's properties were given to the Amtsgericht-Hinterlegungstelle (District Court Depository) for disposition pursuant to applicable German law. The author tried to contact the Viehmann Company but all request were ignored; therefore the fate is of these valuables is unknown.[11]

One page of Erich Viehmann's inventory seized by US authorities and later turned over to the Germans

Friedrich Schwend

Shipment 71 involves one of the most interesting and enigmatic person the author has ever encountered in his vast research; a man named, Friedrich (Fritz) Schwend, born in Munich but spent his early childhood in Innsbruck, Austria. He was described as medium height, age forty-five, blond, hooknose and slender with the aliases "Schwendt" and "Wendig."

Before 1929, he was an international arms dealer who shipped weapons to China and Russia. Schwend married Frauline von Gemmingen, the niece of the then Minister of Exterior, Baron von Neurath. She was also the relative of an extremely rich family in California. Through his new family connections, Schwend became the personal administrator of the wealthy Argentinean wheat magnate of the Bunge family. Prior to the war, working from New York City, Schwend managed this and other investments with a pre-war income exceeding $50,000 a year. This did not include the income from his activities in selling Belgian weapons, and German fighter aircraft to the Chinese.

Upon his return to Europe, Schwend lived in Rome. With his activities in Europe, Schwend spent most of his time at his estate in Merano, Italy, a predominantly German-speaking town; it looks to belong in Austria but is actually ten miles inside Italy, due to the redrawing of borders after World War I. Merano is tucked into the intersection of four mountain valleys spilling down from lower Alpine ranges. It is protected location, about 1,000 feet above sea level and shielded from the north, east and west, has given Merano a climate mild enough to nurture vineyards, as well as palm trees, oleander and fruit trees that blossom against a backdrop of snowy peaks. Bisected by the Passirio River the city of 32,000 residents combines red-roofed arcaded buildings, ancient battlements, stone churches and flower-embroidered parks.[12] After a divorce, Schwend met his second wife in Merano, the former Hedda Neuholt, daughter of Dr. John Neuholt, the former Austrian Consul General then assigned to Washington DC.

In 1941, at the request of the Germans, the Italian police arrested him on charges of being an American spy. After five months in a German jail, he purchased his way to freedom and returned to Rome. In Italy, Schwend met German agent Dr. Wilhelm Höttl, and through him offered his services to Operation Bernhard. This was the codename of a secret plan devised during the World War II by Nazi agencies to counterfeit British currency. It was the largest and most successful counterfeiting operation in history. The clandestine, Friedrich Schwend, always attired in impeccable civilian clothing, organized a master network for the distribution of large blocks of these perfect forgeries. He was undoubtedly selected because of his financial influence, owning considerable real estate in Italy, and was involved in numerous Italian commercial and banking concerns as a partner of his wealthy father-in-law. Schwend now became "Major Wendig" in the German tank corps and legal officer of the Gestapo as a cover for his operation that enabled him to move freely in Greater Germany and its occupied territories.

The counterfeit notes were spent by the millions to purchase weapons, ammunition, military equipment, liquor, gold, and jewelry, and also exchanged for other currencies. The military goods, including food, were mostly used in the immediate area. The gold and currencies would be shipped to the Reichsbank and the chinaware, clothing, shoes, furniture, etc. would be shipped to three storage depots in Austria. As the sole distributor for the counterfeit currency Schwend, and with a wide organization of agents, he worked closely with Ernst Kaltenbrunner and his assistants. The currency sent to Italy, Croatia, and Hungary was delivered directly to Wilhelm Höttl. These distributions of the forgeries enabled Schwend to satisfy the most luxurious wishes of Kaltenbrunner and Höttl.

This began in 1943, with the founding of black market concern by the SS, headquartered in Trieste, known as Saxonia. Its object was to buy goods with counterfeit British pound notes in Italy and export them to foreign countries thereby obtaining foreign currency such as Swiss francs and Swedish kroner. In particular, works of art, leather goods and textiles were bought, and high prices were paid for the goods. The head of the Saxonia organization was none other than SS Major Friedrich (Fritz) Schwend, under the alias name of Fritz Wendig. As American forces pushed north, Schwend headquarters was moved from Trieste north towards Innsbruck, Austria to Merano, Italy. Here Schwend took up residence in the (Schloss) Labers Castle, an SS headquarters established in the castle following Germany's takeover of Italy, after Mussolini's arrest by the King of Italy.

Also in Merano, and working with Schwend, was Dr. John Neuholt, his father-in-law ("brother-in-law!," is handwritten on the source document) and John's son who worked in the Saxonia organization. Here at the Labers Castle, now a hotel, Schwend worked on the top floor in room number 3 from where he and his group organized the "laundering" of counterfeit money under the code name of "Wendig."

Soldiers of the US 88th Infantry Division fought their way up the Italian Peninsular to Merano. Here, they were astonished by the contents of the warehouses; truckloads of silverware, jewelry, hundreds of thousands of meters of silk, hundreds of thousands of suits of clothes and an unusual number of shoes. The Alpine barracks were crammed full with a miscellaneous collection enough to stock a hundred shops with children's bathing suits, bicycles tires, silk stockings, women's attire, canvas shoes, and much more. All of this was controlled by SS Major Friedrich Schwend. It was here that Schwend was arrested shortly after the war, in the company of George Spitz, by soldiers of the 88th Infantry Division. Schwend was carrying a certificate issued on April 28, 1945, identifying him as a representative of the International Red Cross.[13]

Inspecting U.S. officers and soldiers leave Dornsberg Castle, Merano, Italy, in search of other loot hidden by the Germans. They found great quantities of silk, wool and other stolen goods in the castle. Doctor Jaac Van Hartner, an alleged representative of the International Red Cross from Budapest, is in the passenger seat of the jeep directing the party to places where the Germans have hidden more loot.

Doctor Jaac Van Hartner, pictured in the photograph, knew where to look for the hidden assets as he had an inside knowledge of the operation. He was working for Friedrich Schwend and had collaborated with the Nazi in the distribution of the counterfeit British currency. Schwend often used Jews to "circulate" the counterfeit currency as they would never be suspected as being a German agent. The senior, and most successful operative was a Dutch-German Jew named Jaac Van Hartner. On May 17, 1945, Van Harten was arrested by the CIC and a search of his residence turned up a huge stock of black market goods, and tens of thousands in counterfeit British notes. Arrested as a Nazi collaborator, representatives of the Zionist movement came to his aid and he was soon released.[14]

After Schwend's arrest, and in trying to convince the US military authorities of his seriousness in working with them, he turned over the below described gold. Friedrich Schwend signed this statement:

18 July 1945
I, Friedrich Schwendt turned over gold coins which were hidden by me near Imst, Austria. The total Money consisted entirely of gold pieces was checked in my presents. It consisted of three (3) cloth bags bearing tags, (1,000 pcs. per sack) The sacks weigh about 6.8 Kg. The remainder of the loose coins were made and weighed, when wet on an untested scales (testing about 800 pieces to 6 Kg.) The total of unsacked coins or loose coins was about 27.2 Kg. on the untested scales. This made a grand total of 47 Kg.
F. Schwendt (signed)

The following statement, written in German, Schwend's native language was attested to him:

"This is to certify that I fully understand the above statement." Although his name and signature is Schwendt.

The French and Italian gold coins were taken by Capt. Eric W. Timm and Capt. Charles C. Michaelis of the Third Army Special Counter Intelligence Detachment. As with everything else with Schwend, this collection of 7,155 gold coins weighing 103 pounds is obscure. These coins were deposited in the Foreign Exchange Depository on October 17, 1945 as shipment 71.[15]

Schwend was released from prison in September 1945, and he managed to land a job with US forces to mediate between the Italian Partisans and the Americans, and for that reason he stayed out of prison.

Later, Schwend crossed the border to Italy, where Spitz convinced him that, as a high-ranking SS officer, he could not safely remain in Europe. On September 16, 1946, Schwend gave George Spitz power of attorney to obtain several carpets that Schwend claimed he had evacuated in 1945 from his father-in-law's home, and took them to Unterrach, Austria. The carpets were to be sold with Spitz, "quoting the amount."[16]

The carpets in six large wooden crates had been seized by US military authorities. One carpet, a Korassan, Herti design, Mesched border was valued at $1,250, and another Mesched rug was valued at $800. Altogether, these rugs were valued in excess of $3,000 in 1945 money. According to Schwend, the carpets were taken into the custody of Dr. George Gyssling, Consul General and Mrs. Boone, an American citizen who were involved in detaining the rugs. None of this is clear to the author, but as stated before, Schwend is unfathomable.

Apparently, Spitz was unable to obtain the carpets for on April 30, 1948, living in Genoa, Italy; Schwend sent Dr. George Gyssling this letter:

Herewith in attached you will find the letter from Mrs. Boone to whom I had referred for advice regarding the whereabouts of the carpets in question. Will you please call Dr. Wotruba to instruct him to return to you the rugs which remain after the sales completed by Mrs. Boone.

… There is little chance that anything will be restored by Yugoslavia although a claim was lodged by my <u>brother</u>-in-law, [John Neuhold] in his capacity as an Italian citizen. It is for this reason that I appeal to you to do your upmost for the recuperation of the Carpets."[17]

The conniving Schwend had acquired three of the rugs from the heavily looted Jacques Goudstikker Collection along with two paintings; No.2108, Miereveld, *Portrait of a Lady* and No.5573, Moreelse, *Woman and Child*.[18] The Goudstikker Collection from the Netherlands was part of Reichsmarschall Hermann Göring's collection.

Spitz provided Schwend with falsified Jewish papers and a new alias as "Vencel Turi." Another set of fake Red Cross papers listed him as a Croatian exile named "Wenceslas Turi." With the help of the notorious "Ratline," Schwend and his wife escaped through Milan to South America. He lived comfortably in Lima, Peru, where he worked as a senior engineer for Volkswagen. Schwend traveled extensively, and American intelligence believed he was the leader of a pro-Nazi group that helped shield Josef Mengele from arrest.

Schwend's luck ran out when he was hauled before a Peruvian court for his involvement in a murder, and other crimes. During the long trial that followed, the prosecution's lead witness died under mysterious circumstances. A conviction on a minor charge followed and Schwend was expelled from Peru. German authorities then took him into custody for his role in a World War II-era murder in Italy (perhaps the time he had spent in a Rome jail during the war years was related to this matter), but the case had gone cold and Schwend was released after about one year. Peru lifted the expulsion order during his sojourn in a German jail, and Schwend returned to Lima. He lived, some say lavishly, until his death in 1980.[19]

In May 1948, the gold coins, surrendered by Friedrich Schwend, were still in the FED with a note they belonged to the Reichssicherheitshauptamt (Reich Security Main Office). These coins may have been sent to the Federal Reserve Bank in New York, credited on February 26, 1952, under Military Law 53, Shipment XIII.

Doctor Jaac Van Hartner settled in Tel Aviv in 1947 as a rather wealthy person. Here, he demanded compensation of $5 million from the US Army for property seized from him at Merano. He also filed claims with the IGCR for the counterfeit currency he had given Jewish rescue activist during the war. He died as a hero in Israel in 1973 for saving Jewish lives during World War II.

Unfamiliar Individuals

Shipment 54 consisted of an envelope containing money, papers, and various documents received by the Foreign Exchange Depository on July 13, 1945. These items were discovered by Tec 5 Thomas M. Huffman, Headquarters Company, 10th Armored Division on May 6, 1945. While walking near the outskirts of Farchant, Germany, he noticed a bundle of papers and money tied in a white rag beneath a pile of logs. Upon finding the bundle, he immediately brought the complete package to his headquarters for proper disposition through channels.

The rag was examined on March 4, 1947, by officials of the Foreign Exchange Depository where it had been deposited as Shipment 54. It contained no currency, but, a fire insurance policy and seven securities being Belgian stocks and bonds and two savings books and two passports, numbers 3174 and 3175, issued by German authorities to Belgian women, Germaine Ruscart and Jeanne Ruscart. The passports were dated August 20, 1944. The savings books contained a total of 500 Reichsmarks.

The stocks and bonds were released to the Landeszentralbank von Hessen on January 9, 1949. The passports were given to the authorized representative of Belgian government on February 16, 1949. A week earlier, Belgian representatives had written to the chief of the Foreign Exchange Depository that the Belgian securities released to the Landeszentralbank were blocked and could not negotiated, sold or pawned without a seal of approval from Brussels.[20]

Shipment 109 involves the mysterious John Plater-Zyberg as follows in categories A through C.

A. Members of the 15 Infantry Regiment were inventorying a warehouse in Huttau, Austria that had been used by the Todt organization, a combat assigned civilian labor unit. During the search, a locked office was found. Acquiring the key the soldiers found four boxes containing an undetermined amount of European currency. On the afternoon of July 3, 1945, Lt. John Frazer removed the four boxes of money and turned them over to Capt. James W. Coles, 15th Infantry. On July 25, 1945, Coles turned over to the finance officer of the Third Army the following identified as taken from warehouse occupied by Todt Organization in Hottau, Austria.The Todt valuables consisting of paper currency from Croatia, Bulgaria, Bohemia & Moravia, Germany, Slovakia and Hungary were delivered to the Foreign Exchange Depository on July 25, 1948, by Col. L.C. Grimes, Finance Officer and assigned Shipment 109.

B. Stored in the Foreign Exchange Depository on September 15, 1948, were 483,000 French francs deposited in Nuremberg by Capt. Stewart Campbell, Military Government on August 21, 1945. This could be in relation to Capt. Campbell's involvement in Shipment 15.

C. Additionally, US currency was deposited in the Foreign Exchange Depository on September 16, 1948. The money had been placed in the Currency Section on November 26, 1945 for temporary custody by Col. M.I. Hudtloff. The money had been taken under Military Law 53, but it is not known why or how it was deposited in the Currency Section.

The currency follows:

41	$1	41
5	$2	10
68	$5	340
33	$10	330
120	$20	240
2	$50	100
109	$100	10,900
14	$1,000	14,000
		25,961

The US dollars on inventory Form No.15632 was changed to 15826/15827, with the former containing one $1, one $50 and six $100 bills and the later the remaining inventory.

Included with the US currency were two $2 Canadian bills and other European currency including British.

On April 2, 1949, The Foreign Exchange Depository received a letter from Mr. Jo Fisher Freeman, finance advisor to the Military Governor, Berlin requesting release $651.00 US and four Canadian dollars (two $2) that were claimed by John Plater-Zyberg. It was noted that the currency had been collected from Zyberg pursuant to Military Law 53 by Military Government Detachment I18 B3 located in Hochstadt, Germany. At that time, Plater-Zyberg was a displaced person from Belarus, then a country within the Soviet Union. He was now, apparently, living in Paris, France. The FED was requested to release these funds to a representative of the Office of Political Affairs, OMGUS. Thus, the inventory records were split as shown above with the $651 remove with the Canadian currency.

The FED was further instructed:

The Office of Political Affairs, OMGUS prefers not to transmit US dollar currency to the US Embassy in Paris by diplomatic pouch, therefore you are requested to present the 651 dollars to the US Army Finance Office, Frankfurt, Military Post for conversion into Military Payment Certificates. With the Military Payment Certificates you are to purchase a US dollar draft payable to Mr. John Plater-Zyberg.

The request was granted, and on April 21, 1949, the US currency and four Canadian dollars were released to the Office of Political Affairs.[21]

What happened to the remaining $25,310 is undocumented. Who was John Plater-Zyberg?

The author was unable to find this person, but on September 9, 1945, Count Henry Spater-Zyberg's wife, Polish countess Therese Spater-Zyberg was found guilty of stealing art treasures valued at 700,000 Reichsmarks from Reichsmarschall Hermann Göring's plundered art. On the second day of the trial, the countess had burst out in tears stating she had not the slightest notion that the removal of the objects taken from Poland would constitute an act of theft. She admitted receiving the art objects at Göring's chateau at the time US soldiers were staying there, but maintained her claim that she had intended to hand the treasure back to Poland.[22]

In her defense, the attractive blond, twenty-three-year-old countess appealed to an American paratrooper colonel, "My colonel, the man I love, the man I plan to marry, and the man who can explain, I was not stealing" to get her out of this jam.[23] The colonel was never identified. A US Army military court in Salzburg sentenced her to two years imprisonment.

Shipment 166 involves Dr. Gustav Hilger, akin to tens-of-thousands of Germans, had his assets surrendered under Military Law 53. But apparently, being connected with someone in authority and now living in the Unites States his valuables were to be sorted out and returned by officials of the Foreign Exchange Depository.

Hilger was captured in Salzburg, Austria on May 19, 1945; he spent a brief period in a prisoner of war cage in Mannheim, Germany, then transported to the United States, and spent the remainder of the year incarnated at Fort Meade. Hilger provided unusual intelligence information of great value to his American captors. He had served in the Nazi Foreign Office as counselor to Joachim von Ribbentrop, who had been hanged at Nuremburg for war crimes. He returned to Germany in 1946 to work for the US Army, Counter Intelligence Corp as a specialist in Soviet intelligence. Wanted for war crimes in Russia, they requested that he be extradited to the Soviet Zone of Occupation. The Army, considering security outweighed moral consideration, whisked Hilger and his family back to the United States.

Sometime during this activity, the doctor's assets consisting of forty gold Swiss francs, forty gold French francs and $3,300 US dollars, were submitted to the Reichsbank in Augsburg. In retrieving these assets, the FED assigned this transaction Shipment 116 as they pulled the deposit of Hilger. The valuables were to be shipped to Col. Baker, Pentagon Building, Washington, DC. Hilger's assets were placed in a diplomatic pouch and on August 10, 1949, sent by Rhein-Main Security Courier Service to Washington.

The returned FED shipping ticket included this statement:

> Enclosed are shipping tickets signed by Gustav Hilger which are returned in accordance with letter from Frank J. Roberts, Acting Chief, Foreign Exchange Depository dated 10 August 1949. The sealed package was delivered to recipient and contents checked in the presence of the signing witnesses. Mr. Leland H. Carlisle of CIA identified the recipient.

Hilger continued to work for the CIA until December 4, 1953, when he returned to Germany and accepted a position with the West German Foreign Office. He retired in 1956 at the age of seventy and died in Munich in 1965 at age seventy-nine.[24]

CHAPTER 16

Diamonds, Radium, Rare Books, and Castle

Diamonds

Shipment 22: On May 23, 1945, Lt. Charles W. Bowen, Company E, 102nd Infantry Division, along with another officer and two enlisted men, were told to take a truck and report to the commander of the 30th Division Artillery at Gronigen, Germany. The party then questioned the German director of the mine who had no knowledge of the history of the valuables within the tunnels of the mine. Using help from the artillery division, the soldiers removed and loaded the seventy-two sealed boxes onto trucks. Prior to the arrival of Bowen, some officers of the artillery division had opened two boxes and discovered gold and platinum ingots. On May 26, the Foreign Exchange Depository received from Bowen fifty-eight containers (one open and contained broken glass jars), fourteen bags and one empty box. Following is Shipment 22:

1) 17 boxes contained platinum, iridium and rhodium
2) 14 packages contained platinum mash
3) 5 large wooden boxes contained diamonds, mostly identified as Dutch, with one large envelope of diamonds with the name Kessler-Georg.
4) the remaining boxes contained silver, candle holders, tableware, and hundreds of household valuables, generally described as "3 silver sauce bowls of which 2 are identical each carrying double sided handles and having the initials "S" engraved underneath, total weight 2,590 kilograms."[1]

The five large wooden boxes contained the following:

122.8 carats for 95 diamonds with no identifiable owners,
183.06 carats for 301 diamonds with no identifiable owners
1,549.77 carats for 15,032 diamonds with no identifiable owners
633.45 carats for 15,904 diamonds with no identifiable owners
644.25 carats for 15 lots of 818 diamonds with no identifiable owners
537.05 carats for 4,728 diamonds with no identifiable owners
1,914.28 carats for 19 lots of rose diamonds with no identifiable owners
332.33 carats for 3986 diamonds with no identifiable owners, including 1,152 8/8 diamonds and one lot of recut diamonds at 10.06 carats.

Total: 5,916.99 carats for 40,046 diamonds, 1,152,818 diamonds, nineteen lots of rose diamonds, fifteen lots of 818 diamonds and one lot of re-cut diamonds with no identifiable owners.

2,861.34 carats for 47,353 diamonds belonging to 67 individuals.
686.55 carats for 7,649 diamonds belonging to 25 owners.
705.66 carats for 5,900 diamonds belonging to 16 owners,
3,289.16 carats for 130,972 diamonds belonging to 12 owners and 184.5 grams of precious stones belonging to 1 owner.
46.04 carats for: 274 diamonds belonging to 4 owners.
666.31 carats for 21,666 diamonds belonging to 29 owners
31.44 carats for 233 diamonds belonging to 8 owners.

1,342.03 carats for 29,400 diamonds belonging to 23 owners.
2,851.42 carats for 253,744 diamonds belonging to 17 individuals.
1,378.32 carats for 26,018 diamonds belonging to 77 individuals.
1,280.58 carats for 65,578 diamonds belonging to 68 individuals.

Total: 15,138.85 carats for 588,787 diamonds belonging to 346 individuals, 184.5 grams of precious stones belonging to one individual.

The five boxes contained a total 21,055.84 carats of diamonds that had been removed from Arnhem in 1944, by the previously mentioned Mr. Erich Hagen and Herr Plumer. Most of the diamonds were still in the original Dutch envelopes with the owner name, and number of carats. From documentation, it appeared that the Dutch diamonds, along with a large cache of industrial diamonds, were sent by car from Berlin in March 1945, to Stutzerbach. The car stopped for a short time in nearby Strassfurt and the diamond were removed by Dr. R. Heraerus, deputy commissioner, and deposited in the Friedrichshall Salt Mine. Also in the five boxes, were 252 plain white glassine envelopes that did not bear any identification. The diamonds in these envelopes weighed 5,917.03 carats. There was a single envelope containing more than 1,000 diamonds weighing 141.93 carats with the name Martin Wolf.

The Foreign Exchange Depository had previously obtained the work sheets used in Berlin by Helmuth Schlaefer to check the weights of the Dutch diamonds. They also had access to Mr. Schlaefer who stated that some of the diamonds were sorted out and others sold. The German records report that 827.33 carats, belonging to Dr. Wijaberg, a Dutch citizen, had been sold. It appeared from German records that the Wolf diamonds had been sold to him from the collection of Dr. Wijaberg and Partie A, but in these hectic closing days of the war they had remained with the Dutch diamonds.

Schlaefer stated many of the diamonds bearing Jewish names had been segregated by the Nazis from the Dutch boxes and listed as Partie A and Partie B. The Partie A diamonds had a weight of 2,103.32 carats and Partie B 3,758.12 carats for a total of 5,771.44 carats an almost match to the gems in the white envelopes. German records showed that some diamonds from Partie A had been sold. Officials at the Foreign Exchange Depository were almost certain these diamond in the white unidentified envelopes and found in the Dutch boxes were indeed from the Netherlands. They worked the figures from Partie A, Partie B, the remaining Dr. Wijaberg and Martin Wolf's diamonds to within thirty-six carats of the weight of the valuables in the white envelopes.

The previous mentioned envelope of diamonds with the name Kessler-Goerg, came from Prague, Czechoslovakia. In the later part of 1944, Otto Goerg and Ludwig Schmidt traveled to Prague and took delivery of a large lot of jewelry from the Boehmische Escomptebank. They then returned to their diamond cutting firm in Idar-Oberstein, Germany and removed all of the stones from the settings and parceled them out to twenty-six different firms for re-cutting. This procedure was necessary as the stones were all of old fashion designs and re-cutting would enhance their value. In early 1945, two individuals came to Idar-oberstein and took delivery of the modernized stones that Goerg placed in a large manila envelope with the firms name Diamant-Kontor, Kessler-Goerg AFI. He knew nothing of the destination of the finished diamonds in the envelope. Not taken were ninety-eight carats of unfinished gems that remained with his firm. These diamonds were subsequently deposited at the Reichsbank Fulda with one carton of emeralds, one thirty carat opal, one twenty-five carat rose sapphire and one 150 carat topaz. Schmidt stated he was informed these valuables were removed two days prior to the arrival of US troops and sent north towards Berlin.

There was considerable discussion regarding the antique jewelry that was transported back to Germany by Goerg and Schmidt. The concern was that the valuables were liquidated assets previously owned by Jews who emigrated from Czechoslovakia, and placed in a fund established by the Reich protector of Bohemia and Moravia. After much debate, between officials of the Foreign Exchange Depository and Washington D.C. in July 1948, the diamonds from the envelope were returned to Czechoslovakia under claim 139C.[2]

Captain Smit-Kleine (center), head of the Netherlands mission, checks part of the $2,000,000 trove of Nazi looted gems. Looking on are Colonel William G. Brey (left) and Colonel Walter Kluss.

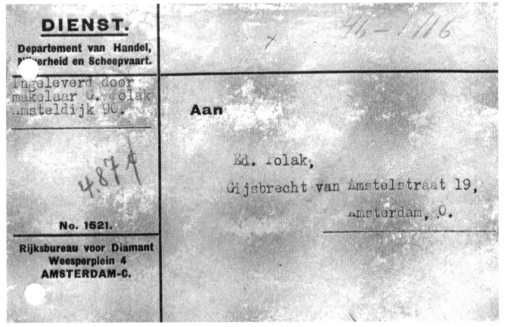

One of the many white envelopes containing Dutch diamonds. Today, these envelopes are in the National Archives.

In 1947, Dutch Captain Rudolf Smit-Kleine brought a claims list of the missing Dutch diamonds with him to the Foreign Exchange Depository. The list was in alphabetic order and the names, addresses, and envelopes in the Foreign Exchange Depository were matched to Kleine's list. The list positively identified 17,096.54 carats of diamonds.

At noon on August 28, 1947, a US Army truck with fifteen boxes of diamonds left Frankfurt with a jeep escort. The jeeps would be replaced by motorcycles upon reaching the Dutch border. Smit-Kleine followed the armed convoy in his car accompanied by Col. William G. Brey, Chief Foreign Exchange Depository. These diamonds were estimated in 1945 at two million dollars. One red, five carat stone alone was valued at $45,000. Another weighed nine carats alone, and thousands of others ranging in color from white through green, black and rose.

But the Partie A, Partie B and Martin Wolf remained in the Foreign Exchange Depository. Although the officials at the Foreign Exchange Depository were mum about the remaining diamonds, the Dutch officials were aware of the gems left behind.

After considerable debate, the US Army returned these diamonds with a 1947 appraised value of $774,857 to the Netherlands government on October 30, 1947.

By August 22, 1950, the thirty-one boxes of platinum, (more valuable than gold), iridium and rhodium had been determined to belong to Roges and I.G. Farben. They were returned to Osmar Beltzener, I.G. Farben control officer. Their disposition was finalized later in Shipment 121.

On November 9, 1949, the "remaining boxes" containing silverware was signed for by Intergovernmental Committee for Refuges, official George Wenzel. It appears the items were melted down into silver bars.

The gold in this Shipment 22, consisting of 5,270.401 Troy ounces of gold, was air freighted to the Bank of England in 1948 and placed into the account of the Tripartite Gold Commission.

Shipment 47: On July 3, 1945, the Foreign Exchange Depository received under Military Law 53 from the Gotha Reichsbank, three bags and three metal safe deposit boxes of industrial diamonds, 142.322 kilograms of platinum and two cardboard boxes of diamond tools. The valuables were delivered by Maj. Mack Terry, of the 102nd Infantry Division. The previous month the treasure had been reported to Lt. R.V. Stone, fiscal officer of Military Government Detachment I8 C9 by Max Uhlig, Chief of the Industrial Diamond Section located in Stutzerbach. Uhlig was not a German civil servant, but had been a diamond merchant prior to transferring in 1943 to the Minister of Armaments.

Lt. Stokes had the items taken from Uhilg and placed in the Reichsbank in Ilmenau pending instructions for the removal. The assessment of the diamonds was estimated to be more than 150,000 carats, and worth several million dollars.

Col. Rodney L. Mott, finance division, US Twelfth Army Group, then traveled to Stutzerbach and interviewed Max Uhlig, Hellmuth and other officials of the Diamond Section located in Stutzerbach. During the investigation, Uhlig claimed he had previously turned in the valuables of the company over to the US authorities under Military Law 53, and had intended to turn over the large cache of diamonds but had overlooked the diamonds, and forgotten about them. Uhlig assured Mott that these were all the diamonds that he was aware of under his administration.

Uhlig disclosed that the diamond tools that had earlier been seized by German authorities, were from a man in Leipzig who had been using them illegally. According to Uhlig, this man was still owed 23,000 Reichsmarks for the tools. Also, he said an inventory of the diamonds had been made in Berlin before the March 1945, shipment to Stutzerbach, but the papers had been burned with the approach of the American soldiers. Uhlig kept this shipment of diamonds from Berlin under his bed! In Berlin, the diamonds had been in the inventory maintained by ROGES (ROhstoff Handels GESellschaft), an armaments company controlled by the Reich Economics Ministry. These industrial diamonds were used to replenish merchants and firms using the diamonds under license from the German government.

A large number of diamonds, 20,000 to 30,000 carats a month, were used for war production in Germany. Before the war, industrial diamonds had been purchased largely from England and Belgium, but during hostilities these diamonds came as the results of an agreement signed in the summer of 1943 with the diamond firm, Forminere, located in Brussels. These large diamonds, as written in an earlier chapter, came from the Belgian Congo and had been seized by the French. Now with the German occupation of France, these gems were forcefully transferred to the rightful owner, Forminere. The bulk had come from this source. The second main source was purchased from various shady characters in France, and came in small lots of 1,000 carats and were sold to German agents in occupied France. These were sold at a very high price; several times the price before the war. Some of the French diamonds came from religious objects, horse bridles and other nefarious sources. The total amounted to approximately 22,000 carats, while the Netherlands supplied approximately 25,500. During the war, a few diamonds had also been obtained from Brazil and shipped through neutral ports. These diamonds at Stutzerbach had been graded and intermingled by ROGES making it impossible to identify them. As noted, the paper invoices regarding the diamonds had been intentionally burned.

In addition to these industrial diamonds, the Foreign Exchange Depository had received 639.6 carats of industrial diamonds from Kugelfischer, Schweinfurt, Germany (FED lot number 21-115).

The Kugelfischer and Stutzerbach industrial diamonds amounting to 165,457.69 carats of diamonds, valued then at $932,378.25, were restituted to the Belgian Mission for Restitution on October 16, 1950. Of these gems, the Netherlands received 1,783.06 carats containing some Dutch markings but designated "Congo Boort." These were appraised on October 16, 1950 with a 1945 value of $4,457.65. They were delivered to the acting consul of the Netherlands that month, although officers at the Foreign Exchange Depository were doubtful of the Dutch claim.

The bars of platinum were placed in the custody of the Bank Deutscher Laender on January 12, 1949.

A letter dated June 14, 1949, to the Foreign Exchange Depository from the Bipartite Control Office, Frankfurt, makes clear in the final settlement of Shipment 115. The letter explained that there were 639.6 carats originally taken by the US Army which were in the custody of the property control officer in Wuerzburg, Germany. The diamonds were to be sent to the FED and, "These diamonds are to be treated in the same manner was the 162,240.75 carats now in your custody and are a part of the original US Army seizure." Thus the FED still had in its possession a whopping 71.53 pounds of these valuable stones. The wooden container with these diamonds was received on June 30, 1949.

During the inventory of these gems, two paper envelopes contained the name of John C. Urbaneck, the German official who had tracked the original Congo diamonds reported in a previous chapter. This tied the diamonds to a Belgian claim. This shipment, containing 638.073 carats, was delivered to a Belgian Restitution Representative on November 10, 1950.[3]

Radium

While out hunting for beer, a German civilian found a metal box containing radium, hidden in a beer box, with other boxes stacked on top, in the brewery at Bad Salzungen. He took the radium in its black box lined with lead and held shut by wire, to Lt.Col. E.W. Moyers, Military Government Detachment 72 and here the radium was placed in the vault of the Deutscher Bank in Meiningen for safekeeping. On June 12, 1945, Capt. Archie E. Russell received verbal orders to delivery the radium, to the Foreign Exchange Depository. On June 15, the radium in the black lead lined box was brought to the Depository. Here, the metal box was initially refused, but after a demanding phone call from Maj.Gen. A.W. Kenner, Chief Medical Division, the radium was accepted as Shipment 30. Inside the box were two large and five small lead cylinders. The large cylinders were empty, but the small canisters each contained one sealed glass tube two centimeters long in which there was an inner sealed tube, one centimeter long containing a grayish-white powder. A letter was immediately written to the general discussing the hazards of handling this material.

As a safety precaution, the radium was stored in the most remote location in the Foreign Exchange Depository as Shipment 30. After considerable correspondence, it was delivered to Capt. Martha E. Howe, Office of the Theater Chief Surgeon, on November 19, 1945 for shipment to the United States.[4]

Seven vials of radium in a lead box were seized by the 11th Counter Intelligence Corps and sent to the Foreign Exchange Depository on March 8, 1948 as Shipment 91. A Geiger counter was used and indicated a moderate to heavy level of exposure. Two days later it was sent to Berlin for evidence in a trial with a note it should be returned after the trial. There is no evidence that the radium was returned to the Foreign Exchange Depository.[5] Thus the only case of failure in security for Col. Brey in obtaining the proper release form.

On November 28, 1947, the US 11th Criminal Investigation Division was notified that Dr. Fritz Bahr, residing in Berlin Charlottenburg, had in his possession about forty-five milligrams of radium that he offered for sale on the black market. From a subsequent investigation, it had been revealed that about fifty milligrams of this substance had been put up for sale by a French Public Safety Officer, who misappropriated it from stocks of war material turned over to his office by the German police. The wholesale price of the radium increased, and finally reached a price of three million Reichsmarks. In addition to the French connection, Dr. Bahr offered about ten milligrams of radium from his own stock. The 1945 value of this radioactive substance of five glass vials, with ten milligrams each was valued at about $300,000.

Nine men including Dr. Bahr were arrested and the radium was seized by Mr. W.T. Babcock, US Occupation Government, Berlin. They were tried, found guilty, and the radium was confiscated and forfeited. These vials in a lead container were tallied in at the Foreign Exchange Depository on March 12, 1948 as Shipment 94. On April 27, 1948, the lead box with the vials were released to George W. Brossard, Chief Prosecutor, Occupation Military Government for delivery to the Public Health Branch, Military Government, Berlin for use in treatment of German civilians in the American Sector of Berlin.[6]

Books

The Mainz Psalter is the earliest dated example of printed matter issuing from the new moveable-print technology of the Gutenberg press. It was ordered by the Mainz archbishop in 1457. In the early Middle Ages, Psalters, containing the Book of Psalms were amongst the most popular types of illuminated manuscripts. They often included a calendar, a litany of saints, and hymns containing words from the Old and New Testaments.

By 1948, the Mainz Psalter was in the United States, but it had originated from the Landesbibliothek in Dresden. During the war, the German government sent the rare books from Dresden for safekeeping to Czechoslovakia. When the Germans were driven out of that country, these books were left in Czech territory and were taken by the Russians. Apparently, some Russian soldier "liberated" the Psalter while it was en route to Moscow, and sold it to Prague bookseller, Vladimir Zikes.

The Czech dealer wrote to New York bookseller Herbert Reichner, asking him if he would be interested in selling a copy of the Psalter. Mr. Reichner answered that of course he would, thinking that it might be merely a facsimile, but being curious to know what it was all about.

When the book arrived in New York, Mr. Reichner was somewhat terrified to find that it was obviously the Dresden copy, in its original pigskin binding. His first inclination was to return it to the Czech dealer, but before doing so he decided to seek the advice of William A. Jackson, Librarian of the Houghton Library of Harvard University. On February 10, 1948, Jackson traveled to Washington and called upon an old friend, who stated that he was in charge of such matters in the State Department. They agreed that a trusteeship should be set up consisting of the Librarians of Congress, the Morgan Library, and Harvard, any two of whom would be empowered to decide when it was proper for the book to be returned to Dresden. The State Department approved that the book would be placed into the custody of the Harvard Library under the control of these trustees, and Harvard would endeavor to reimburse the Czech bookseller $10,000 for his service to civilization in preserving the book intact.

On the April 23, 1948, after some delays, Jackson wrote that he had every confidence from the assurances that the matter would soon be completed. The Department of State had a completely different view on this subject and wrote, in a top secret memo condemning the methods of America's oldest university: "In sharp contrast with the cooperation the Department of State has generally received from American museums and libraries, it may be asserted that the 1475 Mainz Psalter has been recovered by the Department in spite of the lack of cooperation from the Librarian of the Houghton Library of Harvard University."

The seized Mainz Psalter was placed in the custody of Collector of Customs in New York, and from there sent to the Foreign Exchange Depository where it was tallied as Shipment 118 on May 24, 1950. On June, 20, 1950, one steel banded carton said to contain a valuable religious book known as the Mainz Psalter was signed for by representatives of the US Wiesbaden Collection Point.[7] On April 12, 1951, this prized book was signed over to the Minister President of Hesse by Cultural Affairs Advisor, Thomas Carr Howe.

The medieval "Book of Hours" was deposited as Shipment 98 in the Foreign Exchange Depository, on May 14, 1948, by General George H. Weems – under restriction that it only be released by his order. The valuable book was released to Theodore Heinrich MFA & A Branch in Wiesbaden on July 7, 1948. Here it was assigned property number WIE 5546 and identified as from the Belton House, of Flemish origin about 1500. The book was further identified as an illuminated prayer book, containing painted miniatures with scenes of the life of Christ. It was presumed to be German property and transferred to the Hessian Minister President on June 26, 1951.

Castle

One of greatest robberies of all times was the theft of the Hesse Crown jewels, stolen after World War II from the Kronberg Castle by Maj. David Watson, Col. Jack Durant and his lover Capt. Kathleen Nash.

Kronberg Castle was requisitioned as a country club for US Army officers and Capt. Kathleen Nash was appointed hostess of the officer's club. In November 1945, while exploring the castle, Nash and her staff stumbled upon a wooden box full of several individually brown-paper-wrapped packages, containing millions of dollars' worth of valuables. Watson, Durant, and Nash removed the diamonds and other gems by pushing them from their settings or cutting them loose from the various tiaras, necklaces and bracelets and then sold the gold settings in Switzerland.

In January 1946, after the three looters had returned to the US with the bulk of the valuables, a member of the Hesse family reported the missing jewels to the US Army. Investigations by the Army's Criminal Intelligence Division determined the magnitude of the theft, and Watson, Durant and Nash were thereafter arrested. The three were tried in Germany and sentenced to light prison terms. The trials were completed in the spring of 1947.

The Army relentlessly attempted to recover the jewels. Half of them were recovered at the home of Nash's sister. After a further search, the remaining bulk was traced to underground criminal elements in Chicago. Understandably, these larger and more valuable precious stone were never recovered.

The U.S. Army exhibited the valuables recovered in Kathleen Nash sister's attic. When asked how much of the valuables were mailed to her sister, Nash responded: "I think I probably have [mailed] about one-half, I mean the small stuff."

But were all of the valuables stolen? On October 21, 1947, four months after the trial, PFC Raymond L. Floyd, RA 12273302, opened a drawer of a writing desk in a cottage on the grounds of the Kronberg Castle. Here in two boxes he found the following:

Prayer book with velvet cover and 18 carats gold decoration bearing the royal cost of arms of which the first pages are covered with an autograph signed by the Princess of Hesse in 1883 regarding the history of the different owners of the Royal family of Hesse from 1794 to 1938.

A book containing famous autographs bearing signatures of royal and princely personalities as well as those of eminent statesmen of the period beginning 1830 and ending 1845.

A bundle of autographed letters of which his Royal Highness Charles of Hesse is the addressee and prominent personalities of that time.

A Daguerreotype portrait of Prince Ann of Prussia at 10 years of age. The portrait was in a letter case.

Autographed manuscripts of his Highness Charles of Hesse and letters copies dating from 1918 to 1933. Among other are his correspondence with the French occupation authorities of 1918 and copies of his correspondence with Princess Hermine (written about in Shipment 87) as well as those of two letters from Hitler and Hermann Göring.

Three ancient paintings, Wilhelm VII Landgrafen of Hesse, Oval painting on ivory and a rectangular painting on wood.

A miniature of Princess Louis of Hesse in a case.

Four unframed silhouettes in oval form in a case.

Three framed silhouettes in round form.

A framed miniature bearing of a autograph of Wilhelm I, grand duke of Hesse.

Fifteen engraved crystals and a cameo, all set in a velvet stand.

A watch chain adorned with a medal and a pennant, all in 14 carat gold.

One 14 carat gold seal decorated with an agate engraved with coat of arms of the House of Hesse.

A pair of salt cellars in blue crystal with silver lid.

Seventeen ancient miniatures of which 14 are painted on metal, two on ivory and one on a shell.

One 14 carat gold signet ring belonging to Wilhelm of Hesse decorated with an agate engraved with the House Coat of Arms

A 18 carat gold pocket watch bearing enamel coat of arms

gold 18 carat pocket watch, Patek and Phillippe decorated with the Hesse Coat of Arms in enamel.

Two pendants bearing the arms and the device of the House of Hesse. The larger pendant is in metal. The smaller pendant is in 18 carats gold.

One 14 carat gold medallion bearing inside a miniature adorned with roses diamonds and decorated with enamel.

A 18 carat gold power box adorned with blue enamel carved inside in a case.

A 18 carat pocket watch, Breguet, decorated with 78 pearls, blue enamel back with18 carats gold chain.

One ancient silver piece of money with Johann Frederic's effigy, bearing the date of 1544.

One low grade silver memorial medal with the portrait of Ernst Ludwig—Elenore.

A silver, gold and metal center in two pieces, decorated with diamonds, rose diamonds and enamel.

One 14 carat gold and silver medal, decorated with diamonds and rose diamonds, the center in enamel with ribbons

These ornaments were handed over to Capt. R. Martin who made an inventory. He then turned the valuables over to the guards of the 18th Infantry Regiment. Were these items really in the cottage and overlooked for 2½ years or did someone(s) lose their nerve after the above courts-martial?

The items were delivered to the Foreign Exchange Depository on October 22, 1947 by Col. E.H. Harrelson and Lt. W.W. Woodside on behalf of the Command General as Shipment 89. Seven months later on May 18, 1948, these valuables were signed for by US Lt. Alexander S. Gottlieb. They left the Depository and their fate remains unknown.[9]

In a classic case of closing the barn door after the horse is gone, the silverware from the Kronberg Castle officer's club was removed on January 7, 1947 and deposited in the Foreign Exchange Depository for protective custody as Shipment 92. The silver contained the usual fork, knives, spoon, and thirty-one silver candlesticks. These five boxes were also returned on May 18, 1948 and signed for by Lt. Alexander S. Gottlieb.[10]

A Mixture of Gold, Silver, Coins, Religious Objects, and Sundry Items

Gold

Shipment 23A: Discovered on May 12, 1945, at the Reichsbank in Holzminden by Capt. J.C. Wallace, Military Governor of Holzminden, were one box and five bags sealed with Nazi swastikas. Bank officials stated that they had received the packages on March 29, 1945, with instructions to hold the packages in the bank vault for two or three weeks, and then someone would retrieve them. The markings identified the sacks as being from Marseilles, France. Wallace and several senior officers of the Ninth Army examined the containers. Bag one was packed full with 4,615 gold coins that included U.S., 170—$20 gold coins, thirty-five—$10 gold coins, one—$2.50 gold coin and $10,890 in US currency. Additional gold coins were British, French, Italian, Dutch, Portugal, Belgium, Swiss, as well as gold bars and pieces. This bag contained valuable jewels that included twenty-four chronograph watches, twenty-two pearls, forty rubies, twenty-one ladies wristwatches, each eighteen-carat gold and many more gems including a five carat diamond. The remaining bags contained the same high quality ill-gotten gains.

On May 17, 1945, at about 6:00 in the evening, these picking,s estimated to weigh one ton, were delivered to the G-5 Finance Branch, Ninth Army, by Lt. Vincent Monachelle, Military Government Detachment I2 B9. Monachelle was in a big hurry to leave, and when asked if he had an inventory, he replied that one had been made and was inaccurate and not signed. The lieutenant was given a handwritten receipt for the one box and four bags. Later, the box and five bags tied with a string were spot-checked and the inventory did indeed prove to be highly inaccurate. The items were stored in a large wall safe in the executive office. On May 30, 1945, the box and bags were removed from the wall safe, and transferred to the Foreign Exchange Depository as Shipment 23A and were delivered under the command of Capt. George Hackleman.

Previously removed from box five for "special handling," were three large diamond ring and five cut diamonds, two bracelets, one gold necklace, two watches and several more uncut diamonds. These were taken by Maj. James P. Jamieson who traveled by aircraft to transport them to the Foreign Exchange Depository on June 15, 1945, as a partial delivery of shipment 23A.

Many of the items had indeed been taken from Marseille, France. They had been removed by the Germans from the treasury of Bouches-du-Rhône and contained securities, jewels, gold coins, and bank notes. Other parts of the treasure had been seized by the Germans in May 1940, from the Marseille airport along with the Clipper airship that was to fly the cargo to Amsterdam. Unfortunately, by May 10, 1940, Amsterdam was then under German occupation.

On March 30, 1949, the valuables uncovered at the Holzminden Reichsbank, were released to the French Mission for Restitution.[1]

Shipment 23B: On May 11, 1945, Lt. John C. Shinn, Counter Intelligence Corp, 8th Infantry Division, and a German interpreter, Klaus, "acting on the basis of confidential information" dug up a box of gold coins, bars and currency. The valuables were reported to have been previously taken by the Gestapo stationed in Schwerin, Germany.

The box included fifty-three—$10 gold coins, 346—$20 gold coins, more gold coins and 120,000 in Swiss paper currency, valued at $27,840 in 1945 and released to Maj. James P. Jamison, G-5, Twelfth Army Group on May 29, 1945, by William W. Young, USA 20173729, driver, from the 507 Car Company. This box was delivered to the Foreign Exchange Depository on May 30 the same time as shipment 23A. It was assigned shipment number 23B. Very little is documented regarding 23B.

Even Col. William Brey was stymied by this shipment, and tried unsuccessfully to contact Lt. Shinn in civilian life in 1947 seeking additional information.[2]

Shipment 24: In the closing days of the war, PFC Nicholas S. Chopper, and two of his buddies all of Company G, 318 Infantry Regiment, were given orders to remain in the mountainous village of Alt Aussee and guard prisoners, as well as round up other straggling German soldiers as they came into the village. During this time they noticed a bag lying along the side of the road and handed it over to their commanding officer, Capt. Gabriel R. Martinez. The bag contained gold coins as follows: 449 US $20, 237 French 20 franc, thirty-two Swiss 20 franc, twenty-four Italian 20 lire, sixty-five Belgian 20 franc, three Yugoslavian 20 dinara, one Austrian 20 franc.

The gold coins were deposited in the Foreign Exchange Depository on June 1, 1945 as Shipment 24.[3] There is no documentation as to the discarding of these coins but they may have been relinquished to Austria as part of the Allied Gold Pot.

Shipment 72: The Counter Intelligence Corps, Headquarters US Forces Europe recovered 1,750 British Sovereign gold coins based on information from Consul Carl Berthold Franz Rekowski of the German legation in Budapest. The gold coins had been an emergency reserve fund of the former German consulate at Budapest, Hungary. These nickel-sized coins were first introduced in 1816, and became the world's most widely distributed coin.

The forty-five-year-old Rekowski had lived previously in Dallas, New York and Mexico, and his work involved oil shipments to Germany. Leaving the US in 1940, he traveled via Japan and Russia before returning to Germany and being assigned as German counsel in Budapest. With the danger of the advancing Soviet Army, he left Budapest with the emergency funds of gold coins and buried them in a barn at St. Anna just across the Austrian border at Ering, Germany. During an interrogation by US Army personnel, Rekowski disclosed the gold and location. The coins were deposited in the Foreign Exchange Depository on October 20, 1945 by Col. Dupre Sassard, G-2 Seventh Army, as Shipment 72.[4]

Shipment 77: On December 18, 1945, the Office of Political Affairs in Berlin, Germany received a telegram that gold was under US naval guard at the former German embassy in Madrid, Spain. The telegram explained that they had approximately 115,641 English sovereigns, in approximately thirty-two boxes plus a sack and a half. Also, the telegram stated that they had five boxes and one sack of gold coins from a previous delivery. This had been from the former German embassy in Lisbon, Portugal, and contained 5,000 English gold sovereigns, in coin rolls of forty in each packet. The total gold amounted to $43,219, in 1945. The coins from Madrid consisted of 322 miscellaneous coins, and twenty kilograms of gold bars. The telegram insisted that the gold be received immediately by Army officials in Frankfurt as it was "increasingly embarrassing" that the gold was still in Spain.

The naval officials insisted on an expedited transport. They would provide a C-47 and fly the cargo out immediately. These navy plans were not carried out, and later an army C-47, s.n.43-15647, finally left Madrid with the gold on December 26, 1945, at eight in the morning and flew by way of Marseille, arriving in Frankfurt at 3:00pm. It was initially under guard by the navy. Upon unloading the aircraft, the safeguarding of the gold was the responsibility of the US army. The navy insisted upon a signed release for the valuable cargo.[5] These coins and bars were accepted by the Foreign Exchange Depository on December 26, 1945 as Shipment 77. Later, in the Foreign Exchange Depository, a 100kr Austrian Gold Coin and a US $10 gold coin, dated 1915 were added to the collection. The valuables remained in the Depository under protective custody until 1952 when they were shipped by air to the Federal Reserve Bank in New York City.[6]

Shipment 83: In a whimsical turn of events, that underscores the mishmash of "gold fever" that gripped some individuals during the war, the Foreign Exchange Depository added an additional 3.3

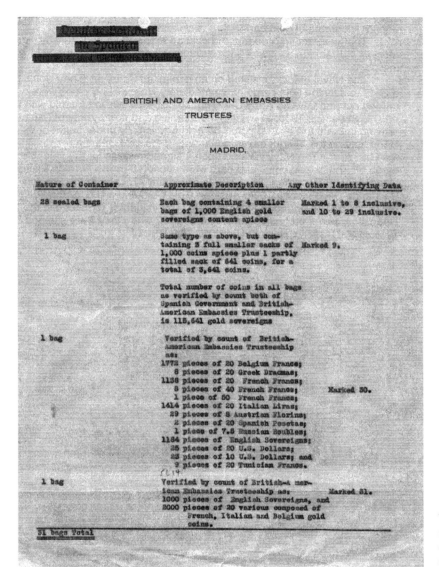

The inventory of the valuables removed from the German embassy in Madrid, Spain and sent to Frankfurt, Germany.

pounds of gold to its vaults on March 12, 1947. A single small gold bar was retrieved from Anton A. Volsic of Louisville, Colorado. He had found the gold near Tetz, Germany, in the spring of 1945; it was stamped "RT 997-6" and bore the imprint of the Prussian state mint.

In the summer of 1946, Volsic took his prize to the United States Mint in Denver, Colorado, and attempted to exchange it for cash. It was explained to him that he could either give the gold to US authorities, or face the possibility of going to jail, because in 1946 it was a criminal offense for an American to own monetary gold. Volsic grudgingly signed a statement relinquishing his right to the gold and assigning it to the United States. Because of his signing this document, the US Army agreed not to prosecute Mr. Volsic.

The Department of State arranged to waive all regulations pertaining to the exportation of gold and the United States mint shipped by air the bar of confiscated gold to Berlin. The gold bar weighing 48.68 Troy ounces was picked up by an armed guard and transferred to the Foreign Exchange Depository as Shipment 83.[7]

Shipment 80: On August 16, 1946, Dr. Waldemar Meier, Prisoner of War, wrote the following:

> On 1 December 1944, I was transferred from NCO-training school at Radolfzell where I was employed as a dentist to the dental services of the medical detachment of the Waffen-SS. On 26 April 1945, after this office was transferred to Munich, I received an order from my chief, SS Oberstrumbannführer Dr. Johannsen to take the gold of the office to Prien/Chiemsee and secure it. If it would be impossible to secure it in Prien, I should bring it to Traunstein, to where I transferred as a dentist. On about 1 may 1945, I dug in the gold at the outskirts of Grabenstaett/Chiemsee, caused by that order. Another part was dug in at a farm in Burghausen.
>
> This concerns the following:
>
> In the wood of Grabenstaett: Plate of gold, gold cast for dental purposes from gold refinery, Degussa. Total weight ca. 30 kg.
>
> At farm in Burghausen: 1 bar silver-gold compound weight ca. 8 kg. Old gold in a small box.
>
> The plate of gold and the gold cast mentioned in paragraph 1 are secured in a box and a wooden box
>
> I submit this report since I have learned that all devices therefore rare metals also have to be reported.

> s/ Dr. Waldemar Meier.

The statement was delivered to Lt. B.T. Causgrove, Provost Marshal, who was skeptical of the buried gold. Dr. Meier was questioned as to the reason for his reporting the gold cache rather than waiting until his release from the POW camp and securing the gold for his personal gains. The doctor stated that, "the knowledge had been weighing on his mind, that the gold was not his personal property, and that he wished to turn it in and clear his conscience."[8]

Dr. Meier did not wait more than a year to disclose the gold just to "clear his conscience." Through underground sources, someone surely informed him the gold had been discovered and removed.

Causgrove convinced his superiors to allow him to search for the gold. On a Friday morning, August 23, 1946, Causgrove, Lt. Gandell, and a few enlisted men along with Dr. Meier searched the wooded area in the vicinity of Grabenstaett. Under Meier's direction, lines were strung for reference points and two empty holes were found. In one hole was a wooden box that the Dr. identified as having originally held part of the gold. The entire area was searched with a Signal Corps mine detector without success.

The party then proceeded to Burghausen and visited the home of Kneittingen a friend of Dr. Probst, another SS dentist, who had accompanied Meier when the gold was buried. The only person at home was Justine Kneittingen, age seventeen, who denied any knowledge of the location of the gold. Lt. Gandell interrogated her for approximately one half hour at which time she admitted knowing where the gold was buried and led them to a spot in the family garden.

After digging in this area to a depth of about two feet, they uncovered one cash box with eleven smaller boxes and one large bar presumable mixed gold and silver was found with a stamp on the bar indicating it weighed 10.75kg. The eleven boxes all contained gold in various forms.

The entire garden was searched with the mine detector without success. Two caches reported by Dr. Meier were not recovered. Causgrove continued his investigation. His results are unknown

The gold was deposited in the Foreign Exchange Depository on October 2, 1948 as Shipment 80. Later the dental gold in Shipment 80 was turned over to the Intergovernmental Committee for Refugees.[9]

Shipment 86: In the closing days of the war, Col. P.C. McElvee, Judge Advocate General, Seventh

Army picked up from the Dachau concentration camp, twelve pounds 1½ ounces of gold teeth and fillings. He delivered this gruesome trove to Headquarters, 7708 War Crimes Group. Two years later on July 19, 1947, these teeth and filings were delivered to the Foreign Exchange Depository as Shipment 86. This gold alloy was disposed of with the Intergovernmental Committee for Refugees.[10]

Shipment 93: A number of gold coins and jewelry, identified as former Jewish possessions from unknown owners safeguarded in the Reichsbank Karlsruhe, was deposited in the Foreign Exchange Depository as Shipment 93 on March 8, 1948, and turned over to the Intergovernmental Committee for Refugees.[11]

Silver

Shipment 56: An officer of the US Army Signal Corps uncovered a large quantity of silver at the Afga photographic plant of I.G. Farben at Wolfen, Germany. The silver was placed in safekeeping by the US Ninth Army and arrangement was made for it to be sold through Twelfth Army Group channels.

Thus approved by the Army, this large amount of silver, 69,212.623 kilograms value in 1945 at $1,466,721.21, was exported through the Office of the deputy purchasing agent for Belgium, the Netherlands, and Luxembourg. The ore was shipped between May 20 and May 25, 1945, before it was known by Army authorities that silver was excluded from commodities exportable from Germany.

It was therefore brought back from Liege, Belgium and delivered to the Foreign Exchange Depository on July 29, 1945, as Shipment 56. The silver was delivered to the Bank Deutscher Laender on September 10, 1948, and used in German industrial plants.[12]

Shipment 85: The origin of the deposit of a large amount of silver into the Foreign Exchange Depository as Shipment 85 is well reported by Lt. Ernest F. Hauser and follows:

> June 19, 1947
> At approximately 11:30pm on June 11, 1947, the undersigned officer apprehended four people driving a Horch Sedan, license no.ASC 2625013. Papers for the vehicle looked forged. It was the standard British Army Book 412. No official stamps were in it. The travel orders were like those usually carried by Poles of the II Corps. At two previous occasions, Kiefersfelden and Wilheim, vehicles and their occupants have been apprehended carrying contraband to Italy with orders issued by either Allied Forces, Headquarters Italy, or Allied Screening Commission. These four men professing to be Norwegians had the same style order and also stated they came from Milan on the 9th, crossing at Füssion, went to Frankfurt and now were on their return trip. The personal identification by the four was identical. All were made out for Scandinavian sounding names. Under questioning the men stated they were Norwegians attached to Allied Screening Commission in Italy. They wore US OD and English Khaki uniforms with English Lieutenant pips sewed on the shoulder straps.

After examining the papers, Hauser requested the four to follow him to a military housing compound where the men were detained for the night. The following morning, the vehicle was searched by US military police and they found under the floor boards, in the trunk and in a tool chest; roughly 1,000 pounds of silver, many silver coins in two five-gallon gas cans.

After a short interrogation the men admitted they were Poles and gave their "true" names of Boleslaw Skalski, Maninek Bulka, Zdislaw Przybyl and Igo Blaugrund. After additional investigation, Skalski admitted his name was Karsz Waclaw.

Waclaw had previously been arrested by US authorities for being illegally involved with carrying tires to Italy, but was released. Karsz had been a resident of Munich since 1945. He was a member of the Provisional Polish Brigade which had quite a black market fame connected with the Brigade members. It was rumored that Karsz was involved with the counterfeiting of various currencies. Przbyl was also a member of the Brigade, involved in the black market when he resided in Italy. He was a long time friend of Karsz.

Blaugrund was a Polish Jew, born August 29, 1917. He had provided the identification papers, travel orders, and car papers for this trip. Blaugrund told the US investigators that he had purchased the silver from inmates of the Jewish Displaced Person Camp, Zeilheim, located near Frankfurt for a sum totaling 300,000 Reichsmarks (1945 value $30,000). He and Bulka, also Jewish, had approached the camp in civilian clothes and asked about buying silver.

Hauser further wrote:

> During the investigation of the original arrestees of the Kiefersfelden incident and some additional Poles still in Italy were brought out as members of an organized black market ring. It is almost impossible to ascertain the vast amount of goods and raw material that have been illegally exported to Italy by this band. Evidence was found in Karsz's papers that he had previous shipments of tin, needles for automatic weaving machines, pencil lead and automobile tires. It seems that this so called Polish Brigade has fostered this action all along and as a matter of fact has supported itself from it.
>
> In view of these facts it seem most important that border post be re-instructed so no foreigner could bluff his way in or out of the US Zone.

The silver, with a total weight of 1,028 pounds twelve ounces, was sent to the Foreign Exchange Depository on July 10, 1947 as Shipment 85. At the FED it was determined that the small, unmarked silver bars were apparently melted down silver objects. On January 12, 1949, these items were transferred to the custody of the Bank Deutscher Laender.[13] The exception to this transfer was two US silver dimes, that would later be turned over to the United States Treasury.

Religious Objects

Shipment 19: In early May 1945, Lt. Lamont Moore, Monuments Fine Art and Archival Officer, was assigned the task of removing the treasure of the Cathedral of Posen from the Brauschweig-Lüneberg salt mine at Grasleben. The request was made at the request of Gen. William H. Simpson, Commander Ninth Army. The treasure consisting of:

> 2 cases marked 1 and 2 labeled Posen Domkirche
> 1 case marked 3 labeled Collect, Schrwa und Lissa
> 2 cases marked 4 and 5, labeled Posen Domkirche
> 2 cases marked 6 and 7, labeled Silber Kirchengerät
> 1 case marked II labeled Lissa Collection
> 4 chest unmarked
> 1 trunk marked Edelmetal 1
> 1 box marked #5 which has been smashed
> 1 object wrapped in burlap said to be Processional Cross
> 87 cases said to contain gold and silver monstrance and shrines.

The above was turned over to the Foreign Exchange Depository on May 14, 1945 by Moore as Shipment 19. On September 4, 1945, these items were shipped to the U.S Wiesbaden Collection Point.[14]

These religious symbols, deposited as Shipment 19, from the Cathedral of Posen, one of the oldest churches in Poland are being displayed for the civilian radio reporters (right) who were guests of General Dwight D. Eisenhower and touring throughout the military government installations in Frankfurt. Civilians were required to wear a type of military uniform during this stage of the war.

Shipment 26B contained the valuables from the Czechoslovakian authorities, as well as citizens, seized by Germany forces during the occupation of that country. Many of these assets were identifiable by name and address of the persecuted victims of the Gestapo. Even the martyred town of Lidice, destroyed by the Nazis in revenge for the killing of Reinhard Heydrich, was listed. From Lidice, as a reminder of this tragedy, were twenty-four wedding rings, other rings and some tooth bridgework. On their retreat from the advancing Soviet Army, the Nazis removed these objects from the property office in Prague and deposited them in the Regensburg Reichsbank.

They were subsequently discovered by the US Army, and on June 9, 1945, the director of Regensburg Reichsbank was ordered to release the Czech valuables to Military Government Detachment F1 D3 for shipment to Frankfurt. Here, on that date, it was deposited in the Foreign Exchange Depository as Shipment 26B. Accompanying the shipment from Regensburg was Lt. John J. Stack.

There were forty-three bars of silver, averaging twenty-five kilograms each, and the non-inventoried items contained nine suitcases, four large wooden boxes, a cardboard carton said to contain jewelry and securities and a sack containing the tabernacle of a Russian Orthodox Church. The jewelry was packed in individual paper with the name of the original proprietor. The silver bars were stamped "HG" by jeweler Hans Grünfeld, in Prague. Additionally, the bars were marked with a number, net weight in grams and refinement.

The tabernacle, a beautiful piece of exquisite workmanship, stood about three feet tall with a base of about one foot. The various inscriptions on the object were of a religious significance. It was a miniature church with a door on one side in which was a space that may have kept communion bread, and was looted from a Russian Orthodox Church in Prague. Its packing on arrival in Frankfurt gave little evidence of its importance or value since it was contained in on old cardboard carton inside a rather dirty burlap bag. Undoubtedly, such an item was irreplaceable as the miniature tabernacle was transferred to the Wiesbaden Collection Point. It was removed by Capt. Edith A. Standen, the then director of the Collection Point.

Chapter 17

This Russian Orthodox Religious Tabernacle stands about three feet high and is constructed of ornamental gold. It contained various inscriptions of religious significance. The cultural and religious significance of this piece makes it of irreplaceable value. This religious ornament was taken for safekeeping by the U.S. Army in Germany during the late combat phase.

Shipment 26B was released in it entirety, by the Foreign Exchange Depository on October 21, 1949, to the Czechoslovakian Mission for Restitution. This restitution included the tabernacle from the Wiesbaden Collection Point.[15]

Shipment 26A: Also in the vault of the Reichsbank Regensburg were thirty bars of gold weighing about 792 pounds that were furnished to Lt. John J. Stack, Military Government Detachment F1D3. These bars were delivered to the Foreign Exchange Depository along with shipment 26B on June 9, by the lieutenant. It was determined the bars belonged to the Berlin Reichsbank. Later smelt numbers identified the gold bars as being of Belgian origin.[16]

The gold in this shipment, consisting of 11,929.545 Troy ounces of gold, was air freighted to the Bank of England in 1948 and deposited into the account of the Tripartite Gold Commission.

CONTAINER NO. 1154

5848	I	9 crosses, 14 carats gold, decorated with imitation stones
	II	4 pairs of earrings, 14 carats gold, and 1 small chain decorated with imitation stones
	III-1	1 pair of cuff links, 14 carats gold and
		1 pair of shirt studs, 14 carats gold, adorned with imitation stones
	-2	10 medallions, 14 carats gold, set with imitation stones
	-3	1 pair of earrings, 14 carats gold and
		10 brooches, 14 carats gold set with imitation stones
	-4	5 barettes, 14 carats gold, decorated with imitation stones
	-5	1 pendentive with chain, 14 carats gold, decorated with imitation stones
5853	I -1	5 rings, 14 carats gold, decorated with cultured and Japanese pearls
	-2	12 rings, 14 carats gold, decorated with topases and amethysts
5854	I	13 rings, 14 carats gold, with cultured and Japanese pearls and diamonds
	II	10 rings, 14 carats gold, adorned with diamonds, topases, aquamarines
	III	8 rings, 14 carats gold, adorned with rose diamonds, cultured and Japanese pearls
	IV	6 rings, 14 carats gold, and 1 pair of earrings, 14 carats gold, adorned with rose diamonds and imitation stones
5855	I	1 watch, women's, 14 carats gold, decorated with diamonds and rubies
	II	1 watch, women's, 14 carats gold, decorated with diamonds and rose diamonds
	III	1 watch, women's, 14 carats gold, decorated with rose diamonds
	IV	1 watch, women's, 14 carats gold, decorated with rose diamonds

- 2 -

Shipment 26: page 181 of 234 typed pages with individual names.

```
13489 (15)  Item 8      Kratkornsky,  XXIII    1 pair of shirt studs, 14
            L II/121    Vaclav                   carats gold, with diamonds
            4259                       XXIV     1 pair of ear-rings, 14 ca-
                                                rats white gold, with Ja-
                                                panese pearls and diamonds
                                       XXV      1 ring, 14 carats gold, with
                                                an imitation stone
                                       XXVI     1 wrist watch, women's, 14
                                                carats gold, with diamonds
                                       XXVII    1 pair of ear-rings, 14 ca-
                                                rats gold
                                       XXVIII   1 brooch, 14 carats gold,
                                                with 1 imitation stone
                                       XXIX     1 cross, 14 carats gold
                                       XXX      1 pendentive with chain, 14
                                                carats gold, with a rose
                                                diamond
                                       XXXI     1 ring, 14 carats gold, with
                                                diamonds
                                       XXXII    2 wedding-rings, 14 carats
                                                gold
                                       XXXIII   1 wrist watch, women's, 14
                                                carats gold

13489 (16)  Item 8      Groeschel,    I        1 cigarette case, 18 carats
            L II/175    Irma                    gold, with enamel
                                       II       2 pocket watches, men's, 14
                                                carats gold
                                       III      2 pocket watches, women's,
                                                18 carats gold, with rose
                                                diamonds and semi-pearls
                                       IV       1 pair of cuff links, 14 ca-
                                                rats gold
                                       V        1 ring, 14 carats gold, with
                                                agate
                                       VI       1 ring, 18 carats gold, with
                                                an imitation ruby and 2
                                                rose diamonds
                                       VII      1 ring, 14 carats gold
                                       VIII     1 medallion, 14 carats gold
                                       IX       1 fountain pen, 18 carats
                                                gold
                                       X        2 metal pencils
                                       XI       2 brooches, 14 carats gold,
                                                with enamel
                                       XII      1 cigarette lighter, 14 ca-
                                                rats gold
                                       XIII     2 medallions, one in 14 ca-
                                                rats gold the other one in
                                                metal
                                       XIV      1 cigarette holder end, 14
                                                carats gold and amber
                                       XV       1 metal monocle
```

Shipment 26: page 181 of 234 typed pages with individual names.

Shipment 26C: During hostilities, members of the US 166th Field Artillery found one bag and one box of gold in a hay wagon by the train station in Haidhausen, Austria. The unit moved back to Furth and the gold consisting of Austrian gold coins and gold bullion was retrieved by Lt. John J. Stack, Military Government Detachment F1 D3. Delivered with the above two shipments, as shipment C, it consisted of 1,817 gold Austrian Ducats, and twelve bars of gold bullion. The bars weighed 290.090 troy ounces with a 1945 value of $10,153.15.[17]

The gold in this shipment consisted of 491.050 Troy ounces of gold was air freighted to the Bank of England in 1948 and deposited into the account of the Tripartite Gold Commission.

Berlin Coin Collection

Shipment 102 was a repackaging of the majority of the rare coins, consolidated into Shipment 97 with the silver coins collected under Military Law 52. They were repackaged under Shipment 102 on May 27, 1948. This was done under written orders on May 10, 1948, by Jack Bennett, Finance Adviser to the Military Governor, as follows:

> Pursuant to authority granted with letter, subject: "Removal from Foreign Exchange Depository, Reichsbank Building, Frankfurt" dated 1 March 1948, you are hereby authorized to release to the duly accredited representative of the Monuments, Fine Art and Archival Section, Restitution Branch, Property Division, OMGUS, the numismatic coins listed in Schedule A, B, C and D attached hereto. The letter and each of the schedules bears my signature.

It is understood that Schedule A and B represent the coins found by US Forces in the Merkers Mine and believed to have originated from the Reichsbank Money Museum, Berlin. While schedule A consisting of fifty-seven pages, is a detail descriptive inventory of the major part of these coins, Schedule B, consist of 11 pages, is less detail, listing the remainder of these coins.

Schedule A and B contain some coins which cannot be termed truly numismatic; however, it is understood that they have been a part of the collection and you are authorized to release them.

Schedule C, consisting of 7 pages, represents an inventory of numismatic coins found in diverse shipments to the FED. It is understood some of these coins may be subject to internal restitution to a Mr. Julius J. Fulton pursuant to the provision of Military Law No.59. A Photostat of coins claimed by Mr., Fulton under this law is attached to Schedule C.

Schedule F, [D] consisting of six pages, represents an inventory of numismatic coins found in shipments 2 D and 2 F to the FED which may have been looted from France.

You will prepare your official shipping ticket covering this release from FED and have signed by the representative of the Monuments, Fine Art and Archival Section who is authorized to accept and receipt for the said assets.[18]

And indeed all these coins were received by the MFA&A representative Theodore A. Heinrich on May 17, 1948.

The Reichsbank Museum Coin Collection had it origin in 1931 when Georg Kropp, Reichsbank official, discovered a collection of rare German gold coins and some gold medals which originated from the deliveries of gold during World War I. Supposing there were additional coins of numismatic value mixed with the considerable quantities of gold coins stored in the vaults for years, Kropp obtained permission to sort through the gold, looking for numismatic and historical coins. In a small and inexpensive way, this resulted in a notable collection of rare coins and the beginning of the Money Museum. Subsequently, a procedure was established that all gold and silver received by any Reichsbank must be examined by bank employees in Berlin, especially trained and chosen for monetary considerations. Several distinguished German aristocratic collectors donated their coins, to include Celtic-Germanic, Brandenburg-Prussian and Hesse collections. Auctions were held to fill gaps in the collection.

But most of the gaps of collectable coins would be filled under the March 21, 1939, Decree of the Reich Minister of Economy Number I/3 which required that all coinage, as well as medals in gold and silver previously obtained from Jewish people, be sent to the Central Purchase Agent in Berlin. It was the function of the Reichsbank in the various German cities to collect these valuables: "In order to avoid a diminution of the valuable coins of especial rareness they must be left in those cabinets and containers which had been used until now. In case of having knowledge of large and valuable collections being Jewish property it is recommended that the Reichsbank branches securing these collections in their own vaults."[19]

The Reichsbank branches would sort the coins and the ones without numismatic value would be smelted. The coins not smelted were sent to the Reichsbank, Berlin. The vast majority of the coins were "purchased," and added to the Reichsbank Museum Coin Collection. The rest were to be auctioned to native and foreign dealers, "as far as possible against a payment in foreign currency." The remainder must have been a rather large lot as they would, "gradually be placed on the market to avoid a sudden fall in prices." These Jewish acquired coins made up portion of the Reichsbank Museum Coin Collection.

Previous chapters noted, as the danger from Allied bombing became more acute in Berlin, most of the valuables of the Reichsbank were removed from safety to the Merkers Salt Mine. In view of the elaborate manner in which the thousands of numismatic coins and medals were arranged for display, however, it was impractical to transport the entire museum collection to Merkers. Only the choicest and rarest specimens, consisting of about 10% of the collection, and filling nine bags, were taken to the mine. The leftovers, together with the voluminous card index records, were left in Berlin. These remaining coins and indexes survived the bombings and remained intact until later removed by Soviet forces. In this move, the Russians disregarded the recorded arrangement of the coins and dumped them all in a random fashion into canvas bags.

In 1947, US citizens, Julius and Grete Fulton, San Francisco, California, filed a claim for the 365 piece gold coin and medal collection that had been taken from them while residing in Frankfurt, Germany. Before they left Germany in early 1939, by law they had deposited their valuable collection with the Deutscher Bank, Frankfurt. Because of the March 21, 1939, decree, the collection in a sealed box had been sent to Berlin.

The Fultons had purchased many of their gold medals and coins from Frankfurt coin dealers. Dealer Busso Peus had sold the Fultons a large part of their collection, and noted of importance, a 1701 Prussia Coronation Medal of Friedrich I, the first King of Prussia. Dr. Busso Peus, in an affidavit signed on December 13, 1946, certified he had recognized on display in the Gold Museum of the Berlin Reichsbank this specific 1701 Coronation Medal that he had previously appraised in the Fulton collection. There are no known records of payment to the Fulton family by the Germans or the United States for these assets.

```
        2) Goldmedaillen & Goldabschläge von Münzen.

307.  Mainz. Joh. Philipp v. Schönbron. Goldabschlag v. Taler  RM    125.—
                    im Gewicht von 5 Dukaten            RM    125.—
308.      -   Lothar Franz v. Schönborn. Desgl.                125.—
309.      -   Karl Friedirch Jos. v. Erthal. Dukat mit Fassg.   12.—
310.-     -   -    -     -    -  Goldabschlag v. Kreuzer          6.—
311.      -   St. Albanstift. Goldgulden 1716                   30.—
312.      -   Friedrich Karl Joseph. Universitätsmed. 1784
                                            27 gr.              90.—
313.      -   Karl v. Dalberg. Med. 1807            38 gr.     275.—
314.  Hessen  Ernst Ludwig. Med. o.J.              85 gr.     500.—
315.  Hamburg. Portugalöser 1679.                  36         180.—
316.      -        -      1903                      35         150.—
317.      -        -      1890                      35         150.—
318.      -        -      1862                      35         150.—
319.      -        -      1851                      35         150.—
320.      -        -      Kath#rinenkirche          35         130.—
321.      -        -      1837                      35         130.—
322.      -        -      1828                      35         130.—
323.      -        -      1876                      35         130.—
324.      -        -      1885                      35         130.—
325.      -        -      1894                      35         130.—
326.      -   Ein u. ein halbfacher Portugalöser 1689 52gr.   200.—
327.      -   Portugalöser o. J. Bismarck          35 gr.     125.—
328.      -   Halber Portugalöser 1784             18          65.—
329.  Baden. Medaille 1714. Freide v. Rastatt      21          90.—
330.  Hindenburg Erinnerungsmedaille               22          75.—
331.      -            -                            12          38.—
332.      -            -                             4          12.—
333.  Baden. Friedrich II. Verdienstmedaille       19          75.—
334.  Geis. Sänger in München       Medaille 1924  10          35.—
335.  Goethe Erinnerungsmedaille                    7          25.—
336.  Emden. Stadtmedaille 1750                     10          30.—
337.  Zeppelin. Med. auf den Weltflug               6          20.—
338.  Preussen. Friedrich III. Vermählungsmed.      7          90.—
339.      -   Friedrich I. Krönungsmedaille von
                  seinem Münzmeister 1701        356 gr.     2200.—
340.      -   Friedr. Wilh. III. Med. 1803        20 gr.       75.—
341.      -   Wilh. I. Krönungsmedaille 1861        41        125.—
342.  Hamburg. Portugalöser 1826                    35        130.—
343.  Lippe-Detmold. Verdienstmedaille 1893         29        100.—
344.  Nürnberg Religiöse Medaille                   15         60.—
345.  Habsburg. Friedrich III. & Maximilian Judenmed. 20     120.—
346.  Nürnberg. Miscellandukat o.J.          3 gr.  12.—
347.      -   Halbe Lammdukatenklippe 1,7 gr.                   7.—
348.      -   Lammdukatenklippe 3,5gr.                         13.—
349.  Holland. Abschlag v. westfries. 6 Stüverstück, 3 gr.    25.—
350.  Russland. Peter d.Gr. Med. 1705. Mitau
                  von Müller Augsburg.          77 gr.        300.—

                                       Übertrag  RM   6770.—
```

The Fulton family kept a complete typed inventory of their valuable coin/medal collection. On this page, item 339 is the Prussian Coronation Medal of 1701.

Sundry Items

Shipment 28: The valuables taken in Erlangen contained more securities that were returned to the Dutch. Two sealed bags containing securities, many that had been confiscated from the Netherlands had been taken to the Berlin Reichsbank and placed into the account of Arthur Seyss-Inquart, who at the time was serving as Nazi governor of the Netherlands. These were later removed from Berlin by Dr. Friedrich Freiherr von Haller and hidden on a farm in Erlangen. Here they were uncovered by members of the US Third Army, and delivered to the Foreign Exchange Depository on June 11, 1945 as Shipment 28. The bags contained foreign currency and hundreds of bonds. A yellow tax seals on most of the bonds proved they had indeed been taken from the Dutch. During September 1948, the entire lot was released to the Netherlands.

Shipment 96: A handful of miscellaneous gold and diamond jewelry and two paintings were deposited in the Foreign Exchange Depository as Shipment 96 on November 26, 1946. The US Army Counter Intelligence Corps (CIC) had ascertained the property was from victims of concentration camps. The two paintings were part of a collection that had been sold by auction under the supervision of the Chief of Police of Pforzheim. Professor Amandus Goetzell the official appraiser of the collection was awarded the two paintings as compensation. The paintings were described as one pencil drawing, 19th century German Landscape, and one drawing by Moritz von Schwind, titled *Presentation in the Temple*. The paintings were signed for by Theodore A. Heinrich and sent to the MFA & A Branch in Wiesbaden on May 27, 1948.[20]

The following letter to Mr. Saul Kagan, Jewish Restitution Successor Organization (former IGCR) was written on July 3, 1951, regarding the paintings:

Dear Mr. Kagan:
Whist cleaning up our storage room we did discover two more drawings (Wiesb. No.5481 & 5482) which were confiscated from a certain Professor Goetzell, Bad Liebenzell. According

to our information these two drawings are former Jewish property. The owners can not be discovered thus and therefore Mr. Howe decided to turn these drawings over into your custody. The drawings are rather small and therefore I think it advisable that we deliver them to your Frankfurt office for further action.

The paintings were given by Thomas Carr Howe to Mr. Saul Kagan on July 5, 1951. A year later German lawyers for Professor Goetzell were trying to obtain the two paintings.[21] The disposal of the jewelry was not reported.

Shipment 32: On June 20, 1945, four bags of silver weighing 240 pounds and two sealed envelopes with Belgian francs and Czech crowns were given to the XXI Corps Artillery by Military Government Detachment 12. No information as to its origin was furnished.

Norman Helmet, 8x8 inches. Note the knob at the top center, with a circular disk in gold colored metal, from which six similarly colored strips of metal studded with small knobs radiate to the lower part of helmet.

This botanical book's title page reads "Elisabethae Blackwell Collection Stirpivn." It is about one foot long, and was printed in Nürnberg in 1760. Illustrated by Nicholas Friedrich Eisneberger, Court Painter of Nürnberg, it is also known as the Blackwell Kreuter Bucher.

Five albums of maps printed in 1641, each about two feet long by one foot wide.

Also recovered at this time by Government Detachment 12 were several antique items that had been turned over to the Degenershausen Natural Park Estate in the closing days of the war by SS General Ludolf von Alvensleben for safekeeping:

Five albums of original maps
Five albums of original botanical objects
One Norman Helmet

The silver was deposited in the Foreign Exchange Depository on June 21, 1945 as Shipment 32A and the cultural objects as 32B. The Norman helmet was later transferred to the Wiesbaden Collection Point, the books were sent to the US Offenbach Archival Depot, and an album of maps was tentatively identified as having been looted from France.

On September 20, 1948, the 240 pounds of silver was sold to the Bank Deutscher Länder.[22]

Shipment 51: Maj. Henry R. Nelson, Field Artillery, delivered a box of money to the Finance Officer, 76th Infantry Division on May 3, 1945. The money had been obtained from a German civilian on April 25, 1945, who had found it in a prisoner of war camp in Hartmannsdorf, Germany. It was assumed that the money had been taken from Allied prisoners. The Hartmannsdorf POW camp had incarcerated 42,053 Allied prisoners. That included 18,341 Russians, 10,690 Frenchmen and 2,264 Americans.

The money and other securities were received by the Foreign Exchange Depository on July 9, 1945, as Shipment 51. It appears these valuables were later consolidated with Shipment 18E (POWs) and the currency was returned to country of origin and remainder released to the Landeszentralbank von Hessen on December 30, 1948.[23] The US currency consisted of sixty-one pennies and that was forwarded to the US treasury.

Shipment 117: This shipment does not have a folder in the Central Files but the Records Relating to Tabulation and Classifications of Deposits under Inventory Forms is for Shipment 117. This shipment was four wooden boxes containing private property and records pertaining to Allied prisoners of war from Stalag VIII C:

Released to Belgium, 1 box, October 16, 1950
Released to France, 2 boxes, October 16, 1950
Released to Britain, 1 box, October 20, 1950
Released to Canada, 1 box, October 27, 1950
Released to US 7771 Berlin Documentation Center, 1 box miscellaneous records, November 2, 1950

CHAPTER 18

Acquired Under US Military Law 53

Shipment 13: An I.G. Farben ledger book contained 204 handwritten pages of entries for foreign currency obtained by that giant chemical firm I.G. Farben, Frankfurt during World War II. The money listed was contained in one large box and was sent to the Foreign Exchange Depository on May 2, 1945, under authority of US Army Military Law 53. The currency was from Italy, Hungary, Switzerland, Belgium, Spain, France, Denmark, Sweden, Norway, Rumania, Greece and Slovakia. With the exceptions of coins, the paper was noted as worthless. The coins then had a total face value of 118.44 Deutschmarks, or approximately $10. There are no records regarding the disposition of this shipment.[1]

Shipment 25: On June 8, 1945, delivered to the Foreign Exchange Depository by Maj. Henry H. Martin Jr. from the Halle Reichsbank were reported to be seventy-seven bags of German silver five mark coins, nineteen bags of silver two mark coins and three packages of foreign currency and securities. The inventory discloses the bags to contain from most of the countries occupied by Germany. The coins were taken under US Military Law 53.[2]

Shipment 33, Leipzig: On June 24, 1945, Capt. Beverly C. Pratt, 690th Field Artillery Battalion delivered to the Foreign Exchange Depository from the Reichsbank, Leipzig thirty-two boxes, two bags, and one package of securities that appeared to have belonged to German citizens. These items were seized under US Military Law 53 and deposited as Shipment 33.

Shipment 34, Reichsbanks Kothen and Dessau: Thousands of envelopes with valuables inside were received from these Reichsbanks, and they listed all types of items and identified the original owner. These contained articles required by US Military 53 that were to be brought to all local banks; consolidated at the closest Reichsbank, then forwarded to the Foreign Exchange Depository. Part of this shipment was taken from the Mansfield Copper Mine under Military Law 53. This shipment contained thirty-four chests of pure silver, six bottles of various granules including platinum and five gold leaves.

The four large gold leaves and one small leaf in this shipment consisted of 894.479 Troy ounces of gold was air freighted to the Bank of England in 1948 and deposited into the account of the Tripartite Gold Commission.

Shipment 50: This shipment was from a large number of sources that were all delivered to the Foreign Exchange Depository on July 6, 1945, by Capt. George Hackleman, 12th Army Group which was composed of the U.S First, Third and Ninth Armies.

Shipment 50A: Maj. Raymond W. Laycock, 23rd Infantry Regiment Intelligence Officer, 2nd Infantry Division, seized 65,150 kroners from a German paymaster.

Shipment 50 B: On May 2, 1945 Maj. W.H. Rice put in writing:

> I certify that the enclosed 10,250 units of alleged Bulgarian Currency were found apparently abandoned in the factory of Walter Waffenwerk at Zella-Mehlis, Germany after the capture of the town by American troops. Found by Battery Commanding Officer, Battery D, 110th AAA Gun Battalion who transferred the funds to me.

Shipment 50C: The Intelligence Section, G-2, of the 30th Division turned over 29,000 Banca D'Italia Lire to the Controller of Finance 12 Army Group on April 23, 1945.

Shipment 50D: Maj. James H. King, 2nd Infantry Division, turned over 118,391 Czechoslovakian kroners to the Controller of Finance 12 Army Group The kroners were reportedly captured Wehrmacht payroll and taken by Capt. Rausch, US Military Intelligence Interrogator at Pilsen, Czechoslovakia.

Shipment 50E: Funds received from Col. Harvey M. Coverley, 2nd Infantry Division, were taken from a captured German vehicle on May 9, 1945, near the town of Ejpovice, Czechoslovakia and contained 157,300 kroners. The box containing the currency was marked "Feldherrnhalle Kommandeur."

Shipment 50F: Accounts of the Nazi party uncovered in the Sparkasse der Mansfelder Seekreises, Hauptzweigstelle Helbra (Savings Bank of Mansfelder Lake District, Main Branch, Helbra, Germany), and consisted of foreign currency in envelopes. In each envelope was a Military Government form showing name of account. All were small amounts of German currency and a few coins, with the exception of Nazi Party Wehrertüchtigungslager (military training bureau) account with a balance of 13,928.63 Reichsmarks. The Savings Bank contained three safe deposit boxes with absent owners. The boxes were sealed by the US Military Government with orders not to be opened without a Military Government officer present. This account was seized under Military Law 53.

Shipment 50G: On April 19, 1945 Col. Norman E. Hart wrote:

> During operations of the 440th Armored Field Artillery Battalion, 7th Armored Division against the enemy Battery C overran the town of Obertiefenbach, Germany on March 27, 1945. In this operation several enemy vehicles were destroyed and captured. One of the vehicles contained two boxes of various types of coins and currency. Upon arriving on the scene two boxes had been broken open. I immediately locked the two boxes and kept them in my possession until I turned them over to the Finance Officer. The large boxes contained currency from every country in Europe, Japan, Fiji, Curacao, and China.
>
> The Finance Officer that took possession of this currency from Colonel Hart was Lieutenant Colonel J.P. Bellamy. Found along with this money were documents and pay vouchers involving British and American prisoners of war located in various Stalag. Bellamy may have passed this information on the Military Intelligence, for in the file is a large manila envelope sent by post to Lt.Col. J.P. Bellamy, 7th Armored Division, Fort Benning, Georgia with a postage date of November 9, year unknown. It is not known how or why but the envelope with its contents fortunately ended up in the files of Shipment 50G. These documents include messages sent to Headquarters in Berlin summing the currency taken from POWs. Many individual receipts for currency taken from British POWs that appear to have been captured in Holland during Operation Market Garden. This is evidenced by their valuables being seized at the POW Processing Center, Krefeld, Germany, not far from the Dutch border.
>
> There are no records as to the disbursement of Shipment 50.[3]

Shipment 53, Reichsbanks Mühlhausen, Erfurt and Eschweg: Lt. Chase turned in to the Foreign Exchange Depository on July 11, 1945, in accordance with Military Law 53 the following:

> 926 bags of foreign currency
> 11 cardboard cartons of foreign currency
> 1 folder of more than 600 Military Government Finance Section (MGAX) forms
> 6 bars of silver

Kriegsgefangenen-Übernahmestelle II, Krefeld

Tagebuch Nr. /

Lfd. Nr.	Nat.	Rang	Name	Vorname	Erkennungs-Nummer
1		Pt	Jenkins	Philip	7798932
2		Pt	Coman	William	14200807
3		Pt	Lynch	Leslie	14756513
4		Pt	Ingram	Leonard	1979320
5		Pt	Isaak	Walter	14714257
6		Pt	Jones	John	14745281
7		Pt	Morris	William	14753741
8			White	Cleo	15017498
9			Palenica	Mathew	35319409
10					
11					
12					
13					
14					
15					
16					
17					
18					
19					
20					
21					
22					
23					
24					
25					
Total		7	mann		

Mit Abgang Nr. 52 weitergeleitet nach

Diez/Lahn am 24. Dez 1944

Army Form A.2038 Serial No. _____

WAR DEPARTMENT DRIVING PERMIT

(Not valid for driving any mechanically propelled vehicle for private purposes)

Issued under the conditions of A.C.I.699 of 1942

The undersigned _____

(description) Major Dover M.C.

2nd Bn Parachute Regt.

being employed on Military Service is hereby authorised by the Secretary of State for War to drive mechanically propelled vehicles of :—

All Groups
Group I
" III
" IV   } (Delete Groups inapplicable)
" VI

when on Government duty, from 1/5/ 194
until 1/5/ 1945

Signature of Holder

Permanent Under-Secretary of State for War.

(24802) Wt.19714 A.& E.W.Ltd.

One of the documents in the envelope marked Fort Benning, Georgia within Shipment 50 regards the processing of prisoners of war. U.S. soldiers, twenty-three-year-old Cleo White and twenty-two-year-old Mathew Palenica, have been struck from the list. Palencia service number is 35319409, not quite as listed.

Another document in the envelope marked Fort Benning, Georgia within Shipment 50 is British Major Dover's War Department Driving Permit.

	50g R-Brot	50g R-Brot	50g R-Brot	50g R-Brot	50g R-Brot	30g Käse	50g Zucker	25g Marmelade	25g Marmelade	
	Urlauber	Urlauber	Urlauber	Urlauber	Urlauber	Urlauber	Urlauber	Urlauber	Urlauber	
50g R-Brot	50g R-Brot	50g R-Brot	50g R-Brot	50g R-Brot	25g Kaffee Ersatz	50g Zucker	25g Marmelade	25g Nährmittel		
	Urlauber	10g Brot	10g Brot				Urlauber	T 25g Nährmittel	Urlauber	

Reichskarte für Urlauber
Gültig im deutschen Reichsgebiet 5. Ausgabe

4 Tage

Diese Karte enthält Einzelabschnitte über insgesamt:
1380 g Brot, davon 900 g R-Brot
150 g Fleisch
81 g Butter
40 g Margarine
100 g Marmelade
100 g Zucker
75 g Nährmittel
25 g Kaffee-Ersatz
30 g Käse

Ausgabestelle EA:
Name: ....
Wohnort: ....
Straße: ....

Ohne Nameneintragung ungültig! Nicht übertragbar! Sorgfältig aufbewahren! Abtrennen der Einzelabschnitte nur durch Kleinverteiler, Gaststätten usw.

This German ration card for four days vacation was enclosed in the envelope from Shipment 50. In typical German fashion, the stamps cover a multitude of rations. A careful look shows that the ration stamps have mostly been marked with a cancellation of that stamp.

1 bag gold and silver coins
180 bags silver German coins
3 wooden boxes foreign currency
1 bag currency and some coins
1 suitcase of assorted valuables.

The currency from Mülhausen included currency from every European country and the United States. The suitcase contained loose paper money, gold watches, bracelets, necklaces, gold pins, rings, gold teeth and bridgework, and an envelope of pearls The origin of the suitcase was unknown but it was identified as "Koffer der Gemeinde Ringleben Kreiss, Weissensee/Thuringia (A suitcase of community valuables from Weissensee, Thuringia).

Russian rubles filled 813 of the bags. The rubles had been sent to Mülhausen from the Strassburg [Strassfurt] Reichsbank. General Sokolvsky of the Soviet Military Administration in Germany sent a letter to the Gen. Lucius Clay, on December 15, 1945, requesting that the currency be returned to the Soviet Union. Clay agreed to this release, and directed the Russian the bags containing only rubles to be released from the Foreign Exchange Depository to Soviet Representatives. The Soviets removed the rubles on February 5, 1946.

Hundred of forms were completed with an inventory of the currency including owner when known and as standard procedure the money was returned to country of origin.[4] A part of Shipment 53 was turned over to the Intergovernmental Committee for Refugees. Turned over to the US treasury was (128) $1, and (15) $2.[5]

Shipment 58, Weimar: Shipment 58 surrender by Capt. Robert Hacken, Finance Officer, Detachment G1E3, in accordance with Military Law from Reichsbank Weimar was delivered on July 31, 1945 to the Foreign Exchange Depository. The shipment consisted of a bag of silver 2 and 5 Reichsmarks coins, French, Rumanian, coins and some securities.[6]

A Russian Ruble used in the identification of Russian currency.

Shipment 62, Reichsbank Hersfeld: On August 24, 1945, received from Lt. Lucius K. Timms, Detachment H-67, taken from the Hersfeld Reichsbank one bag of currency and securities. Assigned Shipment 62 by the Foreign Exchange Depository and stored in vault location 6 ARS. Seized under Military Law 53. On April 13, 1948, it was transferred to the Landeszentralbank von Hessen.[7]

Shipment 63, Reichsbank Fulda: On August 24, 1945, Lt. Sol Kaplan, Detachment G-40, delivered to the Foreign Exchange Depository from the Reichsbank, Fulda twenty-two bags of foreign currency, one bag old silver Reichsmarks, fifteen bags silver German coins, twenty packages to contain securities having belonged to German citizens. These items were seized under US Military Law 53. A change from the standard practice, but the securities were returned unopened on April 13, 1948, to the Reichsbank in Fulda along with the MGAX forms.[8]

Shipment 73, Sulzbach: On July 2, 1945, Maj. E.C. Ophuls visited Sulzbach to investigate some records of the firm Flick Kommandit Gesellschaft. This was done with the help and cooperation of Capt. Minter and Lt. Paul Joseph, 359th Infantry Regiment. After a careful investigation, it was decided to seize one large crate of records, two suite cases of letters, pictures of interest to the Counter Intelligence Corps, and eight million French francs. After some misunderstandings and delays, the items were delivered to the foreign Exchange Depository on October 29, 1945, by Staff Sergeant Phillip Feld, 2nd Battalion, 359th Infantry as Shipment 73.[9]

Shipment 74, Reichsbank Bremen: Received from Reichsbank, Bremen on November 1, 1945 under Military Law 53 the following:

> 299 bags German 5RM silver coins
> 28 bags various coins
> 20 bags currency
> 82 packages currency
> 3 packages forms MGAX (Military Government Finance Forms)

The valuables were delivered to the Foreign Exchange Depository by Lt. Kenneth Stevenson, Military Government Detachment E2C2.

On April 26, 1948, all of the above was returned to the Landeszentralbank von Bremen with the exception of the 299 bags of German silver coins and six East African shillings that were missing from the original shipment.[10]

Shipment 75: Capt. Charles W. Snedeker was introduced previously. He received the following receipt dated August 14, 1944:

> This is to certify that the central court of the Army, Berlin-Charlottenberg 9, Kaiserdamm 49/50 today deposited a secret letter with us, to be called for, this letter containing:

> 1 diamond brooch
> 1 platinum bracelet
> 1 gold coin
> Oberkommando der Wehrmacht

On November 6, 1945, Snedeker, Government Detachment G-236 wrote:

> On or about 5 September 45, Director Hildeprandt, of the Kreissparkasse, Garmisch-Partenkirchen, delivered to my office a sealed envelope deposited by two German Wehrmacht Officers.

In the presences of the bank director the envelope was opened and contents inspected.

A box within the envelope contained one diamond broach with platinum mounting and having a large pearl set in the center. One diamond bracelet mounted in platinum with a blue stone set in center and one small gold coin the size of a 5RM coin.

The above envelope was deposited by the same officers who had deposited the English Pound notes that had been taken from English Flying Officers forced down within German occupied territory.

The English Pound notes discussed in Snedeker's letters is recorded in Shipment 57. These valuables were delivered by Snedeker to the Foreign Exchange Depository on November 5, 1945.[11] Part of Shipment 75 went to the Intergovernmental Committee for Refugees.

Shipment 95: Acquired under Military Law 53 in the City of Cologne were sixty certificates each certifying 2,000 shares (120,000 shares) of capital stock of Ford Motor Company, Antwerp. They were found in a loose binder on the person of Mr. R.H. Schmidt and considered his personal property. Most unusual, the "Tally In" sheet of the Foreign Exchange Depository is not dated or signed. The "Shipping Ticket" for Shipment 95 assigns the Ford stock to the Landeszentralbank von Hessen on November 29, 1948.[12]

Shipment 97, MG Law 53 Consolidation: The puzzle of all the silver German coins of five Reichsmarks and two Reichsmarks acquired under Military Law 53 from the various Reichsbanks, is solved by Shipment 97, Tally In, April 21, 1948. The coins from shipments 25, 34 B, 38, 41-44, 48, 49, 53, 58, 63, 65-68, and 74 were consolidated in Shipment 97. The total face value was 3,596,152.80 RM or a 1945 value of $359,615. The silver contents were at a far greater value.

Also transferred into Shipment 97, was the rare coin collection from Berlin acquired in Shipment 1. Early Shipments 9, 10, 14, 16 (Buchenwald Concentration Camp), 17, 21 A, 21 K, 21 D, 23 A, 31, and 85 were also included. All of these coins were inventoried, boxed and banded by Foreign Exchange Depository personnel.

The coins taken under Military Law 53, totaling 3,596,152.80 RM, in 259 band wooden boxes, was received by the Bank Deutscher Laender on September 10, 1948, signed for by Albert Thoms. The majority of the rare coins noted in the above paragraph were transferred to Shipment 102.[13]

Shipment 103, Law 53 Russian Zone: This was a consolidation of 184 boxes of assets from Military Law 53 received from various Reichsbanks that became cities under the control of the Russian Occupation Zone. The assets were repackaged as Shipment 103. During the Cold War, these would not be released to the Soviet representative of this zone. The boxes with the detailed MAGX forms, were signed for by the Landeszentralbank von Hessen on July 6, 1948.[14]

Valuables collected under Military Law 53 were disbursed as follows: monetary gold was sent to the Tripartite Gold Commission; monetary silver was smelted into bars and infused into the German economy for industrial needs, foreign securities; and currencies, including American dollars, were sent to country of origin. The remainder was sent back to the original Reichsbank.

Shipment 35-46, 48, 49 and 65-69 acquired under Military Law 53 are found in Appendix A.

CHAPTER 19
Shipments of Little or No Value

Shipment 6, Leipzig: On the April 29, 1945, 173 bags of currency were received from the Reichsbank, Leipzig. The money was delivered to the Foreign Exchange Depository by Escort Officer, P.H. Imbrock, Field Artillery, V Corps. The larger bags required two men to lift them, therefore, the currency from these bags were repacked into smaller packages resulting in a total of 328 bags containing currency mostly from Poland.

The history of this mostly worthless currency is unknown as the recognized Poland Government at that time was established in London with the Bank of England handling its financial interest.[1]

Shipment 8, Frankfurt: Mr. Andrew M. Kamarck, Finance Division, and a US citizen working for US forces, delivered one package of an insignificant amount of Danish, Norwegian, Italian, Swedish, Swiss, Slovak, Ukrainian, Hungarian, and Bohemia and Moravia currency to the Foreign Exchange Depository on April 25, 1945. The money had been deposited in the Reichsbankhauptstelle in Frankfurt. The disposal of this shipment is unknown.[2]

Shipment 55, Engraving Plates: On July 21, 1945, Lt. Edwin Sacks, Military Government Detachment E1F3 brought to the Foreign Exchange Depository 382 engraving plates used to print small denominations of German currency. The plates had been found by military police, Third Army, in Bad Toelz, Germany.[3]

Shipment 78, Coupons: Dividend coupons with talons attached were received from Military Government Detachment E-6 on June 17, 1946. The coupons with talons, attached printed slips to apply for new coupons, were found in a safe in a Military Government building in Frankfurt by Capt. Lee H. Morrison. He turned the coupons over as Shipment 78. They were transferred to the Landeszentralbank von Hessen on May 26, 1948.[4]

Shipment 81, German Post Office: On February 4, 1947, the Foreign Exchange Depository accepted unidentifiable bonds and securities that had been found in mail containers taken during the closing days of the war by US forces from German post offices. The containers were deposited by the US Civil Censorship Division. These were in poor condition, and the sender and addresses were unreadable. The sacks delivered to the Depository had been previously plundered. The securities included 228 interest coupons valued at 2875 RM, 4.5% Mortgage Bonds drawn on various German banks and other such securities from various firms. The fate of Shipment 81 is unrecorded.[5]

Shipment 84, German Post Office: On February 4, 1947, the Foreign Exchange Depository had accepted as Shipment 81 unidentifiable bonds and securities that had been found in mail containers taken during the closing days of the war by US Forces from German post offices.

Along with the above items, deposited by the US Civil Censorship Division, were large bags of paper currency and coins of every denomination in containers in poor condition with unreadable senders and addresses. An inventory of the items was made in detail. No additional information was supplied for Shipment 84 also delivered on February 4, 1947. Most of Shipment 84 was turned over to the Intergovernmental Committee for Refugees.[6] Turned over to the US Treasury from this shipment was $65.95.

Shipments 112-114, Coupons: These shipments, taken from various previous shipments, were in regard to coupon sheets of 50% paid shares of I.G. Chemie, Basel. The coupons were sent to the US legation, Bern, Switzerland to be delivered to the Union Bank of Switzerland and had been sent for the purpose of conversion. It is not clear if the Union Bank collected from the I.G. Chemie. But any proceeds were to be deposited with the Union bank. It's a good guess that the account was in the name of the Landeszentralbank as they were the recipients of a large number of securities taken under Military Law 53. All the Foreign Exchange Depository was interested in receiving was a signed receipt for the coupons, and doggedly they did.[7]

CHAPTER 20

Housekeeping at the Foreign Exchange Depository

Shipment 90, IGCR: On December 10, 1947, in room five, the former air raid shelter within the Foreign Exchange Depository building was emptied of all items belonging to the FED. What remained was a large cache of valuables that had not been inventoried, belonging to the IGCR. This included seventy-five boxes of gems, weighing seventy-five pounds each, that had been released from Salzburg in June 1947 taken from the Hungarian gold train. Thus, this was a segregation of gold and silver for the Intergovernmental Committee of Refugees. Released from the room were seventeen boxes filled with fifty-two bars of gold, two boxes containing six bars of silver along with 189 bags with one bar of silver each and two boxes of documents. These valuables were shipped by British European Airways to London on March 12, 1948.[1]

Shipment 99, Documents: Records, correspondence and other papers found in various shipments previously received by FED to be retained for information for later was Shipment 99, dated May 28, 1948.[2]

Shipment 100, Consolidation: A consolidation of all the worthless paper currency collected in the Foreign Exchange Depository, including a $20 Confederate States of American from the Civil War, made up Shipment 100. The money was banded in eight large Air Corps lockers. The cash had

IGCR Reparations Director Abba Schwartz and Colonel William Brey examine some of the valuables released to the International Governmental Committee for Refugees. The chevrons on Brey's jacket sleeve indicate that he experienced six months combat in World War I, and thirty months during World War II.

been under the custody of the Office of Chief Finance and was sent to the Depository on May 21, 1948. Col. Brey had previously questioned the validity of the transfer. The disposal of the worthless currency is not documented.[3]

Shipment 101, Currency: Sent to the Foreign Exchange Depository on May 25, 1948, by the Theater Provost Marshal were several currencies including $5,995.00 US as Shipment 101. On September 7, 1948, this box of currency was returned to the Provost Marshal.[4]

Shipment 104, Missing Precious Metals Documents: There is no file or shipping ticket in the Central Files for Shipment 104 but in the section records relating to Tabulations and Classifications of Deposits, 1949-1955, under Proforma Shipping Ticket No.79 is the following information. The date is in the proper sequence for Shipment 104:

> July 8, 1948, received from the Foreign Exchange Depository the following described assets: 87 books, folders and papers, or microfilm thereof, of the Precious Metals Department of the Reichsbank, Berlin as per Annex A.
> No booking [their underline] is being made for this shipping ticket which had been prepared a matter of record only. Receipt acknowledged by Bank Deutscher Länder as per their letter attached of 8 July 1948.

These books, folders and papers that had been received in Shipment 17 by Lt.Cmdr. Joel Fischer, were the most important papers collected by the Foreign Exchange Depository and would be invaluable to future historians. Of the sixteen sacks found in Magdeburg at the end of the war, two of the sacks were labeled "Melmer" and contained documents concerning SS transactions. These records in these sacks formed the basis of various reports on Nazi gold transactions from the years 1939 through 1945.

In June 1948, Harry E. Hesse, Treasury Department Official, traveled to the Foreign Exchange Depository to investigate the original records of the Berlin Reichsbank regarding the administration of gold. Here he found the records of the Precious Metals Department to be fairly complete. Hesse writes:

> After the immediate requirements of the 1948 investigation had been complete, namely the tracing of gold which the Germans had looted from the Netherlands, the question arose as to the most useful disposition of the original records, in view of the imminent dissolution of the Foreign Exchange Depository of the US Army (OMGUS). In order for the best possible use be made of these records, with the concurrence of the Chief Economic Advisor, Mr. Jack Bennett, requested Col. William G. Brey, to turn these records over to the Bank Deutscher Länder as permanent custodian.
> Prior to this however, I arranged to have all the records photographed on 35mm. film so a set would be available in Washington. ... The actual film is in a cardboard box in the wooden cabinet in Mr. Schwartz's office, Room 5327, Main Treasure. Either as a result of poor technique or of deterioration of the film, a few rolls are very dim and cannot be read.

The above is from a memorandum for the files written on January 16, 1953, Hesse. Why did Hesse write this memorandum in 1953? Only about half the records were filmed and these microfilmed records, contained on some seventy reels, are available today in the National Archives at College Park, Maryland.

The signatures on Proforma Shipping Ticket No.79 are Piper and Thoms, and both employees of Bank Deutscher Länder. The Proforma was a three part carbon document with the third carbon issued to the bank. Thoms continued working with the Bank Deutscher Länder until his retirement

<u>Annex A</u>

Books, folders and papers of the Precious Metals
Department of the Reichsbank, Berlin.

<u>Records Microfilmed</u>

1. ✓ Gold in Barren u. Auslaendischen Muenzen
2. ✓ Kontrolle d. Spitzenbetraege des Bankbestandes
3. ✓ Statistik u.d. Goldbestandes d. Reichsbank
4. ✓ Statistik für Gold u. Silber, Edelmetallankaufskasse
5. ✓ Bestandskontrolle des Goldankaufs, 9. Febr. 1940-2. Jan. 1945
6. ✓   do   , ab 2. Jan. 1945
7. ✓ Statistik Gold u. Silber - Edelmetallankaufskasse
8. ✓ Bestand des Haupttresors (6.Jan. 1932-23. Sept. 1942)
10. ✓ Goldankauf Diverse Goldbarren Hauptbuch No. 30001 -
11. ✓   do   Kontrollbuch No. 30001 -
12. ✓ Hauptbuch Versch. Goldbarren, Hauptkasse Edelmetall
13. ✓ Kontrollbuch Versch. Goldbarren,   do
14. ✓ 900er Goldbarren Hauptbuch No. 15001 - 21000
15. ✓ 900er Goldbarren Kontrollbuch No. 15001 - 21000
16. ✓ Standard Goldbarren Hauptbuch No. 10001 - 15000
17. ✓   do   Kontrollbuch   do
18. ✓ Hochwertige Goldbarren Hauptbuch über 990/1000,No. 20000-30000
19. ✓   do   Kontrollbuch   do   ,No. 1-10000
20. ✓   do   do   do   ,No. 20000-30000
21. ✓ Hochwertige Barren Hauptbuch, Sonderlagerung im Reich
22. ✓ Hochwertige Sonderlagerung im Reich Kontrollbuch
23. ✓ Tagebuch - 1. Juni 1940 - 9. Sept. 1943
24. ✓ Tagebuch - 10. Sept. 1943 -
25. ✓ Tresorarbeitsbuch des Tresors A, 1 Juni 1940 -
26. ✓ Ein- u. Ausgangsbuch des Goldankaufs v. 15. Sept. 1944
27. ✓ Buch über die Lagerung im Tresor A
29. ✓ Gewichtskontrolle Asservate u. Depots
30. ✓ Gewichtskontrolle f. Goldbarren des Goldankaufs
31. ✓ Barkontrolle der Kasse Edelmetall v. 3. Jan 1944
34. ✓ Gold u. Silber Notierungen
38. ✓ Hauptkasse Edelmetall, Bestandsbuch der angekauften Silber-
   münzen
39. ✓ Auswärtiges Amt   (F)
41. ✓ Goldbarren u. Goldmünzen, Bestände b.d. Bankhaushalten
   u.s.w.   (F)
42. ✓ Gold u. Silver Statistische Notizen   (F)
43. ✓ Waagen u. Gewichte - Hauptkasse Edelmetall   (F)
44. ✓ Prüfungsergebnisse des Eichamtes   (F)
45. ✓ Goldankaufspreise   (F)
46. Geschäftsgang u. Dienstanweisung d. Edelmetallankaufs-
   ✓ kasse   (F)
47. ✓ Unterschriftsblätter   (F)
48. ✓ Verschiedene Briefe re Gold   (F)
49. ✓ Beutelbuch (Hauptbuch) A ausl. Goldmünzen
50. ✓ Beutelbuch (Kontrollbuch) A,   do

- 1 -

Page 1 of the controversial microfilmed documents in Shipment 104.

```
 ✓51.  Goldbuch B Hauptbuch                                          (F)
 ✓52.  Beutelbuch B Kontrollbuch                                     (F)
 ✓53.  Beutelbuch Kontrollbuch C                                     (F)
  54.        do      (filmed twice)                                  (F)
 ✓55.  Depot f. Rüstung u.s.w.                                       (F)
 ✓56.  Judengesetze u. Bestimmungen u.s.w.                           (F)
 ✓57.  Silberverfügungen                                             (F)
 ✓58.  Allg. Verfügungen betz. Ankauf v. Goldmünzen, Barren
        u.s.w.                                                       (F)
 ✓59.  Wirtschaft u. Währungsnotizen                                 (F)
 ✓60.  Goldbewirtsch. I                                              (F)
 ✓61.        do      II                                              (F)
 ✓62.  Liste der Abgesandten Goldtransporte
 ✓63.  Hauptkasse Edelmetallankaufskasse (Asserv. u.Depots)
 ✓64.  Quittungsbuch der Edelmetallankaufskasse
 -65.  Same as No. 38 - filmed twice
 ✓66.  Ein- u. Ausgangsbuch des Silberankaufs
 ✓67.  Bestand des Tresors.

 ✓M 1.  Beutelbuch C Hauptbuch                                       (F)
 ✓M 2.  Banca de Italia Mappe                                        (F)
 ✓M 3.  Goldbew. Kriegsmassnahmen                                    (F)
 ✓M 4.  Depot-Mappe (Same as No. 55, filmed twice)                   (F)
 ✓M 5.  Goldbew. Oesterreich                                         (F)
 ✓M 6.  Misc. Data                                                   (F)
 ✓M 7.  Verlagerung Ital. Gold Mailand nach Franzensfeste            (F)


                        Records not Microfilmed

 ✓70.  Gold u. Silber Statistik                                      (F)
 ✓71.  Belgian Gold                                                  (F)
 ✓72.  Italien Gold Transport Franzensfeste - Berlin                 (F)
 ✓73.  Gold u. Silber Notierungen
 ✓74.  Bestandsnachweisung d. Golddepots                             (F)
 ✓75.  Gold u. Silber Verkäufe - Privat                              (F)
 ✓76.  Zeitungsausschnitte v. Gold u. Silber                         (F)
 ✓77.  R/B Hauptkasse, Registratur - Anordnung u.s.w.                (F)
 ✓78.        do             - Verschiedene Papiere                   (F)
 ✓79.  Kontrolle u. Transport - Ital. Gold                           (F)
 ✓80.  Transport von BfZ bis Schweizerischen N/B                     (F)
 ✓81.  Misc. Schedules of Gold bars and Coin                         (F)
 ✓82.              do                                                (F)
 ✓83.  Notverordnungen etc.                                          (F)
 ✓84.  Misc. Papers, Forms of Precious Metals Dept.                  (F)
 ✓85.  D.S.K. Rapport Puhl.                                          (F)
 ✓86.  Statistical Information                                       (F)
 ✓87.  Work Papers - Belgian N/B - W.V. Dunkel                       (F)


 ✓88.  Silber Ankauf - Berlin R/B
 ✓89.  Prussian State Mint Photostats                                (F)
 ✓90.  Photostats Bar Book Pages                                     (F)
 ✓91.  26 Folders re Melmer deposits                                 (F)


    Note:  (F) signifies Folder; all others are Books.




                                    Received above material

                                    [signature]
                               _____  X
                                    Authorized Official
                                    Bank Deutscher Laender

                                    Date:   8. 7. 46
```

Pages 2 and 3 of the controversial microfilmed documents in Shipment 104.

in 1954. During his employment, he accessed the records in 1951 and 1952 in response to several inquires. These records were passed to the historical archives of the Deutscher Bundesbank in 1971. Another group of the documents were received from Thoms' family in 1982. They were a part of his personal trust records.

Then in 1997, the files were needed for a renewed interest in Holocaust Assets. The documents at Archives of the Deutscher Bundesbank including the receipt, the third copy of the transfer, could not be found. The National Archives furnished the Deutscher Bundesbank with copies of the original receipts. After an exhaustive search all that was found was a book entry: "7.1.51 sealed cardboard box of films / signed Beckert Klockmann / destroyed on June 20, 1978. Further written is, "to what in particular the missing numbers were assigned remains unclear; items other than payment document and securities also appear under the numbers 26, 76, 84, 89, 104, 108, and 109."[5] To the author, these numbers appear to be shipment numbers as found in Appendix A, but these shipments do not match up with the valuables from the Precious Metals Department of the Reichsbank.

Shipment 105, Tripartite Gold Commission: Repackaged from previous shipment for bookkeeping purposes, 3,469 boxes of monetary gold as shipment 105 on August 12, 1948. Complete shipment of gold to the Bank of England for the Tripartite Gold Commission. This is described in detail in a subsequent section.[6]

Shipment 106, TGC Repackaged: Repackaged from previous shipment for bookkeeping purposes, 3,469 boxes of monetary gold as shipment 105 on August 12, 1948. Complete shipment of gold to the Bank of England for the Tripartite Gold Commission. Described in detail in a subsequent section.[7]

Shipment 107, Currency from POWs: On September 1, 1948, the Currency Section from the Provost Marshal Headquarters delivered to the Foreign Exchange Depository thirty-four boxes containing currency obtained from German Prisoners of War as Shipment 107. It contained a detail inventory. Disposition of the currency undocumented.[8]

This is a photo of the front and back of some of the money taken from German prisoners of war. This currency was printed by local Gauleiters (Nazi Governors) after the destruction of Berlin printing presses by Allied air attacks.

Shipment 108, Engraving Plates Consolidated: Repacking of ninety-five boxes, each weighing approximately 180 pounds, of engraving plates from previous shipments as Shipment 108 on September 2, 1948. Five day later turned over the German authorities.[9]

Shipment 110, IGCR: These were non-monetary gold assets rejected by the Intergovernmental Committee for Refugees as "being to low in value" that had been previously released to them by the FED from various shipments. They were returned on October 8, 1948 as Shipment 110. FED officials inventoried the six pages of items and returned back to the Committee 10,566 metal coins and a large assortment of currency from around the world.[10]

Shipment 119, Consolidation: There is some confusion with Shipment 119. Again, it is a consolidation from previous shipments, but it is transferred to the Landeszentralbank in 1948 and back to the Foreign Exchange Depository in 1950 for restitution to France.

The consolidation involves twenty-three bars of platinum with a weight of 60,032 grams (132.34 pounds), three units of palladium, three units of iridium, and 1 unit of rhodium. These valuables were released on August 10, 1950, to the French Restitution Representative.[11]

Shipment 120, Unknown: This shipment does not have a folder in the Central Files but the Records Relating to Tabulation and Classifications of Deposits under Inventory Forms for Shipment 120.

Form number 15841, dated September 18, 1950, states, "9 steel-banded cases various sizes, contents unknown."

Form number 15844, dated October 18, 1950, reports, "Two locked half-size Diplomatic Pouches s/c Miscellaneous Foreign Currencies, impounded by US Courts in the American Zone of Germany."

Form number 15845, dated November 8, 1950, reports, "Two boxes nailed and steel-banded numbered 50, 50A. Each box contains four bags of silver grain, each bag stated to represent a weight of 25 kilos. Accordingly total weigh of silver in both boxes would be 200 kilos."

Shipment 121, Consolidation: Shipment 121 is a further consolidation and continuation of Shipment 119. These valuables had been seized as a portion of Shipment 22 from the Friedrichshall Salt Mine along with the Dutch Diamonds. It had been part of the ROGES inventory. The claims from France, Belgium, Yugoslavia, Italy and the Netherlands for these precious metals exceeded the amount on hand, therefore the platinum, palladium, iridium, and rhodium was to be pro-rated to these countries. By country, it was valued in 1950 US dollars for: France, $561,651; Netherlands, $212,147; Belgium, $54,362; Yugoslavia, $122,920 and Italy $22,624 for a grand total of $973,704 for 317,325.79 grams of valuables.

The releases for the above countries were signed for in the first week of December 1950. Most disturbing is the authorized recipient of Shipping Ticket 244 as the representative for Yugoslavia, Mate A. Topic. This individual stole a personal fortune as a direct result of World War II. Topic, with his various names, is discussed further in a later chapter.[12]

Another matter involved in the cleaning up of the Foreign Exchange Depository, were the 1,200 envelopes containing personal effects of German nationals who were prisoners in Nazi concentration camps. On August 31, 1949, the FED was awaiting authorization to release the envelopes to the Red Cross Coordination Committee in the U.S., but their fate and their contents is unknown.

PART III

THE TRIPARTITE GOLD COMMISSION

CHAPTER 21

The Paris Conference of Reparations

"I behold Germany dyed in blood, France utterly ruined. While I contemplate the storm, I am almost ashamed of my own tranquility."—Voltaire, from his Swiss refuge, 1750s.

On February 11, 1945, Franklin D. Roosevelt, Winston Churchill and Joseph Stalin met at Yalta in the Crimea to hammer out both wartime and postwar agreements on Germany, China, Japan, Poland and other issues. Major concerns were the dismemberment of Germany, the establishment of a Polish provisional government, and reparations. At this meeting the question of restitution of monetary gold was not addressed. The Yalta Conference was clearly a victory for Stalin. As early as March 1945, the Poles referred to the Yalta conference as "the second Munich."

The first Allied summit after the European victory was held in July and early August 1945, in Potsdam, a suburb of Berlin. The conference was attended by representatives of the governments of England, the United States and Russia. They met to put into specific terms the chief principles concerning the future government and the obligations of defeated Germany on which they had agreed to at Yalta. At Potsdam, the Allies decided Germany should be compelled to compensate to the greatest extent for losses suffered by the Allies; also that the German people accept the responsibility for this reparation.

To redress the injustice of World War II, the Allies met in Paris during November and December 1945, and formed an organization of nineteen countries entitled to receive reparations from Germany. Russia being the notable exception, was excluded from this organization. The Paris Conference on Reparations was organized along the structure of the Potsdam Agreement and consisted of a three-part agreement. Part I established the general principals of distribution of the reparation. Part II was the procedure for internal organization of the Paris Agreement. Part III of the agreement was the restitution of monetary gold.

Part I of the Paris Agreement was divided in two categories. Category A dealt with German assets from countries outside of Germany. Category B included industry, capital equipment and merchant ships. It was agreed that the industrial equipment and factories would be removed from Germany and the level of industry retained by that country would be seventy-five percent of its 1936 capacity. This would put Germany at a starvation level as it was at the end of the Great Depression.

Categories A and B was then divided into the following percentage shares to be allocated to the following countries:

Country	Category		Country	Category	
	A	**B**		**A**	**B**
Albania	.05	.35	Greece	2.74	.35
U.S.A.	28.00	1.80	India	2.00	2.90
Australia.	.70	.95	Luxembourg	.15	.40
Belgium	2.70	4.50	Norway	1.31	.90
Canada	3.50	1.50	New Zealand	.40	.60
Denmark	.25	.35	Netherlands	3.90	5.60
Egypt	.05	.20	Czech	3.00	4.30
France	16.00	22.80	South Africa	.70	.10
England	28.00	27.80	Yugoslavia	6.60	9.60

Category B included 858 factories and 290 ships for a total value of $44,076,047 (1938 dollar value) to be divided among the members.

The United States received fourteen cargo ships. England received ninety-seven, which included eight passenger liners. One of the factories the United States disassembled was the *Aluminiumwerke Tscheulin* (Aluminium Foil) factory in Deningen, Germany. It was reassembled in the United States, where it had the capacity to produce 750,000 pounds of aluminum foil per month.

The percentage rates for the spoils of war, excluding the monetary gold had been established. The majority of external German assets was within the jurisdiction of the member Allies, but collecting the spoils from the neutral countries of category A would be most difficult.

The agreement for restitution of monetary gold was based on Part III of the Final Act of the Paris Conference and was stated as follows:

> "All the monetary gold found in Germany, except numismatic coins, shall be pooled for distribution among the countries participating in the pool in proportion to their respective losses of gold through looting or by wrongful removal to Germany. Claims for each country participating in the pool shall be accepted by that country in full satisfaction of all claims against Germany for restitution of monetary gold. The governments of the United States, France and England shall take appropriate steps to implement distribution in accordance with these provisions. The countries participating in the pool shall supply the United States, France and England detailed and verifiable data regarding the gold losses looted or removed by Germany."

The quagmire of proving looted losses began at the conference with the French representatives claiming that the Belgian gold belonged to France. In November 1945, the De Gaulle government conceded a Belgian claim and some New York Federal Reserve workmen wrapped up 435,364 pounds of gold bars and transferred them from the French vault to the Belgian vault within the Federal Reserve Bank. (Some of the gold found in the Merkers salt mine and transferred to Frankfurt may have borne Belgian stamps.) The Albanian government claimed a share of the recovered Italian gold. The question of Russia waiving its claim to the Allied gold, and the effect on claims by Poland and Danzig, were problems. The disposition of gold found in Austria needed clarification.

During the Paris Conference the Inter-Allied Reparation Agency was established for the collection of German assets and monetary gold from neutral countries. This agency was to enforce the spirit of the original Bretton Woods Resolution issued on July 22, 1944, by the fourty-four Allied countries and additional clarifications agreed upon in Paris.

Germany's banking and industrial assets in the neutral countries of western Europe totaled one-and-a-half billion dollars, most of it concentrated in Switzerland. By using these types of foreign assets after World War I, Germany had completely rearmed. Within twenty years, and under the surveillance of the Allied Commission, Germany's industry was in a position to construct planes, tanks, ships, artillery and all the tools necessary to wage total war. As World War II ended, German businessmen and bankers merely burrowed these assets deeper in neutral countries. They were masters of the complexity of hiding wealth. The job of uncovering these assets, and the collection of looted gold was taken on by the State and Treasury Departments of the United States. The bulk of the Gold Pot had been amassed by the United States Army during hostilities in Europe.

CHAPTER 22

U.S. Currency

The Paris Reparations Conference had ruled that all paper and non-gold coins would be returned to the Allied nation of origin. The Foreign Exchange Depository had acquired a large sum of US currency and in January 1949, began the preparations for returning it to the United States.

According to the official Reichsbank balance sheet, the total amount of US currency in the Berlin Reichsbank amounted to four million dollars. Of this currency, $2,000,000 was transferred to Merkers and the remainder was sent south into Bavaria. This currency is tabbed from the official balance sheet:

1 bag $100	$1,000,000
1 bag $50	$600,000
1 bag $20	$200,000
3 bags $10	$300,000
7 bags $5	$360,000
26 bags $1 and $2	$261,000
2 bags mixed $	$747,700
2 bags $2	$34,000
1 bag $10 and $20	$120,000
5 bags mixed $	$377,200
Total	$3,999,900

[The Reichsbank total for these exact figures is $4,000,000. The missing $100 in the Reichsbank total is unexplained.]

U.S. currency had been recovered from Shipments, 2A/B, 18B,18F, 27D, 52A, 60 and 61; apparently all this currency had been sent from Berlin in the closing days of World War II. According to statements made by Reichsbank officials Mielke and Goller, while under interrogation by Lt. Dubois in May 1945, forty-one bags of foreign currency had been sent to the Munich Reichsbank several weeks previously. The SS took thirteen of these bags and the remaining twenty-eight bags were taken by US forces as shipment 18F. Some of the currency from these thirteen bags was recovered buried in a barn near St. Johann and taken as shipment 27D. Additional money from the thirteen bags was recovered in shipment 60. Thus, the US currency shipped from Berlin to Munch and recovered in shipments 18B, 52A and 60 disagreed with the Berlin total by $1,168,990. What happened to this more than a million dollars?

While transfering the gold to the Kaiseroda Mine, Merkers in 1945, the Germans also shipped $4,000,000 in US currency from the Reichsbank in Berlin to the mine. The US Army did not recover any of the currency at the Kaiseroda Mine, however; it had been removed by the Germans to other locations prior to the arrival of the 90th Division.

As written previously the US currency was recovered from various locations and deposited in the Foreign Exchange Depository as follows:

I - 2 A/B Recovered by Colonel Bernstein's reconnaissance at the
Halle Reichsbank on April 20, 1945. Currencywas formerly held by
Berlin Reichsbank and transferred to Merkers. With the approaching
Americans it was moved to Halle. $2,000,000

II - 52 A Recovered at Walchensee on June 29, 1945.This currency
had been part of the Reichsbank loot transferred south by "Eagle and
Jackdaw" during the last stages of Germany's struggles to finance the
National Redoubt. $1,261,717

III - 31 Recovered at Reuris, Zell an See on June 18,1945;
part of cache hidden by Josef Spacil asa pay depot. $160,679

IV - 18 A, B, F Recovered at the Munich Reichsbank by
Lt.Herbert DuBois during reconnaissance on April 22, 1945. $116,000

V - 52 C Taken by US Military from Gestapo funds on June 21,
1945, at Bad Aussee, Austria. $14,500

VI - 60 Found by US Military on August 11, 1945,
near Mittenwald while searching for buried documents $4,000

VII - 57 A Found with other assets at Garmisch taken from
deceased British aviators. $3,380

VIII - Taken from various Allied Prisoner-of-War Camps
with no records of ownership. $164.88

Total US currency deposited in the Foreign Exchange Depository $3,562,130.88

Items I-IV and VI was currency acquired in the days immediately following World War II and the
source of this money was reported to be the Berlin Reichsbank. Thus only $18,909.88 of the above
total came from other sources. From Shipments 1 (Merkers $93,255.64) and 16 a total of $97,045.80
were turned over to the Intergovernmental Committee for Refugees.[1]
The aggregate denomination of currency follows:

234,731	$1
19,654	$2
54,345	$5
44,218	$10
14,759	$20
5,460	$50
19,135	$100
41	$500 (40) from Shipment 52 A and 1 from Shipment 31
71	$1,000 (70) from Shipment 52 A and 1 from Shipment 57
Total	$3,561,124

Coins:

1,839	at 1 cent
1	at 3 cents silver 1853 from Shipment 31
655	at 5 cents
524	at 10 cents
190	at 25 cents
13	at 50 cents
8	at $1.00 Total $165.57

Also two envelopes with burned currency said to contain $825.00

Again, the official Reichsbank balance sheet for US currency was $3,999,900 and its largest denomination was $100 bills. How could the Foreign Exchange Depository have (41) $500 and (71) $1000 bills in its accountability of Berlin Reichsbank US currency? The US Army had recovered the majority of the Reichsbank's money— or had they? At this point in compiling all these figures, the author asked himself what's wrong with these dollar amounts?

In a conference of December 29, 1948, to discuss the transfer of the cash to the United States, Mr. Frank Roberts reported: "The money has already been verified by German employees of the FED. We do not have these people with us now, so it will be impossible for them to certify to final packing."[2]

On January 4, 1949, personnel at the Foreign Exchange Depository began recounting the US currency. The dollars had been stored in ten large metal cans. On January 4, 1949, at 10:00 in the morning, four US soldiers and three German nationals started emptying the metal containers and sorted the bills into common denominations. Observing in the vault were Mr. Keller, Roberts, Angotti and Lt. Thies. They completed empting and counting the contents of metal containers one and two. The following day, nine counters reported for work and counted and sorted containers three, four and partially five. They filled three wooden boxes and nailed them shut. They could not stencil the boxes because the stencils had been cut too large. The Corp of Engineers were called and agreed to make new stencils. On January 6, an additional counter was added and containers six and seven were completed. The following day, a Friday, the operation continued and the currency counting of nine containers was completed Monday morning. That same day, January 10, 1949, the coins in metal can ten were validated as the stenciling, banding and numbering of the fourteen boxes was completed.

The currency, by denominations within the fourteen wooden boxes, was loaded at 5:30pm into a six-ton van with an eight-man security guard. The van drove to the railway station, where the money was loaded onto a train that left Frankfurt and arrived the next morning at Bremerhaven, Germany. The currency was placed aboard the *General Harry Taylor* and the eight military police were released from their security obligations. The currency was then shipped to New York City and deposited into the Federal Reserve Bank.[3]

During the sorting of the legal tender did Mr. Frank J. Roberts became suspicious as the $500 and $1,000 bills surfaced? After all he had been with the Foreign Exchange Depository since it reorganization in March 1946. And he had bought the official line that the majority of the Berlin Reichsbank stash of US currency had been recovered in Shipment 2 and 52A. The Berlin Reichsbank currency was established by records that had been stored in the Merkers Mine. The evaluations in the early stages were made by the intelligence gathering of naval Lt.Cmdr. Joel H. Fischer and Lt. Herbert G. DuBois, with the assistance of Albert Thoms. Now Frank Roberts had a second opinion about the money.

Two months after the money had been shipped to Washington DC, on March 28, 1949, Roberts wrote a memo—"U.S. Dollars Found in Germany." Let's examine that memo.[4]

Roberts explains that $4,000,000 was sent to Merkers from the Berlin Reichsbank on February 9, 1945. All of the foreign currency including the US money was removed from Merkers Mine (Ort H or German location H) with $1,000,000 deposited in Halle and another $1,000,000 to be sent to

Nordhausen, that was seized also in Halle. Also sent from Merkers Mine, was $2,170,800 that was deposited in Magdeburg and subsequently returned to the Berlin Reichsbank on April 11, 1945. Two days later, on April 13, 1945, this foreign currency, along with the US $2,170,800, was loaded aboard two trains and sent south in the direction of Bavaria.

To prove this, Frank Roberts compared the Berlin Reichsbank balance sheet from February 9 to the balance sheet of April 13 and notes these seven identical entries; (1) $35,200, (2) $14,000, (3) $712,500, (4) ten and twenty dollars for a total $120,000 (5) a miscellaneous stack of dollars for $27,200, (6) one and two dollar bills for a total $14,000 and (7) a stack of one dollar bills for $7,000. Roberts concluded the currency sent south was a part of the February 9, balance sheet.

Roberts finished the report: "It is appreciated that the data and exhibits as submitted through voluminous by no means presents a clear picture of the disposition of the foreign currency after it left the Reichsbank, Berlin. Obviously, a considerable portion has never been found and in various respects, a conclusion as to source can not be fully substantiated."

But what was the point? His three pages of rambling cover letter with ninety pages attached is a rehash of the history of the currency. It is not understood by the author. Thus, the obvious question is neither Berlin Reichsbank balance sheet reported any $500 or $1,000 bills. What was the source of these large bills? Of the (71) $1,000 bills only one was accountable and it came from Shipment 57 in an Allied prisoner of war circumstance.

The large bills were inventoried on July 22, 1946, in Shipment 52A.[5] Were they a part of the original deposit or were they substituted prior to the inventory in the metal containers for smaller currency to avoid suspicion as a $1,000 or $500 bill would be difficult to spend or deposit? The serial numbers of these large bills were recorded. Did a German employee, US soldier or officer make off with a fortune in US currency while assigned to the Foreign Exchange Depository?

CHAPTER 23
Gold Shipment to the Bank of England

After the war, the unlimited, abusive printing of currency had destroyed the Reichsmarks and the German economy. During 1947, the Foreign Exchange Depository began to secretly collect the marks and had them ground up and made into paper.

In an attempt to bolster the German economy, the US took a bold step. On November 21, 1947, the Foreign Exchange Depository, under a top-secret order, began to accumulate and store, in several thousand wooden boxes, a new German currency. This Deutschmark was distributed in West Germany on June 18, 1948, at an exchange of 10 Reichsmarks for one new Deutschmark. The printing of the currency was carefully controlled. The Russians asked for the new plates but the Allies refused. Additionally, the currency was not convertable in the Russian occupation zone. This financial conflict worsened U.S.-Russian relations that had begun to deteriorate at the end of World War II. The Russians demonstrated their military power by challenging the Allies' right to use routes through Russian-occupied Germany into Berlin. This consisted mainly of harassment and the closing of roads, canals, and railroads for unexplained technical difficulties and repairs. The day after the currency reform of June 18, Russia completely cut off all land traffic to Berlin and thus began the famous Berlin blockade and subsequent airlift.

The Cold War between Russia and the United States began with the ending of World War II. Tension between the two countries had increased daily during postwar years and within this atmosphere, and just prior to the beginning of the Berlin blockade, the decision was made to ship the Allied Gold Pot from Frankfurt to the Bank of England.

In January 1948, Col. Brey received a letter from the Department of Defense directing the Foreign Exchange Depository to deliver the monetary gold from Frankfurt to the vaults of the Bank of England. Brey estimated that 1,600 wooden boxes would be needed for the transfer; so they were ordered and sawdust secured for packing. Boxes designated to hold bars of gold were stenciled, beginning with number 1001; those for bags of gold began with number 2001.

On January 19, bagging of the gold coins began. The coins were not weighed, but the weight of an earlier inventory, the so-called Howard Report, was used. Packing took until January 26, and totaled 820 boxes. Packing the gold bars began on January 27, continued until February 6, and totaled 732 boxes of gold bars, weighing 132,000 pounds.

Packing teams, consisting of two US civilians, three military officers and seven enlisted men selected, sorted, packed, banded, and stored the wooden boxes of gold coins and bars. This concluded the packaging of the monetary gold. Coins of numismatic value, and a small amount of gold considered non-monetary, was stored in vault 12 for further examination.

During the collection of the gold, a meeting was arranged between the US Army and the Tripartite Commission to transport the gold to England. The cost of insurance, the number of shipments based on the maximum allowed for insurance coverage, and approved strong rooms on the army vessels were discussed. The cost of insuring the gold established by the US Army was 34.5 cents per $100 value. Military representatives suggested all the gold be shipped at once on a fast passenger ship, without insurance coverage. The Tripartite Gold Commission stated they would never approve the shipment of the gold in this haphazard manner.

During the Army negotiations, the Federal Reserve Bank received quotes for shipments from three commercial airlines. These airlines were lower than the Army or any commercial shipping rates obtainable. But a higher bidder, Pan American contracted to fly the gold on a DC-3 type aircraft with 6,600 pounds on each flight for $800 per flight. In relation to this contract Fred B. Smith wrote:

One fact had always puzzled me. Of the airline rates which we supplied the Tripartite Commission, the lowest rate was quoted by American Overseas Airlines and Pan American was the highest rate quoted. I was, therefore, very much surprised to learn that the contract was awarded to Pan American.[1]

Flights were to begin immediately, but were delayed due to a disagreement between the US Army and the Tripartite Commission on receipt forms and other necessary documents. Four months later, the Foreign Exchange Depository was informed that an agreement on the forms and documentation had been reached and that shipment was to begin.

The boxes of gold were loaded onto trucks at the depository. Under security guard of the 709th Military Police, two truckloads were delivered daily to the Rhein-Main Air Base near Frankfurt. The gold was transferred by a forklift to a storage room, and then shipped out in two different planeloads, one shipment at 2:00pm and the other at 6:00am the following day. Shipments continued daily until July 13, when technical difficulties arising from the Berlin airlift caused cancellation of shipments for that day. Due to the Berlin crisis, additional military police guarded the gold at the Rhein-Main Air Base. The fifty-second flight, shipping ticket numbered 133, contained the sixty-four bars of gold recovered by Col. Bernstein at the Eisenach Reichsbank on April 10, 1945, as Shipment 9. These bars numbered Q4781 through Q4789, Q4901 through Q4905, Q4883-99 and 11090 and had been the property of Dollfuss Mieg Company, France. The fifty-third, and final flight by Pan American, was made on August 3, 1948. The gold shipped to the Bank of England for deposit to the Tripartite Commission exceeded 342,543 pounds of fine gold.[2]

Transfer of the gold from Frankfurt to London was uneventful except that on July 28; one bar of gold was missing from flight number 46. The Foreign Exchange Depository was notified by Pan American on July 30 that bar number 862-D was missing from box number 1496 upon its arrival in London.

The US Army Criminal Investigation Division was told about the gold by Capt. Francis D. Ruth, security officer of the Foreign Exchange Depository. He reported that two trucks of gold had left the depository at 11:45am on July 28 for the trip to the Rhein-Main Air Base. One truckload was flown out at 2:00pm and the truckload with the missing bar was put in the storage room for the 6:00am flight the following day. The missing bar contained approximately 400 ounces of gold and was valued at $14,000.

The investigation of the gold was assigned to US military agents Hector J. Deleo and Eugene R. Bonner of the 31th CID stationed in Wiesbaden, Germany. The two agents interviewed a Pan American representative and were told that the box was offloaded with thirty-five other boxes containing gold directly from the aircraft into an armored truck under security of customs officials and British police. Box numbers 1496 and 1489 were loose as the boxes were being unloaded from the aircraft into the truck. The ends of the boxes were immediately nailed tight in the presence of all the security personnel. Loading was completed and the armored truck was locked and preceded directly to the Bank of England. Upon arrival, box number 1496 which showed signs of damage was checked immediately. Only five bars of gold were in the box, instead of the six that had been placed in every box. The investigators thus concluded that the security measures taken in England were such that it was improbable the wooden box had been opened and the bar removed after its arrival at the London Airport. The agents then turned their attention to investigating loading at the Frankfurt Air Base.

Four Germans had loaded the boxes of gold onto the forklift pallets in the storage room on the morning of July 29, 1948. They were questioned and all stated one box containing the gold had a loose end. The end was opened only about one-half inch away from the top and sides, but was still held together by interlocking dovetailed ends. During the loading process the four Germans were observed by the 709th Military Police. By more backtracking, the CID agents learned that the gold had been guarded in the storage room the night previous to the theft by Cpl. Joseph V. Ellis and Pvt.

Howard E. Garrett, both from A Company, 709th Military Police Battalion. The CID agents left to interrogate both men, but they were AWOL.

Ellis was apprehended on August 8, 1948, and interrogated by Agents Deleo and Bonner. Ellis said he knew nothing of the disappearance of the gold bar, but had heard rumors a bar was missing. Ellis's story was checked out and the agents verified Ellis had been in the vicinity of Frankfurt while AWOL and had not spoken with anyone about the missing gold.

The CID agents then went to Garrett's quarters and searched his room. His footlocker contained two US silver dollars, two US silver half dollars, five German silver Reichsmarks, and a small piece of gold weighing two ounces assayed at .9998 fine. Garrett returned to Company A on August 10, and, under questioning by the CID agents, said he had been in Paris for a good time and did not know anything about the missing gold.

The agents proceeded then to interrogate Garrett's girl friend, Miss Asta Zwinscher, who said Garrett had talked to two of her friends about gold. She showed the two agents the house where the two women lived. The CID men interrogated the two and they admitted that Garrett had come by their house on the evening of July 29, 1948, and talked to them from the street, as they were looking down out their window. Garrett had asked them if they had any scales and if they would weigh some gold for him. He then showed the girls two pieces of gold approximately three inches long. The two women did not own any scales and so Garrett had walked away.

On September 3, Garrett was asked again by the CID and admitted that he had two pieces of gold and that he and PFC Williams A. Saunders, Company A 709th Military Police, had received the gold from an Italian in trade for a watch. The exchange had taken place at the Frankfurt railway station during June of 1948. Garrett further stated that Saunders still had the gold. Garrett again denied having any knowledge of the gold found in his foot locker and stated that as far as he knew the gold was placed in his foot locker by someone who did not like him.

Saunders was then located and questioned about the gold allegedly acquired from the Italian at the Frankfurt railway station and confirmed Garrett's statement. The two pieces of gold were surrendered to the two agents. The bars were approximately three inches long and were assayed at .5854 fine, much too poor a grade to qualify for the gold contained at the Foreign Exchange Depository.

The gold found in Private Garrett's locker was .9998 fine and the records at the Foreign Exchange Depository showed that bar number 862-D was .900 fine. On September 3, 1948, Garrett willingly submitted to taking a polygraph test. Agent Mervin Cumpton, who administered the test, concluded that Garrett had taken the missing bar of gold from the storage room at the Rhein-Main Air Base, but due to a lack of solid additional evidence, no arrest was made and no one was confined as a result of this investigation by the 31st CID, US Army.[3] Despite all of this inquiry, the missing bar was never found. The gold was insured by Lloyds of London, who compensated the Gold Commission $12,926.66 for the missing bar.[4]

Thus, all of the Allied Gold Pot from Germany, minus one bar, and the shipments to the Netherlands and France, were deposited in the name of the Tripartite Commission in the Bank of England. The total cost of transportation and insurance amounted in all to $158,080.78.[5]

Remaining in the Foreign Exchange Depository in Frankfurt was a fortune in silver, platinum, diamonds and paper currency.

CHAPTER 24
The Tripartite Gold Deposits

An account was opened at the Bank of England for the Tripartite Gold Commission in the name of His Majesty's Treasury on May 20, 1948, with the first deposit from Romania. The bulk of the gold from Frankfurt, detailed above, would arrive during July.

The Bank of England procedure for receiving gold was different than the Federal Reserve Bank, New York, (explained later with that section) as they would accept as good delivery twenty-six categories of gold and give a firm credit in Troy ounces. Bars that were not good delivery would be melted down and converted into acceptable bars. Good delivery bars were not kept separate. When an order was given to transfer the gold to another customer, the Tripartite Gold account was debited and the gold transferred was not necessarily the same gold deposited by the customer. In 1955, this practice stopped and specific bars were set aside for the Tripartite Gold Commission.[1]

In regards to gold coins, they were received in bags with the weight indicated by labels tied to the bags. Because of the large number of coins, the bank was unable to examine the individual coins. The Tripartite Commission agreed to relieve the Bank of England of the responsibility and liability in respect to any counterfeit coins. Later upon delivery, counterfeit coins were found. The Bank credited the Tripartite Commission account with the amount of fine ounces on the bag tags as, "the calculated contents of sundry gold coins set aside for the account."[2]

The deposit to the Bank of England from Frankfurt was supposedly made because; "Experts of the Commission who were unanimous in their opinion that the Commission could not satisfactory carry out that part of its functions which consisted in announcing the value of the pool of monetary gold and in distributing it."[3] The Commission expressed the concern that the Frankfurt Depository was cramped and the inexperienced personnel, and the equipment proved unsatisfactory. It was further emphasized that the verification of the weight of the bars and coins were suspect and that the accuracy could only be validated in a central bank. Also, the resmelting and conversion into good delivery bars would require a central bank such as the Bank of England. After the matter had been carefully considered by the Tripartite Gold Commission, the Foreign Exchange Depository gold described in a prior chapter was shipped to the Bank of England.

The Bank of England received the last shipment of gold on August 3, 1948, and proceeded to inventory the gold, but found itself faced with a number of difficult problems. A large number of bars, particularly the Prussian mint bars, were not good delivery bars and had to be melted into Bank of England essayed bars. Some of the gold coins, medals and tokens were unidentifiable and others defaced. After validation, those not of numismatic or historical value were melted into bars. An additional 141 Prussians bars contained both silver and gold. These were smelted into good delivery gold and silver bars.

The Bank of England levied a safe custody fee of .0025 for every gold ounce delivered and deposited into the Tripartite Gold Commission's account. This charge was assessed every three months for a fee resulting in .01 per year. At this price the 1948 Frankfurt deposit alone would amount to a whopping $580,692.46. Apparently, there was some concern regarding this large fee for the Bank as the first nine months reported a safe custody charge of only $193,873. The Commission must have balked for on March 18, 1949, the Bank of England refunded the Commission $111,873.28 of the safe custody charges, resulting in a fee to the Bank of England of $27,202. This was solely the safe custody fee for, "handling, assay, melting, refining and other exceptional charges were of course claimed separately by the Bank in accordance with its usual practice."[4] The first nine months of deposit was very profitable for the Bank, but thereafter the safe custody charge was reduced to a reasonable flat fee of $8,060 a year. The additional fees were not addresses.

In New York, the first Tripartite Gold Commission account was opened, without prior intervention of the Commission, at the Federal Reserve Bank of New York on June 6, 1947. The Bank wrote on June 26, 1947, stating that it had been requested by the Banque Nationale Suisse at Berne, to release not less than 1,659,119.140 fine ounces of gold from its account with them and to hold such amount at the disposal of the Commission. The bank added that it had been informed that this transfer represented a payment agreed between the Allied Governments concerned and Switzerland under the Washington Agreement of 1946, and that pursuant to an authorization and instructions of the United States Treasury Department, acting as fiscal agent of the United States, it had opened a gold account on its books, on June 6, 1947, in the name of the Commission. The only account opened in the name of the Tripartite Gold Commission.

The rules governing the holding of gold bars and coins in the United States were different than the rules in Europe. The Federal Reserve Bank of New York held only United States Assay Office gold bars, which are the only bars of good delivery on the American market. The bars are set aside in the bank's vaults under earmark for the account holders' account and the latter receive from the bank a list of the bars held and a firm credit in respect of these bars in Troy ounces of fine gold. The FRBNY upon receiving foreign bars and coins, had these melted down and converted into United States Assay Office bars. This operation entailed certain costs and a small loss of gold in the melting process.

There are about twenty-six different types of gold bars that are good delivery on most of the European markets, and most gold coins have a recognized value and are preferred by many countries to bars. Since the countries with which the Commission was concerned were all European and, therefore, accustomed to receiving bars recognized as good delivery bars on the main European' markets, as well as foreign gold coins having a recognized value, the Commission asked whether there would be any objection to the setting aside by the Federal Reserve Bank of New York of bars and coins answering the above description, intact, for its account, as well as all United States coins which are only redeemable at their face value in the United States. This procedure was agreed upon, but the bank only gave a "said to contain" credit for such bars and coins. Miscellaneous gold bars, that were not good delivery on the European markets, and mutilated and unidentifiable coins, were converted into United States Assay Office bars.

Confusing, but the Bank of France was apparently the international bank for the Belgium and Luxembourg governments and housed their allotment of the Allied Gold Pot. Also, the bank opened an account for the Tripartite Gold Commission.

France's first deposit was the large transfer of gold from the Foreign Exchange Depository that consisted of a deposit of 1,267,151.553 Troy ounces of bars and 1,169,704.252 Troy ounces of gold on November 19, 1947. This was not considered as a part of the Banks gold as it was immediately credited to Belgium and Luxembourg as their gold reserves. This gold transfer will be addressed in a later chapter.

The Bank received its first deposit as a result of Military Law 53. The Tripartite Gold Commission requested this gold be delivered to the Bank of England. In August 1951, after much discussion and disagreements an account for the Tripartite Gold Commission was opened at the Bank of France in Paris. The total gold collected by the Bank of France amounted to 75,500.338 of fine ounces of gold with a 1945 value of $2,642,511.83.

Gold Deposited by Countries

Romania: A portion of the Belgian gold seized in France by the Germans was sent to the Berlin Reichsbank. There the gold was sent to the Prussian Mint to be resmelted; thus destroying the original identity of the bars. Some of the new bars were forwarded to the National Bank of Romania in Bucharest. There, it was deposited in the National Bank of Switzerland, credited to the National Bank of Romania.

On November 26, 1947, in Berne, Switzerland, the officials of the Government of Romania requested that US embassy officials act as their custodians in receiving 578,796.850 Troy ounces of gold stored in the National Bank of Switzerland. The US Embassy requested the gold to be sent to the Bank of England and deposited into the Gold Pot. The Swiss agreed to transfer the gold to the Bank of England for a then whopping $46,400. All agreed, and the gold that was comprised entirely of Prussian Mint Bars, was delivered to the account of the Bank of England on April 22, 1948. The bars were not considered good delivery; there they were smelted into good delivery bars with a weight of 578,700.153 Troy ounces of gold bars. Therefore, the Romanian deposit lost 96.697 ounces ($4,351.37) in the smelting and $46,400 in transfer fees, a total loss of $50,751.37 in 1945 dollars. It seems odd that a country under Soviet occupation would deliver gold to the Allied Gold Pot.[5]

Switzerland: Negotiations, known as the Washington Accord, began immediately with Switzerland. The essential provision of the accord provided that all German assets in Switzerland be sold by the Swiss, and the proceeds be split 50/50 by the Swiss and the Allies. In addition, the Swiss were to place at the disposal of the Allies 138,260 pounds of gold payable on demand at the New York Federal Reserve Bank. The United States let Switzerland know that collecting the gold would not be a problem. In the early days of World War II, Switzerland had transferred her gold reserves to the New York Federal Bank for safekeeping and it was merely a matter of moving the gold from one pile to another by US banking officials.

At the beginning of the conference, the Swiss agreed to the 50/50 split of German assets, but negotiations with respect to the looted gold was extremely difficult. The Swiss Government maintained they were obligated under Swiss law to buy and sell gold freely for all customers in order to preserve the stability of the Swiss franc. The Swiss maintained that they never knowingly accepted looted gold from the German Reichsbank. The Swiss Minister, Walter Stucki, responded in a convincing rebuttal that the Allies were sabotaging international law and holding it to be a crime that Switzerland did not enter the war. Mr. Stuchi's convincing ethical statements may have been made to protect the profits of the Swiss National Bank. During the first months of 1945 the profits made from dealing with Germany were 4,429,526 Swiss gold francs.

The Allies, in the course of the Washington Accord, presented decisive proof of the methods Germany used to appropriate the gold and sell it through Switzerland in order to utilize the wealth in promoting the conquest of Europe. The Allies stated that they were not asking payment by Switzerland for a victory that benefited four million Swiss, but wanted complete cooperation to reimburse the Allied countries their stolen wealth. The Swiss continued to refuse to recognize any legal liability to restore the looted gold. The United States was aware that unless an agreement could be negotiated with the Swiss to provide the restitution of looted gold, the agreement with any other neutral country on this subject would collapse.

After the initial agreement on foreign assets, many conferences took place with the Swiss Government but questions on currency exchange rates and custodial problems due to dual citizenship were not resolved. German records indicated more than $750,000,000 was in numbered accounts protected by the Swiss bank secrecy law and the United States intended to obtain half of this wealth. The Swiss continued to delay it obligations for restitution.

The United States took drastic action to pressure them to be more responsive by freezing all their assets in the United States and placing prominent Swiss firms and individuals on a black list for aiding and abetting the enemy. This action was injurious to the Swiss economy and provoked political and social unrest.

Regardless of the measures, the German assets were never split, but the accord was signed in Washington, DC, on May 25, 1946, and the Allies removed all restrictions on Switzerland. They continued to prevent the implementation of the accord and these difficulties raised serious doubts in the minds of the Allies as to the good faith of the Swiss. Despite these problems, 138,260 pounds of gold were transferred from the Swiss pile to the Allied Gold Pot in New York on June 6, 1947.

Although Switzerland had not been at war, either with Germany and the Axis countries, or with the United States, Great Britain, Russia and their allies, it was in fact the conclusion of the Washington agreement that sounded the knell of the long period of war. It was only at that point that Switzerland was able to normalize its relations with the coalition of victorious countries. In that sense, the agreement, signed in Washington and ratified in Berne by the Federal Chambers, convened in an extraordinary session at the end of June 1946, represented an obligatory means of emerging from the shadow of German hegemony during the war to the new parameters of an Allied (or American) peace after 1945.

Now earmarked in the Federal Reserve Bank of New York vaults from the Swiss account were 4,031 United States Assay Office gold bars containing 1,659,121.321 Troy ounces of fine gold. This was 2.181 ounces more than requested. Due to the small amount the Swiss never requested a refund.[6,7]

Sweden: Shortly after the Swiss Accord, negotiations commenced in Washington with representatives of Sweden on the subject of German assets in Sweden, and looted gold. The attitude of the Swedish representatives appeared to be considerably more sympathetic to the views of the Allies than the Swiss. They agreed to the liquidation of all German assets in Sweden, and that $3,770,000 be allocated to nine selected members of the Paris Agreement, provided the funds be used to purchase Swedish goods for export to Germany as a preventative of disease and unrest. Thus, the Swedish government insured that the purchase of these goods would profit their economy and minimize the impact of their allocation. It was also agreed that the German owners of property liquidated would be compensated with German paper currency (which would soon have no value).

With regards to looted gold purchased by the Swedish Government, they agreed to the effects of Bretton Woods Resolution VI. The Allies had proof that the Swedish had acquired 19,170 pounds of looted Belgian gold from Germany. They agreed to transfer this amount of gold to the Allied Gold Pot on the basis that this was the total obligation of the Swedish government. These negotiations resulted in an agreement signed on July 16, 1946.

After this accord was signed, however, the Allies, using information derived from captured Reichsbank records, discovered that Sweden had acquired 23,810 pounds of gold looted from Holland. The Allies filed claims that more than doubled the original signed arrangement. The Swedish in rebuttal stated that the language was clear in the accord and that Sweden was not obligated to resolve the issue, and offered no compromise. Nevertheless, Swedish merchants made a profit from the German liquidation and the Swedish government appeared to be fair from the standpoint of moral principles.

On December 12, 1949, the Sveriges Riksbank, Sweden, transferred 230,049.065 ounces from its account at the Federal Reserve Bank into the Tripartite Commission Gold Pot. On October 14, 1947, the 401 bars of gold had been shipped from Sweden aboard the luxury liner, *Drottningholm* and deposited into the Swedish account at the FRB. Two months later, 170 bars originally imported from Argentina and shipped on the steamship *Mormacrio,* arrived in New York and were credited to Sweden's account at the Federal Reserve Bank.[8]

The second delivery of Swedish gold was received by the Federal Reserve Bank on May 2, 1955. The gold bore markings of assayers acceptable by the Bank of England but questioned by the New York bank officials. In question were seven bars with Prussian mints and a stamp and numbers of the Swedish Mint (Köngl Myntet). Officials at the Federal Reserve Bank wrote the Bank of England and France questioning the assay marks. The Bank of England responded that the bars were considered good delivery bar in London. The Bank of France reluctantly agreed the bars were of good delivery due to the Swedish Mint mark. Thus, the delivery was accepted and entered on the books of the Federal Reserve Bank as 192,904.484 Troy ounces added to the Gold Pot.[9]

The last delivery to the Federal Reserve Bank, New York was made on April 29, 1955 when Sweden transferred 479 bars of gold from its account in that bank to the Gold Pot for a total of 192,904.484 ounces.[10]

Portugal: After the cessation of hostilities in Europe, the United States sent a telegram to Portugal setting forth the objectives outlined in Bretton Woods Resolution VI. The Portugal government agreed to participate in a discussion and a meeting convened in Lisbon on September 3, 1946. The accord with them required the liquidation of all German assets in Portugal. The Portuguese Government would receive 180 million *escndos* ($7,200,000) and the remainder of the German assets would be allocated to the Allies. The Portuguese government had acquired 93,520 pounds of looted gold from Germany during the war and the Allies reconstructed a bar-by-bar reconciliation tracing the gold from its original looting by the Germans, including resmelting operations, to the final acquisition by Portugal. The reconciliation of the gold was done in Washington through records obtained from numerous sources, including the Reichsbank Records.

The Portuguese relied on two basic rebuttals. The first, they did not have knowledge that the Bank of Portugal had indeed acquired looted gold, and second, even if they were willing to admit the question in view of the evidence presented by the Allies, they continued to claim "purchase in good faith." They would not back down and did not compensate the Allied Gold Pot with any acquired looted gold or the liquidation of any German assets at that time.

The Allies continued to demand compensation from Portugal. Finally on December 24, 1959, the Bank of England received 318 bars of gold from the Banco de Portugal. There was a problem, as the bars were short of the required amount by 61.856 Troy ounces, which was less than one bar of gold. This was resolved by the Portugal Government selling 61.856 Troy ounces of gold on the London market. From this transaction the Gold Pot was credited with an additional $2,164.96.[11,12]

Spain: After preliminary discussions in Madrid in November 1946, the procedure to be followed in establishing the amount of looted gold in Spain was agreed upon by British, French and US representatives. The Spanish government was unwilling to cooperate because they felt they had a counter-claim with regards to gold taken from Spain during her Civil War. Additionally, some Spanish vessels had been turned over to the Allies, and Spain considered them as payment for any looted gold that might have been acquired by Spain during the war.

The Spanish government was persuaded by the American delegation to turn over its record of gold acquisitions. They could not reconcile the gold reserves from 1941 to the end of 1945. Because of the difficulty in identifying the gold, the delegation was forced to drop the reconciliation of the Spanish records. From other records, though, the Allies knew that Spain had obtained 53,600 pounds of looted gold. The gold had been obtained from the Swiss National Bank, The Bank of Portugal and the Banco Aleman Trans-Atlantico. The gold from the latter bank was identified as looted from the Netherlands and was still in its original form, and the markings had not been changed since it was forcibly removed from Holland and acquired by the Spanish government. These eight bars of gold, weighing 101.6 kilograms, were physically transferred to the Bank of England on January 21, 1949, and deposited into the Allied Gold Pot.[13]

German-owned insurance, chemical and pharmaceutical firms operated openly in Spain. The Spanish government claimed the removal or liquidations of proprieties were not within the limits and possibilities of the Spanish economy. All German assets remained in Spain.[14]

Yugoslavia: On September 18, 1951, the Gold Pot was credited with 1,656.230 troy ounces of fine gold. It appears the account was debited the same day for the same amount with the debit going to Yugoslavia.[15]

Czechoslovakia: This transaction is the most difficult to track. It is referenced from page 23 of a report titled Annex 22 with no date: (CL 206860) This gold was delivered (date unknown) and amounted to 119,279.728 Troy ounces of gold.

Further described: "The circumstances in which this gold was recovered by Czechoslovakia and held by the Commissioner to be gold that should be considered as having been received by

Czechoslovakian on account of the share of the pool are described on pages 28-32 of the Commission's adjudication of the claims of the Czechoslovakian."[16]

The 279.728 Troy ounces of gold was delivered and credited to the Tripartite Gold Commission's account with the Bank of England.[17]

The Bank for International Settlement is the world's oldest international financial institution, owned and controlled by central banks. The BIS was created in 1930 in implementation of the Young Plan, which was adopted at the second Hague Conference in January of that year, and which provided for a settlement of the problem of German reparations ensuing from the First World War. The BIS took up its activities in Basel, Switzerland, in May 1930. By early 1932, twenty-four European central banks and two banking syndicates representing Japan and the United States had subscribed to the BIS's capital. The primary tasks of the BIS, as summed up in its original statutes, were to promote the cooperation of central banks and to provide additional facilities for international financial operations. Allied representatives met in Washington with representatives of the Bank of International Settlements to discuss its participation with Germany during World War II. During the heated discussion, on June 24, 1948, the BIS agreed to deliver to the Bank of England 120,243.777 ounces of gold bars in full settlement for looted gold it had acquired from Germany.[18] Some of the bars were Prussian Mint bars that had been delivered to the BIS. These bars were melted into good delivery bars and incurred a few ounces of loss in weight.[19]

Gold Delivered from Austria

A month after hostilities had ended in Europe, on June 6, 1945, Bernd Gottfriedsen, introduced in a previous chapter, was in Bad Gastein, Austria. This Alpine village was a fashionable resort area and had escaped the ravages of World War II. He lived here in comparative luxury with fashionable hotels and homes. For some unexplained reason, in great confidences, Gottfriedsen told Herbert Heroz, a twenty-two-year-old tradesman that he had hidden, on specific orders from Joachim von Ribbentrop, two large caches of gold. One on the dairy farm of Alois Ziller in Hintersee, and the other in the cellar of a house at 89 Böcksteiner Street, Bad Gastein. Why would Gottfriedsen inform a youthful Heroz and not someone else? His story is full of holes, but it's all we have and it is consistent with Gottfriedsen's sworn statement.

The following day, the young Heroz, ascertained personally that the location in Bad Gastein did not seem to have been disturbed. The next morning, he traveled the sixty-nine miles north to Hintersee. Heroz went to Ziller dairy farm where in the shed; he tapped on the ground and determined the soil had not been disturbed. As Heroz tells the story, he then spent the next ten days in vain to get the Austrian authorities to place the gold in the safety of local officials. He was told that only the Occupying Authority was qualified to safeguard the treasure.

Therefore, on June 17, 1945, Heroz went to the headquarters of the Detachment of CIC (Counter Intelligence Corps), 3rd Infantry Division; US Army located in Salzburg and told agent Mr. James Devan that he knew the location of two large caches of gold. Devan had heard too many gold stories and gave the youthful Heroz no credit for his story. Now, strangely, Gottfriedsen appears on the scene and confirms Heroz's information. The three men drove in an army car the eighteen miles to Hintersee, arriving that afternoon. Ziller saw then approaching and recognized Gottfriedsen, with the Army officer. He was introduced to Heroz who walked straight to the wooden shed. Here Heroz, acting as the one in charge, uncovered the packing crates in the shed and lifted a bag of gold from one of the containers. This surprised Mr. Devan, as he had Heroz replace the gold bag and close the door to the shed. He told Heroz to go to Hintersee and have the Bürgermeister send some men residing in the village to help in the removal the gold. Meanwhile, Devan dispatched an armored truck from the 15th Regiment with an escort of eight US soldiers to the dairy farm. Six to eight men arrived as Ziller and Herzog had shoveled all the dirt from the hole. They loaded the eighty-one sacks onto the truck.

One sack had torn spilling golden lira coins on the ground. Ziller replaced the torn bag with a new sack of his. Herzog noticed that the bags contained seals bearing the inscription Banca d' Italia.

Upon a request by Devan, Heroz handed him a written statement affirming the delivery of eighty-one bags of gold with the approximate weight of five tons. Again, it is not comprehensible that Heroz had taken command of the gold deposit?

Late on June 17, the three men now along with another CIC agent, Mr. Cary, left the dairy farm in Devan's car, accompanying the armored truck and escort. Early in the morning of June 18, they arrived and delivered the truckload of gold to Lt. William Lipper, Head of the CIC Detachment, in Salzburg.

The following morning, CIC agents, Cary, Devan, Gottfriedsen and Heroz, still acting as the person of authority, left Salzburg, and drove south eighty miles to the village of Bad Gastein. Arriving here, Heroz directed them to the house at 89 Böcksteiner Street, where Gottfriedsen had buried the gold previously on May 1, 1945. The packing case in the cellar was dug up and it contained thirteen small bags of gold coins some small bars of gold and one bar of silver. Heroz estimated the total weight at about 330 pounds.

Again, and properly so, Devan requested an inventory list that Herbert Herzog wrote up:

> According to the labels
> 3 sacks each   5,000 gold dollars
> 10 sacks each   20,000 gold francs
> 20 loose gold bars
> 1 sack containing gold bars
> 1 packet with 12 gold bars
> 1 box with gold bars 12X10X5.5 with the inscription: valuables 15 IV belonging to Minister Dienstmann, Minister of Foreign Affairs, forwarded by Minister Koch, German Legation, Berne.
> 1 box 12X10X5.5
> 1 box 13X7X7
> 1 box 11X10X5
> 1 bar of silver 5.189 kilograms
>
> (sd) Herbert Herzog

Within two days both deposits of gold were turned to the Officer of the Finance Division, 3rd Infantry Division stationed in Salzburg. From this day forth it would be known as The Salzburg Gold. During the investigation of these two deposits of gold Gottfriedsen was notified by the CIC that the gold remaining at the Julianna Farm in the village of Heiligenstedten, Schleswig/Holstein had been recovered and his name connected with the gold. Herbert Heroz immediately, with the help of a lawyer, filed for a finders fee in this recovery. This is customary a 10% reward of the total value, which would have been $485,532 in 1945. A whopping sum considering a new Ford or Chevrolet could be purchased for $800. Was Bernd Gottfriedsen in cahoots with Heroz in a ruse to collect this fee? Heroz with a lawyer tried for years to collect but there is no evidence that a fee was every paid.[20]

The Salzburg Gold was considered to be looted by the Germans who tried to hide it from the advancing Allies in the closing days of the war. These bars found by the US Counter Intelligence Corps (CIC) in the hiding place in Bad Gastein were identified as German Legation in Bern. The bars in four boxes contained sixty bars, each weighing one kilogram or 32.151 Troy ounces. The boxes were wrapped in brown paper with the markings, "Sender, German Legation in Bern."[21] They had been sent to Berlin and removed by Bernd Gottfriedsen. The gold was turned over to the Austrian Government in early 1947 by the US military authorities, which were not fully aware of all the implications involved. The Tripartite Commission considered this gold to be a part of the Gold Pot. This gold was deemed to be an advanced payment by the Tripartite Commission. Thus, the net result of the decision was that the pool was credited (and the Government of Austria's account debited) on the Commission's books, on August 4, 1953, with the fine gold content of a delivery made to Austria on February 19, 1947 of 138,723.461 Troy ounces or 4.76 tons of fine gold.[22]

Thus this gold along with along with Shipments 27A, 27B, 27C and Shipment 77 constituted the German Foreign Office gold recovered by US Forces and amounted to 5.63 tons. This with the 4.76 tons from Austria and a reported two tons recovered in the British Zone amounted to 12.39 tons recovered from the Ribbentrop Gold Fund or German Foreign Office. The two tons from the British Zone were discussed in a previous chapter involving Bernd Gottfriedsen who had taken it to Heiligenstedten and stored in the cellar of the Julianna farm. From German records it was estimated the Ribbentrop gold fund totaled fifteen tons of gold consisting of 515,000 British sovereigns and another half in gold bars. Thus, missing was 2.61 tons of gold or 76,125 Troy ounces with a 1945 value of $2,664,375.00.[23][24]

After the war a large number of former German diplomats were living quite well in Spain, Ireland, Argentina, Sweden and Switzerland from unknown sources. They most likely were living from these resources. Former Foreign Office official, Dr. Gustav Hilger, as noted in a previous chapter, was in the United States working for American intelligence. He recovered his Nazi tainted valuables with his US connections.

Regarding the Gold Deposit on December 7, 1946, in a letter from General Mark Clark, United States Forces Austria, stated:

> There is no doubt in my mind that this gold is part of that formerly owned by the Austrian National Bank and looted by the Germans. In view of the fact that restitution of the gold would benefit the Austrian economy and constitute further proof that the United States intends to carry out it announced policies in Austria, I unhesitatingly recommend the gold be returned to the Austrian Government. I would be placed in an embarrassing position here if we now fail to carry out the restitution of the gold.

The following reply from the War from Civil Affairs Division arrived on January 16, 1947:

> Since you have established to your satisfaction the Austrian National Bank gold in question did not leave Austria this gold is not subject to transfer to European Gold Pot under Paris Reparations Act Part 3, par G. You are therefore authorized to restore gold to Austrian Government with appropriate ceremony.[25]

The gold delivered to Austria by the commander in chief of US Forces, Austria consisted of 161 British gold sovereign coins, 2,580 French gold coins of various denominations and sixty-seven gold bars, weighing one kilo each. These bars were packed into four boxes. Box five contained two large gold bars; one weighs 11.625 kilos and the other, 11.77 kilos.

Unfortunately, for Austria, at a later date this gold was sent to the Bank of England. This shipment entry identified as "Chief of US Forces" was used by the Tripartite Gold Commission to identify the gold delivered to the Bank of England during March of 1950. It had been kept in the Salzburg Branch of the Austrian National Bank. US civilian James A. Garrison had these gold coins removed (61.842 Troy ounces) from the vault and along with the bars they were sent to England on a US B-17 bomber. The gold coins and bars weighed 2,964.905 ounces and arrived on March 14, 1950.[26][27]

On October 8, 1947, Bernard Koller attempted to cross into the American Zone, Austria from the British Zone. He was apprehended by British military guards with gold coins valued then at $20,492.05. The coins consisted of 1,673 English Sovereigns and 199 US $20 dollar gold coins. Koller was arrested and the gold coins seized and deposited in the National Bank, Graz, Austria.

In January 1952, a British agent drove to Graz and delivered the gold to the British Embassy in Vienna. Here the forty pounds of gold was placed in a diplomatic pouch and delivered to the Bank of England about March 11, 1952.[28]

Then, on April 18, 1952, official of the Tripartite Gold Commission were informed that an additional 2,500 Sovereigns, 105 Turkish and 501 Swiss 20fr gold coins had also been appropriated from Bernard Koller upon his arrest in 1947. Due to various Austrian Court issues the gold coins were not pursued by the Allied powers.[29,30]

In 1955, 15,640 gold coins weighing 3,149.812 ounces were sent to the Federal Reserve Bank in New York and added to the Gold Pot. It was reported that the coins have been recovered from a German Me 108 courier plane that had been shot down in April 1945. The Me 108 was found in Lake Atter at a depth of seventy meters. This fact alone signifies the gold as Nazi gold and susceptible to the Allied Gold Pot. The plane was not the actual true story, but loosely connected with the account. In September 1955, divers found a Luftwaffe plane below the surface of Lake Atter. This made the news and somehow erroneously reported by the Tripartite Commission as the source for this deposit.

Actually, the source began on February 8, 1949, when two Hintersee Austrian police were searching for a reported stolen motor. From tips they suspected the motor was buried in the vicinity of an old abandoned millhouse with a water wheel. The mill was located on a farm, known as the Posch farm but owned by a Mr. Weissenbacher. The police noticed some ground that was disturbed and begin digging. After removing a small amount of dirt they hit a rusty metal box of the type used by the Wehrmacht to transport anti-aircraft rounds. The rusty container held gold coins, with an additional eighty-six coins in the soil surrounding the box. This gave the impression that the box had been buried for several years.

The gold was removed and placed into the protective custody of the United States Forces Austria, Property Control Officer in Salzburg. Then in September 1949, the Austrian Federal Police arrested Anton Steiner, one of the policemen that recovered the gold coins back in February. A subsequent investigation revealed he had stolen many of the coins. The Federal Police recovered 681 coins from Steiner's property and they were added to the money already in Salzburg.

These gold coins were packaged and flown by KLM airlines to the Federal Reserve Bank in February/March 1955, for on April 14, 1955, KLM was requesting recompense from the Tripartite Gold Commission for $629.83. Payment was being withheld as the "French Commissioner was delaying signature on payment order to Federal Reserve and requesting costly shipment to New York."[31] These coins in their entirety were released in full to Czechoslovakia on February 19, 1982.[32]

Military Law 53 Gold

Because of Military Law 53, thousands of Germans in the US Zone turned in silver, U.S currency, gold coins and gold bars to their local bank. The central banks were scattered in the American Zone, such as Mannheim, Ulm, Karlsruhe, but the largest bulk of the coins were confiscated in Munich. It was sent to Finance Division, External Claims Branch, Frankfurt/Main.

The total gold seized in the US Zone under Military Law 53 was 13,592.33 ounces in gold bars and 27,365.94 ounces in coins. In the US Zone not all coins seized under Military Law 53 were allocated to the Gold Pot. Coins classified as Napoleon D, British, Austrian, Danish, US dollar, Turkish, Austrian, and German Reich gold coins were acceptable to the Gold Pot. Coins considered as non-monetary were excluded and that included, all coins before the middle of the 19th century, coins in the denominations of 5, 40, 50, 80, and 100 francs, the 37½ ruble, South and Central American coins, German East African and many more numismatic classifications.

A portion of this gold may have been returned to the legitimate owners, but this is highly unlikely and unknown.

In January, 1952, most of these gold bars and coins were packed into seventeen boxes measuring 13¼ x 8½ x 7½ inches and sent from the Finance Division, External Claims Branch, Frankfurt/Main, Germany to the Federal Reserve Bank in New York to be added to the Gold Pot.

The boxes were labeled BB 1 through BB17 and contained the following valuables.

BB 1 contained gold coins as follows; German Mark, German ducat, French franc, Swiss franc, Belgian franc, and Dutch gilder with a total weight of 1,107.27 ounces.

BB 2 contained British Sterling, Russian ruble, Austrian kroner, Austrian shilling, Austrian ducat. Hungarian franc, Turkish pound, Turkish pastier, Spanish pieta, Spanish?, Italian lira, Danish kroner, Swedish?, Bulgarian? and Greek drachma weighing 1,434.24 ounces.

Boxes B.B. 3 through B.B.17 contained 18,806.44 ounces of gold bars.

The gold was shipped from Rhine-Main Airport, Frankfurt on February 2, 1952 on Pan American flight number 123 arriving in Idlewild Airport (later John F. Kennedy International Airport).

These gold coins were estimated by the US authorities to have a value of $79,832. The coins in boxes B.B.1 and B.B.2 were examined in the Federal Reserve Bank by Mr. Vernon Brown of the Chase National Bank, and he concluded that forty-two of the gold coins had some numismatic value. This value, estimated by a phone call, was $792.50. The US treasury immediately expressed a special interest in purchasing all of the gold coins. The total ounces added to the Gold Pot at the Federal Reserve Bank was 20,999.768 ounces.[33]

In 1951, the British Financial Advisor Control Commission for Germany wrote the Tripartite Gold Commission informing then they had 75,312.632 ounces of gold to allocate to the Gold Pot. The decision was made to deposit the gold in the Bank of France due to the cost of transportation. After several delays and an exchange of encrypted telegrams the exchange took place. On October 18, 1951, the Royal Air Force flew the first batch to Orly Airfield, near Paris and stored it in the vaults of the Bank of France. After a delay, due to bad weather, the next aircraft arrived with the second and last consignment of gold on October 25, 1951. The British authorities made no charges for the transportation of gold, considering the flights as a part of training. But some authority allocated DM49 ($12.25) to reimburse police escorts for guarding the gold.

Maybe the Bank of England sent the gold to France with a premonition of problems. Difficulties began immediately with the Financial Advisor, Germany, notifying the Bank of France that ten coins of numismatic had been sent by mistake. They requested the bank to set these coins aside and arrange for their return. This was followed on May 19, 1952, with notification that nine gold coins and one gold bar be returned to Germany as they had been taken from nationals of neutral countries. Five gold coins belonging to some unknown person from the Neuengamme concentration camp should also be returned. This camp was close to the village of Neuengamme, near Hamburg. The Financial Advisor, Germany also requested that a few gold coins of historic or numismatic value be returned. Some of these coins were returned on April 27, 1953.

The Bank of France would not return the gold bar requested but a gold bar of same weight and origin was "reinstated" to the British in Germany from a Hanover branch of the Swiss firm Günther Wagner of Zurich. After much haggling, and three years later on May 11, 1956, the requested bar was returned to Germany. The five coins taken from the Neuengamme concentration camp stayed in the Gold Pot. Of the nine coins returned in 1953, only two of the owners were identified, so the remaining seven were returned to the Gold Pot, this crediting the Pot with 0.918 Troy ounces. Thus 75,312.623 Troy ounces of gold were allocated to the in the Bank of France to the Gold Pot from the British Zone valued in 1945 at $2,635,941.81.[34]

On September 6, 1951, the High Commissioner of the French Republic in Germany wrote the Tripartite Commission stating that 6.30 kilograms of gold collected in the French Zone were available for the Gold Pot. He asked for instruction on the disposal of the gold. The High Commissioner was informed that an account had been opened at the Bank of France and was instructed to deliver the gold to that bank in France. Thus added to the Pot from the French Zone of Occupation was 105.184 Troy ounces ($3,681.44).[35,36]

Assorted Deposits to the Gold Pot

On March 1, 1951, the Federal Reserve Bank received six packages containing 150 gold bars from Tokyo, Japan. These bars were from the disposal of German assets in Japan. Several sixty-ounce bars were minted by the Imperial Mint of Osaka. Approximately, 110 bars were in the ten-ounce category. The bars were sent in their entirety to the US Assay Office and converted into US Assay bars. After smelting, the total ounces of gold were 4,813.463. The Bank also received a check for $2.02 from the US Assay Office for gold that was too small to cast. The amount of the check was credited to the Gold Pot.[37][38]

The gold from the former German embassy in Madrid, Spain and deposited in the Foreign Exchange Depository as Shipment 77, was delivered by air transport to the Gold Pot at the Federal Reserve Bank, New York on November 27, 1952. Twenty-one bars were identified as Gabriel bars and considered not good delivery. The bank was instructed to melt these bars and coins that were broken, unidentified and defaced into "good delivery bars. The final credit to the Gold Pot was 644.531 ounces of gold bars and 1,216.435 Troy ounces of coins"[39,40]

On August 7, 1953, the French Commissioner wrote the Tripartite Commissioner informing him that in 1949 American military authorities in Germany had turned over 163.496 ounces of gold valued then at $5,722.36. The gold coins and bars were delivered to the Bank of France on January 20, 1954.[41,42]

On August 2, 1955, the French Commissioner notified the Tripartite Commissioner that fifty gold coins had be surrendered to the French authorities by M.L'Abbe Weygand, parish priest of the church in Petersberg-Fulda, Germany.

These were part of a hoard of coins looted by German soldiers from a French chateau during the recent war. They divided them amongst themselves with each receiving fifty coins. One soldier on leave in Petersberg-Fulda, gave the coins to the then Priest Bruehler for safekeeping before returning to the front. Bruehler hid the coins in a safe place. The soldier never returned. When it was time for Bruehler to leave the parish, he came across the coins and handed them to his successor M.L'Abbe Weygand, who gave them to the French authorities, pursuant to Military Law 53. These were not included within this category.

There were some questions from the Tripartite Gold Commissioners about the coins, but on March 15, 1956, coins weighing 9.385 ounces, valued then at $328.48 were added to the Gold Pot as a single separate entry.[43,44]

This deposit is a bit confusing. It appears the German prisoners of war had gold confiscated from them by French officers. The gold was deposited in the Lille branch of the Bank of France. On January 6, 1956, the Tripartite Commission was notified by French authorities of this credit. On April 13, 1956, 7.845 ounces of gold coins were added to the Gold Pot as they were delivered to the Bank of France, Paris.[45,46]

In the early-1980s, two independent researchers established that two gold bars which had formed part of a shipment from the Reichsbank in Berlin to a "safe area" in the south of Germany in the last weeks of the war had apparently not been included in the gold of this shipment which had in due course ended up in the Bank of England via the Foreign Exchange Depository in Frankfurt. It was eventually discovered that the bars were in the possession of the German financial authorities. Following protracted negotiations with the German Government, which was concerned not to find itself subject to claims for these bars from third parties, they were handed over to the US Embassy in Bonn on 27 September 1996. They were then shipped to the Bank of England for incorporation into the Gold Pot.

The bars improperly bore the Prussian State Mint insignia, and the date-stamp 1938. Such bars had not been acceptable in the past as good delivery bars on the London market. However, as they also bore the assay mark of the German specialist assayers, Degussa, for the year 1956, they were deemed acceptable. They weighed net 797.539 ounces of fine gold. The Reichsbank records show that these bars were originally Belgian Central Bank gold bars that had been looted by the Nazi regime, re-smelted by the Reichsbank and given false identification markings.[47]

In a remarkably short period of time, a considerable quantity of looted gold was taken into custody by the Allied authorities or identified as having been deposited in third countries. By July 1948, a total of 9,849,169 ounces of gold in bars, coins or pieces had been deposited with the Federal Reserve Bank of New York or the Bank of England, or was still held at the Foreign Exchange Depository in Frankfurt by US military authorities. The grand total in the gold pool rose further, to 10,816,223.863 ounces by December 1974, and in 1996 another two bars of gold, weighing net 797.539 ounces of fine gold were added making the total 10,817,021.402 ounces.

CHAPTER 25

The Tripartite Gold Commission Distributions

The average citizen would not have been aware of Nazi gold or the Tripartite Gold Commission without the intervention of US Senator Alfonse D'Amato of New York. On March 1996, D'Amato, after talks with the head of the World Jewish Congress, decided the issue surrounding Jewish assets in Swiss banks needed addressing. The Senator thus began an extensive research project regarding the looting of Jewish assets during World War II. Public interest grew and in October 1996, President William J. Clinton appointed Stuart E. Eizenstat, the Under Secretary of Commerce for International Trade, to head an eleven-member Interagency Group on Nazi Assets. This action started one of the largest research projects in the history of the National Archives. It also forced the secretive Tripartite Gold Commission to take action in resolving the final settlement of the fifty-year-old Gold Pot.

The Allies recalled that in 1918 the victors had demanded reparations by Germany and were to be paid in gold, but these future exchanges were never paid, therefore, in 1945 the Allies decided that Germany's payment for aggressive war should be carried out by handing over compensation, in kind, to the greatest extent. At the same time, it was decided that Germany should be disarmed by eliminations of its war industries. The intent was to safeguard the security of Europe by breaking up Germany's war potential. It was realized that the compensation of monetary gold presented features differing from those of the restitution of identifiable works of art and other recognize objects since gold coins and bars would not generally be determined in the same manner. Therefore, a plan was devised whereby all gold found in Germany would be pooled and distributed on a pro rata basis to those countries entitled to participate in the Gold Pot.

To address some of these problems, the Tripartite Commission had been established, consisting of three members nominated by the governments of France, England and the United States. The Commission was headquarters in the Residence Palace, 155 rue de la Loi, Brussels, Belgium. It was charged with the full responsibility for transacting all phases of restitution of monetary gold to the claimant countries as outlined in the Paris Reparation Conference. The governments of the United States of America, France and the United Kingdom were to receive claims and distribute the gold. In order to implement part III of the agreement, the three governments founded, on September 27, 1946, the Tripartite Commission for the Restitution of Monetary Gold. Its establishment was announced in the *Department of State Bulletin*, *Le Journal de la Republique Françoise* and *The London Gazette*. As stated previously, the Commission only dealt with monetary gold, not silver, platinum or diamonds.

For the sake of convenience, the Tripartite Commission was organization in Brussels in co-location with the Inter-Allied Reparation Agency (IARA). The first commissioners were concurrently also the three governments' representatives on the IARA. However, the Tripartite Commission was constitutionally separate from and independent of the agency. It was agreed that the Gold Commission would have access to the IARA staff for shorthand, typists, translators, interpreters, accountants, drivers, messengers and other administrative needs. However, the Army at the Foreign Exchange Depository in Frankfurt, Germany would provide most of the needed information. After all they had in their possession the preponderance of German financial records and German Chief Financial Officer of Foreign Transactions, Albert Thoms on their staff. The most influential member of the Tripartite Gold Commission was its Deputy Special Assistant, Col. J.A. Watson, British Empire Officer of the Legion of Merit, Chevalier de la Legion d'Honneur, Croix de Guerre, Licencié en Droit de la Faculté de Paris.[1]

The status of the Tripartite Commission as an international organization attracting privileges and immunities in respect of its official functions was recognized in Belgian law on August 1, 1952; this law being retroactive to September 27, 1946. The commissioners and the secretary general of the Tripartite Commission were also specifically accorded the appropriate privileges and immunities.

On March 13, 1947, the Tripartite Commission issued a questionnaire to potential claimant countries seeking information that would allow it to make awards from the gold pool on a proportional basis. Claims were submitted in due course by Albania, Austria, Belgium, Czechoslovakia, Greece, Italy, Luxembourg, the Netherlands, Poland and Yugoslavia. The following countries did not submit a claim; Australia, Canada, Denmark, Egypt, New Zealand, Norway, South Africa, France, the United States and the United Kingdom. In a political statement of the time, Pakistan stated that since India had refrained from admitting a claim they also had no request to formulate.

The claims were for monetary gold only as defined by the Commission. "All gold which at the time of its looting or wrongful removal, was carried as a part of the claimant country's monetary reserve, either in the accounts of the claimant government itself or in the account of the claimant country's central bank or other monetary authority at home or abroad."[2] The commission decided not to define looting or wrongful removal.

Until August 15, 1971, the world's economy was basically on a modified gold standard, which indicated the standard economic was based on a fixed weight of gold. During this time the United States Treasury set this standard with an ounce of gold valued at $35. The US treasury would purchase or sell to any country any amount of gold for $35 per Troy ounce. The questionnaire brought forth many questions. Some countries did not understand the Tripartite Gold Commission's definition of monetary gold. Of concern was gold belonging to organizations and individuals that was seized by the Nazis from the country's central bank and found it way into the Reichsbank gold reserves.

The Italians had an interesting dilemma; what was the status of the gold they had looted while a German ally, then was subsequently looted by the Germans. Also, gold claimed by Italy, while a German ally, which was taken against a dollar credit in the United States. Belgium inquired about its gold that had been deposited in the Reichsbank before the war and then seized during hostilities. What about gold that was claimed by two countries? For instance, Belgium had purchased several large sums of gold in good faith from the Reichsbank in 1940. Unbeknownst to the buyer, the gold had been looted from Austria and Czechoslovakia. All three countries would submit claims for the same gold.

Poland had concern regarding the gold taken by the Nazis from the Free City of Danzig. Questioned was gold transferred to the Reichsbank prior to the beginning of World War II. After all, the Bank of Danzig opened a gold deposit with the Berlin Reichsbank in December 1934. At the time of the invasion the account had 352 bars of gold on inventory when the account was closed on September 4, 1939. These questions would have to be focused on by the Tripartite Gold Commission in addressing the validation of the claims.

The first problem concerned the gold collected from private individuals by the Central Banks of the Netherlands, Austria, Belgium and Yugoslavia that continued to function after the occupation of Germany. This gold was subsequently transferred to the Reichsbank in Berlin. Due to the laws of the other countries invaded by Germany, this was not an issue as it was illegal for a private citizen to own monetary gold. This same law also existed in the United States and Germany at that time. Consequently, private citizens were compelled to surrender their gold coins and bars to the Central Government controlled banks. These four countries requested the gold belonging to individuals by considered monetary gold be returned to the claimant countries bank. The Tripartite Gold Commission could not entirely agree with the claimant four countries.

The claimant countries requested multiple claims, and during the evaluation the Commission rejected many portions of these but not outright the complete claims, with one exception. Once the claims were validated they exceeded the Allied Gold Pot by 35.86 percent; they were appropriated by the differences of 64.14 percent to each country. This meant that of the total gold reserves in Europe in 1939, that 35.86 percent had vanished and was unaccountable. The final total of the Gold Pot was 10,817,021.139 Troy ounces or 370.869 tons of gold consisting of about 40% coins and 60% bars.

Regardless of these issues, it became clear by the middle of 1947 that there was an urgent need to distribute some of the gold to meet the requirements of the claimant governments and it was decided by the three governments, the United States, Britain and France, that a preliminary distribution of gold should be made even before the totality of claims could be fully considered and adjudicated upon. The Commission was discontented with this decision, but the allotment began with the first shipment from Foreign Exchange Depository, Frankfurt to Paris, France for deposit to the accounts of Belgium and Luxembourg.

The French, Gold Conundrum

As addressed in previous chapters, an explanation is needed on the deliveries to France on behalf of Belgium and Luxemburg from the Foreign Exchange Depository, although the author himself is confused with the issue. This gold from the National Bank of Belgium gold reserves, and those of the Savings Bank of Luxemburg went to the Bank of France, which it was holding, for safe keeping, shortly before the German invasion. The French authorities, in turn, transferred both of these quantities of gold, with holdings of their own, down the Senegal River to the interior town of Kayes, in Senegal (today Mali), where they considered the gold would be safe. But the Vichy Government, under pressure from the Germans, caused this gold to be brought back to France where it was seized, under various pretexts, by the Reichsbank. After the war, the National Bank of Belgium brought pressure to bear on the Bank of France for restitution in its entirety of these two quantities of gold. France did so with the understanding that Belgium and Luxemburg would lodge claims for this gold before the Commission, and under arrangements concluded between the three above mentioned banks would return to France such gold as would be allocated to the two countries. Without doubt a complicated transaction?

Thus, the delivery orders in favor of the Bank of France were issued in October 1947, upon the Federal Reserve Bank of New York and the Military Governor, United States Zone of Occupation, Germany as the Frankfurt Exchange Depository gold had not yet been transferred to the Bank of England, special receipting arrangements had to be made at Frankfurt.

Pursuant to the terms of the Paris Reparations Conference, the Tripartite Commission initiated the first allocation of monetary gold to France for deposit to Belgium, Luxembourg, and also made a distribution to the Netherlands. The gold allowance was to be composed of forty-eight percent gold coins and fifty-two percent gold bars. The Tripartite Commission agreed to transfer the gold to France, as describes above, based on a prior agreement in which France paid Belgium and Luxembourg in full for the gold turned over to Germany in 1941. The governments of Belgium and Luxembourg requested that the Foreign Exchange Depository deliver the gold directly to the French in order to avoid a series of physical transfers. The commission had stated that the gold must be "good delivery," meaning conforming to the assay certifications of the Bank of England, Dutch Mint, French Mint, Swedish Mint, Swiss Mint or United States Assay Office.

Upon receiving this information for the initial distribution of gold, Col. William Brey requested additional security officers to help with this transfer. Five officers reported to the depository and were briefed immediately on the task ahead. Brey estimated that approximately 6,000 gold bars and 2,000 large bags of coins would be required to satisfy the needs for the participating countries. He established an operating procedure for the preparation, security, and distribution of the gold.

Gold coins were stored in vault compartments 3, 4, 5, 12, and 13, each containing more than one type coin. The bags weighed from 90 to 112 pounds. The 2,000 bags were to be subdivided and each bag re-packed into five smaller bags. The five smaller bags would then be prorated by weight among the five recipient countries, thus insuring the same percentage of individual gold coins to each participating country. All weights were to be metric.

A U.S Army security officer was stationed at the door of each section with a folder of the compartment's inventory. The officer selected two bags of coins and they were loaded into a metal box by a laborer. The officer marked the inventory list to signify that the bag of coins had been removed from the compartment. The metal box was then placed on a hand truck and a second security officer accompanied the pushcart and laborer to the weight department on an upper floor via the elevator. The bags of coins were then released to a third security officer acting as the US recorder for a weight team, and the laborer returned for more bags of gold coins.

The weighing department had three independent operating teams working, each team consisting of the US Army recorder, four French nationals who weighed and recorded the gold coins, and one German who sealed each bag. Once it was sealed, a tag previously prepared by the French was affixed to it and the bag was put in a wooden box. When the box had ten bags of coins, representing the entire contents of the original two bags, it was delivered to the US banding officer. The banding officer verified that each wooden box contained ten sealed bags, and then he banded it with two metal strips. The boxes were returned to the original compartments by the security officer and laborer who brought the gold up from the compartments.

The recorders in the weight department delivered the completed pre-numbered columns to Frank Roberts of claims. The columns showed total box gross weight and total box fine weight. Fine weight differed from the gross according to the actual gold content of the coins. Most of the coins were 900 fine, but some of the English coins were 916.66 fine. All returnable gold was defined in fine gold weight. The gold coins selected for participating countries were coins from Austria, England, Italy, Germany and the United States.

The security and procedure for packing the gold bars was not as stringent as for the gold coins. Each bar weighed from twenty to forty pounds, making it more difficult to steal than a coin. The bars were in the compartments in piles of thirty bars each and separated into two categories: German origin gold bars and non-German gold bars. An inventory sheet was used to indicate the removal of each stack of thirty bars. Two displaced person laborers stacked the pile of thirty bars onto a table in the corridor at vault level. The gold had been weighed during a previous inventory, and this inventory was accepted by the French as correct. Each bar was numbered and six bars each were transferred into a pre-numbered wooden box containing sawdust for cushioning. The US banding officer certified each box. Then the boxes were filled completely with sawdust and banded with two metal strips before being returned to the original compartments. Sixty-eight percent of the gold bars were of German origin and the remaining was of non-German origin. Each gold bar ranged from 916.1 to 999.8 fine.

At 8:00am, November 19, 1947, the release of the gold to France was started promptly and continued without interruption. A metal roller conveyer was positioned at the compartments and used to remove the boxes of gold from the vaults to ten two-and-a-half ton trucks. They were loaded with thirty boxes each and accompanied by military police security. The trucks delivered the gold to the transport train at the Frankfurt Railway Station, and then returned for more. Lightly falling snow did not disrupt the loading schedule for the 541 boxes of gold bars and 550 boxes of gold coins, as one truck was loaded every five minutes. Once the wooden boxes containing the gold were put onto the train, they were rechecked by a French representative at each baggage car. At 1:45pm the train left Frankfurt for France under French supervision.[3]

The Netherlands Distribution

On November 21, 1947, the transfer of the Dutch gold began with the arrival and disbursement of the US military police security detail. The gold was to be transported to Holland by a convoy of five large trucks. Loading began at 1:15pm and the cargo consisted of 209 boxes of gold bars and 223 boxes of gold coins. It ended at 4:30pm, and on orders from Col. Van Limberg, general inspector of the Netherlands Army, the convoy departed from the Foreign Exchange Depository.

Lt. Reed A. Speirs, and twelve enlisted men were assigned to escort the convoy to Nijmegen, Netherlands, just inside the Dutch border. Thereafter, security for the gold would be the responsibility of the Dutch. In Frankfurt, the military escorts rode at the front, center, and rear of the convoy, with one military policeman assigned to ride in the cab of each truck.

The procession proceeded at 30mph through the night. The trip was uneventful until it reached the British zone at 3:45am on November 22. The British had not received advance notice of the shipment and detained the convoy. After a twenty-minute delay and additional information from the military police, they were allowed to proceed. It reached Nijmegen at 5:00 in the morning. Speirs was then relieved of his security responsibility by Col. Van Limberg of the Dutch Army and the security of the convoy was transferred to the armed guards from the Netherlands Bank.[4]

After the trucks from Holland left, a search of the displaced persons who helped in the transfer was made and a small Austrian gold coin was found on one of the laborers. He was arrested by the Criminal Investigation Division, and a search was made in the vault area. A small sock with 125 Austrian gold coins was found on a shelf and four more coins of a similar nature were discovered loose on the same shelf. The investigation revealed that one bag of gold coins was missing from those that had been set aside

Gold to France being loaded on a truck for transport to the railway station during a light snow.

for the Austrian claim. The search uncovered gold coins in the old bags, so all the old, original bags were re-examined and several coins were discovered. In continuing the search, 20,000 Allied military marks were found

The Netherlands received this gold against signature of the standard form of combined waiver and receipt, two delivery orders, one upon the Bank of England and one from the Military Governor, United States Zone of Occupation, Germany. After certain exchanges of letters, it was agreed that the Netherlands would be shown on the Commission's books as having received 69.6821 Troy ounces over and above the amount mentioned on the receipts signed at Frankfurt. The net results of all these operations were that the Netherlands received in part of the preliminary distribution, 1,153,906.527 Troy ounces of gold.

In May 1948, the Commission decided to allocate the Netherlands a further amount of gold. This second delivery of gold to the Netherlands was suspended at the request of the United States until 1949. On December 30, 1949, two orders one upon the Bank of England and the other to the Federal Reserve Bank of New York were sent to the Netherlands, requiring that government to sign a standard form of waiver and receipt. The gold was delivered and ten counterfeit coins were found in this shipment from the Bank of England. Additionally, the Netherlands complained they had received 4.023 ounces more than stipulated by the Bank of England. The total amount received in the second delivery was 985,289.133 Troy ounces of gold.

The Tripartite Commission rejected a significant part of the Netherlands contested claim. The negative response of the Commission is difficult to follow, but it appears that the Netherlands were

Gold loaded into a Dutch truck for return to the Netherlands.

most unhappy with what they considered a small settlement for Switzerland's contribution to the Allied Gold Pot. The Dutch threatened to take this issue to The Hague International Court, but unknown to the Dutch, members of the Tripartite Gold Commission had visited the international Court of Justice at The Hague, prior to making the decision to reject the Netherlands' claim.[5] Also of concern, was the Commission's initial stand on the Netherland gold taken by the Germans from the sunken Dutch pilot boat "19." The Commission interpreted the 307,714.795 Troy ounces of gold as being salvaged by the Germans and thus not looted or wrongfully removed to the Reichsbank in Berlin.

Following lengthy discussions, the Commission accorded the Netherlands a special hearing of its case in May 1963. After due consideration, the Tripartite Commission maintained its rejection of the relevant part of the Netherlands' claim and so informed them in July 1965. The Netherlands Government did not respond for some time and the Commissioners decided to leave the initiative with that Government. In July 1972, the Minister of Finance of the Netherlands enquired about the delivery of its allocation. Information was immediately provided by the secretary general. Eventually, in May and August 1973, the Bank of England and the Federal Reserve Bank of New York delivered to the Netherlands 78,102.499 ounces and 53,460.758 ounces of fine gold respectively, a total of 131,563.257 ounces as their third distribution.[6]

As part of the final payout on April 30, 1998, The Netherlands received 38,013.550 Troy ounces of gold and £5,089.32 from the Bank of England.

Their total settlement was 2,099,579.650 Troy ounces or 19.41% of the Gold Pot

Albania

Albania original recognized request was for 50,616.538 Troy ounces of gold. The actual distribution of the share attributed to Albania was delayed because of a counter-claim by England and Italy to all of the Albanian gold.

Known as the Corfu Channel Case, the British Navy with minesweepers, had cleaned the Corfu Channel, but later on October 22, 1946, in this same area two British destroyers hit sea-mines damaging the ships and killing naval personnel. The English accused Albania of re-laying the mines and brought suite in the International Court of Justice that ordered Albania to pay the UK £843,947 in compensation for damages. In the 1940s, this would amount to 97,174.470 Troy ounces of gold. England filed claim for the all of the Albanian gold to settle this issue.

Italy further asserted that the National Bank of Albania had been headquartered in Rome and Italy was the major stockholder of that bank. The allegation is unclear although the Commission wrote a twenty page report regarding this claim was arbitrated by Professor Sauser-Hall, Professor of Law in the University of Geneva and Neuchätel, Member of the Permanent Court of Arbitration, Member of the Institute of International Law.

Regardless of the third party claims and counter claims, finally, on October 29, 1987, Albania received 49,804.149 ounces of gold from the Bank of England in respect of its combined preliminary and quasi-final shares.[7]

Then on July 13, 1998, Albania received 1,571.543 Troy ounces and £2,106.24 From the Bank of England. This was the last entry in the Tripartite Commission Gold Book.

Albania received a total of 51,375.692 Troy ounces of gold or .47% of the Gold Pot

Austria

Strangely, Austria was not considered an ex-enemy nation although they are German through blood and language and strongly participated in the defense of Nazism during World War II.

On February 2, 1948, Austria was allocated 152,630.007 Troy ounces of gold bars from the Federal Reserve Bank, New York. On March 7, 1948 the Federal Reserve Bank allocated an additional 244,211.408 ounces of bars. The Bank of England, on August 17 and October 14, 1948, delivered coins with respectfully 330,862.199 and 358,434.052 Troy ounces of gold. Austria obtained these four deliveries between January and September 1948. As a result of all these operations, Austria received 1,086,137.670 troy ounces of gold in the preliminary distribution. On October 18, 1948, an additional 197,725.755 Troy ounces was delivered.

On August 4, 1953, the Commission debited the Austrian Government with the amount of the so-called "Salzburg Gold." This gold had been handed to the Austrians by the American authorities in February 1947, but was subsequently found to be gold that should have been put into the Gold Pot. It was considered as having been received on account of its shares by Austria.[8]

The Salzburg Gold consisting of 138,723.461 Troy ounces was added to the total deposit of the Gold Pot, not credited to any bank, but the account of Austria was also decreased by this amount. On July 7, 1958, (entry 180) this transaction was reversed thus voided the August 4, 1953, entry (154) and Austria received credit for the gold that never left the bank vault in Salzburg.[9]

On June 25, 1998, an additional 26,697.741 Troy ounces and £23,000.32 was transferred to the Austrian Account.

A total of 1,640,079.339 Troy ounces of gold was allocated to Austria for 15.16% of the Gold Pot.

Belgium

The Belgium Government's first claim from the Gold Pot has been discussed in previous chapters. The amount of gold for that transaction was 2,925,742.000 Troy ounces. On September 19, 1954, Belgium was given another 803,805.640 Troy ounces. Now in 1958, Belgium was allotted additional 237,416.797 ounces of gold and requested it to be delivered to its account with the Bank of France. The gold distribution made on July 1, 1958, was from the Bank of England, Federal Reserve Bank, New York and the remaining ounces of gold that depleted the Commission's gold account in the Bank of France that was an additional 74,491.412 Troy ounces.

On April 30, 1998, final tally, Belgium received an additional 67,231.138 Troy ounces of gold and £18,119.01 from the Bank of England and Federal Reserve Bank of New York.

Belgium/France received a total of 4,169,686,986 Troy ounces or 38.55% of the Gold Pot.

Czechoslovakia

On February 3, 1948, the government of Czechoslovakia submitted a claim for 1,447,049.752 Troy ounces of gold.

The case of Czechoslovakia was a straightforward one. The Munich Agreement of 1938 awarded Nazi Germany the western border region of Czechoslovakia, collectively known as the Sudetenland. Within a year, Adolf Hitler and his German forces moved into the remainder of Czechoslovakia. Germany simply took over the banking system. The Germans split Czechoslovakia by creating the so-called Protectorate of Bohemia and Moravia within the framework of the Third Reich and also the Independent State of Slovakia. They then issued a decree abolishing the National Bank of Czechoslovakia's powers and privileges outside the territory of the Protectorate and changing its name to the National Bank of Bohemia and Moravia. In Slovakia, the puppet government created by decree the National Bank of Slovakia. Thus, the original National Bank of Czechoslovakia was abolished with Germany in complete control of the country's gold deposits.

This banking arrangement gave Germany many advantages, not the least, another venue to transfer gold to the Swiss National Bank, and make monetary transactions with the Bank of International Settlement, under the guise of the National Bank of Bohemia and Moravia and National Bank of Slovakia. These accounts were most active in 1938-1940. During June 1940, thousands of kilograms of Czech gold were sent to the Reichsbank in Berlin and Swiss National Bank.

The Gold Commission awarded the Czechoslovakian Government 1,224,626.017 Troy ounces of gold. This amount as with all claims would be prorated to the claimant governments.

In anticipation of this claim on May 17, 1948, the order was given upon the Federal Reserve Bank of New York. Czechoslovakia signed the standard form of combined waiver and receipt. The amount was delivered and the preliminary distribution was 195,283.845 Troy ounces of fine gold.[10]

An additional share of the gold was set aside in 1958 for delivery to Czechoslovakia. There was considerable confusion in the delay of the gold. The Czech Government owed the British £19.7 million from a World War II debt. England insisted on delivery of the allocated gold in order to resume negotiations for the war debt. Apparently, not happy with the British reasoning regarding the gold and also cognizant that US citizens also had claims against the Czechs, the United States suspended delivery of the allocated gold.[11]

By 1980, gold had hit a record $850 an ounce. The Czech allocation was now valued at $502,837,211.50. This year the United States and the Czechoslovak Socialist Republic agreed on a settlement regarding outstanding claims. The US would receive $81,500,000 from Czechoslovak in full settlement of all mutual claims of both countries. One of the more interesting settlements was the release of the crown account of the United States Army with the Zivnostenska Banks the amount of 7,161,557 crowns.[12]

After years of haggling, finally in February 1982, Czechoslovakia received an additional 263,939.461 ounces of gold from the Federal Reserve Bank of New York and 327,633.729 ounces from the Bank of England, making a total of 591,573.190 ounces in respect of its quasi-final share.[13] This shipment included the gold coins seized in 1948 from the old abandoned millhouse in Hintersee, Austria.

On June 25, 1998, the Czech Republic received 10,485.566 Troy ounces of gold and £24,289.40 from the Bank of England. The Slovak Republic received 5,240.413 Troy ounces and £12,559.88.[14]

Czechoslovakia took delivery of 797,342.610 Troy ounces for a 7.37% total of the Allied Gold Pot.

France

As German forces were crushing the French army, Italy decided to join its victorious Axis partner and declared war on England and France as Italian forces invaded France in June 1940. This was a small-scale invasion, and it is unclear how Italy acquired some of France's gold reserves, but they apparently did. Quickly defeated by Germany, France surrendered and in the negotiation maintained the quasi nation status known as the Vichy government, and the country maintained it large colonial empire. The Vichy French position was unclear and on July 3, 1940, a British naval task force attacked the French Navy, its former ally. The attack resulted in the deaths of 1,297 French servicemen, the sinking of a battleship, and the damaging of five other ships.

As noted before, the French acquisition from the Gold Pot is difficult to follow, considering that country did not make a formal claim to the Commission and also France was a member of the three members Tripartite Gold Commission. The Gold Book transactions regarding France are difficult to audit, taking into consideration the many multiple entries from/to Belgium and Luxembourg. This complicated accounting had to be advantageous for the three countries?

As part of this Commission, France registered a claim for gold allocated to Italy, and on June 30, 1948, it was issued 463,644.348 Troy ounces of gold from Italy drawn on the Bank of England's share of the Gold Pot.

This was France's total distribution and amounted to 04.29% of the Gold Pot.[15]

Greece

Greece followed with a claim and that was quickly discarded by the Commission. But the country did submit another for gold that had been deposited in the Bank of Greece and registered to an individual. This too was rejected.

On May 10, 1947, the Royal Hellenic Government filed two claims for the restitution of 238,292.794 Troy ounces of gold, valued in 1945 at $8,340,247.79.

The first was labeled Claim A and involved the National Bank of Greece, The second, a small claim, identified as Claim B, involved gold coins taken from other banks.

Claim A began on October 31, 1940, when the National Bank of Greece, as a precautionary measure, in view of the threat of a German invasion, packed their gold coins in twenty-seven small bags, numbered 1-27 and placed these bags into three large boxes. The silver coins were bagged and likewise placed into seven boxes, but the Tripartite Gold Commission was not concerned with the silver coins as their mission was only gold. The ten boxes bound with steel wire were sealed with Spanish wax, bearing the bank's seal, the letters E.T.E. The boxes were placed under the custody of a competent bank official ready for immediate transfer if needed.

On April 12, 1941, Nicolas Lavdas, submanager of the National Bank of Greece delivered the ten boxes of valuables to the Bank of Greece for safekeeping. The Bank of Greece had been the central bank of Greece since 1927. A few days later, these ten boxes were shipped by the Bank of Greece to the island of Crete and deposited in the vaults of one of its branch banks in the city of Heraclion.

A month later, Germany launched the then largest airborne invasion, onto the Island of Crete. The British and Greeks defended the island, and after one day of fighting the Germans had suffered heavy causalities. The following day, the main airfield fell to the Germans enabling them to fly in reinforcements. In ten days, the Germans managed to overwhelm the defenders and the battle for Crete was over.

Subsequently, on June 17, 1941, Germans Major von Künsberg and Major Krüger arrived in Heraclion and proceeded to the Bank of Greece's branch office. They requested the key to the vault and made a search of it in the presence of the manager of the branch. The ten cases originally from the National Bank of Greece were seized and removed by the German authorities. The bank officials requested the return of the ten cases of valuables through the German Occupation Authorities, but the gold or silver was not returned.

Claim B was for 29.569 Troy ounces of gold that had been deposited in branches in Arta, a city in northwestern Greece (the Pireaus Bank) and Candia, a branch bank in Crete. The coins in the Candia branch included two US twenty dollar gold pieces, one had been deposited by the director of the Pananion Hospital from a deceased patient and the other deposited in favor of the heirs of Nicolaidis. The coins from Candia were taken by the Germans on August 11, 1941, and coins from Arta were seized by German authorities on April 18, 1944.

In its reply to the Tripartite Gold Commission, the government of Greece described itself as the owner of the gold in claim A and claim B as within the meaning of the Tripartite Agreement for the restitution of gold. Thus, the Commission questioned the monetary gold looted by Germany as belonging to the country of Greece. The Commission was aware that the Bank of Greece had sent twenty-five tons of its own gold abroad and in safety prior to the German invasion. The Commission concluded that the Royal Hellenic government failed to prove the looted gold belonged to the monetary authority of Greece.[16]

An amount of 1,216.324 Troy ounces of fine gold was allocated to Greece, but Greece did not press for the delivery of this amount, which was a small one, and the matter remained unresolved. On June 11, 1958, and additional 391.213 Troy ounces were distributed to Greece. This was delayed for purely practical reasons because the amount concerned was very small. Gold amounting to 1,607.537 Troy ounces was delivered to the Bank of Greece on June 29, 1959.

On June 26, 1998, an additional 116.172 troy ounces and a check for £20,351.59 were delivered from the Bank of England.[17]

Greece received 1,607.530 Troy ounces that was .01% of the total Allied Gold Pot.

Italian Account

The Italian case was unique in the era. Italy was an ex-enemy country and partner with the Axis Power of Germany, Italy and Japan. Italy took considerable quantities of gold from the Allied countries and incorporated it into the gold reserves of the Bank of Italy. After the Armistice between the legitimate government of Italy and the Allies, the country was still headed by Mussolini and his Fascist government. The Germans subsequently looted the gold from the Bank of Italy.

On February 10, 1947, Italy signed a peace treaty that it would restore to the governments of France and Yugoslavian all monetary gold looted or wrongfully removed by Italy. Once this was complied with, Italy would be allowed to draw from the Allied Gold Pot.

The Italian case was a complicated one and can best be described by taking the events in order.

According to the claim filed by the Italian Government, an agreement had been reached in December 1940, between the Reichsbank and the Istituto Nazionale per i Cambi con L'Estero (Istcambi) whereby seven million US dollars was placed at the disposal of the German embassy in Washington DC. These funds were to be used in swaying the election against President Franklin Roosevelt. The German embassy disposed of most of the money but due to the shortness of time, before the declaration of war in one year, was unable to spend it all and $3,021,120 remained unaccounted for. Therefore, the Italian government, representing Istcambi requested settlement of this amount in gold and Swiss francs.

During the war years, the Germans admitted they did not know what had happened to the US dollars in Washington DC and suggested Italy settle in gold for $2,000,000 which was agreed upon and the gold was duly delivered to the Bank of Italy. It was later transferred back to Germany based on the February 5, 1944 assignment of the Bank of Italy's gold to the German Ministry of Foreign Affairs, as a trustee.

In their claim, the Italian government contended the dollars were used for the benefit of the Germans and the gold became part of Germany's monetary reserves. The Commission was unfavorably impressed by this claim and rejected the request.

In a letter dated March 29, 1949, the Italian ambassador informed the Tripartite Gold Commission that $3,021,120 had been found in Washington DC where it had been taken by the Office of Alien Property in 1942. On February 12, 1956, the money was returned to the Liquidators of Istcambi.[18]

In October 1947, the Commission set aside gold for Italy pursuant to Paragraph D of Part III of the Paris Agreement, but no allocation was made since Italy was not yet entitled to participate in the pool. Then on June 30, 1948, France was issued 463,644.348 Troy ounces of gold, and on September 23, 1948, Yugoslavia was credited with 269,841.177 Troy ounces of gold from Italy's allocation.

The gold was removed from the Bank of England.

After these two transactions, all that remained in the Italian account was 14,917.959 Troy ounces. This gold was transferred to Italy from the Bank of England on October 8, 1948, and this small amount was all Italy had received at that time.

On July 7, 1958, 403,320.247 Troy ounces of gold was transferred to the Banca d'Italia, Roma by the Bank of England. Then on June 25, 1998, Italy received 24,581.655 Troy ounces of gold and £2,388.12 from the Bank of England.[19]

Italy's share was 442,820.446 Troy ounces of gold that was 4.09% of the total Gold Pot.

Luxembourg

The Luxembourg government first claim from the Gold Pot was discussed in a previous chapter. The amount of gold for that transaction was 62,034.854 Troy ounces of gold. In 1958, Luxembourg was allotted additional 24,113.056 ounces of gold and requested it to be delivered to its account with the Bank of France. The gold asked for was delivered to the Bank of France on July 2, 1958.

On June 26, 1998, Luxembourg received an additional 2,006.325 Troy ounces of Gold and £51,374.75 from the Bank of England.

Luxembourg received 138,941.668 Troy ounces for 1.28% of the Gold Pot.

Poland

Poland was one of the very few countries in Europe that was able to save the gold reserves of their central bank prior to the German invasion. Poland did not participate in the preliminary distribution because its claim was not properly formulated until 1950. The initial claim included a request for 4,382,146.757 Troy Ounces of gold (1945 value $153,375,136.50). This request was for trinkets, bangles, rings and gold teeth that had been taken from concentration camp victims, smelted and deposited into the Reichsbank under the infamous aforementioned name "Melmer." The Commission considered this gold from individuals and rejected the claim in its entirety.

The second claim, in respect of gold originating in the former Free City of Danzig, was validated by the Tripartite Commission, but it decided in its adjudication of June 1958 that neither the government of Poland, nor any other government, had proved that it was entitled to claim in respect of the Danzig gold, and that an appropriate share of the gold pool should be set aside in the custody of the three governments pending resolution of the issue. The ambassador of Poland protested this decision by stating in writing that his government considered the Commission's decisions were without foundation in law and in fact.[20] The Polish government further pointed out that the gold looted from concentration camp victims was not monetary gold at the time of the looting, but was subsequently smelted into gold bars and formed part of the monetary gold reserves of the Third Reich. This gold ended up in the Merkers salt mine; recovered by US Forces and deposited in the Gold Pot.

After all, Germany had invaded Poland on September 1, 1939, and in a brutal attack defeated the country in less than a month. The military was followed closely by the *Devisenschutzkommando* or Nazi Treasury Agents. They forcibly opened every vault, safe and safe deposit box in every bank and financial institution in Poland. The agents finished the job in three to four months. With German efficiency, every item was inventoried, and all the valuables shipped back to Germany.[21]

Cooler heads prevailed, and eventually, in June 1976, the Tripartite Commission decided that as no other claimant had come forward and as the Polish People's Republic had exercised authority in Danzig for over thirty years, the gold should be delivered to the Government of Poland. A supplement to the original adjudication was signed by the three Commissioners. In August 1976, Poland received 50,237.827 ounces from the Federal Reserve Bank of New York and 29,327.197 ounces from the Bank of England (a total of 79,565.024 ounces) in respect of the combined preliminary and quasi-final shares relating to Danzig.[22]

On June 5, 1998, Poland was granted an additional 1,233.530 Troy ounces of gold and a payment of £4,782.90 from the Bank of England.[23]

A total of 80,771.252 Troy ounces for a .75% total of the Allied Gold Pot.

Yugoslavia

In addition to the gold mentioned in a previous chapter, another source of gold from Yugoslavia that went to Germany was the Bor Copper Mines. The mines had been sold by the Kingdom of Yugoslavia to a French company in 1903. The company, La Compagnie Françoise des Mines de Bor, operated the Bor Copper Mines with the understanding that gold extracted from the copper must be sold to the National Bank of Yugoslavia. The mine yielded about 1.5 Troy ounces of gold for every ton of copper. The gold was removed by an efficient electrolysis process, thus making it a most profitable byproduct.

This agreement was enforced until Germany invaded France in 1940. The conquering Germans forced the stockholders of the French company to sell them their shares of stock in La Compagnie Françoise des Mines de Bor, renamed de Bor Kupferbergwerke und Hütten A.G (BOR A.G.). Thus during the occupation of France and a year later the occupation of Yugoslavia the Germans removed from the Mines de Bor 68,208.375 Troy ounces of gold with a 1945 value of $3,034,793.

Part of the gold, 14,325.440 Troy ounces was reported as looted. The gold bars, were marked BOR followed by two digits. The German director reported that 643.015 Troy ounces were given to Hermann Göring. Franz Neuhausen's function under the Four-Year Plan was to insure that Germany acquired the raw materials needed for war production. With the help of Göring, Neuhausen purchased many shares in mining companies, iron and steel mills. He was also the President of the Bor A.G. mines. Always present at Göring's birthday parties each year, the wealthy industrialist Franz Neuhausen would give Göring, on his fiftieth birthday, January 12, 1943, a large twenty kilogram bar of gold, the by-product of this copper mine.

On May 8, 1947, the Federated People's Republic of Yugoslavia filed a restitution claim for 394,326.470 Troy ounces of gold. The claims were for gold seized from the National Bank of the Kingdom of Yugoslavia and National Bank of Serbia. Some of the Yugoslavian gold had been looted by Italy when they were allied with Nazi Germany. When the tide of the war turned, Italy quit Nazi Germany and joined the US Allied Forces. At that time Germany seized the Yugoslavian gold from the Italians as described above in the section regarding Italy.

On September 23, 1948, Yugoslavia was credited with 269,841.177 Troy ounces of gold from Italy's allocation and an additional 6,919.813 ounces from a source that is not quite clear but is on page 15 of the Gold Book Spread Sheet. The 276,760.751 Troy ounces of gold was delivered from the Bank of England.

On November 17, 1950, Yugoslavia received an additional 1,629.648 ounces of gold. British authorities in Germany through a misunderstanding had also delivered Yugoslavia sixteen bars of gold containing 1,656.130 ounces of fine gold. This the total amount delivered in the preliminary distributions to that country was 278,416.881 ounces of gold.[24]

On November 5, 1958, an additional 56,263.667 was transferred to Yugoslavia from the Bank of England.

The remaining share, originally destined for the former Yugoslavia, amounting to 1,209.781 ounces of fine gold and £33,612.04, was retained in associated gold and sterling non interest-bearing accounts held by the three governments at the Bank of England to await an arrangement between the successor states.[25] These valuables were delivered on July 13, 1998.

The Yugoslavia total was 665,153.706 Troy ounces of gold for 6.15% of the total Gold Pot.

Slavic Republic

The Slavic Republic on June 24, 1998 was allocated 5,240.413 Troy ounces of gold for a .05% of the Gold Pot.

One of the more interesting characters representing the Yugoslavia Government in the restitution of valuables was Mate Topic. On August 17, 1949, Topic, counselor to the Yugoslavia Military Mission in Berlin and wearing the uniform of a Yugoslavia major, visited Mr. Frank J. Roberts, Acting Chief of the Foreign Exchange Depository in Frankfurt, Germany. Topic made inquiries to Yugoslavia Claims 1701, 1702 and 1703. These claims were currently being evaluated by the Tripartite Gold Commission in Brussels, Belgium. Topic stated that Claim 1701 consisting of eighty-five bars of gold could not be considered in the category of gold because of low gold contents of the bars. He further informed Mr. Roberts that he was obtaining new evidence regarding these three claims. Topic was told to submit his finding directly to the Tripartite Gold Commission as soon as possible.

Topic returned on August 30 and hand delivered a letter addressed to Mr. Roberts regarding, two new claims, numbers 1704 for the Bor Mine Gold and 1705 that involved three bars of gold from the Hermann Göring collection. Included with the letter were sworn statements addressed to Mr. Mate Topic favoring his position including a statement from Franz Neuhausen's wife, Helene. Topic had even notarized some of the signatures of the statement addressed to himself. Of interest, Topic had XXed out the preprinted name Major B. Brejc and typed his name below the XXs. Roberts forwarded these documents to the Commission in Brussels.

Topic's request 1704 was immediately rejected as explained by the Commission; this claim in a previous form had been accepted by the Commission from the Yugoslavia Representatives. The objectives of this claim had already been agreed upon. It appears that claim 1705 was ignored by the Tripartite Gold Commission.

In September, Topic filed another request for four bars of silver with the Foreign Exchange Depository, claiming these bars of silver that had been given to Göring for his birthday. To support this claim he submitted a March 16, 1949 statement from Richard Schultz stating that he had handed the silver bars to Göring's valet, and that the bars were packed in the treasure train that was seized by US forces in Berchtesgaden, Germany.

Surprisingly, Topic informed Mr. Roberts that he had identified one of the silver bars packed in a small wooden case. He further said that the bar was safeguarded in the US Army Central Collection Point in Munich, Germany. Roberts wrote Mr. Stephen P. Munsing a letter on October 19, 1948, informing him of Topic's conversation regarding the bar of silver. Topic seemed to have an inside connection in the Central Collection point.

Now, most likely with inside information in the Foreign Exchange Depository, Topic filed a claim for ten bars of valuable platinum and three bottles of Iridium. His claim matched the inventory exactly. Platinum in 1949 had a greater value than gold. Today it is on even par with gold. Iridium is a member of the platinum family and is one of the rarest elements on earth. On December 13, 1950, Topic signed for the platinum and Iridium valued then at about $45,000 and left with the ninety pounds of valuable ore.[26]

Topic was not only working the Foreign Exchange Depository in Frankfurt but a year prior in December 1949, Mate Topic turned up at the Munich Central Collection Center, claiming to be the Yugoslav government's representative in charge of restitution. Topic presented a list of 166 objets d'art that he claimed had been looted from Yugoslavia by the Nazis. This included one silver bar with an inventory number of 5058/20/25. Topic had been able to compile the lists because he had a young German art historian, Dr. Wiltrud Mersmann, who worked as a junior curator at the Central Collecting Point helping him.

Regardless, on June 2, 1949, the bulk of the requested art that had arrived at the Collection Point from the Hitler Collection at Alt Aussee, was loaded onto trucks and disappeared. The receipt granting the art to Yugoslavia was signed by Stephen Munsing.

On March 24, 1956, Mate Topic, now named Topic Ante Mimara, was tracked to Tangier by the US Department of State. In an interview, Topic stated that all the objects he took in 1949 were signed by receipts, loaded onto trucks and escorted by US military police to the Yugoslav border and turned over to Yugoslavian authorities. He further lied that Dr. Veljko Petrovic, Director, showed him the objects on display in June or July 1946 at the Academy of Belgrade and that the valuable tapestries and textiles had been cut in sizes to fit the floor of the offices of the museum. He had returned to Belgrade in 1950 and now has no idea as to where the objects are now located.

In an unsigned letter dated March 10, 1954, "Restitution in Error to Yugoslavia," to Mr. Crutcher writes: "It would be impossible to expect a satisfactory answer from Yugoslavia without providing photographs, a full description, and justification of the request. ... However the Yugoslav claims are not in the Munich Collection Point files. We cannot find any trace of this folder of the original claim." The 166 objects stolen by Topic have never been recovered.

Regardless of Topic's conman abilities, in 1963, Thomas Hoving, curator of the Metropolitan Museum's Cloisters (and later director of the Metropolitan), purchased one of the most marvelous and enigmatic works of art ever created—the Bury St. Edmunds ivory cross from Topic Ante Mimara for $600,000. Mimara refused to give Hoving or the museum any details about the provenance of the piece, which had been missing for eight centuries, saying only that it had been purchased from an Eastern European monastery. James Rorimer, director of the Metropolitan, called the cross one of the most important acquisitions the museum had ever made. Topic Ante Mimara used the proceeds to purchase Schloss Neuhaus, the castle near Salzburg where his widow, Mrs. Dr. Wiltrud Mersmann Mimara, now lives. The junior curator and former employee from the Munich Collection Point had done quite well for herself.[27]

As seen from the above paragraphs the US government had a difficult job in the restoration of valuables seized by the Nazis and now looted by the looters.

CHAPTER 26

Winding Up of the Tripartite Commission

The general of a military occupying force has more power and authority than any king, emperor or despot ruler. Thus, two years after hostilities, using captured financial German records, US General and Military Governor, Lucas Clay had reinstated four countries, including Hungary, with 57% of the monetary gold under his command that also constituted 31% of the total Gold Pot. Then politics took place as the Gold Pot was placed under the authority of the US Department of State. Under their authority, it would take fifty years to settle the remainder of the claims for the Gold Pot.

By 1971, the Tripartite Commission's staff had been reduced considerably and consisted of no more than a secretary general, his personal assistant and a staff member responsible for the archives and accounts. By the end of 1971, the personal assistant had retired without replacement, and the staff member was retained on a "short part-time basis." By 1974, the staff member was employed on the basis of ad hoc consultation, leaving the Secretary General, Col. John Watson, as the sole remaining official of the Tripartite Commission. When he fell ill in 1976, a successor was found in Mr. Colin Harris, who took office with effect from January 1977. Mr. Harris unfortunately died in office in the spring of 1992.

For much of the period post-1971 the Tripartite Commission was unable to undertake the distribution of gold while the resolution of problems outside its control were undertaken by the three governments of the U.S., England and France.

At the Bank of England, there were two sterling accounts that were used as the main operating accounts: one was an interest-bearing deposit account in which were placed the proceeds of the sales of gold bars over the years. This account was used to feed the financial credit that funded expenditures in sterling such as gold storage charges at the Bank of England, and also funded the current account held at the Morgan Guaranty Trust Company in Brussels that was used to meet the administrative expenses of the Tripartite Commission. When the Morgan Guaranty Trust ceased its "High Street" banking operations in Brussels in 1995, the Tripartite Commission avoided the expense of opening a new account in Brussels by thereafter using the Bank of England's current account for all current expenditures. After all, the gold had been distributed with the exception of the final share of the successor states to the former Yugoslavia, when the Commission was wound up, there remained £78.09 in the deposit account and £350,044.46 in the current account. The total of £350,122.55 was then distributed pro rata to the claimant countries by check.

At an enlarged meeting of the Tripartite Commission on June 27, 1997, in which representatives from various capitals took part, it was agreed that the Tripartite Commission should launch the final distribution by informing the claimant governments by diplomatic note of the amount of gold due to them in the final distribution, and that the Tripartite Commission was ready to proceed. Simultaneously, the three governments would inform the claimant governments by diplomatic note of the findings of the British and US researchers, and suggest that they might wish to consider placing all or some of their final share in a fund being established to aid needy victims of Nazi persecutions. This exercise took place in early August when the chairman and secretary general of the Tripartite Commission called together the diplomatic representatives in Brussels of the claimant countries (with the exception of those of the successor states to the former Yugoslavia) and handed over copies of the diplomatic notes referred to above.

In the first forty-nine years of its existence, the commission had made nineteen partial settlements to eight countries. Then in one year, 1998 with the spotlight shining on them the commission would make eleven final payments to ten countries.

The three governments then agreed that the archives of the Tripartite Commission should be transferred immediately upon its closure to the Archives Nationales Françoise, and be available immediately to the public. The archives included all the documents relating to each claimant country's claim, the Tripartite Commission's adjudication thereon, the distributions of gold made to each country, and the minutes of all the meetings of the Tripartite Commission from 1946 to 1998; the 1971 Report to the three governments, which includes all the adjudications and the history of the Tripartite Commission's proceedings up to 1971; the Final Report to the three governments of 1998, files relating to the Commission's dealings with the Federal Reserve Bank of New York, the Bank of England and the Banque de France; and "The Gold Book"—the ledger in which are recorded all the movements of gold into and out of the Tripartite Commission's accounts Tripartite Commission Staff.

At an international Nazi gold conference held in London in December 1997, several countries agreed to relinquish their claims to their share of the remaining 5.5 metric tons (worth about sixty million dollars) still held by the Tripartite Gold Commission (TGC) and donate it to a Nazi Persecution Relief Fund to help survivors of the Holocaust. Almost all of the claimant nations similarly agreed to such a policy during the course of 1998. Early in September 1998, in a ceremony held in Paris, the TGC announced its task was completed and folded. Thus, the Merkers story ends on a noble, selfless, just, and moral note, as upwards of fifteen countries were willing to forego receiving gold stolen from their nations by the Nazis and allow it to be used as compensation for victims of Nazi persecution.

Appendix A
The Foreign Exchange Depository—List of Shipments

Following is a list of shipments with the date of receipt, the source, amount of gold deposited to the Allied Gold Pot and a summary of contents. Alphabetic subdivisions of the contents of a given shipment indicate the items came several different sources.

Shipment   Date Source

1. April 15, 1945 Merkers
   - 3682 bags and cartons of German currency
   - 80 bags of foreign currency
   - 4173 bags with 8307 gold bars
   - 55 boxes of gold bullion
   - 3326 bags of gold coins
   - 33 bags silver and gold coins
   - 5 bags Maria Theresa Thalers
   - 63 bags of silver bars
   - 1 bag containing six platinum bars
   - 8 bags of gold rings
   - 185 parcels of plates and dies
   - 48 containers of misc. supplies
   - 207 containers of SS loot: jewelry, gold teeth etc

2. April 25, 1945 Reichsbank, Halle
   - A 43 bags of currency
   - B 22 bags of currency
   - C 64 large gold bars
   - D 2 chest of currency and gold
   - E 7 bags of currency and gold
   - F 4 bags of currency, silver and gold

3. April 27, 1945 Stadt & Kreissparkassee Hof
   - 2 chest of gold plate service and 1 gold chalice, 24 gold plates, 41 gold knives,
   - 41 gold spoons and 41 gold forks

4. April 27, 1945 Reichsbank, Plauen
   - 28 bags of gold coins
   - 22 bags of silver coins

5. April 29, 1945 Reichsbank, Nordhausen
   - 242 bags of currency
   - 3 bags of platinum
   - 21 containers of records
   - 1 envelope of French checks

6. April 29, 1945 Reichsbank, Leipzig

   - 328 bags of currency

7. April 30, 1945 Reichsbank, Eschwege
   - 82 large gold bars

8. April 25, 1945 Reichsbank, Frankfurt
   - 1 package of foreign currency

9. April 24, 1945 Reichsbank, Eisenach & Erfurt
   - 2 bags of currency

10. May 2, 1945 Reichsbank, Coburg
    - 82 large gold bars
    - 1 box of currency

11. May 2, 1945 Factory, Wurtingen
    - 297 large bars of silver
    - 645 small bars of silver

12. May 2, 1945 Salt mine, Bernterode
    - 3 boxes art objects containing crown jewels

13. May 3, 1945 I G Farben Company
    - 1 box of currency

14. May 3, 1945 Reichsbank, Wurzburg
    - 111 bags of currency
    - 24 bags of coins

15. May 3, 1945 Reichsbank, Nuremberg
    - 37 bags of gold coins
    - 1 bag of currency
    - 2 boxes of gold

16. May 7, 1945 Buchenwald
    - 319 boxes containing currency, jewelry, coins currency, gold teeth, toys, etc

17. May 9, 1945 Reichsbank, Magdeburg
    - 5273 small bars of silver

769	large bars of silver
34	miscellaneous bars of silver
536	boxes containing silver coins, silver bars, scrap silver and 707 bars of silver
1	metal box of currency and coins
94	packages of records
10	packages of printing plates
1	small cardboard crate of plates
14	bags of assays
3	German record books
1	package of foreign securities
1	envelope containing silver inventory

18. May 13, 1945 Reichsbank, Munich

A	11	bags of foreign currency
B	5	bags of foreign currency
C	104	bags of foreign currency and coins
D	5	bags of foreign currency
E	4	boxes contents unknown
F	3	valises contents unknown
	28	bags of foreign currency

19. May 14, 1945 Salt Mine, Grasleben

4	cases labeled "Posen Domkirche"
1	case labeled "Collection Schrwa und Lissa"
2	cases labeled "Silber Kirchengeraeta"
1	case labeled "Lissa Collection"
4	chests, unmarked
1	trunk labeled "Edelmetall"
1	box marked number 5
1	Processional cross
87	cases of monstrance and shrines

20. May 16, 1945 National Bank of Hungary

A	633 cases of gold bullion and coins
B	2 cases of foreign currency and coins
C	19 cases containing gold bars, gold coins, and silver
D	3 containers of platinum
E	1 package belonging to the Hungarian Military Police
F	28 cases of deposits forOrphans of Budapest
G	1 sack containing:
	a. 1 case sealed envelopes re: Jewish properties
	b. 1 package belonging to Minister President Ferenc Szalazi
	c. 1 case deposit by Commercial Bank of Budapest
H	2 envelopes containing securities
	1 box containing valuables

21. May 19, 1945 Seventh U.S Army, various places

A	4	boxes containing currency, jewelry,
B	2	mail bag and 3 boxes of coins
C	3	boxes of currency
D	8	bags of coins
E	3	bags of currency
F	1	bag of currency
G	3	bags of currency
H	1	wooden case currency
I	7	bags of currency
J	2	bags of currency
K	11	boxes of gold and silver ingots

22. May 26, 1945 Salt mine, Friedrichshall

58	containers and 14 bags of gold, diamonds, silver and platinum

23. May 30, 1945 Reichsbank, Holzminder

A	1	box and 4 bags of jewelryand gold coins
	1	bag of jewelry
B	3	bags of gold coins and gold bars property of Schwerin Gestapo

24. June 1, 1945 Alt Aussee, Austria

1	bag of gold coins

25. June 8, 1945 Reichsbank, Halle

96	bags of German coins
3	packages of foreign currency

26. June 9, 1945 Reichsbank, Regensburg

A	15	bags of gold bars
B	9	suitcases,
	4	wooden boxes,
	1	cardboard carton of jewelry
	1	sack with tabernacle from Russian Orthodox Church
C	1	bag Austrian gold coins
	1	bag gold bars

27. June 10, 1945 7th US Army, Innsbruck

A	25	boxes gold bars
	8	bags of gold coins
	18	large gold bars
	6	small gold bars
	1	bag gold scraps
	15	bags of currency

Dorenwald

B	79	gold bars

Lindau

C	16	boxes gold bars
	28	bags of gold coins
	60	gold bars

St. Johann
D 1 large green box and one
1 white pine box of currency
Oberbichl
E 1 box currency
Ober Siegsdorf
F 1 box Hungarian currency
Wallgau
G 364 bags of gold bars

28. June 11, 1945 Erlanger
2 bags currency

29. June 15, 1945 Reichsbank, Zwickau
41 bags of gold bars

30. June 15, 1945 Deutsche Bank, Meiningen
1 box foreign currency
1 metal box radium

31. June 18, 1945 Rauris, Zell am See
19 bags gold coins and bars
1 mail sack of currency
3 boxes of currency
3 bags jewelry and silverware
1 mail sack of wrappings from currency and coins
2 boxes and 10 bags silver coins and bullion
1 envelope with gold coins, currency, and jewelry

32. June 21, 1945 XXI Corps, Mansfield
A 4 bags silver bullion
B 5 albums maps
5 albums of botanical subjects
1 Norman Helmet
C 2 sealed envelopes with currency

33. June 22, 1945 Reichsbank, Leipzig
32 boxes, 2 bags, and 1 package of foreign
exchange assets of affiliated Reichsbanks

34. June 23, 1945 Reichsbank, Kothen 809.479
A 3 bags currency
28 small gold bars
B 17 bags currency
4 boxes currency
9 bags of coins
C 2 1/2 truck loads securities
D 73 boxes silver bars
40 chest silver bars
E 1 box silver granules
1 bag securities

35. June 23, 1945 Reichsbank, Nordhausen
2 bags currency, gold coins and securities
Received on June 23, 1945 two bags of securities and currency acquired under Military Law 53, from Reichsbank, Nordhausen and deposited as shipment 35.

36. June 23, 1945 Various banks, Eisenach
4 bags currency
2 packages of securities
1 envelope securities
1 bag currency
Received on June 23, 1945 seven bags of securities and currency acquired under Military Law 53, from Reichsbank, Eisenach and deposited as shipment 36.

37. June 25, 1945, Schmalkalden
A 3 envelopes currency
B 1 large bag of currency
Received on June 25, 1945 three bags of securities and currency acquired under Military Law 53, from Reichsbank, Schmalkalden and deposited as shipment 37.

38. June 22, 1945 Reichsbank, Naumburg
4 boxes of currency
Received on June 22, 1945 four boxes of securities and currency acquired under Military Law 53, from Reichsbank, Naumburg and deposited as shipment 38.

39. June 25, 1945 State of Saxony, Bad Elster
2 boxes securities
Shipment 39 State of Saxony, Bad Elster—Received on June 25, 1945 two boxes of securities and currency acquired under Military Law 53, from State of Saxony, Bad Elster and deposited as shipment 39.

40. June 26, 1945 Reichsbank, Jena
40 bags silver RM coins
1 bag currency
Received on June 26, 1945 forty bags German silver coins, one bag currency acquired under Military Law 53, from Reichsbank, Jena and deposited as shipment 40.

41. June 28, 1945 Reichsbank, Sonneberg
A. 21 bags silver 5RM coins
B. 111 bags silver 2RM coins
C. 445 bags silver 5RM coins
D. 7 bags of silver bullion and 1 bag coins
E. 1 box currency

Received on June 28, 1945 twenty one large bags German silver coins 5DM, 111 large bags silver coins 2DM, 445 small bags silver coins 5DM , seven bags silver bullion, one bag miscellaneous silver coins, one bag securities and currency acquired under Military Law 53.

42. June 29, 1945 Reichsbanks
Zawickau
A 2 bags silver and gold coins
4 bags currency
Crimmitschau
B 4 bags currency
1 package of gold coins
Werdau
C 1 bag of currency
Gera
D 235 bags of German silver coins
1 bag currency
3 bags various coins
1 bag securities
2 bags foreign currency
Merane
E 1 bag foreign currency
In June 1945 the Foreign Exchange Depository received under Military Law 53 from Zwackau, two bags gold and silver coins, four bags foreign currency; Crimmitschau, four bags foreign currency and coins, one bag gold coins; Werdan, one bag currency, coins, securities; Werdau, 235 bags German silver coins, three bags of gold coins, one bag foreign coins and currency, one bag securities, two bags foreign currency; Merne, one bag foreign currency acquired under military Law 53.

43. June 29, 1945 Reichsbanks
Weissenfels
A. 1 bag foreign currency
Zeitz
B. 8 bags silver German coins
1 bag foreign currency
Weissenfels, Zeitz—In June 1945 the Foreign Exchange Depository received under Military Law 53 from Weissenfels, a box of coins, currency and securities.

44. June 30, 1945 Reichsbank, Weimar
8 bags silver German coins
2 boxes foreign currency
In June 1945 the Foreign Exchange Depository received under Military Law 53 from Weimar Reichsbank, eight bags of securities and German silver coins and eight sacks of silver coins.

45. June 30, 1945 Reichsbank, Leipzig
44 boxes foreign exchange assets
1 bag silver coins
In June 1945 the Foreign Exchange Depository received under Military Law 53 from Leipzig Reichsbank, 44 boxes of securities and one bag of German silver coins.

46. July1, 1945 Financial Institutions, Landkreis Schleiz
1 metal case and 1 bag foreign currency
In June 1945 the Foreign Exchange Depository received under Military Law 53 from Landkreis Schleiz, one metal case and one sack of foreign currency and coins.

47. July 3, 1945 Reichsbank, Gotha
1 small box diamonds
3 bags foreign currency

48. July 3, 1945 Reichsbank, Greiz
1 tin box foreign currency
1 paper box foreign currency
3 packages foreign currency
348 bags of German silver coins
In June 1945 the Foreign Exchange Depository received under Military Law 53 from Greiz Reichsbank, 348 bags of silver coins, foreign currency and 9.3 grams of gold.

49. July 5, 1945 Reichsbank, Saalfeld
1 envelope foreign currency
6 bags of silver coins
In June 1945 the Foreign Exchange Depository received under Military Law 53 from Reichsbank Saalfeld six bags with 78,000 silver German coins and an envelope with a few gold coins currency.

50. July 6, 1945 Finance Officers U.S Army
2nd Division
A 1 package Czech currency
56th Dis Sec
B 1 package foreign currency
30th Division
C 1 package Italian currency
2nd Division
D 1 package Czech currency
2nd Division
E 1 package foreign currency
MG Det A1A1
F 1packet foreign assets
7th Armor Div
G 1 box foreign currency

51. July 9, 1945 Hartmannsdorf
1   box foreign currency

52. July 7, 1945 U.S Army
    Walchensee
    A   72   bags foreign currency
        4   boxes gold
        6   boxes foreign currency
        2   bags gold coins
    Mittenwald
    B   20   boxes gold
    Bad Aussee
    C   1   bag gold, silver, currency, jewelry
Munich
    D   1   tin box, charred currency and coins
    Dachau
    E   4   boxes
2   cartons of jewelry

53. July 11, 1945 Reichsbank, Eschwege
    926 bags of Russian currency
    11   cardboard cartons contents unknown
    1   folder miscellaneous papers
    6   bars of silver
    1   bag of coins
    180 bags of German coins
    3   wooden boxes contents unknown
    1   bag currency and coins pearls and 4 gold
         watches

54. July 13, 1945 Farchant
    1   envelope of securities

55. July 21 1945 MG Det Elf 3, Bad Tolz
    382 engraving plates for German currency

56. July 29, 1945 I G Farben
    1939 silver bars
    102 boxes silver
    33   sacks of silver
    27   bundles sheet silver
    102 pipes of silver
    94   bundles of silver wire

57. July 30, 1945 US Army
    Garmish
    A. 1 wooden box British sterling pound notes
    Munich
    B. 15 bags British silver coins
    C. 10 packages foreign currency

58. July 31, 1945 Reichsbank, Weimar
    1   bag various coins
    1   bag foreign currency

59. August 3, 1945 7th Army Interrogation Center
    1   iron chest containing the Holy Crown and
         Crown
             Jewels of St. Stephen
    2   documents in Hungarian
    1   small sealed glass tube containing particles
         of gold
    3   padlocks with keys to chest
    1   key for chest lock

60. August 11, 1945 Mittenwald
    $4,000 U.S currency

61. August 20, 1945 Linz Austria
    Money taken from Pierre Laval

62. August 24, 1945 Reichsbank, Hersfeld
    1   bag currency and securities

63. August 24, 1945 Reichsbank, Fulda
    22   bags currency
    1   bag coins
    15   bags German coins
    20   packages securities

64. August 24, 1945 Hanau
    1   box diamonds

65. September 25, 1945 Reichsbank, Schweinfurt
    284 bags German 5RM silver coins
    78   bags German 2RM silver coins
         Seized under Military Law 53.

66. September 27, 1945 Reichsbank, Wuerzburg
    23   boxes German 5 RM silver coins
         Seized under Military Law 53.

67. September 27, 1945 Reichsbank, Aschaffenburg
    20   boxes German 5RM silver coins
         Seized under Military Law 53.

68. September 28, 1945 Reichsbanks
    Aschaffenburg
    A. 6 boxes German 2RM silver coins
    Wuerzburg
    B. 8 boxes German silver coins
         Seized under Military Law 53.

69. October 5, 1945 Reichsbank, Regensburg
    10   boxes printing plates
    1   roll partially printed notes
         Seized under Military Law 53.

70. October 11, 1945 Cartels Branch
    1   sack Göring jewels

71. October 17, 1945 SCI Det 3rd Army
    8   bags gold coins

72. October 20, 1945 St. Anna
    1   bag gold coins

73. October 30, 1945 Sulzbach
    1   bag French francs

74. November 1, 1945 Reichsbank, Bremen
    299 bags German 5RM silver coins
    28   bags various coins
    20   bags currency
    82   packages currency
    3   packages forms MGAX2

75. November 5, 1945 Garmish Partenkirchen
    1   brooch diamond
    1   bracelet platinum
    1   coin gold

76. November 8, 1945 Kirchberg
    1   chest of silverware with emblem of
         Polish crown
    1   small brown box of four men's watches,
         one gold women's watch, set with 50
         diamonds,
    2   gold cuff links
    1   small black suitcase containing $1,000
         U.S.dollars, ten English pounds notes, one
         diamond brooch, and other personal
         effects of Eva Braun

77. December 26, 1945 British and American
    Embassies
    Madrid, Spain
    31   bags of foreign currency

78. June 17, 1946 U.S Army
    1   box coupons and German stock

79. October 9, 1946 Border Police
    380 items of Gold Tableware, silver and
    jewelry

80. October 2, 1946 Assistant Chief of Staff
    1   box SS dental gold

81. February 19, 1947 Civil Censorship Division
    1   wooden box containing securities

82. March 24, 1947 Hungarian National Bank
    2,269   gold Turkish pounds
    749 gold Japanese yen
    1,115   gold Columbian pesos

83. March 11, 1947 Tetz Germany
    1   gold bar bearing Prussian State Mint

84. May 16, 1947 German Post Office mail
    containers
    Currency, silver scrap, securities

85. July 10, 1947 US Constabulary Regiment
    Approximately 1,000 pounds of silver coins

86. July 19, 1947 Dachau Concentration Camp
    12 pounds gold teeth and fillings

87. July 22, 1947 US Counter Intelligence Corps
    One sealed package jewelry
    Two boxes containing jewelry

88. September 22, 1947 Bavarian Landsbank
    Jewelry

89. October 22, 1947 Kronberg Castle
    2 boxes antique jewelry

90. December 10, 1947 Intergovernmental
    Committee Refugees
    Storage compartment set aside

91. December 30, 1947 Counter Intelligence
    Division
    8 vial of radium and mesothorium

92. January 7, 1948 Kronberg Castle Officers Club
    5 boxes tableware

93. March 8, 1948 Land Property Officer Stuttgart
    Jewelry

94. March 15, 1948 US Provost Marshall
    1 lead box with radium

95. March 15, 1948 Unknown
    1 stock certificate book of Ford Motors

96. April 20, 1948 Property Control, Pforgheim
    2 pictures

97. April 20, 1948 Various shipments
    All German silver coins extracted from other
    shipments

98. May 6, 1948 Provost Marshall General
George H. Weems
40 items of jewelry
Manuscript Book of Hours

99. May 20, 1948 Various shipments
Records, correspondences and other papers

100. May 21, 1948 Central Disbursement Office
11 boxes of currency

101. May 25, 1948 Theater Provost Marshall
Currencies including $5,995.00 U.S.

102. May 27, 1948 [illegible]
10 boxes numismatic coins of the Berlin Coin
Collection

103. July 6, 1948 Russian Zone Reichsbanks
184 boxes Law 53 assets

104 April 27, 1945 Reichsbank Plauen
Records Precious Metals Department

105. August 11, 1948 Currency Section
14 packages counterfeit plates

106. August 12, 1948 Various shipments
Monetary gold 3,469 boxes

107. September 1, 1948 Currency Section
34 boxes various currency

108. September 16, 1948 Various departments
95 boxes of engraving plates

109. September 9, 1948 Currency Section
1 box currency

110. October 8, 1948 Various Shipments
Items rejected by IGCR

111. January 20, 1949 US Formally Germany
Hohenzollern Silverware and Porcelain

112. January 7, 1949 Various German banks
Securities I.G. Chemie, Basel

113. February 18, 1949 Landeszentralbank
Securities I.G. Chemie, Basel

114. March 10, 1949 Landeszentralbank
Securities I.G. Chemie, Basel

115. June30, 1949 Office Military Government
Bavaria
639.6 carats of diamonds

116. July 27, 1949 L C B. Augustsburg [?]
Dr. Gustav Hilger CIA

117 April 20, 1950 Credit Bank Munich
5 cases Allied P O W effects from Stalag VIII C

118. May 10, 1950 Held for Chief Property Division
HICOG
Mainz Psalter alleged printed 1457

119. July 26, 1950 Deutscher Bank
Platinum, and other precious metals

120. August 1, 10,. October 18, 1950 Budget and
Finance
Sealed case miscellaneous accounts

121. November 20, 1950 Various Shipments
Platinum and other precious metals

Appendix B
Deposits to the Allied Gold Pot

(i) Switzerland

(ii) The French, Gold Conundrum

(ii) The Netherlands Distribution

(iii) Romania

(iv) Gold Shipment to the Bank of England

(v) Bank of International Settlement

(vi) Spain

(vii) The Swedish Contribution

(viii) Gold delivered to Austria by the Commander of Chief
of US Forces

(ix) Gold from German Assets in Japan

(x) From Yugoslavia

(xi) Deposit from Military Law 53—British Element

(xii) Seized from a German agent in the British Zone

(xiii) Deposit from Military Law 53—US Zone

(xiv) Deposit from Military Law 53—France

(xv) German Embassy of Lisbon, Madrid and two coins
from US Zone

(xvi) The Salzburg Gold Delivery

(xvii) Gold handed over to French authorities by Americans

(xviii) Gold from Hintersee, Austria

(xix) From Sweden's Second Delivery

(xx) Gold Received from Priest

(xxi) Gold found in Germany by French Officers

(xxii) From Czechoslovakia

(xxiii) Portugal

Two Found Bars

Appendix C
Kaltenbrunner Missing Treasure

Contents of Shipment 21 A

Silver coins:

1. 97 Polish Zloty at 10: 1970
2. 500 Polish Zloty at 5: 2500
3. 152 Polish Zloty at 10: 1520
4. 924 Polish Zloty at 2: 1548
5. 28½ Silver Bars (6 in. long by ¼ in. diameter)

Gold coins:

7. 74 US $20: 1480
   1 Austria-Hungary ducst
8. 743 British sovereigns
   280 US at $20: 5600
   12 French francs at 10: 120
6. Neth. Guilders at 5: 30
   72 French francs at 20: 1440
   97 Brit. half-sovereigns
   242 Neth. Guilders at 1: 242
9. 31 Silver bars (6 in. x ¼ in. diameter)
   I knife Handle—"Silver"
10. 318 Rubles at 5: 1590
    122 Rubles at 10: 1220
    14 Rubles at 15: 210
12. Miscellaneous gold pieces as follows:
    2 Rubles at 50
    1 Eng. Sov. at 1
    1 French Fr at 20
    1 French Fr at 10
    2 Polish Zl at 20
    1 Polish Zl at 10
    4 Aust-Hun Korona at 20
    1 Napoleon at 40 fr: 40 fr
    1 Napoleon at 50 fr: 50 fr
    1 Austrian Kronen: 100 kr
    1 Austrian Shilling: 100 s
    21 Austrian Goldpieces said to be ducats
    1 Sealed sack labeled "Gold Pd Stig 2500"

Gold Coins

13. 475 US at $20: $8500
    225 US at $10: $2250
    394 Rus. Rubles at 5: 1970 rbls
    51 Rus. Rubles at 10: 510 rbls
    16 Rus. Rubles at 15: 240 rbls

Currency

14. U.S.: $1271
    Swiss: 9045 fr
    English: 220 pounds
    Swedish: 655 kronen
    Danish: 130 kronen
    Norwegian: 50 kronen
    Silver Coins:
15. French 1 at 20 fr: 20 fr
    French 1 at 1 fr: 1 fr
    German 2 at 1 RM: 2 RM
    German 1 at ½ RM: ½ RM
    Polish 2 at 5 Zl: 10 Zl
    Polish 1 at 1 Zl: 1 Zl
    Bulgarian 1 at 5: 5 Lewa
    Bulgarian 1 at 100: 100 Lewa
    Bulgarian 8 at 1: 3 Lewa
    Lithuanian 1 at 10: 10 Der
Gold Coins:
    French 59 at 20 fr: 1180 fr
    U.S. 88 at $20: $1760
    Peru 1 at ½ : ½
    Denmark 1 at 20 kr: 20 kr
    Brit. 474 at 1 sov: 474 sov.
    Brit. 20 at ½ sov: 10 sov.
16. Silver Coin:
    German 1 at 10 Rm: 10 Rm
    French 746 at 20 fr: 14920 fr
    Spanish 6 at 5: 30 pesetos
    Spanish 3 at 2: 6 pesetos

Spanish 26 at 1: 26 pesetos

Polish 4 at 10 Zl: 40 Zloty

Polish 22 at 5 Zl: 110 Zloty

Polish 25 at 2 Zl: 50 Zloty

Aust 1 at 2: 2 shillings

Italian 1 at 2: 2 Lire

Russian 20 at 5 Rbls: 100 Rubles

Slovakeian 1 at 5 K: 5 Korons

Polish: 3 damaged coins, values unknown

Polish: 2 Medals

17. Silver Coin:

Polish 55 at 1 Zl: 55 Zloty

Polish 148 at 2 Zl: 296 Zloty

Polish 236 at 5 Zl: 1180 Zloty

Polish 17 at 10 Zl: 170 Zloty

Russian 31 at 5 Rbls: 155 Rbls

Unknown 4 pieces

18. Silver Coin:

Polish 76 at 1 Zl: 76 Zloty

Polish 1001 at 2 Zl: 2002 Zloty

Polish 13 at 5 Zl: 65 Zloty

Polish 1 at 10 Zl: 10 Zloty

19. Miscellaneous costume jewelry—small value

20. Miscellaneous unset precious or semi-precious stones and gold medallions

21. Large number of precious or semi-precious stones, value unknown

22. Silver bar—weight 30 lbs.

23. 4 bracelets, jeweled, gold

4 rings, jeweled, gold

2 watch chains, gold

2 necklaces with jeweled pendant

1 gold piece pendant

1 pr. gold cuff links

½ gold locket, jeweled

1 gold pendant, jeweled

gold bracelets, jeweled

5 gold pins or pendants

1 gold ring

1 gold mesh purse

In suede purse:

1 broken gold ring

2—2 ear drops

2 gold rings, jeweled

1 pearl and sapphire bracelet, broken

1 jeweled bracelet

2 jeweled rings

1 small piece, silver

2 compacts, gold

24. 32 silver purses; 1 gold ring; 26 strings of pearls;

145 tableware pieces; 20 silver pieces.

25. Miscellaneous bracelets—mostly broken—scrap gold, 30 pieces

26. 8 small clocks—valueless—1 silver medallion

27. 26 pieces costume jewelry

28. 194 miscellaneous rings

29. Miscellaneous costume jewelry

30. 29 Miscellaneous cigarette and vanity cases

31. Miscellaneous costume jewelry

32. Watch chains, wt. about 5

33. 44 watches

34. Scrap gold and silver, costume jewelry, wt. approx. 2

35. Miscellaneous costume jewelry, wt. approx. 12

36. Miscellaneous fountain pens and pencils, used.

37. Miscellaneous costume jewelry, wt. approx. 3

38. 200 watches and/or watch cases, approx. 10

39. 29 pieces of silver (compacts and cigarette cases)

40. Miscellaneous spectacle frames, wt. approx. 1

41. 21 pieces, cigarette and vanity cases, appear to be silver

42. 246 rings, also assorted earrings, wt. approx. 5

43. 17 bottles, approx. 6 ox. cap., silver chips

44. 11 spools of gold thread, also loose gold thread

45. Scrap gold, silver coin bracelet, semi-precious stones, trinkets, total wt. approx 1 pound

46. Approximately 300 assorted rings

Appendix D
Spreadsheets of all Monetary Gold Transactions

From Tripartite Commission Gold Book
   and Mr. Roberts Worksheet of about 1948

Troy Ounces		Total	
Gold Recovered From:	**Bars**	**Coins**	**Troy Ounces**
w1 Merkers	3,267,928.488	3,568,781.346	6,836,709.834
2 Reichsbank Halle	25,682.530	0.000	25,682.530
4 Reichsbank Plauen	0.000	25,296.075	25,296.075
5 Reichsbank Nordhaus	21.494	0.000	21.494
7 Reichsbank Eschwege	32,482.035	0.000	32,482.035
10 Reichsbank Coburg	32,667.532	0.000	32,667.532
15 Reichsbank Nuremburg	404.706	43,183.497	43,588.203
21 Reichsbank Munich	146.853	28.053	174.906
22 Friedrich	5,276.401	0.000	5,276.401
26 Reichsbank Regensburg	11,929.545	0.000	11,929.545
26 Haywagon	290.090	200.960	491.050
27 Innsbruck	7,409.391	36,130.265	43,539.656
27 Dorenwald	31,707.201	0.000	31,707.201
27 Lindau	24,191.270	25,150.842	49,342.112
27 Wallgau	290,584.409	0.000	290,584.409
29 Reichsbank Zwicka	32,637.948	0.000	32,637.948
31 Salzburg	332.667	0.000	332.667
34 Reichsbank Kothen	894.479	0.000	894.479
52 Garmisch	0.000	5,697.387	5,697.387
52 Garmisch	0.000	23,020.722	23,020.722
20 Hungarian Gold	885,845.989	33,445.902	919,291.891
Gold Delivered to Gold Pot in Frankfurt	4,650,433.028	3,760,935.049	8,411,368.077
20 Hungarian Gold	885,845.989	33,445.902	919,291.891
Subtotal For Gold Pot	3,764,587.039	3,727,489.147	7,492,076.186
Adjustment for differences in above worksheets	111.044	41,718.604	41,829.648
Total for Gold Pot from FED, Frankfurt	3,764,698.083	3,769,207.751	7,533,905.834
Withdrawal France Nov 19, 1947	1,267,151.553	1,169,704.252	2,436,855.805
Withdrawal Netherlands Nov 21, 1947	491,206.970	453,497.948	944,704.918
Transfer to Bank of England	2,005,894.380	2,146,022.912	4,151,917.292
Remaining in FED (melting adjustments?)	445.180	-17.361	427.819

Salzburg Gold Added to Gold Pot—			
Aug 4, 1953	2,731.687	135,991.774	138,723.461
Transferred to Austrian Government			
July 7, 1958	-2,731.687	-135,991.774	-138,723.461
0.000	0.000	0.000	

Deposited in Federal Reserve Bank in New York	**Bars**	**Coins**	**Troy Ounces**
1 Switzerland FRB June 6, 1947	1,659,121.321	0.000	1,659,121.321
7 Sweden FRB Dec. 12, 1949	230,049.065	0.000	230,049.065
9 Japan FRB March 1, 1951	4,815.541	0.000	4,815.541
13 Law 53 from US Zone FRB			
Feb 26,1952*	18,514.852	2,280.993	20,795.845
15 Embassy, Lisbon, Madrid,			
two coins US Zone FED Oct 24 1952	644.531	1,216.435	1,860.966
18 Hintersee, Germany FRB Feb 2 1955	0.000	3,149.812	3,149.812
19 Sweden Second Delivery, FRB April 29, 1955	192,904.484	0.000	192,904.484
Total In FRB At New York	2,106,049.794	6,647.240	2,112,697.034
*FRB figures are 20,999.76 Ounces?			

Deposited in Bank of England

	Bars	Coins	Troy Ounces
*Deposited from FED to Bank of England	2,005,894.380	2,146,022.912	4,151,917.292
5 Bank of International Settlement July 48	120,243.777	0.000	120,243.777
12 British Zone, Austria from an agent	0.000	585.487	585.487
22 Czechoslovakia	119,279.728	0.000	119,279.728
23 Portugal	128,562.491	0.000	128,562.491
3 Rumania April 1948	578,700.153	0.000	578,700.153
6 Spain Feb 1949	3,267.271	0.000	3,267.271
8 Austria By Command of US General,			
March 1950	2,903.063	61.842	2,964.905
10 Yugoslavia	1,656.130	0.000	1,656.130
Two Found Bars 1980s	797.539	0.000	797.539
Total in Bank of England	2,961,304.532	2,146,670.241	5,107,974.773

Deposited in Bank of France

	Bars	Coins	Troy Ounces
From FED to France Nov 19, 1947	1,267,151.553	1,169,704.252	2,436,855.805
20 French Parish Priest—M.L'Abbe Weygand	0.000	9.385	9.385
21 French POW	0.000	7.845	7.845
17 Gold given to French by Americans	160.689	2.807	163.496
11 Law 53 from British	1,086.512	74,226.111	75,312.623
14 Law 53 From French Zone	0.620	104.564	105.184
Credited to Belgium Immediately	-1,240,755.548	-1,145,312.813	-2,386,068.361
Credited to Luxembourg Immediately	-26,396.005	-24,391.439	-50,787.444
Subtotal	1,247.821	74,350.712	75,598.533

To Belgium June 30, 1958	-1,247.821	-74,243.591	-75,491.412
Total Bank of France	0.000	107.121	107.121

Withdrawals from Allied Gold Pot	**FRBNY**	**Bk. Of England**	
Albania Oct 29 1996	0.000	49,804.149	49,804.149
Albania June 24, 1998	0.000	1,571.543	1,571.543
Austria—February 2, & Aug 17,1948	152,630.007	689,296.251	841,926.258
Austria—March 7 & Oct 14, 1948	244,221.408	190,784.716	435,006.124
Austria August 7, 1958 Salzburg	0.000	0.000	138,723.461
Austria, Oct 7, 1958	0.000	197,725.755	197,725.755
Austria June 24, 1998	0.000	26,697.741	26,697.741
Belgium to Bk of France—November 20, 1947	539,673.638	0.000	539,673.638
Withdrawal for Belgium 1947 From FED, Frankfurt, Germany	0.000	0.000	2,386,068.361
To Belgium June 30, 1958 From Bk of France	0.000	0.000	75,491.412
Beligum to Bk France July 1956	0.000	803,805.640	803,805.640
Belgium June 30, 1958 to Bk of France Gold Book has 36,451.906	96,451.906	200,964.891	297,416.797
Belgium April 30 1998	27,269.548	39,961.590	67,231.138
Czechoslovakia—May 17, 1948	195,283.854	0.000	195,283.854
Czechoslovakia—February 18, 1982	263,939.461	327,633.729	591,573.190
Czech June 24, 1998	0.000	10,485.566	10,485.566
Italian Share Given to France		463,664.348	463,664.348
Greece 1948 allocated and delivered June 29, 1959	0.000	1,607.530	1,607.530
Italy Oct 8, 1949 After distribution to Fr & Yug	0.000	14,917.944	14,917.944
Italy July 7, 1958	0.000	403,320.847	403,320.847
Italy June 24, 1998	0.000	24,581.655	24,581.655
Luxembourg Nov 1947 FED Germany			62,034.854
Luxembourg From Bank of France			50,787.444
Luxembourg July 2, 1958	0.000	24,113.045	24,113.045
Luxembourg June 26, 1998	0.000	2,006.325	2,006.325
Netherlands Nov 21, 1947 FRN NY & FED Frankfurt Germany	209,201.609	0.000	944,704.918
Netherlands—January, 10 1950	225,055.148	760,243.149	985,298.297

Netherlands—April 21, 1973—19 US Bars, 117 various	53,460.386	78,102.499	131,562.885
Netherlands 1998	38,013.550	0.000	38,013.550
Poland—August 3—19, 1976	50,237.827	29,327.197	79,565.024
Poland June 24, 1998	0.000	1,206.228	1,206.228
Slavic Republic June 24, 1998	0.000	5,240.413	5,240.413
Yugoslavia, Sept 23, 1948 From Italy		276,760.751	276,760.751
Yugoslavia June 14, 1950 Misunderstanding		1,656.130	1,656.130
Yugoslavia 1951		1,629.648	1,629.648
Yugoslavia December 5, 1958	0.000	56,263.667	56,263.667
Yugoslavia, 1982		327,633.729	327,633.729
Yugoslavia July 13, 1998		1,209.781	1,209.781
Expenses, Shipping, Storage & Commission Cost			45,556.795
Withdrawals	2,095,438.342	5,012,216.457	10,601,820.435
Deposited FRBNY, Bank of England & FED, Frankfurt, Ger	2,112,697.034	5,107,974.773	10,817,021.139
Differences	17,258.692	95,758.316	215,200.704

Withdrawals from FED Frankfurt Allocated to a Claim

	Bars	Coins	Total
Withdrawal for Belgium 1947	1,240,755.548	1,145,312.813	2,386,068.361
To Belgium June 30, 1958 From Bk of France	1,247.821	74,243.591	75,491.412
Luxembourg 1947	26,396.005	24,391.439	50,787.444
Withdrawal Netherlands Nov 21, 1947 FRB Above (Total 1,153,976.209) 453,497.948	944,704.918		491,206.970
Salzburg Gold tansferred to Austrian Government July 7, 1952 138,723.461		2,731.687	135,991.774

Total of Gold Pot

	Troy Ounces Bars	Troy Ounces Coins	Ounces Total
Tripartite Commission Report March 23, 1971			
RG 59 Enter 5382 Box 3 Clinton Library 201503			
1 Switzerland FRB June 6, 1947	1,659,121.321	0.000	1,659,121.321
2 *To France for(Belgium,Luxemberg) & Netherlands	1,758,474.352	1,623,183.899	3,381,658.251
3 Rumania	578,700.153	0.000	578,700.153
4 Frankfurt FED	2,010,610.525	2,141,676.100	4,152,286.625
5 Bank of International Settlement	120,243.777	0.000	120,243.777
6 Spain	3,267.271	0.000	3,267.271

7	Sweden FRB Dec. 12, 1949	230,049.065	0.000	230,049.065
8	To Austria By Command of US General	2,903.063	61.842	2,964.905
9	Japan FRB March 1, 1951	4,815.541	0.000	4,815.541
10	Yugoslavia	1,656.130	0.000	1,656.130
11	Law 53 from British	1,086.512	74,226.111	75,312.623
12	British Zone, Austria from an agent	0.000	585.487	585.487
13	Law 53 from US Zone FRB Feb 26,1952	18,514.852	2,280.993	20,795.845
14	Law 53 From French Zone	0.620	104.564	105.184
15	Embassy, Lisbon, Madrid, two coins US Zone FED Oct 24 1952	644.531	1,216.435	1,860.966
16	Salzburg Gold	2,731.687	135,991.774	138,723.461
17	French Zone, Germany	160.689	2.807	163.496
18	Hintersee, Germany FRB Feb 2 1955	0.000	3,149.812	3,149.812
19	Sweden Second Delivery, FRB April 29, 1955	192,904.484	0.000	192,904.484
20	French Parish Priest—M.L'Abbe Weygand	0.000	9.385	9.385
21	French POW	0.000	7.845	7.845
22	Czechoslovakia	119,279.728	0.000	119,279.728
23	Portugal	128,562.491	0.000	128,562.491
24	Two Bars Recovered 1996	0.000	797.539	797.539
	Total	6,833,726.792	3,983,294.593	10,817,021.385

*This was a split shipment between FED, Frankfurt & FRBNY

Tons	370.841

Appendix E
Statistical Figures Complied by the
Foreign Exchange Depository

Units are not defined and are not universal by count or value.

Foreign Exchange Depository
Balance Sheet August 31, 1949

Asset Accountability Accounts

Debits	Units	Credits	Units
Silver Bullion	2	Merkers Mine	62,003
Silver Scrap	141	Law 52	539,118
Mixed Bullion	3,779	Law 53	1,417
Silver Coins	2,738	German Banks [law 52]	1,306,979
Other Coins	246,904	Allied Countries	1,597
Currency	1,904,241	Enemy Countries	7,111
Securities	6,099	Concentration Camps	9,408
Precious Silver	60	Other Sources	210,151
Jewelry	16	Other Sources Marks	28,697
Other Assets	1,461	Journal Entry	10
Other Assets Collections	1,050	-	0
Total Units	2,166,491	-	2,166,491

Restitution Accountability

Released Debits			Dollars
Restitution	12,994,247	-	$64,084,630.60
Transfers	196,371	-	$7,933,055.53
Other	4,284	-	$3,516,502.00
On Loan	942	-	$580,000.00
Returned to German Banks	76	$2.00	
Tripartite Gold Commission	3,469	$263,680,452.94	
Totals	13,199,389	-	$339,794,643.07

Released Credits			
Monuments Fine Art & Archives	1,111	$152,666.78	
Occupation Military Government	946	$580,001.00	
U.S. Army	3,229	-	$16,005.00
InterGovermential Com. Refuges	1,197,341	$806,369.00	
Currency to Foreign Ex. Dep.	80,716	$8.00	
Reichsbank Fulda	43	-	$1.00
Reichsbank Hersfeld	33	-	$1.00
Reichsbank Bremen	104	-	$1.00
Landerbank Vienna	2	-	$0.00
Stadtsparkasse Halle	1	-	$0.00
Kreissparkasse Ploehnen	2	-	$0.00

Debits	Units	Credits	Units
Comersbank Berlin	1	-	$0.00
Deutsch Bank Fuerth	1	-	$0.00
Sparkasse Hanover	1	-	$0.00
Nordiska Poeringsbank	1	-	$0.00
Postsparkassentamt Vienna	4	-	$1.00
Amtsgericht	223	-	$270,400.00
Landeszentralbank Frankfurt	102,402	-	$4,098,505.75
Tripartite Gold Commission	1,953	-	$145,325,827.64
Erfassungsgesellschaft	3,477	-	$10.00
Bank Deutscher Laender	1,277	-	$3,284,455.00
Creamation	4,232	-	$2.00
City of Berlin	44	-	$800,000.00
OFA OMGUS Berlin	8	-	$2,716,500.00
Individuals	110	-	$656.00
U.S.A.	396,458	-	$3,516,305.88
England	245,589	-	$1,301,402.00
Australia	22	-	$34.00
Belgium	1,466,717	-	$1,101,279.00
Canada	4,480	-	$8,750.00
Denmark	105,677	-	$274,000.00
India	26	-	$10.00
The Netherlands	872,868	-	$37,110,954.22
Norway	565,994	-	$1,935,001.00
Switzerland	19	-	$52,125.00
South Africa	1,787	-	$11,600.00
Albana	73,855	-	$2.00
Czechoslovakia	38,903	-	$502,703.00
France	5,243,141	-	$99,861,761.25
Germany	11	-	$1.00
Greece	23,280	-	$2.00
Hungary	9,580	-	$35,757,569.55
Italy	214,471	-	$240,008.00
New Zealand	3	-	$2.00
Yugoslavia	29,290	-	$21,291.00
Poland	2,508,598	-	$3,404.00
Roumania	1	-	$1.00
Turkey	1	-	$1.00
USSR	1,204	-	$5.00
Luxembourg	152	-	$21.00
Totals	13,199,389	-	$339,749,643.07

Endnotes

The source material used for *The Monetary Men* was obtained from thousands of source documents over that past forty year. Therefore the author cannot include all of the documents. Consequently the footnotes are not complete or comprehensive, but do list the main records and publications.

Fortunately today, most of source documents for this book are digitized at the William J. Clinton Presidential Library and Fold-3. Images of the documents can be found by a subject or name search.

The CL followed by a number is the pdf file of the source document in the Clinton Library.

Introduction
1. Leland Howard: Report dated August 15, 1945
2. Diplomatic Papers: Foreign Relations of the United States, Volume III, 1945

Chapter 2
1. OMGUS RG 260, Central files, 940.03 Claims the Netherlands Gold and Alfred Draper: Operation Fish
2. Adjudication, Tripartite Commission for the Restitution of Monetary Gold by the Grand Duchy of Luxemburg, undated, RG 59, box 22
3. Memorandum Belgium Mission, S. Buquenne, February 16, 1948, RG 260
4. German Documents: 1943, RG 260, National Archives Suitland

Chapter 3
1. Wilfred V. Oven, German war correspondent, newspaper, "Panzer am Balkan." The Treasure in the Mountain Eyre, CL 208567—208568
2. Adjudication Yugoslavia, CL 208588
3. Ustasha, RG 319 IRR, Box 62, CL 230642
4. OSS MEMORANDA FOR THE PRESIDENT: FROM PETER TO TITO. CIA WWW
5. Declaration of Mato Crnek, Adjudication Yugoslavia, CL 208594
6. OSS MEMORANDA FOR THE PRESIDENT: FROM PETER TO TITO. CIA WWW
7. Marion H. Scott, Fugitive Enemy Officials, July 25, 1945, IRR Nonperson File Ustasha, National Archives

Chapter 4
1. NARA, RG 165 Decimal file CAD 386.3
2. Working Papers Italian Gold Report, RG260, DN1942, 940.606, National Archives—OMGUS 03 56—59
3. Working Papers Italian Gold Report, RG260, DN1942, 940.606, National Archives—OMGUS 03 56—59
4. NARA, RG 165 Decimal file CAD 386.3
5. "Swiss Gold Traffic With Germany," 1945, RG 43, National Archives
6. Tripartite Commission Adjudication, Italy, RG 59, Box 21,National Archives
7. Working Papers Italian Gold Report, RG260, DN1942, 940.606, National Archives
8. Working Papers Italian Gold Report, RG260, DN1942, 940.606, National Archives
9. Commission Adjudication, Italy, Statement Bernd Gottfriedsen, page 5, RG 59, Box 21,National Archives
10. Tripartite Commission Adjudication, Italy, RG 59, Box 21,National Archives

Chapter 5
1. Erich Hagen, Written Report, September 29, 1944, RG 260—Records of the Foreign Exchange Depository, Central Files, 940.4022, Shipment 22

Chapter 6

1. RG 260, OMGUS, Foreign Exchange Depository Central Files 900.45 Inspector General Inspection
2. RG 260, OMGUS, Foreign Exchange Depository Central Files 900.10
3. RG 260, OMGUS, Foreign Exchange Depository Central Files 900.45 Inspector General Inspection

Chapter 7

1. Bernard Bernstein, Statement of Dr. Werner Veick, April 10, 1945
2. Bernard Bernstein, Statement of Dr. Werner Veick, April 10, 1945
3. Post, April 3, 1945
4. Ray Griffin: Unpublished notes
5. Bernard Bernstein, Joint Statements, April 12, 1945
6. "G-4 Functions in ETOUSA Operations," April 9 to April 22, 1945, National Archives
7. Post, April 3, 1945

Chapter 8

1. Bernard Bernstein: Taped interview, May 19, 1984
2. Bernard Bernstein: Taped interview, May 19, 1984
3. Bernard Bernstein: Taped interview, May 19, 1984
4. General George Patton: War as I Knew It, 1947
5. Bernard Bernstein: Telephone interview, July, 1986
6. Ray Griffin: Unpublished notes
7. Bernard Bernstein: Taped interview, May 19, 1984
8. Captain L.F. Murrary: "Report of Investigation of Alleged Discrepancies in Currency and Coins Found in Mine at Merkers," May 7, 1945, National Archives
9. SHAFE G-5 Finance Germany, "Discovery of Gold and Other Valuables," May 1945, National Archives

Chapter 9

1. RG 260—Records of the Foreign Exchange Depository, Central Files, 940.402, Shipment 2
2. RG 260—Records of the Foreign Exchange Depository, Records Relating to Currency Section, Shipment 2, Page16
3. RG 260—Records of the Foreign Exchange Depository, Records Relating to Currency Section, Shipment 2, Page11
4. Shipping Ticket 217 Foreign Exchange Depository
5. RG 260—Records of the Foreign Exchange Depository, Central Files, Inventory of Assets Released, 1945—1945, A1 Entry 593
6. RG 260—Records of the Foreign Exchange Depository, Central Files, 940.409, Shipment 9RG 260—Records of the Foreign Exchange Depository, Central Files, 940.403, Shipment 3
7. 87th Infantry Division: "Inventory at Reichsbank Vault at Plauen, Germany," April 26, 1945
8. RG 260—Records of the Foreign Exchange Depository, Central Files, 940.404, Shipment 4
9. RG 260—Records of the Foreign Exchange Depository, Central Files, 940.4017, Shipment 17
10 SHAFE: Telegram—G5 General F.J. McSherry, April 1945
    OMGUS: Telegram—Economics Division, Restitution Branch, March 1945
11. RG 260—Records of the Foreign Exchange Depository, Central Files, 940.407, Shipment 7 and 940.4010, shipment 10
12. RG 260—Records of the Foreign Exchange Depository, Central Files, 940.4014, Shipment 14
13. Commanding Officer, Detachment E1B3, Company B, 3rd ECA Regiment, May 2, 1945
14. RG 260—Records of the Foreign Exchange Depository, Central Files, 940.4015, Shipment 15

15. SHAFE: "Reconnaissance to Discover Further German Gold and Loot," May 1945 National Archive. Joel Fisher: Interview, June 1983 and Herbert DuBois: Taped Interview, May 18, 1984

16. RG 260—Records of the Foreign Exchange Depository, Central Files, 940.4028, Shipment 28

Chapter 10

1. New York Herald Tribune, May 30, 1945
2. RG 260—Records of the Foreign Exchange Depository, Central Files, 940.405, Shipment 5
3. RG 260—Records of the Foreign Exchange Depository, Central Files, 940.4011, Shipment 11
4. Walter Hancock: "A Monuments Officer in Germany," College Art Journal, May 1946 Walter Hancock's MFA&A Report, May 12, 1945
5. RG 260—Records of the Foreign Exchange Depository, Central Files, 940.4012, Shipment 12
6. Will Lang: "The Case of the Distinguished Corpses," LIFE, 1948
7. RG 260—Records of the Foreign Exchange Depository, Central Files, 940.4016, Shipment 16

Chapter 11

1. OMGUS: Mielke's "Report Concerning the Transport of Valuables from Berlin to Munich," April 1945 and OMGUS: "Gottfried's Report," April, 1945 & Seventh Army Interrogation Center: Dr. Funk—Interrogation by Paul Kubala, May 21, 1945
2. RG 260, Foreign Exchange Depository, Records Relating to Currency Section, Shipment 18, page 11
3. RG-260, Box 399, FED Status as at 30 June 1948 of Assets held by FED, File 910.911
4. Report on Reconnaissance Trip: "In Quest of Gold, Silver and Foreign Exchange," May 9 to May 17, 1945

Chapter 12

1. RG 260—Records of the Foreign Exchange Depository, Central Files, 940.4027, Shipment 27
2. RG 260—Records of the Foreign Exchange Depository, Central Files, 940.4027, Shipment 27
3. RG 260—Records of the Foreign Exchange Depository, Central Files, 940.4027, Shipment 27
4. RG 260—Records of the Foreign Exchange Depository, Central Files, 940.4027, Shipment 27
5. Seventh Army Interrogation Center: "Interrogation of Gottlob Berger by Paul Kubal," June 5, 1945
6. Elroy P. Perez, T Force: "Chronological Report on Mittenwald Mission," June 6, 1945
7. 10th Armored Division: William R. Geilu's memo, June 6, 1945
8. RG 260—Records of the Foreign Exchange Depository, Central Files, 940.4027, Shipment 27
9. RG 260—Records of the Foreign Exchange Depository, Central Files, 940.4027, Shipment 27

Chapter 13

1 RG 260—Records of the Foreign Exchange Depository, Central Files, 940.4031, Shipment 31
2. Emanuel E. Minskoff, "Preliminary Report on External assets of Ernst Kaltenbrunner, 1945" & Dale F. Shughart "recollections of a Former U.S Counter-Intelligence Officer During World War II" unpublished manuscript, courtesy Dale F. Shughart Jr, Carlisle, PA.
3. RG 260—Records of the Foreign Exchange Depository, Central Files, 940.4021, Shipment 21
4. RG 260—Records of the Foreign Exchange Depository, Central Files, 940.4021, Shipment 21
5. RG 360 Records of the Foreign Exchange Depository, Inventory Forms of Assets Released, Assets released to US Government.
6. 512 Military police: Robert Allgeir's "Report of Incident," June 29, 1945
7. 574 AAA: "Interrogation of Hans Neuhauser," summer, 1945 RG 260—Records of the Foreign Exchange Depository, Central Files, 940.4052, Shipment 52
8. RG 260—Records of the Foreign Exchange Depository, Assets Released to the U. S. Government, page 47

9. RG 549, USAREU, Judge Advocate Division, War Crimes Branch
10. Assets from Dachau, July 21, 1946; RG 260—Records of the Foreign Exchange Depository, Central Files, 940.4052, Shipment 52
11. RG 260—Records of the Foreign Exchange Depository, Central Files, 940.4060, Shipment 60
12. RG 260—Records of the Foreign Exchange Depository, Central Files, Assets Released to US Government.
13. RG 260—Records of the Foreign Exchange Depository, Central Files, 940.4057, Shipment 57

Chapter 14
1. Dr. Julius Torzsay Biber, To the International Red Cross, May 30, 1945
   Dr. Julius Torzsay Biber, To Colonel Ball, May 29, 1945
   Dr. Julius Torzsay Biber, To the International Red Cross, May 30, 1945
   SHAFE: Telegram—G5 General F.J. McSherry, April 1945
   OMGUS: Telegram—Economics Division, Restitution Branch, March 1945
   William I. DeHuszar: 80th Counter Intelligence Corp, Memorandum for the Officer in Charge, May 14, 1945
   Paul D. Harkins, Tally, Transport and Delivery of Treasure, May 12 1945
   Major Lionel C. Perera, Receipt for Valuables, May 14, 1945
   Juilis Biber, To the International Red Cross, may 30, 1945
   W.R. Loeffler, Hungarian national Bank, July 30, 1946
   Vilag, August 8, 1946, Magyar Nemzet, August 8, 1946, Szabad Szo, Evening edition, August 8, 1946 and from a four page document titled, Background, no date, no signature
   Bank of Hungary: Letter, April 24, 1947,
   Jack Bennett: "Restitution of Hungarian Gold," July 25, 1946, NAS
   Walter L. Kluss: "Plans for movement of Hungarian Silver and other Valuables," April 2, 1947, NAS
   Karl Kristof, Vilag, April 24, 1947
2. RG 260—Records of the Foreign Exchange Depository, Central Files, 940.4082, Shipment 82

Chapter 15
1. Alford, Kenneth D and Savas, Theodore P. Nazi Millionaires. Casemate, 2002
2. RG 260—Records of the Foreign Exchange Depository, Central Files, 940.4076, Shipment 76
3. RG 260—Records of the Foreign Exchange Depository, Central Files, 940.4079, Shipment 79
4. RG 260—Records of the Foreign Exchange Depository, Central Files, 940.4087, Shipment 87
5. RG 260, OMGUS Cultural Affairs Branch, Records Relating to MFA&A, Hohenzollern Silver taken by 127th Regiment.
6. RG 260—Records of the Foreign Exchange Depository, Central Files, 940.40111, Shipment 111
7. RG 260—Records of the Foreign Exchange Depository, Central Files, 940.4088, Shipment 88
8. Flight of Axis Capital, April 30, 1945, CL 6997222
9. RG 407, 65th Infantry Division, National Archives
10. RG 260—Records of the Foreign Exchange Depository, Central Files, 940.4061, Shipment 61
11. RG 260—Records of the Foreign Exchange Depository, Central Files, 940.4064, Shipment 64
12. Ralph Blumenthal; The New York Times, June 22, 1986
13. OSS Washington Secret Intelligence, WASH-SPDF-INT-1: Documents 2501—2540
14. Ronen Bergan, Ha'aretz Magazine, Nazi collaborator or Hero, April 28, 2000
15. RG 260—Records of the Foreign Exchange Depository, Central Files, 940.4071, Shipment 71
16. USACA Property Control Branch
17. USACA Property Control Branch
18. RG 260, Ardelia Hall Collection, Daily file: September 21, 1946—November 29, 1946
19. Alford, Kenneth D and Savas, Theodore P. Nazi Millionaires. Casemate, 2002
20. RG 260—Records of the Foreign Exchange Depository, Central Files, 940.4054, Shipment 54

21. RG 260—Records of the Foreign Exchange Depository, Central Files, 940.40109, Shipment 109
22. Broadcast Unit, Foreign Office and Ministry of Economic Warfare, September 20, 1945
23. Associated Press, Salzburg, September 18, 1945
24. RG 260—Records of the Foreign Exchange Depository, Central Files, 940.40116, Shipment 116 & Robert Wolfe, Gustav Hilger: From Hitler's Foreign Office to CIA Consultant, June 1,2006

Chapter 16
1. Inventory Form number 6092, 11 April 1947, RG 260—Records of the Foreign Exchange Depository, Central Files, 940.4022, Shipment 22
2. RG 260—Records of the Foreign Exchange Depository, Central Files, 940.04, Claims, Czechoslovakia: Diamonds (no.139-C)
3. RG 260—Records of the Foreign Exchange Depository, Central Files, 940.40115, Shipment 115
4. RG 260—Records of the Foreign Exchange Depository, Central Files, 940.4029, Shipment 29
5. RG 260—Records of the Foreign Exchange Depository, Central Files, 940.4091, Shipment 91
6. RG 260—Records of the Foreign Exchange Depository, Central Files, 940.4094, Shipment 94
7. Alford, Kenneth D. Allied Looting in World War II: McFarland, 2011 & RG 260—Records of the Foreign Exchange Depository, Central Files, 940.40118, Shipment 118
8. RG 260—Records of the Foreign Exchange Depository, Central Files, 940.4098, Shipment 98
9. RG 260—Records of the Foreign Exchange Depository, Central Files, 940.4089, Shipment 89
10. RG 260—Records of the Foreign Exchange Depository, Central Files, 940.4092, Shipment 92

Chapter 17
1. RG 260—Records of the Foreign Exchange Depository, Central Files, 940.4023, Shipment 23
2. RG 260—Records of the Foreign Exchange Depository, Central Files, 940.4023, Shipment 23
3. RG 260—Records of the Foreign Exchange Depository, Central Files, 940.4024, Shipment 24
4. RG 260—Records of the Foreign Exchange Depository, Central Files, 940.4072, Shipment 72
5. Message Received and Restricted Memo, December 18, 1945, CL 215885 & 215896
6. RG 260—Records of the Foreign Exchange Depository, Central Files, 940.4077, Shipment 77
7. RG 260—Records of the Foreign Exchange Depository, Central Files, 940.4083, Shipment 83
8. B.T. Causgrove, Buried Dental Supplies of Waffen SS, August 16, 1946
9. RG 260—Records of the Foreign Exchange Depository, Central Files, 940.4080, Shipment 80
10. RG 260—Records of the Foreign Exchange Depository, Central Files, 940.4086, Shipment 86
11. RG 260—Records of the Foreign Exchange Depository, Central Files, 940.4093, Shipment 93
12. RG 260—Records of the Foreign Exchange Depository, Central Files, 940.4056, Shipment 56
13. RG 260—Records of the Foreign Exchange Depository, Central Files, 940.4085, Shipment 85
14. RG 260—Records of the Foreign Exchange Depository, Central Files, 940.4019, Shipment 19
15. RG 260—Records of the Foreign Exchange Depository, Central Files, 940.4026, Shipment 26
16. RG 260—Records of the Foreign Exchange Depository, Central Files, 940.4026, Shipment 26
17. RG 260—Records of the Foreign Exchange Depository, Central Files, 940.4026, Shipment 26
18. RG 260—Records of the Foreign Exchange Depository, Central Files, 940.40102, Shipment 102
19. RG 260—Records of the Foreign Exchange Depository, Central Files, 940.084 Claims, Individuals, Fulton, Julius
20. RG 260—Records of the Foreign Exchange Depository, Central Files, 940.4096, Shipment 96
21. Ardelia Hall Collection, Cultural Objects Movement and Control, Outgoing Shipments 329—334, (July 2, 1951—July 5, 1951)
22. RG 260—Records of the Foreign Exchange Depository, Central Files, 940.4032, Shipment 32
23. RG 260—Records of the Foreign Exchange Depository, Central Files, 940.4051, Shipment 51

Chapter 18
1. RG 260—Records of the Foreign Exchange Depository, Central Files, 940.4013, Shipment 13
2. RG 260—Records of the Foreign Exchange Depository, Central Files, 940.4025, Shipment 25
3. RG 260—Records of the Foreign Exchange Depository, Central Files, 940.4050, Shipment 50
4. RG 260—Records of the Foreign Exchange Depository, Central Files, 940.4053, Shipment 53
5. RG 260—Records of the Foreign Exchange Depository, Assets Released to US Government page 72.
6. RG 260—Records of the Foreign Exchange Depository, Central Files, 940.4058, Shipment 58
7. RG 260—Records of the Foreign Exchange Depository, Central Files, 940.4062, Shipment 62
8. RG 260—Records of the Foreign Exchange Depository, Central Files, 940.4063, Shipment 63
9. RG 260—Records of the Foreign Exchange Depository, Central Files, 940.4073, Shipment 73
10. RG 260—Records of the Foreign Exchange Depository, Central Files, 940.4074, Shipment 74
11. RG 260—Records of the Foreign Exchange Depository, Central Files, 940.4075, Shipment 75
12. RG 260—Records of the Foreign Exchange Depository, Central Files, 940.4095, Shipment 95
13. RG 260—Records of the Foreign Exchange Depository, Central Files, 940.4097, Shipment 97
14. RG 260—Records of the Foreign Exchange Depository, Central Files, 940.40103, Shipment 103

Chapter 19
1. RG 260—Records of the Foreign Exchange Depository, Central Files, 940.406, Shipment 6
2. RG 260—Records of the Foreign Exchange Depository, Central Files, 940.408, Shipment 8
3. RG 260—Records of the Foreign Exchange Depository, Central Files, 940.4055, Shipment 55
4. RG 260—Records of the Foreign Exchange Depository, Central Files, 940.4078, Shipment 78
5. RG 260—Records of the Foreign Exchange Depository, Central Files, 940.4081, Shipment 81
6. RG 260—Records of the Foreign Exchange Depository, Central Files, 940.4084, Shipment 84
7. RG 260—Records of the Foreign Exchange Depository, Central Files, 940.40112—114, Shipment 112—114

Chapter 20
1. RG 260—Records of the Foreign Exchange Depository, Central Files, 940.4090, Shipment 90
2. RG 260—Records of the Foreign Exchange Depository, Central Files, 940.4098, Shipment 99
3. RG 260—Records of the Foreign Exchange Depository, Central Files, 940.40100, Shipment 100
4. RG 260—Records of the Foreign Exchange Depository, Central Files, 940.40101, Shipment 101
5. Bundesarchin, a Research Report, August 1998
6. RG 260—Records of the Foreign Exchange Depository, Central Files, 940.40105, Shipment 105
7. RG 260—Records of the Foreign Exchange Depository, Central Files, 940.40105, Shipment 105
8. RG 260—Records of the Foreign Exchange Depository, Central Files, 940.40107, Shipment 107
9. RG 260—Records of the Foreign Exchange Depository, Central Files, 940.40108, Shipment 108
10. RG 260—Records of the Foreign Exchange Depository, Central Files, 940.40110, Shipment 110
11. RG 260—Records of the Foreign Exchange Depository, Central Files, 940.40119, Shipment 119
12. RG 260—Records of the Foreign Exchange Depository, Central Files, 940.40121, Shipment 121

Chapter 22

1. RG 260—Records of the Foreign Exchange Depository, Central Files, 940.151, Restitution: Currency, page 32
2. 260—Records of the Foreign Exchange Depository, Central Files, 940.151, Restitution: United Stated Currency, page 23
3. RG 260—Records of the Foreign Exchange Depository, Central Files, 940.151, Restitution: United Stated Currency.
4. RG 260—Records of the Foreign Exchange Depository, Central Files, 940.151, Restitution: United Stated Currency, page 69.
5. RG 360 OMGUS Records of the Foreign Exchange Depository, Inventory Forms of Assets Released, Assets released to US Government, page 23

Chapter 23

1. Fred B Smith: "Inquiry from the House of Representatives Armed Services Committee," April 14, 1948
2. Edwin P. Keller: "History of Gold Operation no. 2," 1948
   Pan American: Charter Contract, July 2, 1948
3. Hector J. Deleo and Eugune R. Bonner: 31 CID, "Criminal Investigation Report," November 16, 1948, NAS
4. Decision to Transfer Frankfurt Gold, 1971 Tripartite Commission Report? CL 206844
5. Decision to Transfer Frankfurt Gold, 1971 Tripartite Commission Report? CL 206844

Chapter 24

1. Tripartite Commission for the Restitution of Monetary Gold, no date RG 59, Box 7, CL 211578
2. Tripartite Commission for the Restitution of Monetary Gold, no date RG 59, Box 7, CL 211578
3. Decision to Transfer Frankfurt Gold, 1971 Tripartite Commission Report? CL 206844
4. Tripartite Commission for the Restitution of Monetary Gold, no date RG 59, Box 7, CL 211579
5. Tripartite Gold Commission (iii) Romania
6. The Gold Account, RG 59, Entry 5382, Box 3, CL 201493
7. Tripartite Gold Commission (i) Switzerland
8. Tripartite Commission Gold Activity, Fed Res Bank Box 2, CL 205452
9. Tripartite Gold Commission (vii) The Swedish Contribution
10. Tripartite Gold Commission (xix) From Sweden's Second Delivery
11. Page 24 of a report titled Annex 22 with no date: (CL 206865)
12. Tripartite Gold Commission (xxiii) Portugal
13. Tripartite Commission Restitution, about 1958, RG 59, box 7, CL211595
14. Tripartite Gold Commission (vi) Spain
15. Tripartite Gold Commission (x) From Yugoslavia
16. Tripartite Commission for the Restitution of Monetary Gold, no date, RG 59, Box 7, CL211619
17. Tripartite Gold Commission (xxii) From Czechoslovakia
18. Robert J. Schwartz: "Draft, Safehaven and Looted Gold," January 29, 1952
19. Tripartite Gold Commission (v) Bank of International Settlement
20. Tripartite Commission Adjudication, Italy, RG 59, Box 21,National Archives
21. Gold Deposit, James A. Garrison, Oct. 12, 1949, RG 260—CL 227875
22. Page 19 of a report titled Annex 22 with no date: (CL 206860) and Minute, January 8, 1953, CL 215159

23. RG 260—Records of the Foreign Exchange Depository, Central Files, 940.65 German Foreign Records, Office of Chief of Counsel for War Crimes, Perry Laukhuff, December 28, 1948
24. Tripartite Gold Commission (xvi) The Salzburg Gold Delivery
25. RG 260—Records of the Foreign Exchange Depository, Miscellaneous 25. Records regarding Operations, payments and shipments, Restitution Austria
26. Tripartite Gold Commission, March 14, 1950, CL 204047 & 227851—227858
27. Tripartite Gold Commission (viii) Gold delivered to Austria by the Commander of Chief of US Forces.
28. Gold held to be German Reich, CL 206855
29. Page 14 of a report titled Annex 22 with no date: (CL 206855)
30. Tripartite Gold Commission (xii) Seized from a German agent in the British Zone
31. Gold Found in Hintersee, Austria, May 3, 1954, RG 57, Lot 70D 516, Box 16
32. Tripartite Gold Commission (xviii) Gold from Hintersee, Austria
33. Tripartite Gold Commission (xiii) Deposit from Military Law 53—US Zone
34. Tripartite Gold Commission (xi) Deposit from Military Law 53—British Element
35. Law 53 Gold Delivered, CL 206852—206853 & 206858
36. Tripartite Gold Commission (xiv) Military Law 53 from the French Zone
37. Tripartite Gold Account Activity, CL page 205450
38. Tripartite Gold Commission (ix) Gold from German Assets in Japan
39. AMEMBASSY, TGC gold shipment, May16, 1952 FOI Dept of State and CL 206859
40. Tripartite Gold Commission (xv) German Embassy of Lisbon, Madrid and two coins from US Zone
41. Page 19 of a report titled Annex 22 with no date: (CL 206860)
42. Tripartite Gold Commission (xvii) Gold handed over to French authorities by Americans
43. Deposit of French Coins, November 17, 1955, RG 57, Lot 70D 516, Box 16
44. Tripartite Gold Commission (xx) Gold Received from Priest
45. Page 23 of a report titled Annex 22 with no date: (CL 206864)
46. Tripartite Gold Commission (xxi) Gold found in Germany by French Officers
47. Tripartite Commission for Restitution, October 4, 1996, CL 201744

Chapter 25
1. Tripartite Commission Restitution, about 1958, RG 59, box 7, CL211546
2. Tripartite Commission Restitution, Chapter III, about 1969, RG 59, box 2, CL 211741
3. Edwin P. Keller: "History of Gold Pot Delivery 1," December 29, 1947, NAS
4. Reed A. Spiers: "Convoy Frankfurt/Nijmegen, Netherlands," November 24, 1947
5. Tripartite Commission Restitution, about 1958, RG 59, box 7, CL208210
6. Tripartite Commission Meeting, 1971 Report, CL 201493—201534
7. Tripartite Commission Meeting, 1971 Report, CL 201493—201534
8. Tripartite Commission Meeting, 1971 Report, CL 201493—201534
9. Handwritten in French, Tripartite Gold Commission detail ledger from 1947 thru 1998. CL 211470—2111533
10. Adjudication Tripartite Commission, the Government of Czechsolvakia, RG 59 box 13, CL 208483—208513
11. Aide Memoire, April 7, 1960, RG 59, Box 6, CL 208114
12. Agreement 1981, Freedom of Information received by author
13. Tripartite Commission Meeting, 1971 Report, CL 201493—201534
14. Gold Book Spread Sheet, page 61
15. Tripartite Commission Meeting, 1971 Report, CL 201493—201534
16. Adjudication Tripartite Commission, the Royal Hellenic Government, June 19, 1958, RG 59 box 12, CL 208449—208481
17. Gold Book Spread Sheet, page 61

18. Tripartite Commission for the Restitution of Monetary Gold, no date RG 59, Box 7, CL 211777
19. Gold Book Spread Sheet, pages 11—21, 53, 61
20. Tripartite Commission for the Restitution of Monetary Gold, no date RG 59, Box 7, CL 208157
21. Tripartite Commission for the Restitution of Monetary Gold, no date RG 59, Box 13, CL 208547
22. Tripartite Commission Meeting, 1971 Report, CL 201493—201534
23. Gold Book Spread Sheet, page 61.
24. Tripartite Commission Meeting, 1971 Report, CL 201493—201534
25. Most of the material in this chapter regarding Yugoslavia is from a 68 page document, Adjudication by the Tripartite Commission for the Restitution of Gold on Claim Submitted by the Government of the Federation People's Republic of Yugoslavia, June 9, 1958, CL 208560—208628
26. Topic—RG 260, Finance OMGUS, CL 220679—220685 and RG 260 DN1924, Disk 45—46
27. William G. Daniels, Chief Property Division, To Dept of State, June 30, 1950; Consolation Interrogation Report Number 2, The Göring Collection; Holmes, Secretary of State, March 27, 1956; Mr. Crutcher, unsigned letter, Restitution in Error to Yugoslavia, March 10, 1954

Bibliography

Akinsha, Konstantin, and Grigorii Kozlov, *Beautiful Loot: The Soviet Plunder of Europe's Art Treasures*, New York, Random House, 1995.

Alford, Kenneth D., *The Spoils of World War II*, New York, Birch Lane Press, 1994.

— *Great Treasure Stories of World War II*, Mason City, IA, Savas Publishing Company, 2000.

— *Nazi Millionaires*, Haverty, PA, Casemate, 2002.

Alford, Kenneth D., *Hermann Göring and the Nazi Art Collection*, Jefferson , NC, McFarland and Company, 2012.

Alford, Kenneth D. *Allied Looting in World War II*. Jefferson, N.C.: McFarland and Company, 2012.

Ambrose, Stephen E., *Band of Brothers*. New York, Simon & Schuster, 1992.

American Heritage, *World War II*, New York, 1966.

Botting, Douglas, *The Aftermath: Europe*, Time-Life, Virginia, 1982.

Bradley, Omar N., *A Soldier's Story*. New York, Holt and Company, 1951.

Bradley, Omar N., and Clay Blair, *A General's Life: An Autobiography by General of the Army Omar N. Bradley*, New York: Simon and Schuster, 1983.

Butcher, Harry C., *My Three Years with Eisenhower: The Personal Diary of Captain Harry C. Butcher, USNR, Naval Aide to General Eisenhower, 1942-1945,* New York, Simon and Schuster, 1946.

D'Este, Carlo, *Patton: A Genius for War*, New York, HarperCollins, 1995.

— *Eisenhower: A Soldier's Life*, New York, Henry Holt, 2002.

Draper, Alfred, *Operation Fish*, London, 1973.

Duberman, Martin, *The Worlds of Lincoln Kirstein*, New York, Alfed A. Knopf, 2007.

Ducret, S., *German Porcelain*: New York: Universal Book, 1962.

Edsel, Robert M., *Rescuing Da Vinci: Hitler and the Nazis Stole Europe's Great Art, America and Her Allies Recovered It*. Dallas: Laurel Publishing, 2006.

Eisenhower, Dwight D., *Crusade in Europe*. New York: Doubleday & Co., 1948.

Eriken, Svend, *Sèvres Porcelain*, Boston, Faber and Faber, 1987.

Flanner, Janet, *Men and Monuments*, New York, Harper & Brothers, 1957.

Göring, Emmy, *My Life with Göring*, London, David Bruce & Watson, 1972.

Harrison, C.A., *Cross Channel Attack*, Washington DC, US Government Printing Office, 1951.

Hitler, Adolf, *Mein Kampf*, Translated by Ralph Manheim, New York, Houghton Mifflin, 1943.

Holladay, Joan A., *Illuminating the Epic*, Seattle, University of Washington Press, 1996.

Howe, Thomas Carr Jr., *Salt Mines and Castles*, The Bobbs-Merrill Company, New York, 1946.

Hunt, Irmgard A., *On Hitler's Mountain*, New York, William Morrow, 2005.

Konstantine Akinsha and Grigorii Kazlov, *Beautiful Loot*, New York, Random House, 1995.

Kurtz, Michael J., *America and the Return of Nazi Contraband: The Recovery of Europe's Cultural Treasures*, Cambridge, UK, Cambridge University Press, 2006.

McDonald, Charles B., *The Last Offensive*, United States Army, Washington DC, 1984.

Mitchell, Arthur H., *Hitler's Mountain*.

Mosley, Leonard, *The Reich Marshal*, New York, Doubleday & Company, 1974.

Nazi Conspiracy and Aggression, Washington, DC, US Government Printing Office, 1946.

Nicholas, Lynn, *The Rape of Europa*, New York, Vintage, 1995.

Nuremberg 14 November 1945 - 1 October 1946, Nuremberg, International Military Tribunal, 1947.

Rapport and Norwood, *Rendezvous with History*, Old Saybrook, Konecky & Konecky, 1948.

Report of the American Commission for the Protection and Salvage of Artistic and Historic Monuments in War Areas, Washington, DC, US Government Printing Office, 1946.

Rorimer, James J. Survival, *The Salvage and Protection of Art in War*, New York, Abelard Press, 1950.

Sayer, Ian and Botting, Douglas, *Nazi Gold*, New York, 1984.

Shirer, William L., *Berlin Diary: The Journal of a Foreign Correspondent: 1934-1941,* Norwalk, CT, The Easton Press, 1991.

— *The Rise and Fall of the Third Reich: A History of Nazi Germany*, Norwalk, CT, The Easton Press, 1991.

Skorzeny, Otto, Skorzeny, *Secret Memoirs*, New York, 1950.

Smyth, Craig Hugh, *Repatriation of Art from the Collecting Point in Munich after World War II,* New Jersey, Abner Schram Ltd., 1988.

Speer, Albert, *Inside the Third Reich*, New York, Macmillan, 1970.

Stanley-Moss W., *Gold is Where You Hide It*, London, 1968.

Stanton, Shelby L., *World War II Order of Battle*, New York, Galahad Books, 1984.

Trial of the Major War Criminals before the International Military Tribunal.

Thalhofer, Robert L., *Company A!,* Xlibris Corporation, 2010.

Wynne, Frank, *I Was Vermeer*, New York, Bloombury, 2006.

Thyssen, Fritz, *I Paid Hitler*, New York, 1941.

Toland, John, *The Last 100 Days*, New York, 1965.

— *Adolf Hitler*, New York, 1976.

— *No Man's Land*, New York, 1980.

Yeide, Nancy H., *Beyond the Dream of Avarice,* Dallas, TX, Laurel Publishing, 2009.

Ziemke, Earl F., *The US Army in the Occupation of Germany*, US Government Printing Office, 1975.

Index